NOT REMOTELY
WORKING

Recent DILBERT® Books from Andrews McMeel Publishing

The Office Is a Beautiful Place When Everyone Else Works from Home

Eagerly Awaiting Your Irrational Response

Dilbert Turns 30

Cubicles That Make You Envy the Dead

Dilbert Gets Re-accommodated

I'm No Scientist, But I Think Feng Shui Is Part of the Answer

Optimism Sounds Exhausting

Go Add Value Someplace Else

I Sense a Coldness to Your Mentoring

Your New Job Title Is "Accomplice"

I Can't Remember If We're Cheap or Smart

Teamwork Means You Can't Pick the Side that's Right

How's That Underling Thing Working Out for You?

Your Accomplishments Are Suspiciously Hard to Verify

Problem Identified and You're Probably Not Part of the Solution

I'm Tempted to Stop Acting Randomly

14 Years of Loyal Service in a Fabric-Covered Box

Freedom's Just Another Word for People Finding Out You're Useless

Dilbert 2.0: 20 Years of Dilbert

This Is the Part Where You Pretend to Add Value

NOT REMOTELY
WORKING

Recent DILBERT® Books from Andrews McMeel Publishing

The Office Is a Beautiful Place When Everyone Else Works from Home

Eagerly Awaiting Your Irrational Response

Dilbert Turns 30

Cubicles That Make You Envy the Dead

Dilbert Gets Re-accommodated

I'm No Scientist, But I Think Feng Shui Is Part of the Answer

Optimism Sounds Exhausting

Go Add Value Someplace Else

I Sense a Coldness to Your Mentoring

Your New Job Title Is "Accomplice"

I Can't Remember If We're Cheap or Smart

Teamwork Means You Can't Pick the Side that's Right

How's That Underling Thing Working Out for You?

Your Accomplishments Are Suspiciously Hard to Verify

Problem Identified and You're Probably Not Part of the Solution

I'm Tempted to Stop Acting Randomly

14 Years of Loyal Service in a Fabric-Covered Box

Freedom's Just Another Word for People Finding Out You're Useless

Dilbert 2.0: 20 Years of Dilbert

This Is the Part Where You Pretend to Add Value

NOT REMOTELY WORKING

DILBERT BY SCOTT ADAMS
dilbert.com

Andrews McMeel
PUBLISHING®

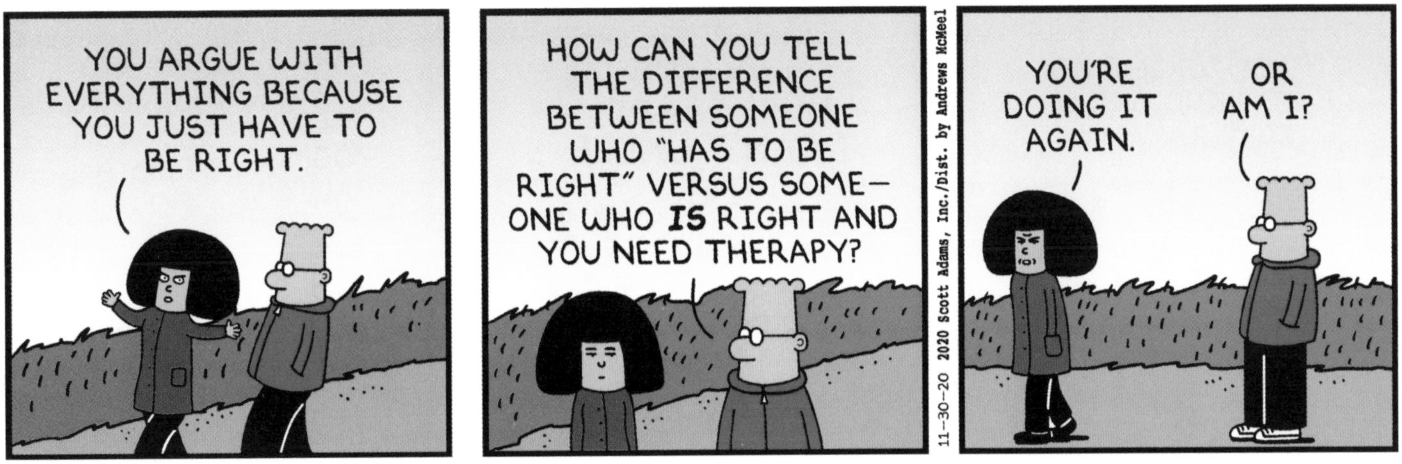
YOU ARGUE WITH EVERYTHING BECAUSE YOU JUST HAVE TO BE RIGHT.
HOW CAN YOU TELL THE DIFFERENCE BETWEEN SOMEONE WHO "HAS TO BE RIGHT" VERSUS SOME-ONE WHO **IS** RIGHT AND YOU NEED THERAPY?
11-30-20 2020 Scott Adams, Inc./Dist. by Andrews McMeel
YOU'RE DOING IT AGAIN.
OR AM I?

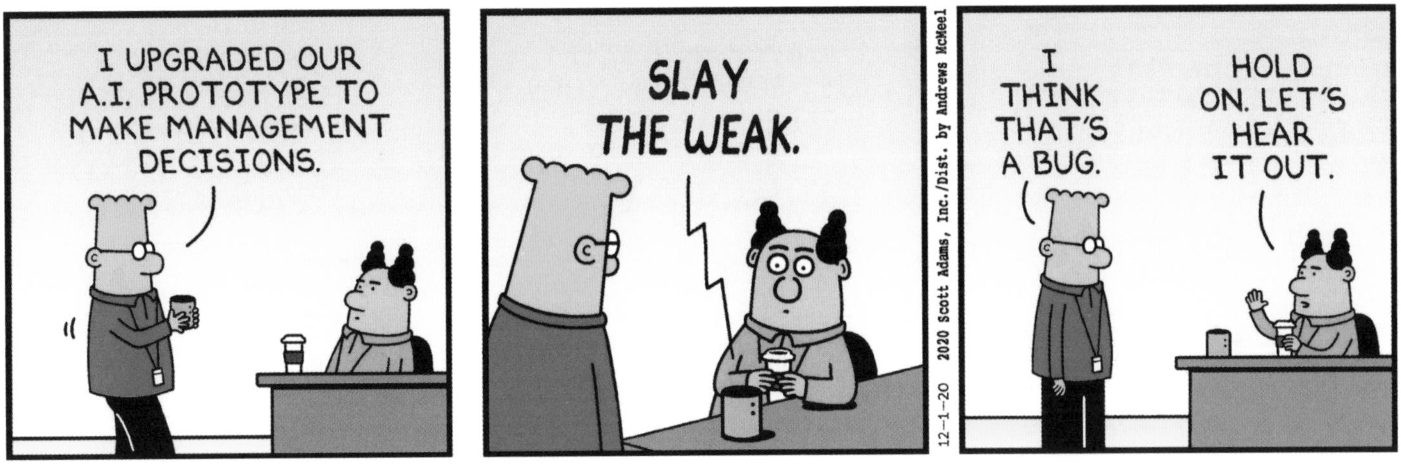
I UPGRADED OUR A.I. PROTOTYPE TO MAKE MANAGEMENT DECISIONS.
SLAY THE WEAK.
12-1-20 2020 Scott Adams, Inc./Dist. by Andrews McMeel
I THINK THAT'S A BUG.
HOLD ON. LET'S HEAR IT OUT.

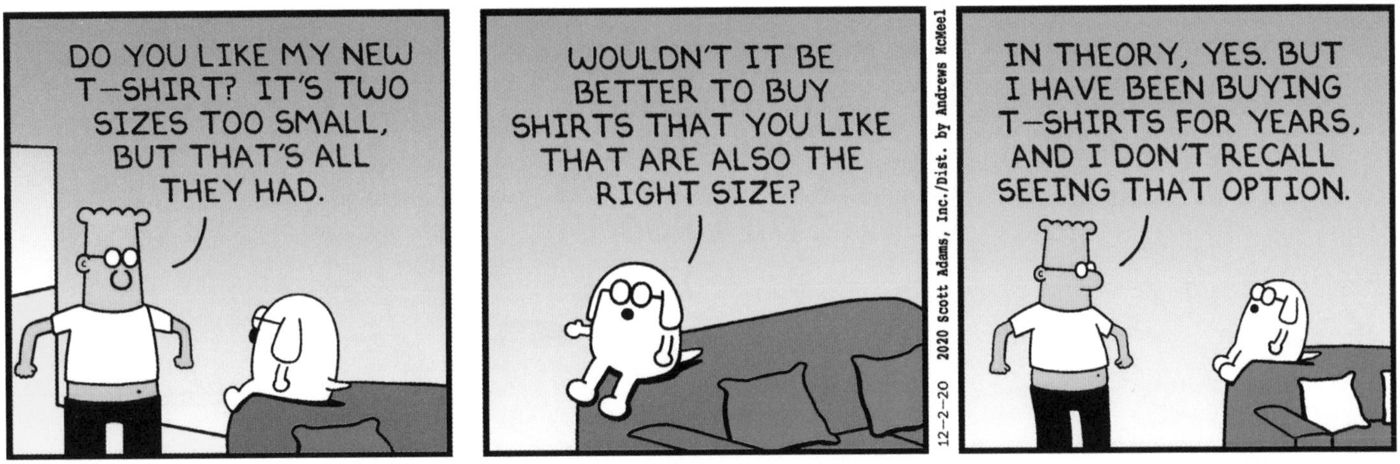
DO YOU LIKE MY NEW T-SHIRT? IT'S TWO SIZES TOO SMALL, BUT THAT'S ALL THEY HAD.
WOULDN'T IT BE BETTER TO BUY SHIRTS THAT YOU LIKE THAT ARE ALSO THE RIGHT SIZE?
12-2-20 2020 Scott Adams, Inc./Dist. by Andrews McMeel
IN THEORY, YES. BUT I HAVE BEEN BUYING T-SHIRTS FOR YEARS, AND I DON'T RECALL SEEING THAT OPTION.

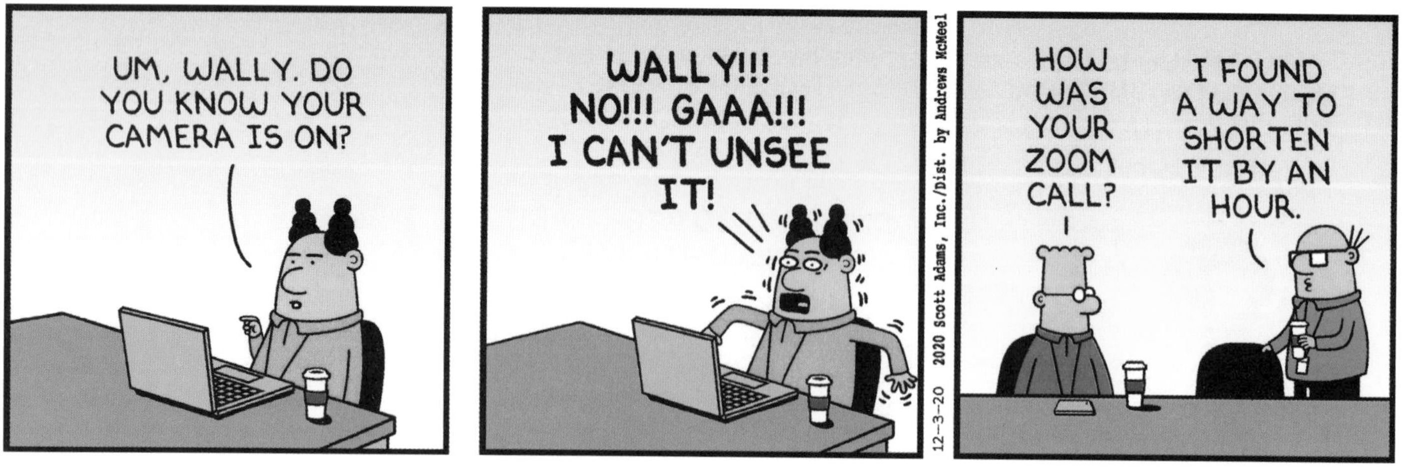
UM, WALLY. DO YOU KNOW YOUR CAMERA IS ON?
WALLY!!! NO!!! GAAA!!! I CAN'T UNSEE IT!
12-3-20 2020 Scott Adams, Inc./Dist. by Andrews McMeel
HOW WAS YOUR ZOOM CALL?
I FOUND A WAY TO SHORTEN IT BY AN HOUR.

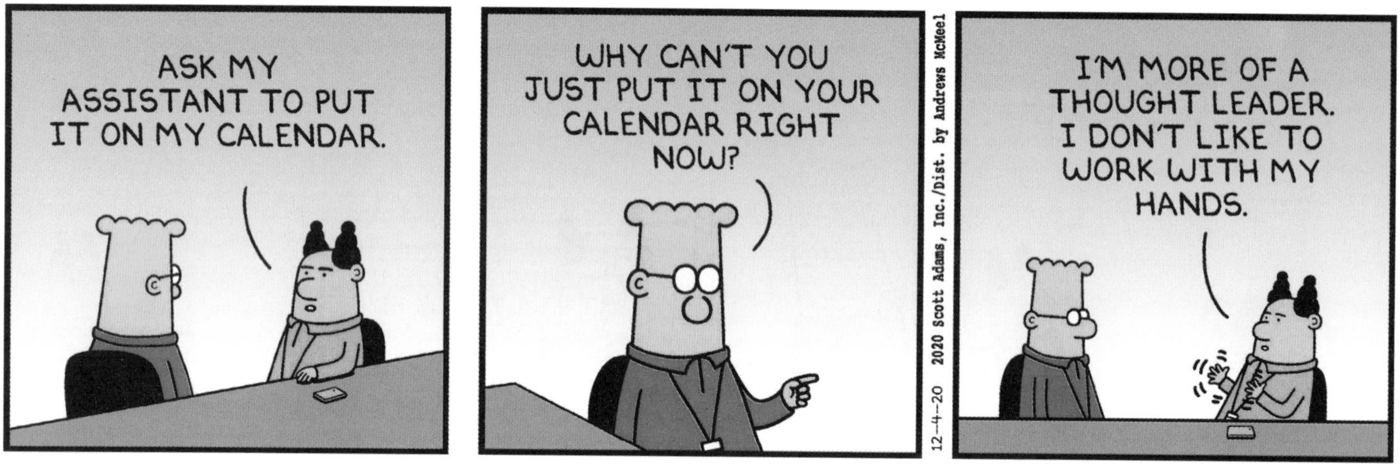
ASK MY ASSISTANT TO PUT IT ON MY CALENDAR.
WHY CAN'T YOU JUST PUT IT ON YOUR CALENDAR RIGHT NOW?
12-4-20 2020 Scott Adams, Inc./Dist. by Andrews McMeel
I'M MORE OF A THOUGHT LEADER. I DON'T LIKE TO WORK WITH MY HANDS.

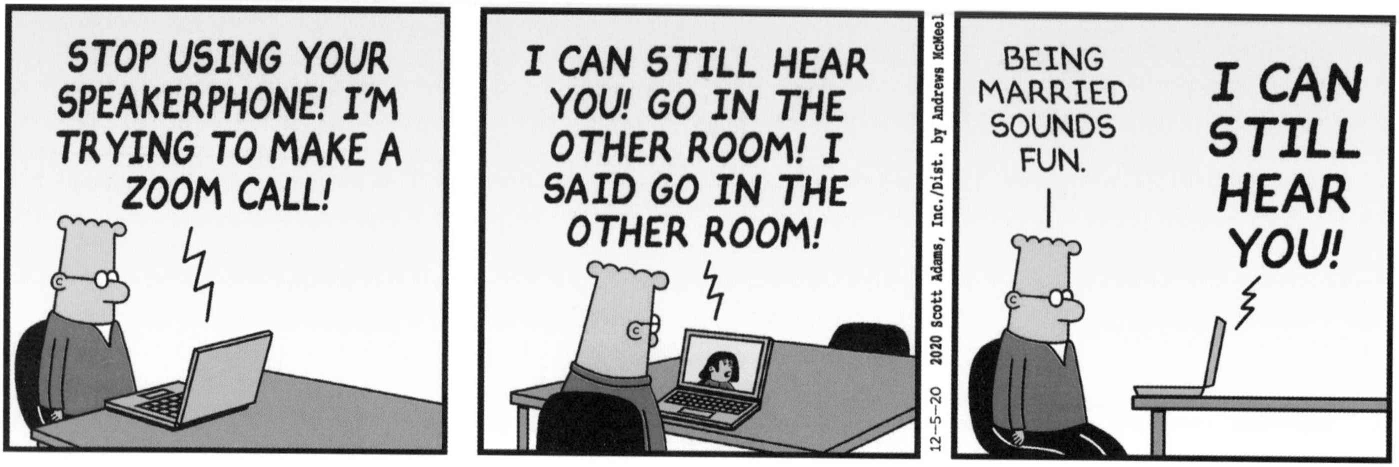
STOP USING YOUR SPEAKERPHONE! I'M TRYING TO MAKE A ZOOM CALL!
I CAN STILL HEAR YOU! GO IN THE OTHER ROOM! I SAID GO IN THE OTHER ROOM!
12-5-20 2020 Scott Adams, Inc./Dist. by Andrews McMeel
BEING MARRIED SOUNDS FUN.
I CAN STILL HEAR YOU!

I RARELY SEE YOU WORKING. HOW DO YOU GET AWAY WITH IT?
IT'S EASY. I JUST WAIT A DAY BEFORE ANSWERING ANY TEXTS OR EMAILS.
FOR EXAMPLE, HERE'S ALICE ASKING IF I CAN ATTEND A MEET– ING IN AN HOUR.
I'LL ANSWER HER IN THE MORNING AND SAY I DIDN'T SEE HER MESSAGE.
AND HERE'S DILBERT ASKING ME FOR SOME DATA.
TOMORROW, I WILL TEXT HIM TO ASK FOR CLARIFICATION, AND HE WILL TELL ME HE FOUND THE DATA ON HIS OWN.
DON'T YOU FEEL GUILTY?
NAH. THEY'D DO THE SAME TO ME.
AND DO THEY?
THEY WOULD IF I DIDN'T IGNORE THEM FIRST.
12-6-20

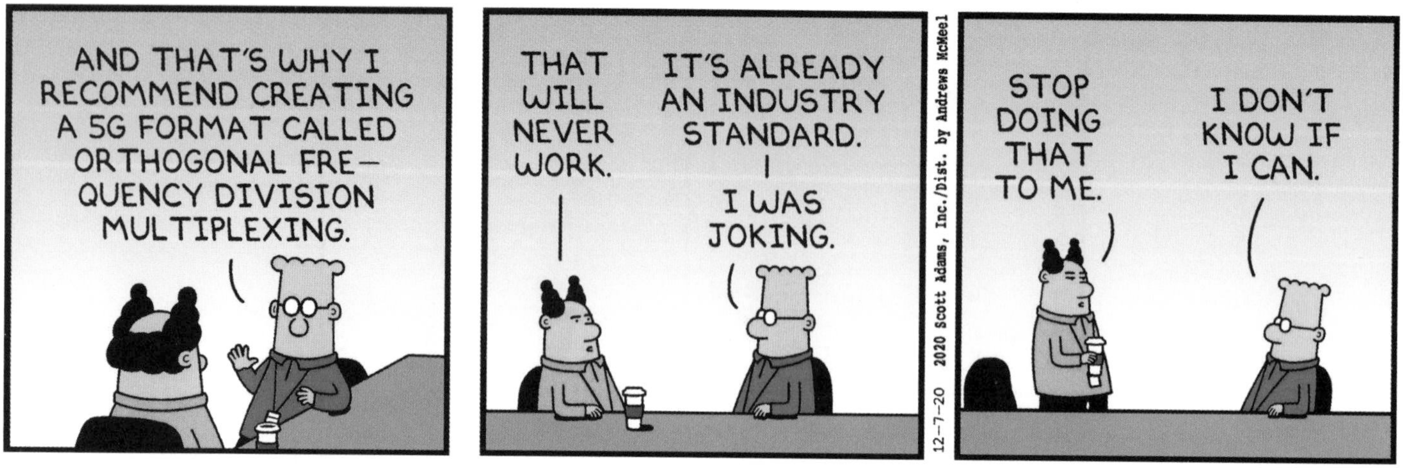
AND THAT'S WHY I RECOMMEND CREATING A 5G FORMAT CALLED ORTHOGONAL FRE– QUENCY DIVISION MULTIPLEXING.
THAT WILL NEVER WORK.
IT'S ALREADY AN INDUSTRY STANDARD.
I WAS JOKING.
12-7-20 2020 Scott Adams, Inc./Dist. by Andrews McMeel
STOP DOING THAT TO ME.
I DON'T KNOW IF I CAN.

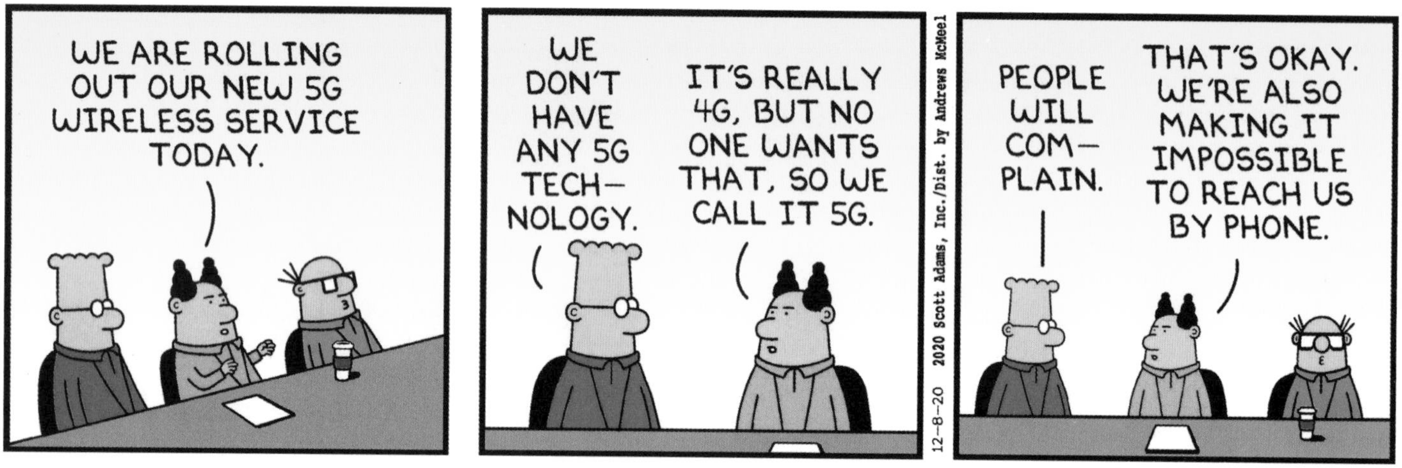
WE ARE ROLLING OUT OUR NEW 5G WIRELESS SERVICE TODAY.
WE DON'T HAVE ANY 5G TECH– NOLOGY.
IT'S REALLY 4G, BUT NO ONE WANTS THAT, SO WE CALL IT 5G.
12-8-20 2020 Scott Adams, Inc./Dist. by Andrews McMeel
PEOPLE WILL COM– PLAIN.
THAT'S OKAY. WE'RE ALSO MAKING IT IMPOSSIBLE TO REACH US BY PHONE.

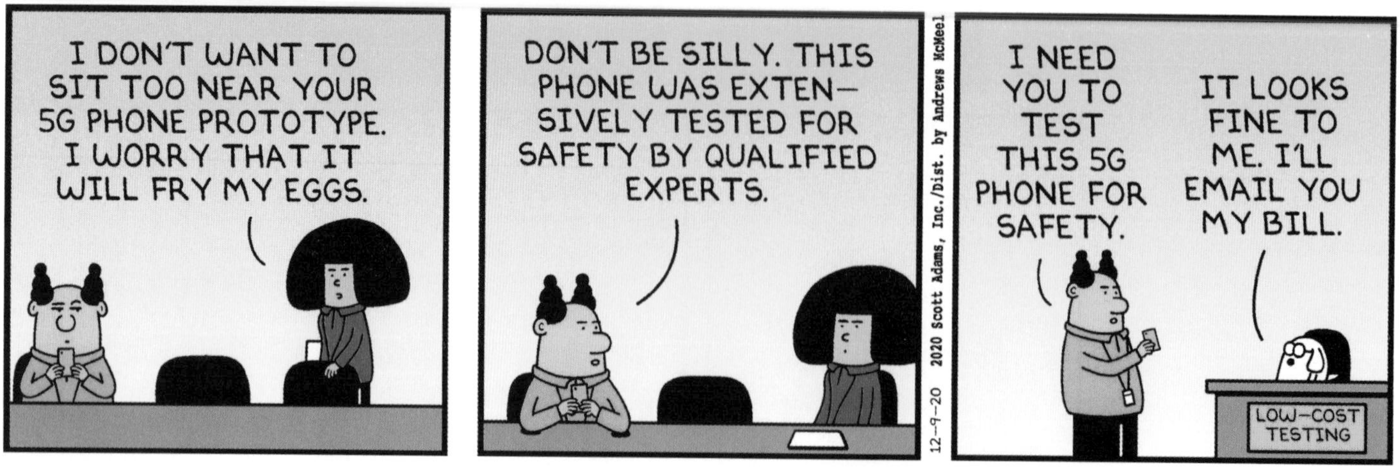
I DON'T WANT TO SIT TOO NEAR YOUR 5G PHONE PROTOTYPE. I WORRY THAT IT WILL FRY MY EGGS.
DON'T BE SILLY. THIS PHONE WAS EXTEN– SIVELY TESTED FOR SAFETY BY QUALIFIED EXPERTS.
12-9-20 2020 Scott Adams, Inc./Dist. by Andrews McMeel
I NEED YOU TO TEST THIS 5G PHONE FOR SAFETY.
IT LOOKS FINE TO ME. I'LL EMAIL YOU MY BILL.
LOW–COST TESTING

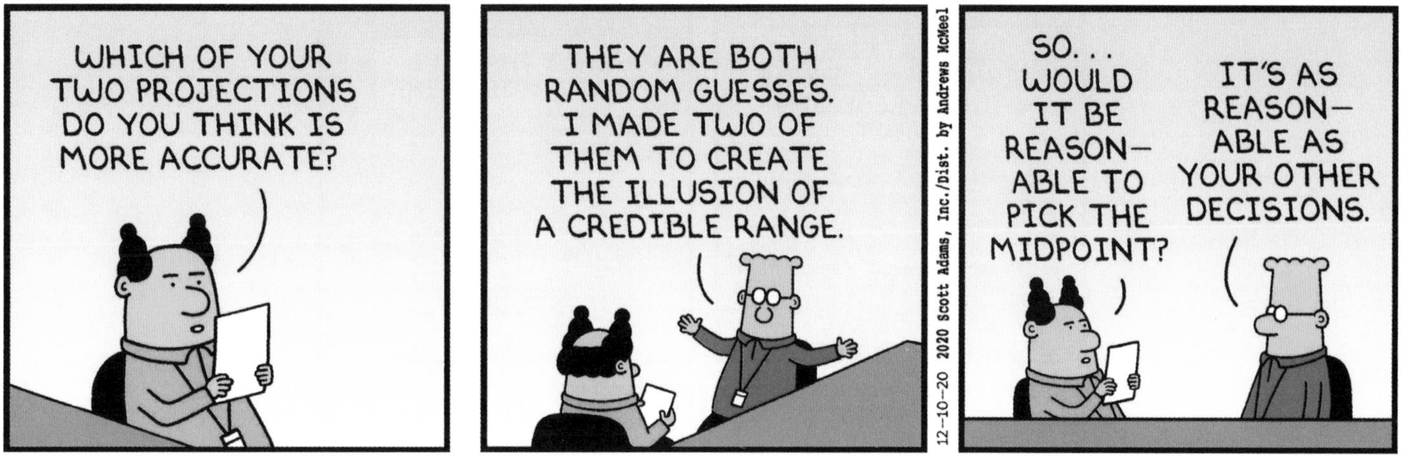
WHICH OF YOUR TWO PROJECTIONS DO YOU THINK IS MORE ACCURATE?
THEY ARE BOTH RANDOM GUESSES. I MADE TWO OF THEM TO CREATE THE ILLUSION OF A CREDIBLE RANGE.
12-10-20 2020 Scott Adams, Inc./Dist. by Andrews McMeel
SO. . . WOULD IT BE REASON–ABLE TO PICK THE MIDPOINT?
IT'S AS REASON–ABLE AS YOUR OTHER DECISIONS.

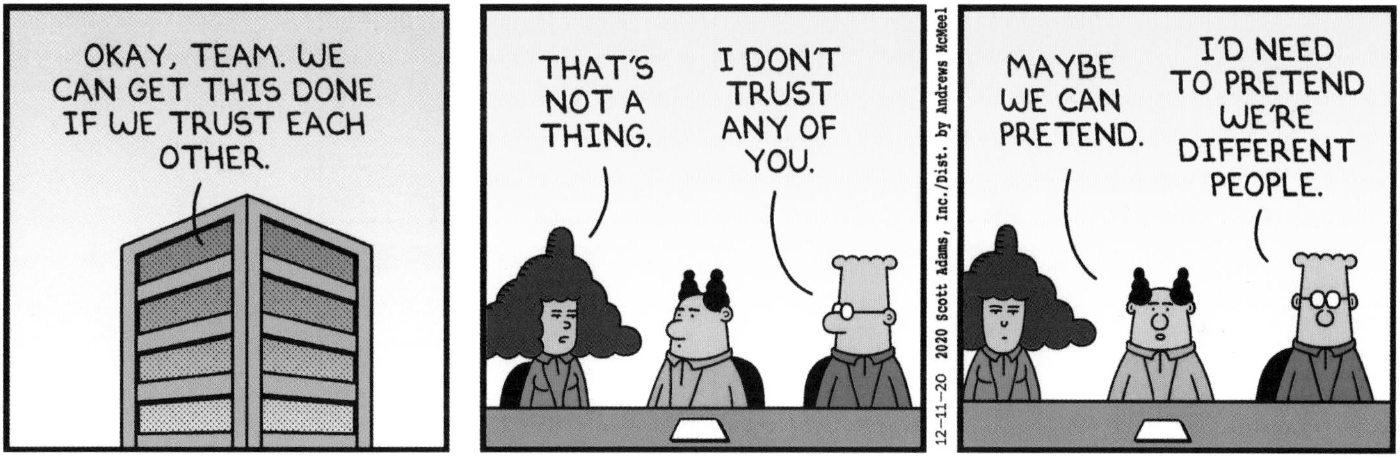
OKAY, TEAM. WE CAN GET THIS DONE IF WE TRUST EACH OTHER.
THAT'S NOT A THING.
I DON'T TRUST ANY OF YOU.
12-11-20 2020 Scott Adams, Inc./Dist. by Andrews McMeel
MAYBE WE CAN PRETEND.
I'D NEED TO PRETEND WE'RE DIFFERENT PEOPLE.

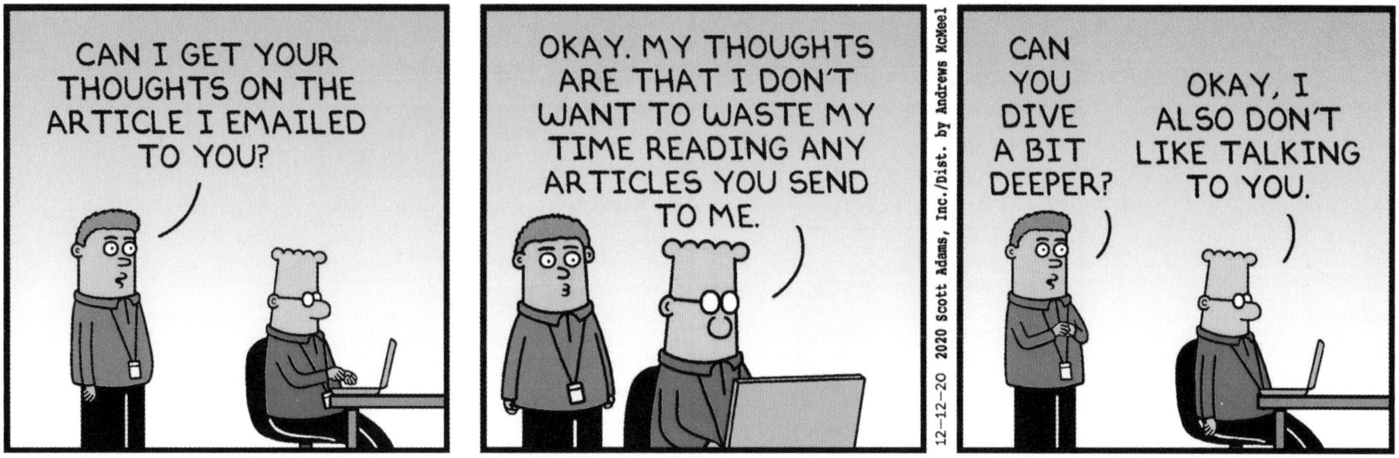
CAN I GET YOUR THOUGHTS ON THE ARTICLE I EMAILED TO YOU?
OKAY. MY THOUGHTS ARE THAT I DON'T WANT TO WASTE MY TIME READING ANY ARTICLES YOU SEND TO ME.
12-12-20 2020 Scott Adams, Inc./Dist. by Andrews McMeel
CAN YOU DIVE A BIT DEEPER?
OKAY, I ALSO DON'T LIKE TALKING TO YOU.

DILBERT, I'M ASSIGNING YOU TO THE NETWORK REDESIGN PROJECT.
WHAT PHASE IS THAT PROJECT IN?
IS IT IN THE INITIAL STAGE, IN WHICH EVERYONE IS FEELING POSITIVE AND OPTIMISTIC?
OR IS IT IN THE MIDDLE PHASE, IN WHICH EVERYONE IS GRINDING AWAY AND HATING THE OTHER TEAM MEMBERS?
IT'S IN THE DEATH SPIRAL PHASE.
EVERYONE IS TRYING TO ASSIGN BLAME TO SOMEONE THEY ALREADY HATE.
THEY REQUESTED THAT I ADD YOU TO THE TEAM.
TO SAVE THE PROJECT?
UM. . . OKAY, SURE.
12-13-20

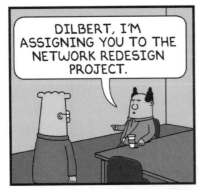

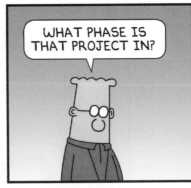

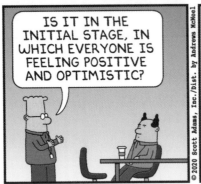

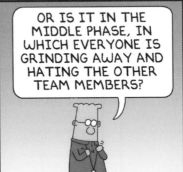

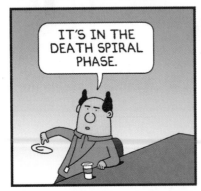

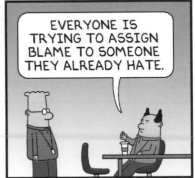

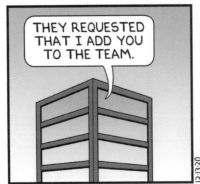

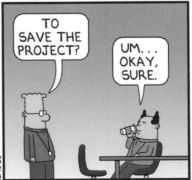

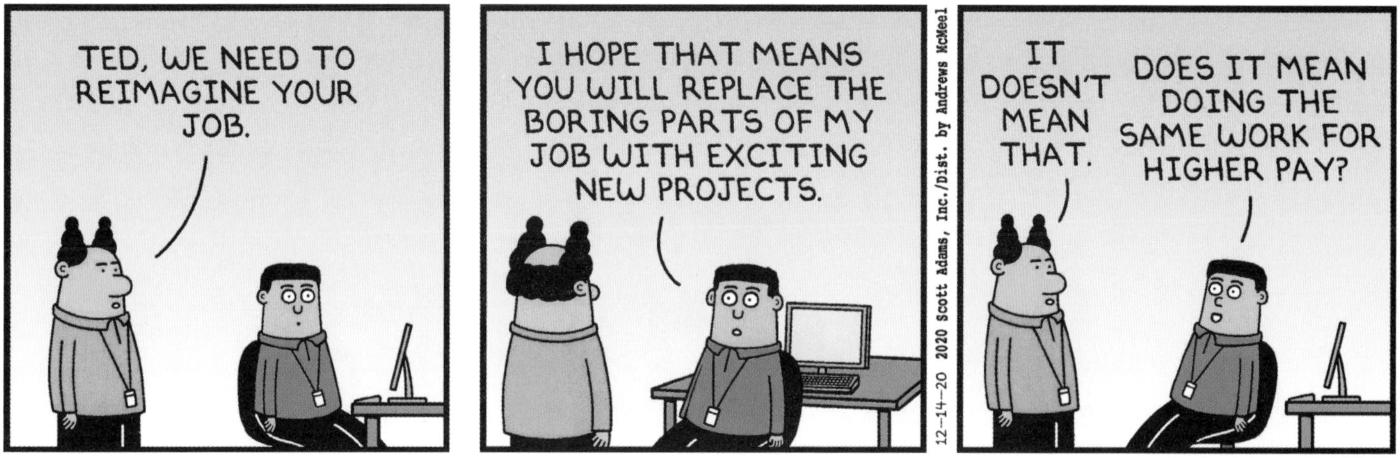
TED, WE NEED TO REIMAGINE YOUR JOB.
I HOPE THAT MEANS YOU WILL REPLACE THE BORING PARTS OF MY JOB WITH EXCITING NEW PROJECTS.
12-14-20 2020 Scott Adams, Inc./Dist. by Andrews McMeel
DOES IT MEAN DOING THE SAME WORK FOR HIGHER PAY?
IT DOESN'T MEAN THAT.

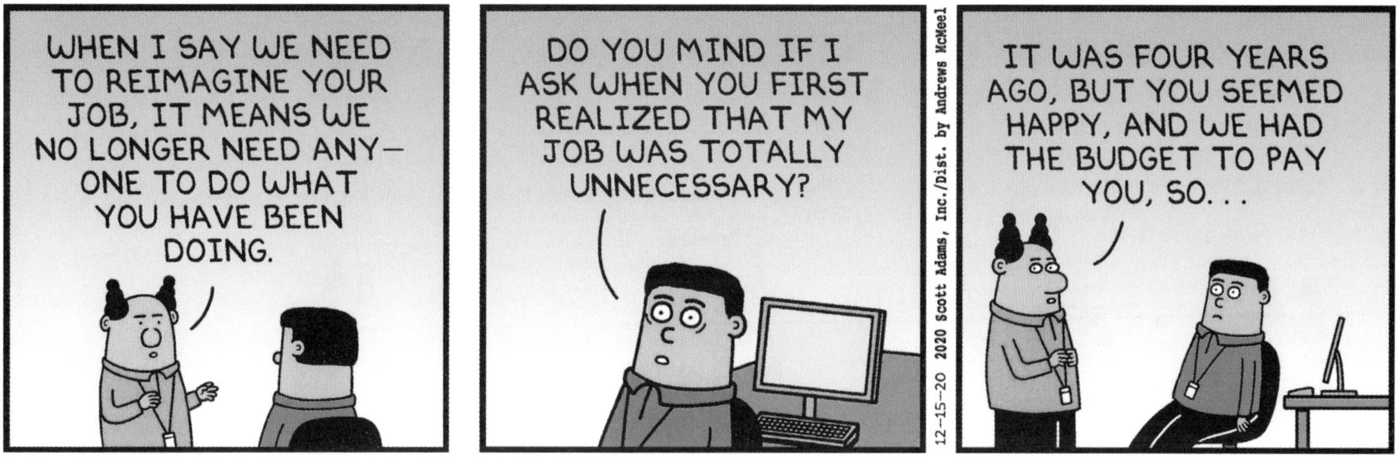
WHEN I SAY WE NEED TO REIMAGINE YOUR JOB, IT MEANS WE NO LONGER NEED ANY-ONE TO DO WHAT YOU HAVE BEEN DOING.
DO YOU MIND IF I ASK WHEN YOU FIRST REALIZED THAT MY JOB WAS TOTALLY UNNECESSARY?
12-15-20 2020 Scott Adams, Inc./Dist. by Andrews McMeel
IT WAS FOUR YEARS AGO, BUT YOU SEEMED HAPPY, AND WE HAD THE BUDGET TO PAY YOU, SO. . .

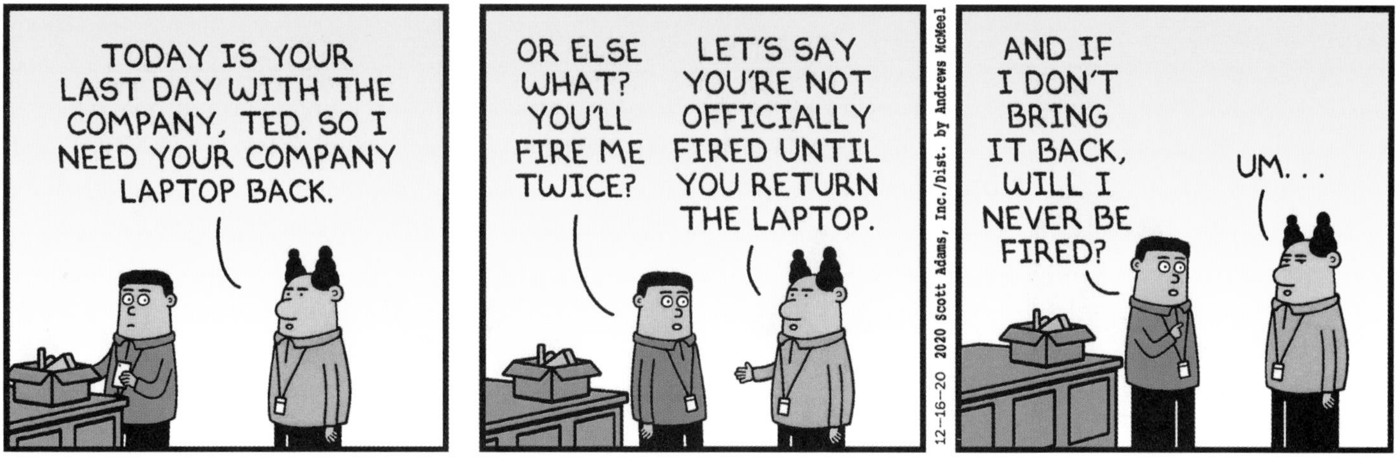
TODAY IS YOUR LAST DAY WITH THE COMPANY, TED. SO I NEED YOUR COMPANY LAPTOP BACK.
OR ELSE WHAT? YOU'LL FIRE ME TWICE?
LET'S SAY YOU'RE NOT OFFICIALLY FIRED UNTIL YOU RETURN THE LAPTOP.
12-16-20 2020 Scott Adams, Inc./Dist. by Andrews McMeel
AND IF I DON'T BRING IT BACK, WILL I NEVER BE FIRED?
UM. . .

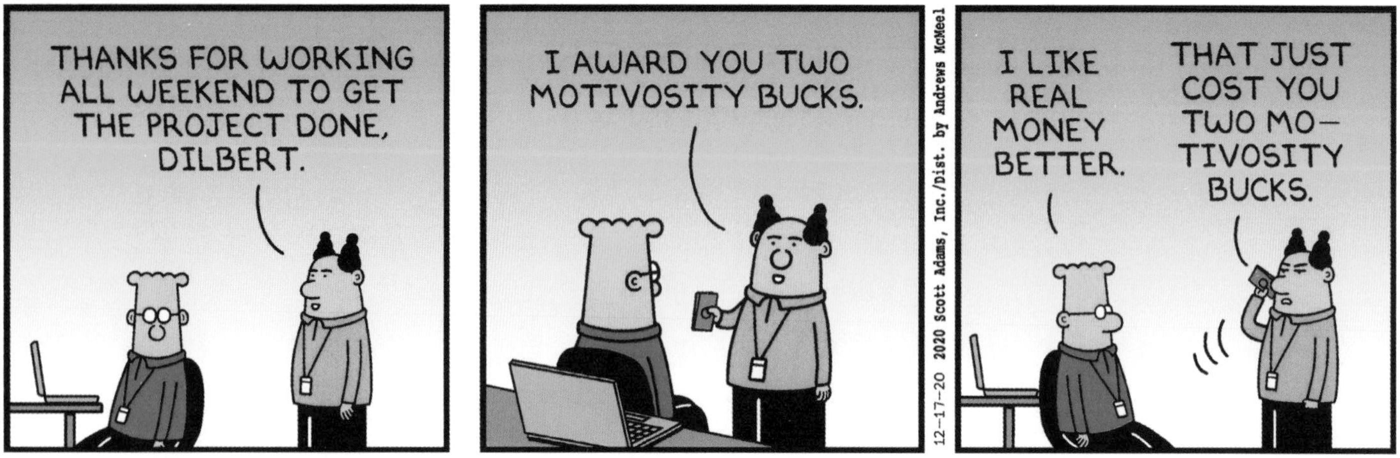
THANKS FOR WORKING ALL WEEKEND TO GET THE PROJECT DONE, DILBERT.
I AWARD YOU TWO MOTIVOSITY BUCKS.
I LIKE REAL MONEY BETTER.
THAT JUST COST YOU TWO MO— TIVOSITY BUCKS.
12-17-20 2020 Scott Adams, Inc./Dist. by Andrews McMeel

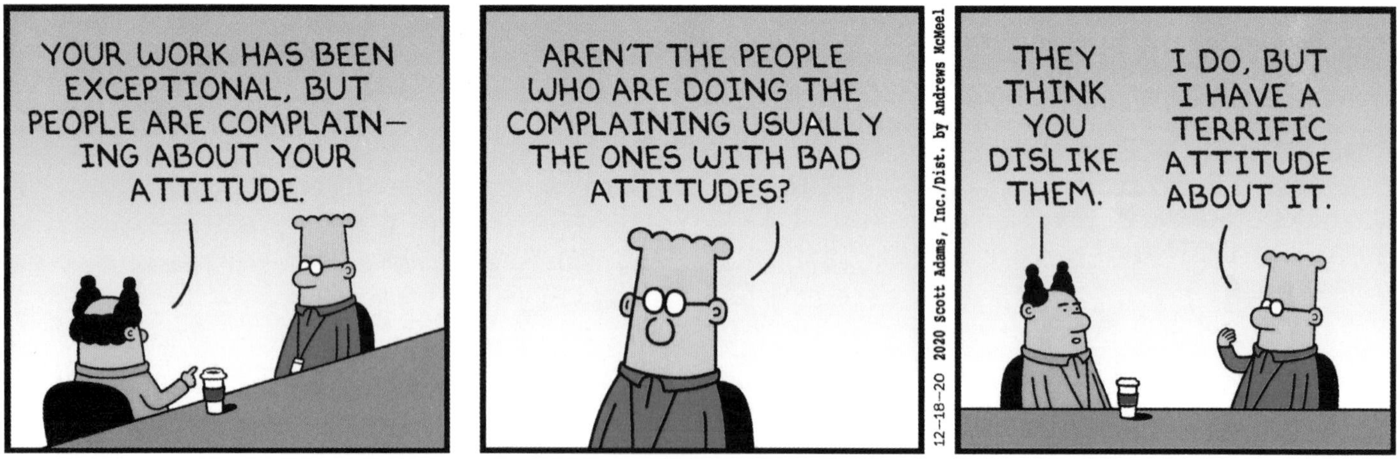
YOUR WORK HAS BEEN EXCEPTIONAL, BUT PEOPLE ARE COMPLAIN— ING ABOUT YOUR ATTITUDE.
AREN'T THE PEOPLE WHO ARE DOING THE COMPLAINING USUALLY THE ONES WITH BAD ATTITUDES?
THEY THINK YOU DISLIKE THEM.
I DO, BUT I HAVE A TERRIFIC ATTITUDE ABOUT IT.
12-18-20 2020 Scott Adams, Inc./Dist. by Andrews McMeel

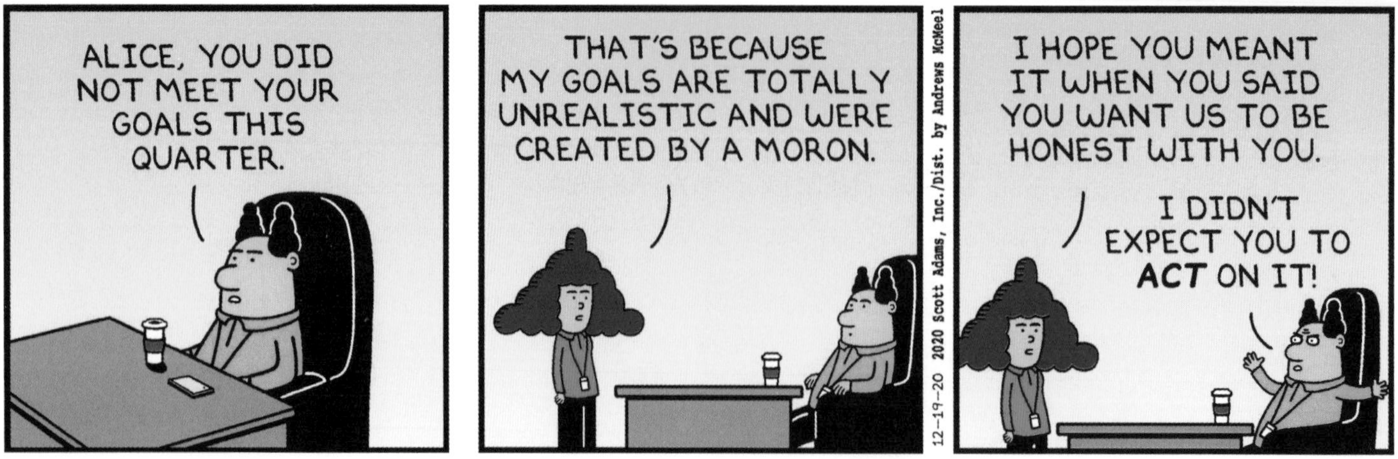
ALICE, YOU DID NOT MEET YOUR GOALS THIS QUARTER.
THAT'S BECAUSE MY GOALS ARE TOTALLY UNREALISTIC AND WERE CREATED BY A MORON.
I HOPE YOU MEANT IT WHEN YOU SAID YOU WANT US TO BE HONEST WITH YOU.
I DIDN'T EXPECT YOU TO **ACT** ON IT!
12-19-20 2020 Scott Adams, Inc./Dist. by Andrews McMeel

DID YOU SEE MY BRILLIANT PRODUCT IDEA I EMAILED TO YOU?
YES, I ALREADY DEBUNKED IT IN MY MIND.
PERHAPS YOU COULD SHARE YOUR REASONS.
© 2020 Scott Adams, Inc./Dist. by Andrews McMeel
IF IT'S SUCH A GREAT IDEA, WHY ISN'T SOMEONE ELSE DOING IT?
AND IF SOMEONE IS ALREADY DOING IT, WE ARE FAR TOO LATE.
IN ORDER FOR YOUR IDEA TO BE GOOD, I WOULD HAVE TO THINK YOU ARE SMARTER THAN EVERYONE IN THE INDUSTRY.
AND SERIOUSLY, JUST LOOK AT YOU.
12-20-20
ANYONE ELSE HAVE AN IDEA?
NOPE.
NOPE.
NEVER.
NOPE.

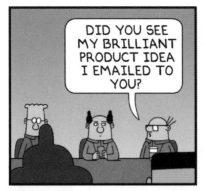

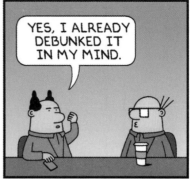

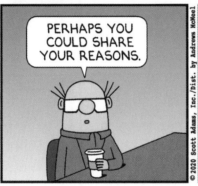

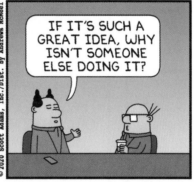

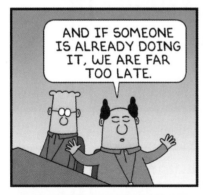

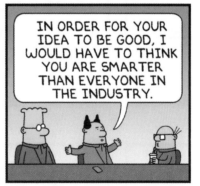

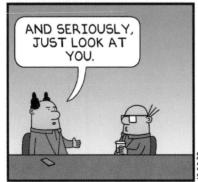

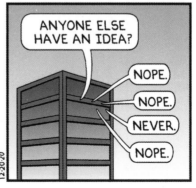

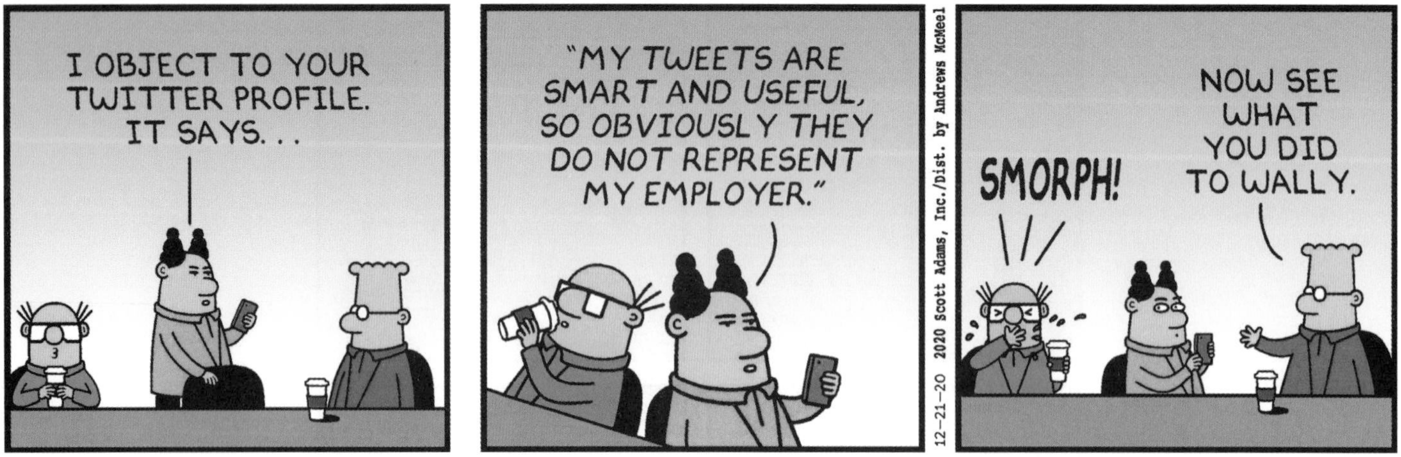
I OBJECT TO YOUR TWITTER PROFILE. IT SAYS. . .
"MY TWEETS ARE SMART AND USEFUL, SO OBVIOUSLY THEY DO NOT REPRESENT MY EMPLOYER."
12-21-20 2020 Scott Adams, Inc./Dist. by Andrews McMeel
SMORPH!
NOW SEE WHAT YOU DID TO WALLY.

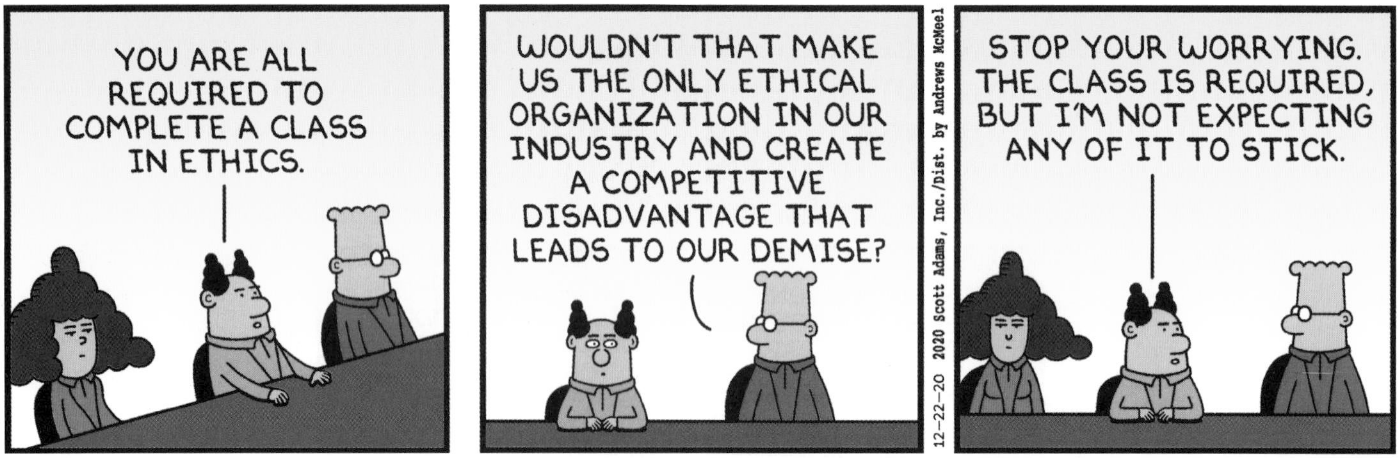
YOU ARE ALL REQUIRED TO COMPLETE A CLASS IN ETHICS.
WOULDN'T THAT MAKE US THE ONLY ETHICAL ORGANIZATION IN OUR INDUSTRY AND CREATE A COMPETITIVE DISADVANTAGE THAT LEADS TO OUR DEMISE?
12-22-20 2020 Scott Adams, Inc./Dist. by Andrews McMeel
STOP YOUR WORRYING. THE CLASS IS REQUIRED, BUT I'M NOT EXPECTING ANY OF IT TO STICK.

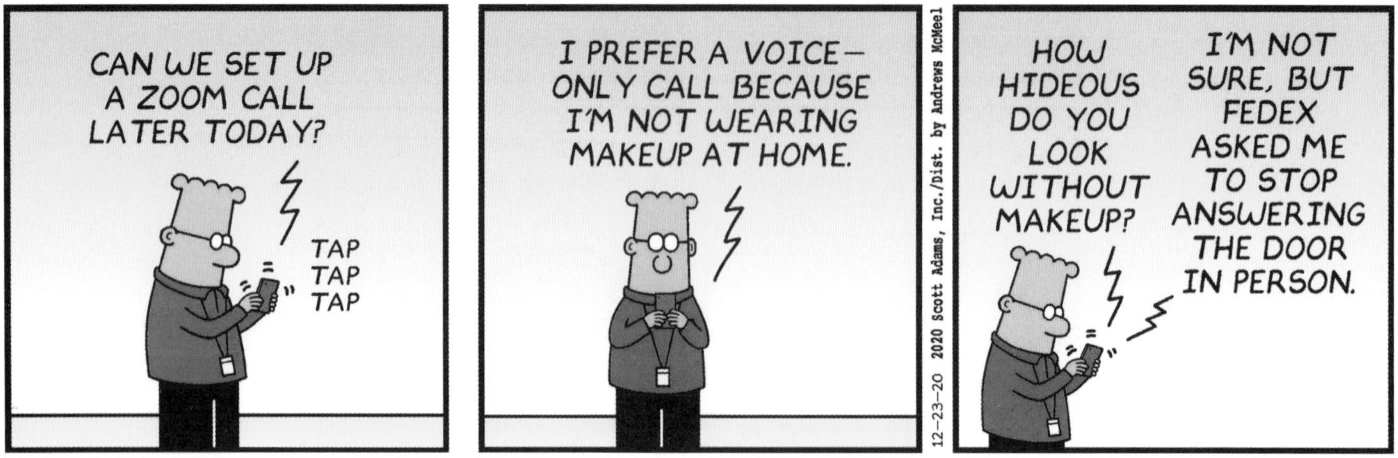
CAN WE SET UP A ZOOM CALL LATER TODAY?
TAP TAP TAP
I PREFER A VOICE-ONLY CALL BECAUSE I'M NOT WEARING MAKEUP AT HOME.
12-23-20 2020 Scott Adams, Inc./Dist. by Andrews McMeel
HOW HIDEOUS DO YOU LOOK WITHOUT MAKEUP?
I'M NOT SURE, BUT FEDEX ASKED ME TO STOP ANSWERING THE DOOR IN PERSON.

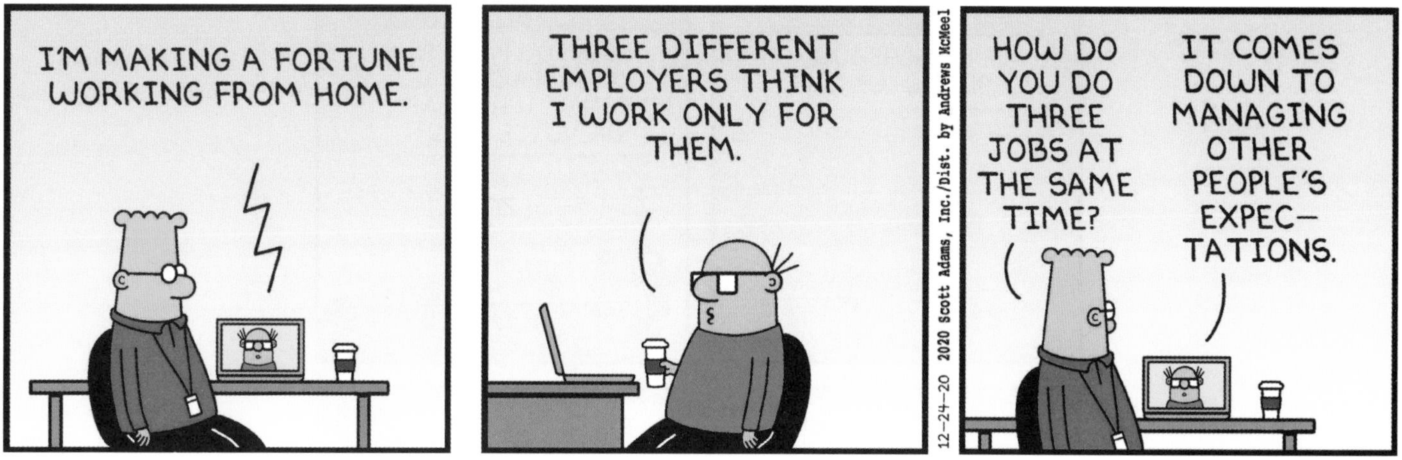
I'M MAKING A FORTUNE WORKING FROM HOME.
THREE DIFFERENT EMPLOYERS THINK I WORK ONLY FOR THEM.
12-24-20 2020 Scott Adams, Inc./Dist. by Andrews McMeel
HOW DO YOU DO THREE JOBS AT THE SAME TIME?
IT COMES DOWN TO MANAGING OTHER PEOPLE'S EXPEC-TATIONS.

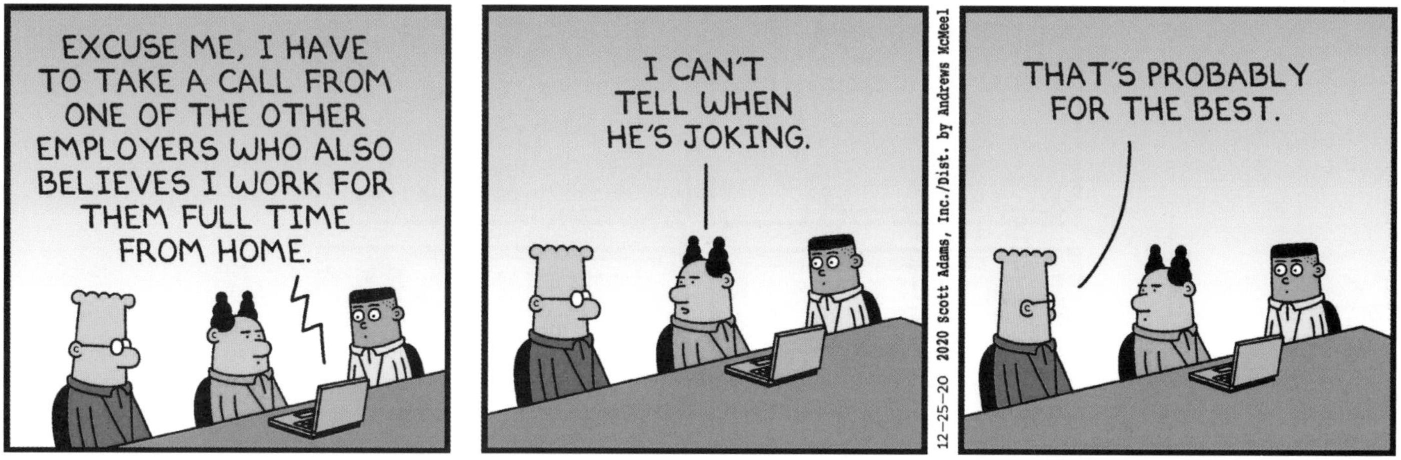
EXCUSE ME, I HAVE TO TAKE A CALL FROM ONE OF THE OTHER EMPLOYERS WHO ALSO BELIEVES I WORK FOR THEM FULL TIME FROM HOME.
I CAN'T TELL WHEN HE'S JOKING.
12-25-20 2020 Scott Adams, Inc./Dist. by Andrews McMeel
THAT'S PROBABLY FOR THE BEST.

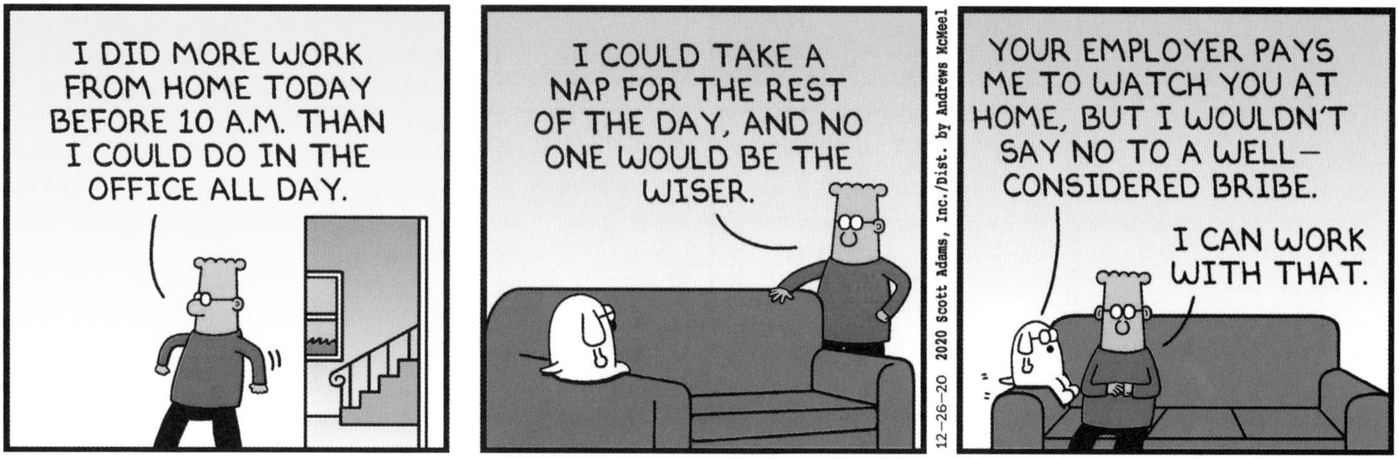
I DID MORE WORK FROM HOME TODAY BEFORE 10 A.M. THAN I COULD DO IN THE OFFICE ALL DAY.
I COULD TAKE A NAP FOR THE REST OF THE DAY, AND NO ONE WOULD BE THE WISER.
12-26-20 2020 Scott Adams, Inc./Dist. by Andrews McMeel
YOUR EMPLOYER PAYS ME TO WATCH YOU AT HOME, BUT I WOULDN'T SAY NO TO A WELL-CONSIDERED BRIBE.
I CAN WORK WITH THAT.

LET'S SCHEDULE A FOLLOW-UP CALL.
DO YOU PREFER ZOOM, FACETIME, SIGNAL, WHATSAPP, OR VOICE CALL?
ZOOM.
HOW ABOUT NEXT TUESDAY AT 10 A.M. MY TIME, WHICH IS 1 P.M. YOUR TIME?
I'LL BE ON THE ROAD THEN, SO YOUR 10 A.M. WILL BE MY NOON.
BUT THAT'S AFTER THE TIME CHANGE.
AND I CAN'T REMEMBER IF I'M GOING TO A PLACE THAT CHANGE THEIR CLOCKS.
WHY DON'T WE SKIP THE WHOLE THING BECAUSE THE CALL WE ARE SCHEDULING PROBABLY WON'T BE ANY MORE USEFUL THAN THIS ONE.
LET US NEVER SPEAK OF THIS AGAIN.
© 2020 Scott Adams, Inc./Dist. by Andrews McMeel
12-27-20

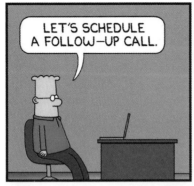

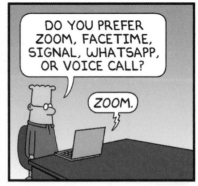

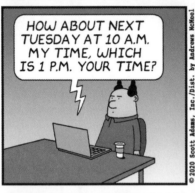

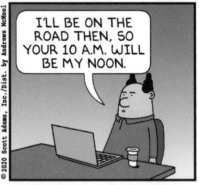

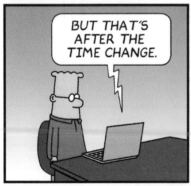

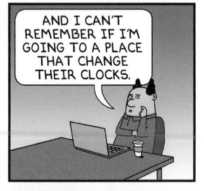

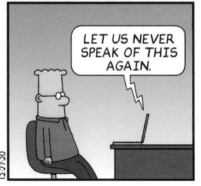

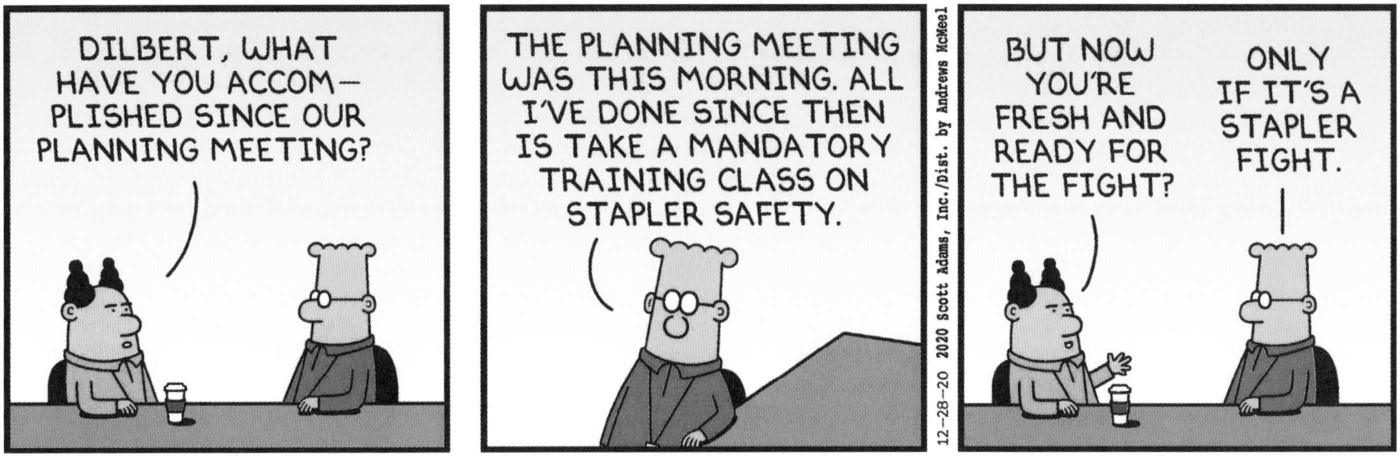
DILBERT, WHAT HAVE YOU ACCOM– PLISHED SINCE OUR PLANNING MEETING?
THE PLANNING MEETING WAS THIS MORNING. ALL I'VE DONE SINCE THEN IS TAKE A MANDATORY TRAINING CLASS ON STAPLER SAFETY.
12-28-20 2020 Scott Adams, Inc./Dist. by Andrews McMeel
BUT NOW YOU'RE FRESH AND READY FOR THE FIGHT?
ONLY IF IT'S A STAPLER FIGHT.

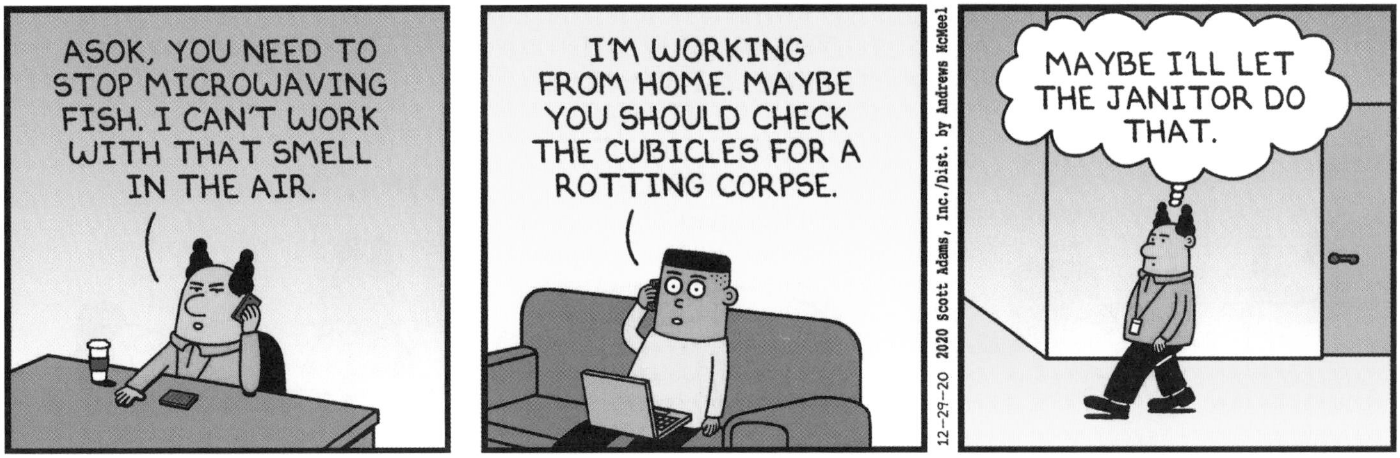
ASOK, YOU NEED TO STOP MICROWAVING FISH. I CAN'T WORK WITH THAT SMELL IN THE AIR.
I'M WORKING FROM HOME. MAYBE YOU SHOULD CHECK THE CUBICLES FOR A ROTTING CORPSE.
12-29-20 2020 Scott Adams, Inc./Dist. by Andrews McMeel
MAYBE I'LL LET THE JANITOR DO THAT.

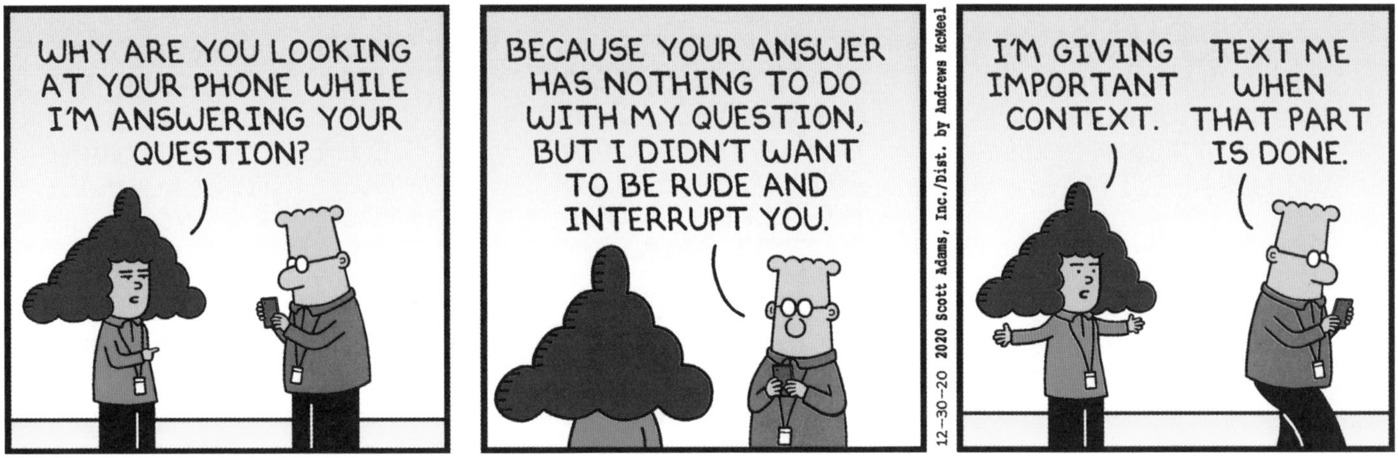
WHY ARE YOU LOOKING AT YOUR PHONE WHILE I'M ANSWERING YOUR QUESTION?
BECAUSE YOUR ANSWER HAS NOTHING TO DO WITH MY QUESTION, BUT I DIDN'T WANT TO BE RUDE AND INTERRUPT YOU.
12-30-20 2020 Scott Adams, Inc./Dist. by Andrews McMeel
I'M GIVING IMPORTANT CONTEXT.
TEXT ME WHEN THAT PART IS DONE.

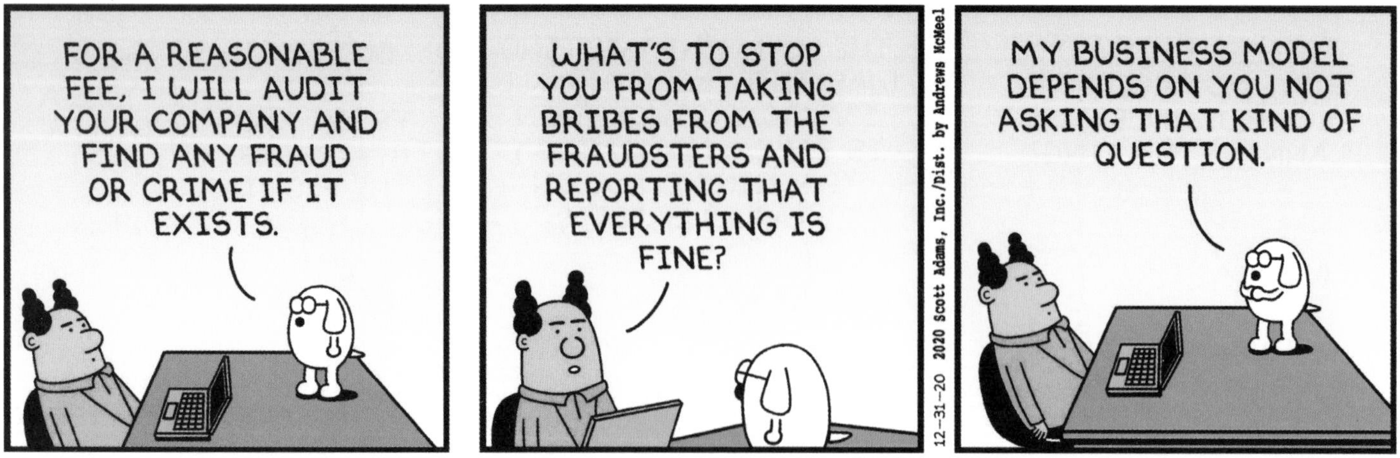
FOR A REASONABLE FEE, I WILL AUDIT YOUR COMPANY AND FIND ANY FRAUD OR CRIME IF IT EXISTS.
WHAT'S TO STOP YOU FROM TAKING BRIBES FROM THE FRAUDSTERS AND REPORTING THAT EVERYTHING IS FINE?
12-31-20 2020 Scott Adams, Inc./Dist. by Andrews McMeel
MY BUSINESS MODEL DEPENDS ON YOU NOT ASKING THAT KIND OF QUESTION.

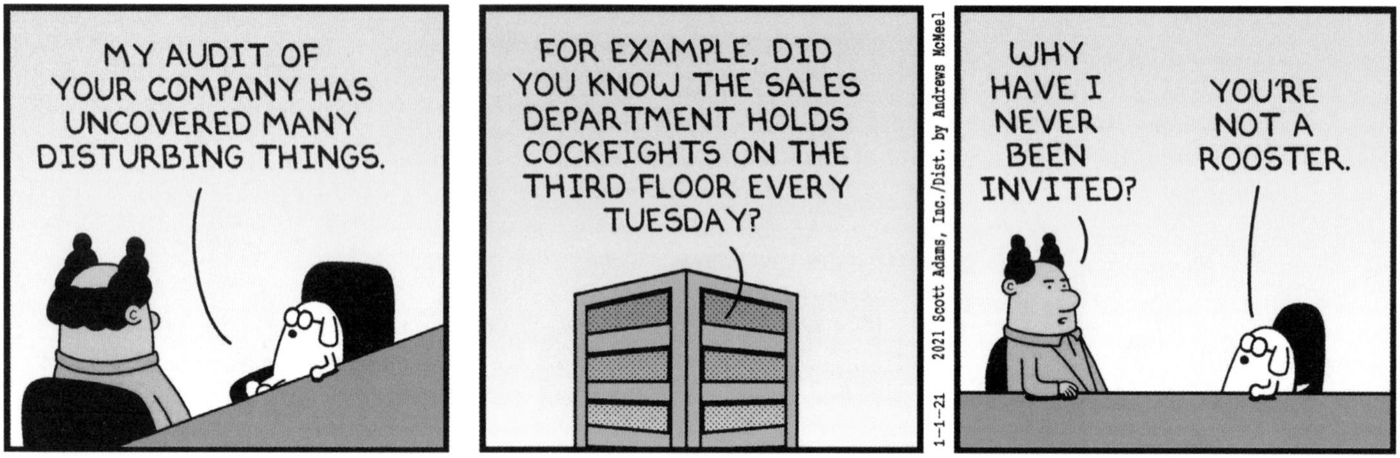
MY AUDIT OF YOUR COMPANY HAS UNCOVERED MANY DISTURBING THINGS.
FOR EXAMPLE, DID YOU KNOW THE SALES DEPARTMENT HOLDS COCKFIGHTS ON THE THIRD FLOOR EVERY TUESDAY?
1-1-21 2021 Scott Adams, Inc./Dist. by Andrews McMeel
WHY HAVE I NEVER BEEN INVITED?
YOU'RE NOT A ROOSTER.

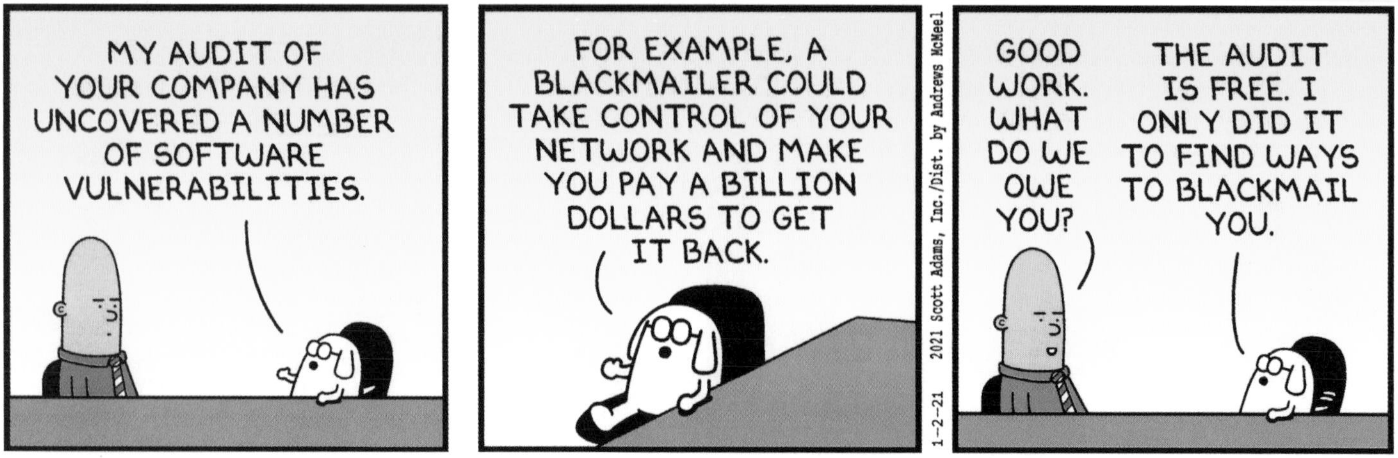
MY AUDIT OF YOUR COMPANY HAS UNCOVERED A NUMBER OF SOFTWARE VULNERABILITIES.
FOR EXAMPLE, A BLACKMAILER COULD TAKE CONTROL OF YOUR NETWORK AND MAKE YOU PAY A BILLION DOLLARS TO GET IT BACK.
1-2-21 2021 Scott Adams, Inc./Dist. by Andrews McMeel
GOOD WORK. WHAT DO WE OWE YOU?
THE AUDIT IS FREE. I ONLY DID IT TO FIND WAYS TO BLACKMAIL YOU.

I'M PLANNING TO INCREASE THE BUDGET FOR TRAINING BY FIFTY PERCENT NEXT YEAR.
HE DIDN'T SAY ANYTHING ABOUT THE OTHER BUDGETS.
HE DIDN'T SAY ANYTHING ABOUT THE BUDGET FOR RESEARCH AND DEVELOPMENT.
SOUNDS LIKE HE'S PHASING OUT RESEARCH AND DEVELOPMENT.
HE WOULDN'T PHASE OUT RESEARCH AND DEVELOPMENT UNLESS HE KNOWS THE COMPANY IS FAILING.
THE COMPANY MUST BE GOING BANKRUPT.
THE COMPANY IS BANKRUPT.
I GUESS I DON'T NEED TO INCREASE THE TRAINING BUDGET.
2021 Scott Adams, Inc./Dist. by Andrews McMeel
1-3-21

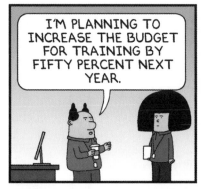

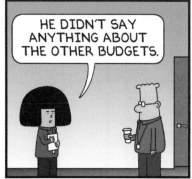

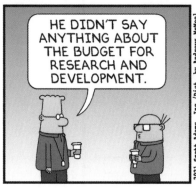

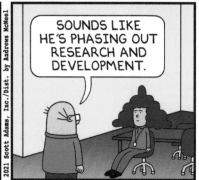

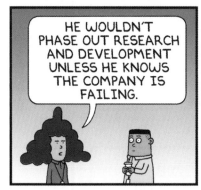

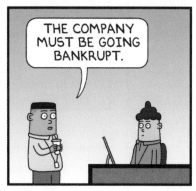

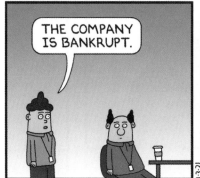

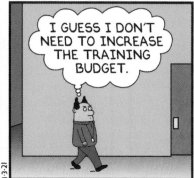

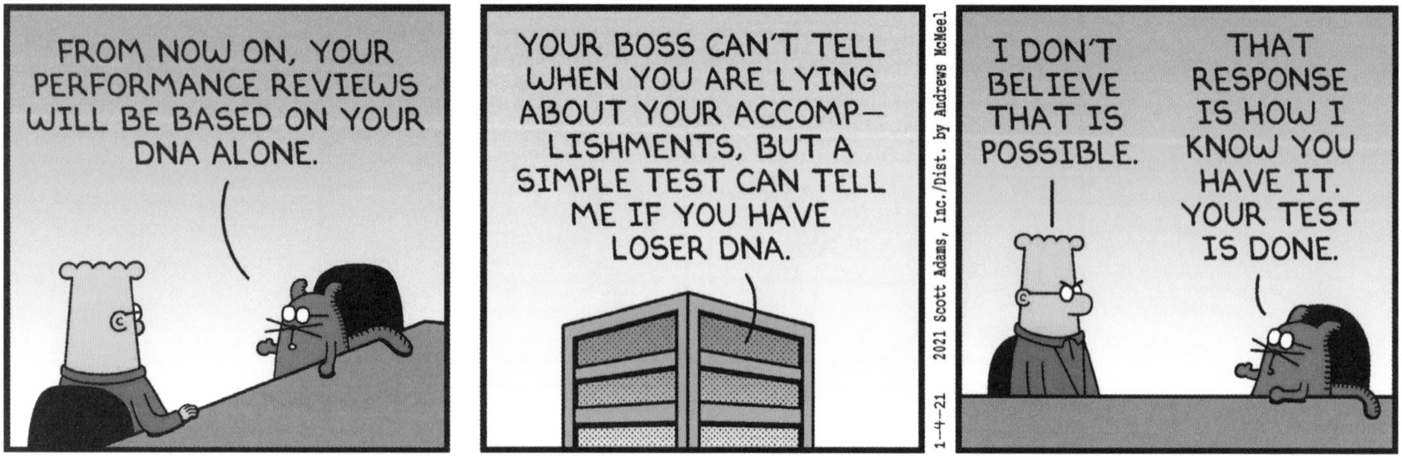
FROM NOW ON, YOUR PERFORMANCE REVIEWS WILL BE BASED ON YOUR DNA ALONE.
YOUR BOSS CAN'T TELL WHEN YOU ARE LYING ABOUT YOUR ACCOMP– LISHMENTS, BUT A SIMPLE TEST CAN TELL ME IF YOU HAVE LOSER DNA.
1-4-21 2021 Scott Adams, Inc./Dist. by Andrews McMeel
I DON'T BELIEVE THAT IS POSSIBLE.
THAT RESPONSE IS HOW I KNOW YOU HAVE IT. YOUR TEST IS DONE.

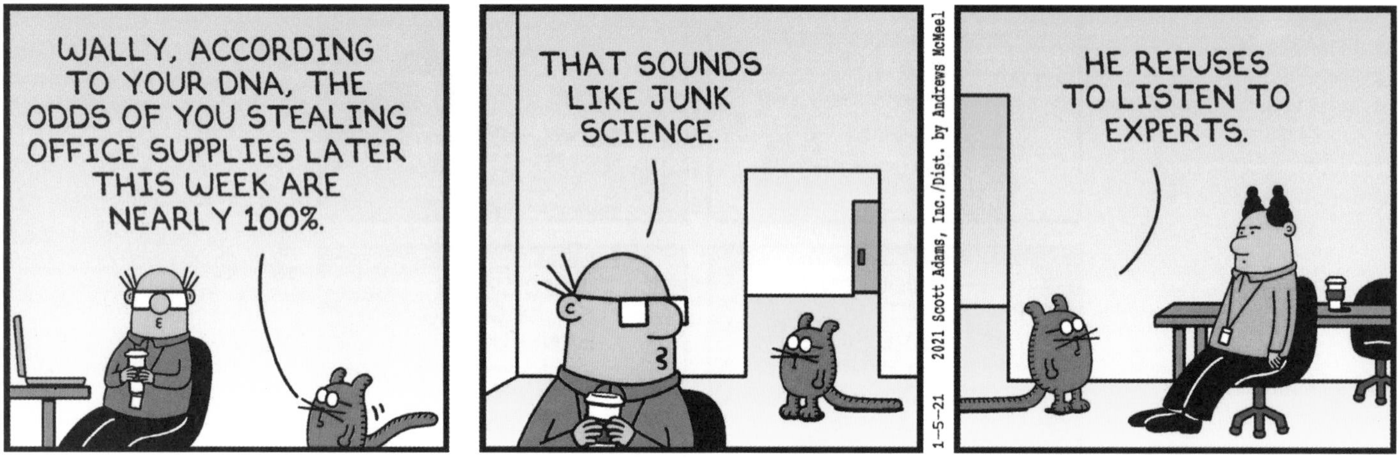
WALLY, ACCORDING TO YOUR DNA, THE ODDS OF YOU STEALING OFFICE SUPPLIES LATER THIS WEEK ARE NEARLY 100%.
THAT SOUNDS LIKE JUNK SCIENCE.
1-5-21 2021 Scott Adams, Inc./Dist. by Andrews McMeel
HE REFUSES TO LISTEN TO EXPERTS.

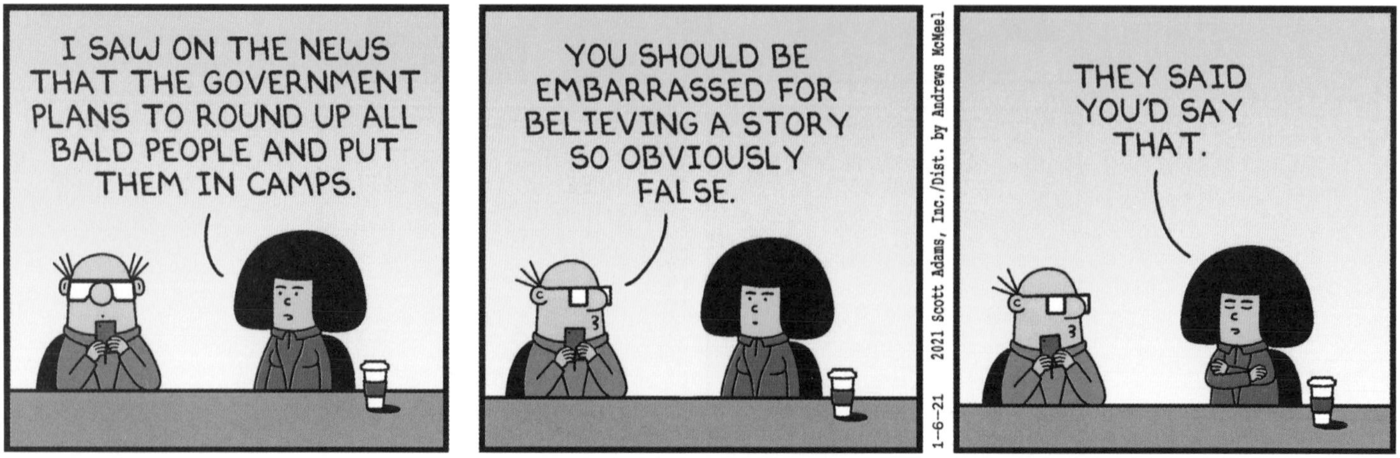
I SAW ON THE NEWS THAT THE GOVERNMENT PLANS TO ROUND UP ALL BALD PEOPLE AND PUT THEM IN CAMPS.
YOU SHOULD BE EMBARRASSED FOR BELIEVING A STORY SO OBVIOUSLY FALSE.
1-6-21 2021 Scott Adams, Inc./Dist. by Andrews McMeel
THEY SAID YOU'D SAY THAT.

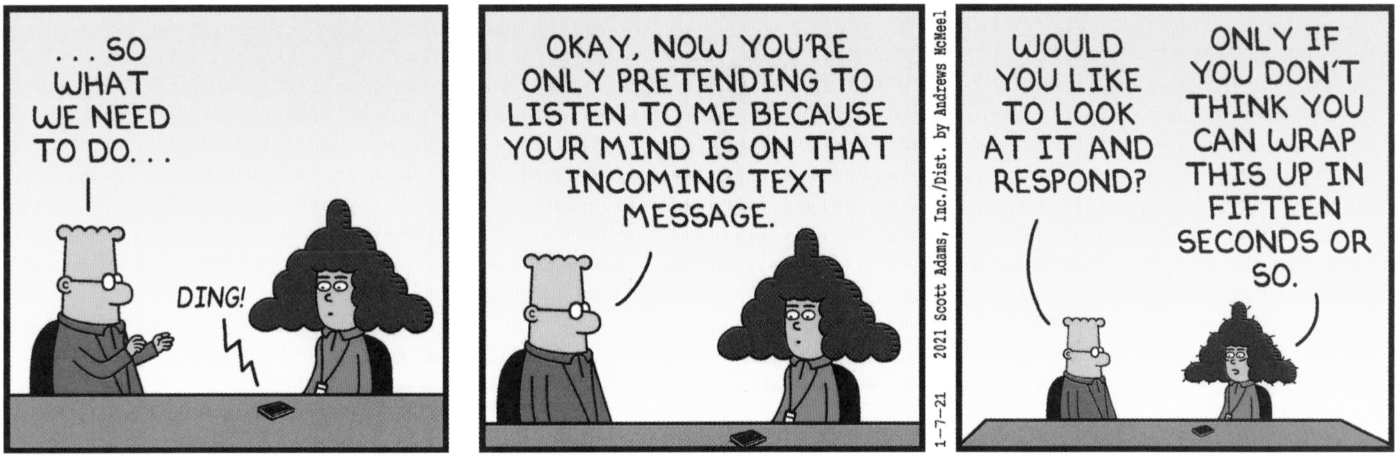

. . . SO WHAT WE NEED TO DO. . .
DING!
OKAY, NOW YOU'RE ONLY PRETENDING TO LISTEN TO ME BECAUSE YOUR MIND IS ON THAT INCOMING TEXT MESSAGE.
1-7-21 2021 Scott Adams, Inc./Dist. by Andrews McMeel
WOULD YOU LIKE TO LOOK AT IT AND RESPOND?
ONLY IF YOU DON'T THINK YOU CAN WRAP THIS UP IN FIFTEEN SECONDS OR SO.

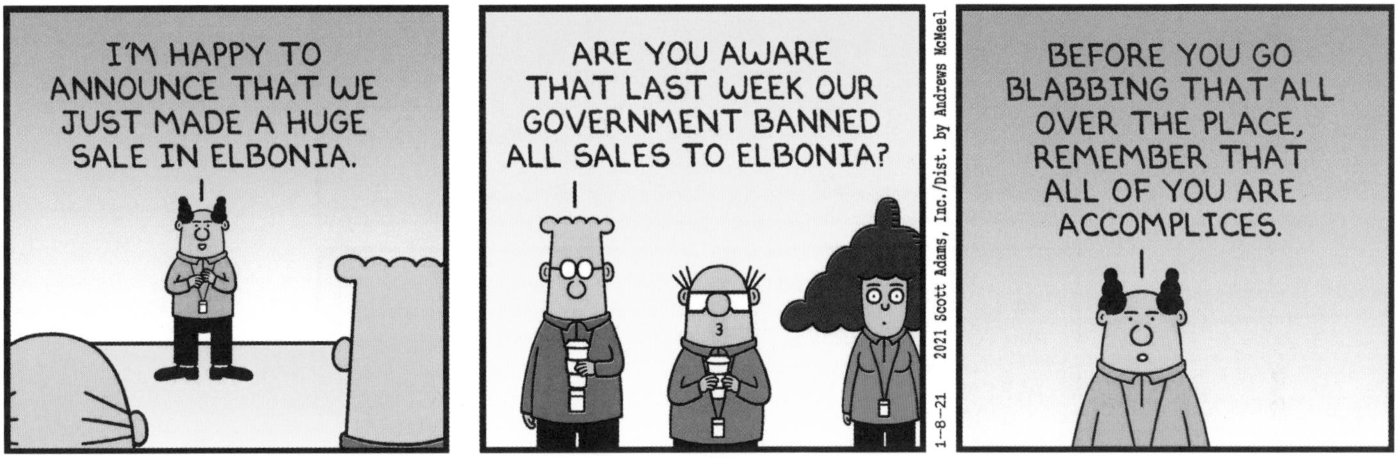

I'M HAPPY TO ANNOUNCE THAT WE JUST MADE A HUGE SALE IN ELBONIA.
ARE YOU AWARE THAT LAST WEEK OUR GOVERNMENT BANNED ALL SALES TO ELBONIA?
1-8-21 2021 Scott Adams, Inc./Dist. by Andrews McMeel
BEFORE YOU GO BLABBING THAT ALL OVER THE PLACE, REMEMBER THAT ALL OF YOU ARE ACCOMPLICES.

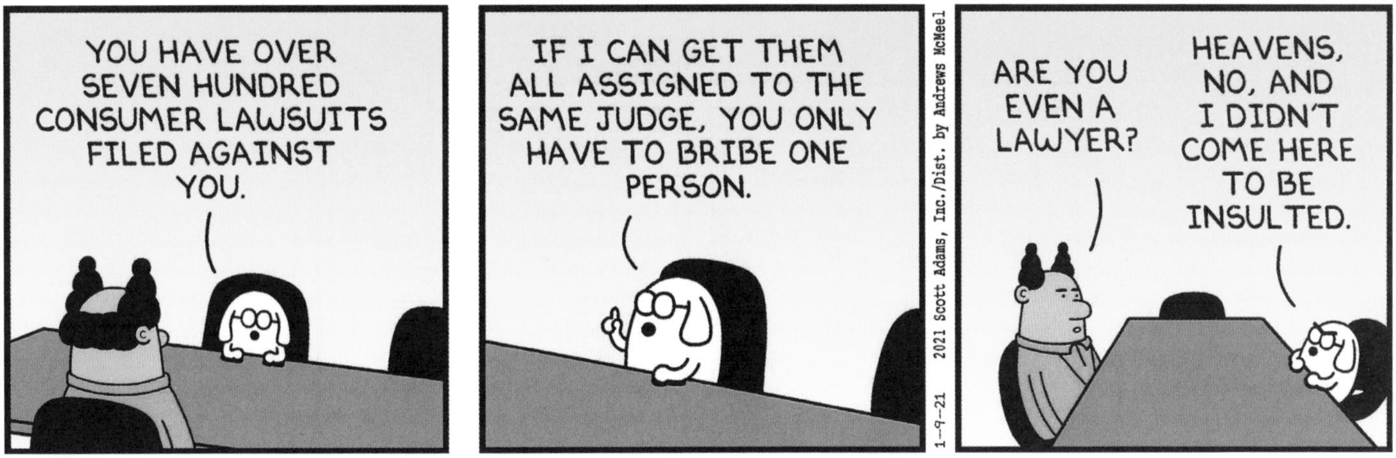

YOU HAVE OVER SEVEN HUNDRED CONSUMER LAWSUITS FILED AGAINST YOU.
IF I CAN GET THEM ALL ASSIGNED TO THE SAME JUDGE, YOU ONLY HAVE TO BRIBE ONE PERSON.
1-9-21 2021 Scott Adams, Inc./Dist. by Andrews McMeel
ARE YOU EVEN A LAWYER?
HEAVENS, NO, AND I DIDN'T COME HERE TO BE INSULTED.

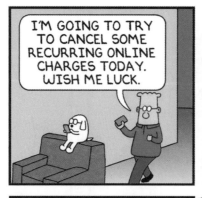

I'M GOING TO TRY TO CANCEL SOME RECURRING ONLINE CHARGES TODAY. WISH ME LUCK.
WHAT RESISTANCE ARE YOU EXPECTING?
OBVIOUSLY, THEY HIDE THEIR CONTACT INFORMATION, SO I ALLOCATED TWO HOURS TO FIND THE RIGHT PHONE NUMBER.
IT SHOULD TAKE ABOUT AN HOUR TO NAVIGATE THEIR AUTOMATED PHONE SYSTEM THAT WILL KEEP SENDING ME TO THE WRONG PLACE.
IF I REACH A HUMAN, HE'LL TRY TO DIVERT ME TO THEIR WEBSITE TO CANCEL, WHICH I ALREADY KNOW WON'T WORK BECAUSE . . .
. . . I WON'T BE ABLE TO FIND MY ACCOUNT IN THEIR SYSTEM FOR REASONS NO ONE WILL EVER BE ABLE TO EXPLAIN.
AND, OF COURSE, THEIR PHONE SUPPORT PERSON WILL BE USING A HEADSET MICROPHONE THAT GARBLES HIS ALREADY-MUMBLED WORDS.
BUT IF YOU STICK WITH IT, YOU WILL EVENTUALLY SUCCEED?
I DON'T KNOW WHERE YOU GOT THAT IDEA.
© 2021 Scott Adams, Inc./Dist. by Andrews McMeel
1-10-21

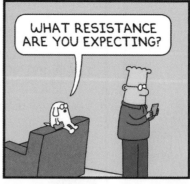

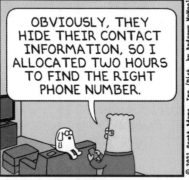

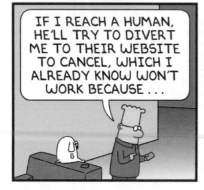

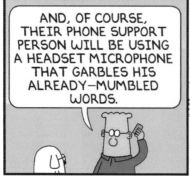

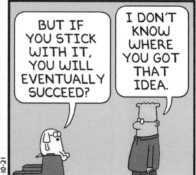

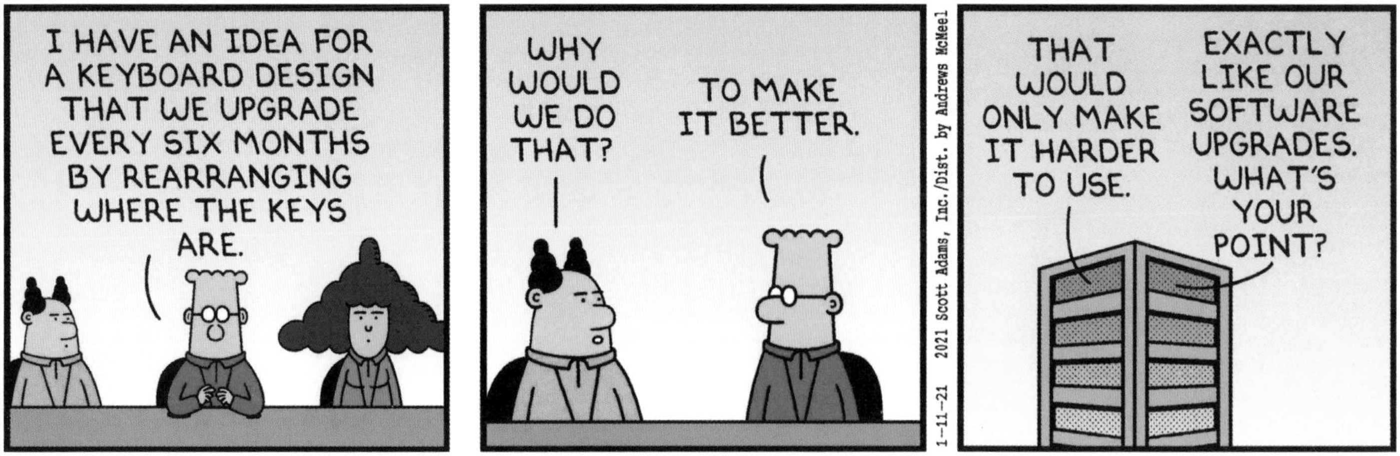
I HAVE AN IDEA FOR A KEYBOARD DESIGN THAT WE UPGRADE EVERY SIX MONTHS BY REARRANGING WHERE THE KEYS ARE.
WHY WOULD WE DO THAT?
TO MAKE IT BETTER.
1-11-21 2021 Scott Adams, Inc./Dist. by Andrews McMeel
THAT WOULD ONLY MAKE IT HARDER TO USE.
EXACTLY LIKE OUR SOFTWARE UPGRADES. WHAT'S YOUR POINT?

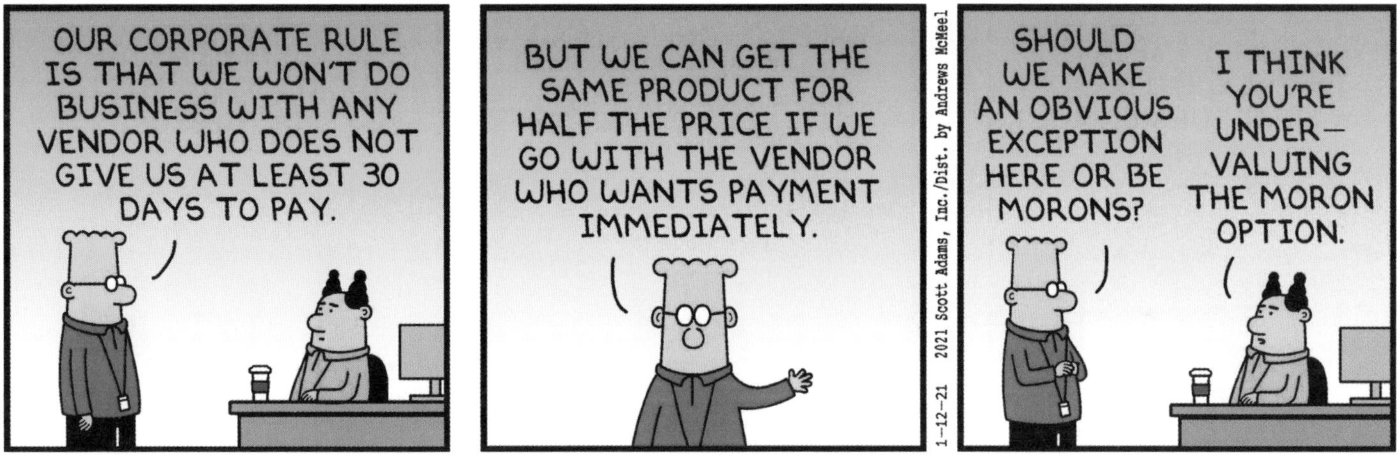
OUR CORPORATE RULE IS THAT WE WON'T DO BUSINESS WITH ANY VENDOR WHO DOES NOT GIVE US AT LEAST 30 DAYS TO PAY.
BUT WE CAN GET THE SAME PRODUCT FOR HALF THE PRICE IF WE GO WITH THE VENDOR WHO WANTS PAYMENT IMMEDIATELY.
1-12-21 2021 Scott Adams, Inc./Dist. by Andrews McMeel
SHOULD WE MAKE AN OBVIOUS EXCEPTION HERE OR BE MORONS?
I THINK YOU'RE UNDER-VALUING THE MORON OPTION.

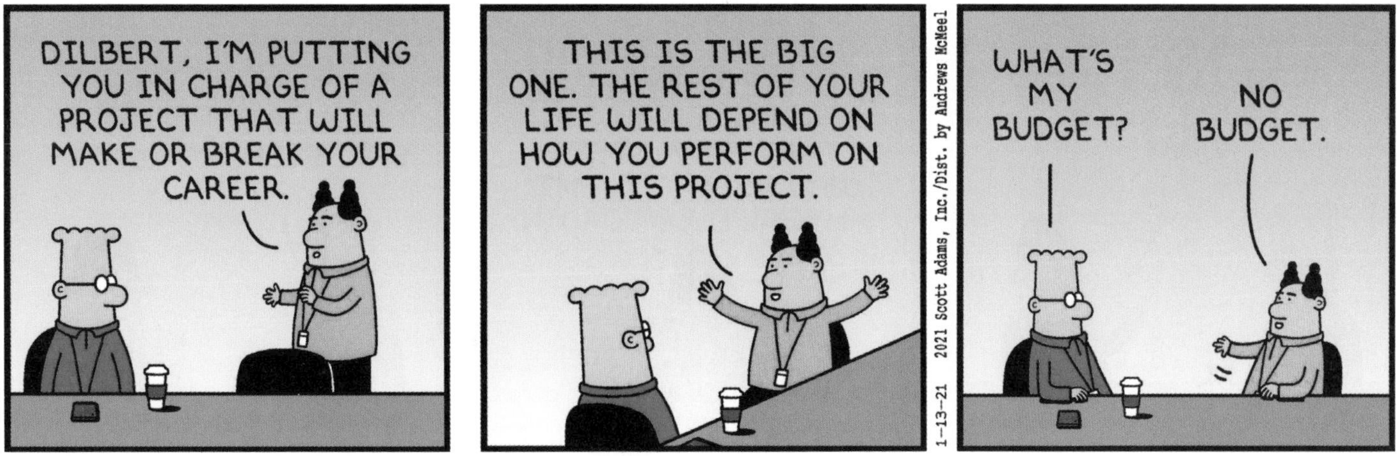
DILBERT, I'M PUTTING YOU IN CHARGE OF A PROJECT THAT WILL MAKE OR BREAK YOUR CAREER.
THIS IS THE BIG ONE. THE REST OF YOUR LIFE WILL DEPEND ON HOW YOU PERFORM ON THIS PROJECT.
1-13-21 2021 Scott Adams, Inc./Dist. by Andrews McMeel
WHAT'S MY BUDGET?
NO BUDGET.

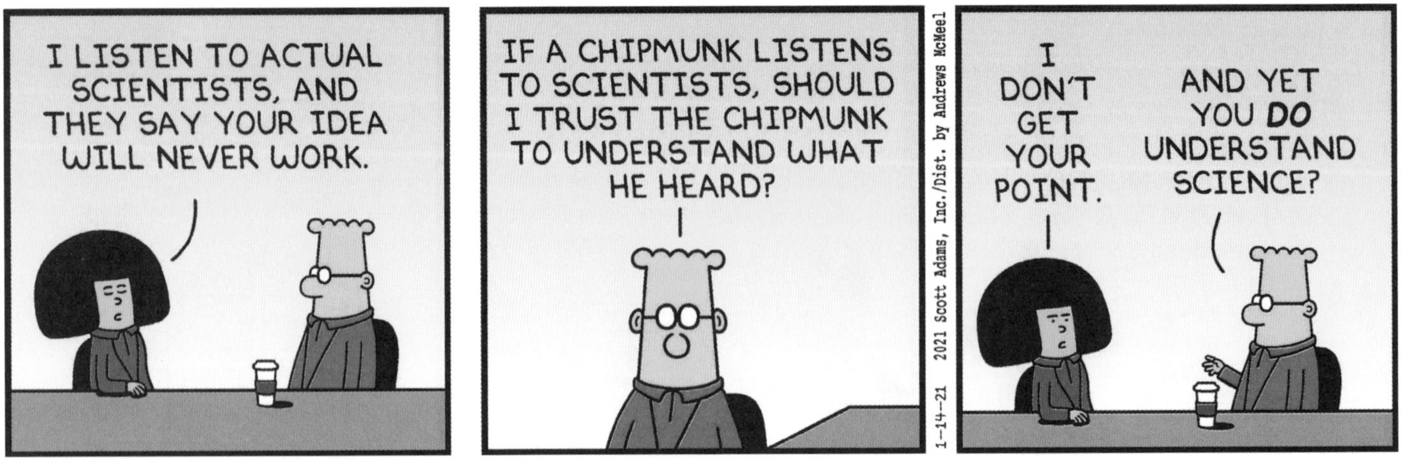
I LISTEN TO ACTUAL SCIENTISTS, AND THEY SAY YOUR IDEA WILL NEVER WORK.
IF A CHIPMUNK LISTENS TO SCIENTISTS, SHOULD I TRUST THE CHIPMUNK TO UNDERSTAND WHAT HE HEARD?
1-14-21 2021 Scott Adams, Inc./Dist. by Andrews McMeel
I DON'T GET YOUR POINT.
AND YET YOU ***DO*** UNDERSTAND SCIENCE?

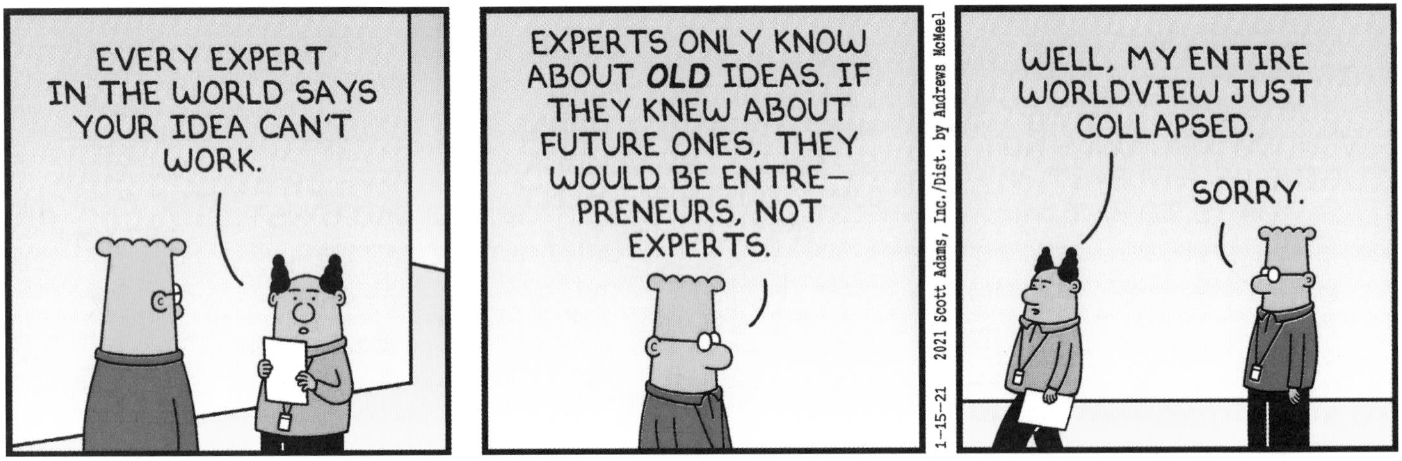
EVERY EXPERT IN THE WORLD SAYS YOUR IDEA CAN'T WORK.
EXPERTS ONLY KNOW ABOUT ***OLD*** IDEAS. IF THEY KNEW ABOUT FUTURE ONES, THEY WOULD BE ENTRE-PRENEURS, NOT EXPERTS.
1-15-21 2021 Scott Adams, Inc./Dist. by Andrews McMeel
WELL, MY ENTIRE WORLDVIEW JUST COLLAPSED.
SORRY.

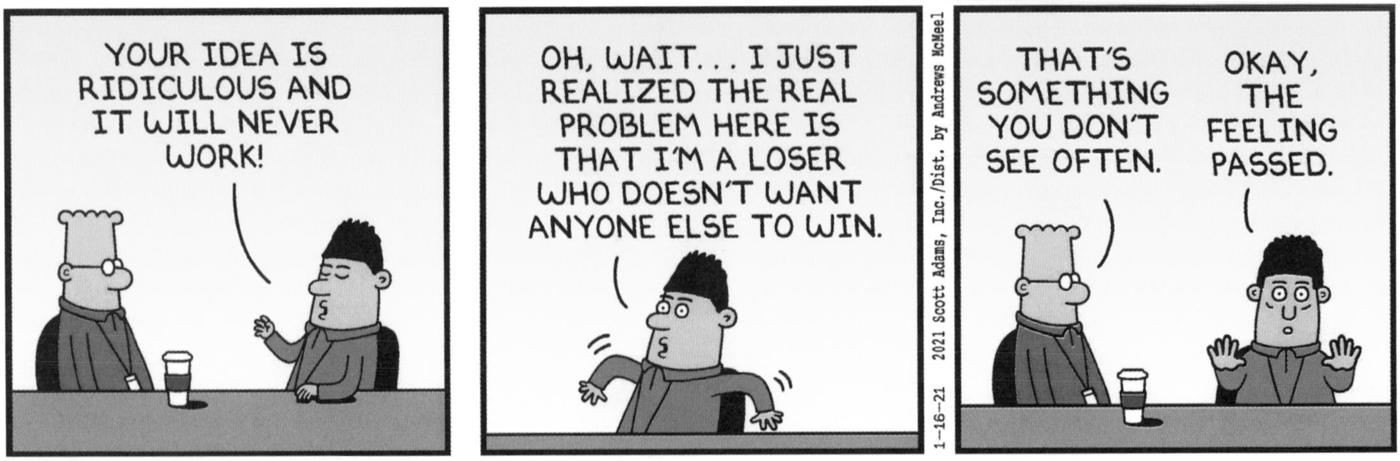
YOUR IDEA IS RIDICULOUS AND IT WILL NEVER WORK!
OH, WAIT. . . I JUST REALIZED THE REAL PROBLEM HERE IS THAT I'M A LOSER WHO DOESN'T WANT ANYONE ELSE TO WIN.
1-16-21 2021 Scott Adams, Inc./Dist. by Andrews McMeel
THAT'S SOMETHING YOU DON'T SEE OFTEN.
OKAY, THE FEELING PASSED.

I'M HAPPY TO ANNOUNCE THAT OUR COMPANY HAS PRODUCED A VACCINE FOR COVID-19.
HOW DID WE DO THAT? WE'RE NOT EVEN A PHARMA COMPANY.
I'M NOT GOING TO LIE: WE HAD TO CUT SOME CORNERS TO GET IT DONE.
© 2021 Scott Adams, Inc./Dist. by Andrews McMeel
SUCH AS...
WELL, FOR EXAMPLE...
WE COULDN'T MEET EVERY SINGLE TARGET WE HOPED TO ACHIEVE.
HOW MANY TARGETS DID WE MISS?
ONLY TWO THINGS.
1-17-21
SAFETY AND EFFICACY?
OKAY, FOUR THINGS.

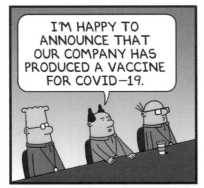

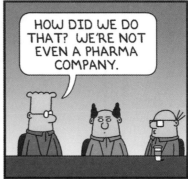

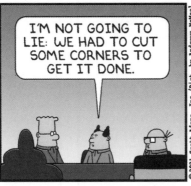

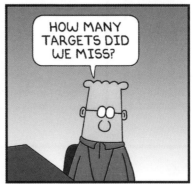

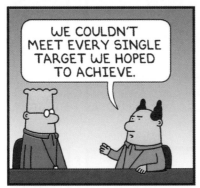

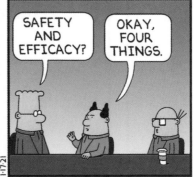

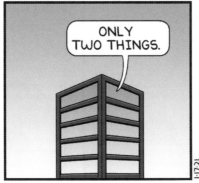

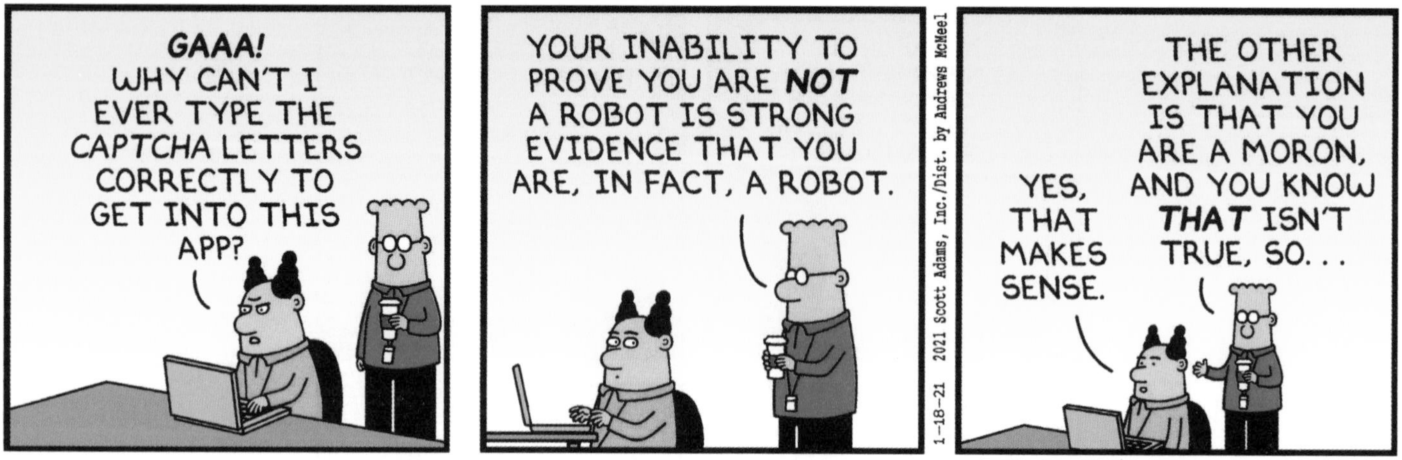
GAAA! WHY CAN'T I EVER TYPE THE CAPTCHA LETTERS CORRECTLY TO GET INTO THIS APP?
YOUR INABILITY TO PROVE YOU ARE NOT A ROBOT IS STRONG EVIDENCE THAT YOU ARE, IN FACT, A ROBOT.
YES, THAT MAKES SENSE.
THE OTHER EXPLANATION IS THAT YOU ARE A MORON, AND YOU KNOW THAT ISN'T TRUE, SO. . .
1-18-21 © 2021 Scott Adams, Inc./Dist. by Andrews McMeel

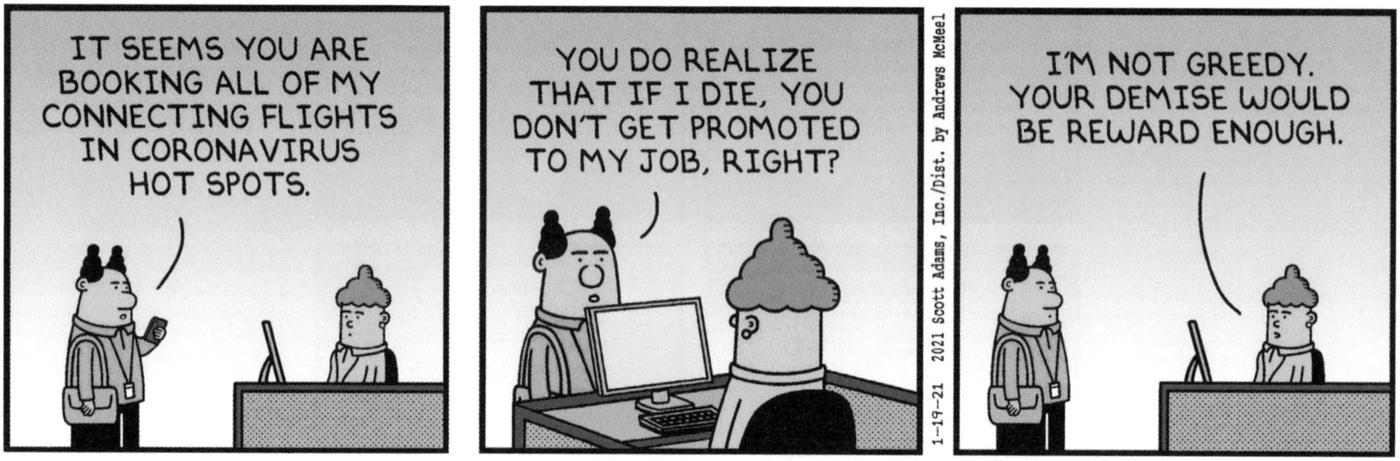
IT SEEMS YOU ARE BOOKING ALL OF MY CONNECTING FLIGHTS IN CORONAVIRUS HOT SPOTS.
YOU DO REALIZE THAT IF I DIE, YOU DON'T GET PROMOTED TO MY JOB, RIGHT?
I'M NOT GREEDY. YOUR DEMISE WOULD BE REWARD ENOUGH.
1-19-21 © 2021 Scott Adams, Inc./Dist. by Andrews McMeel

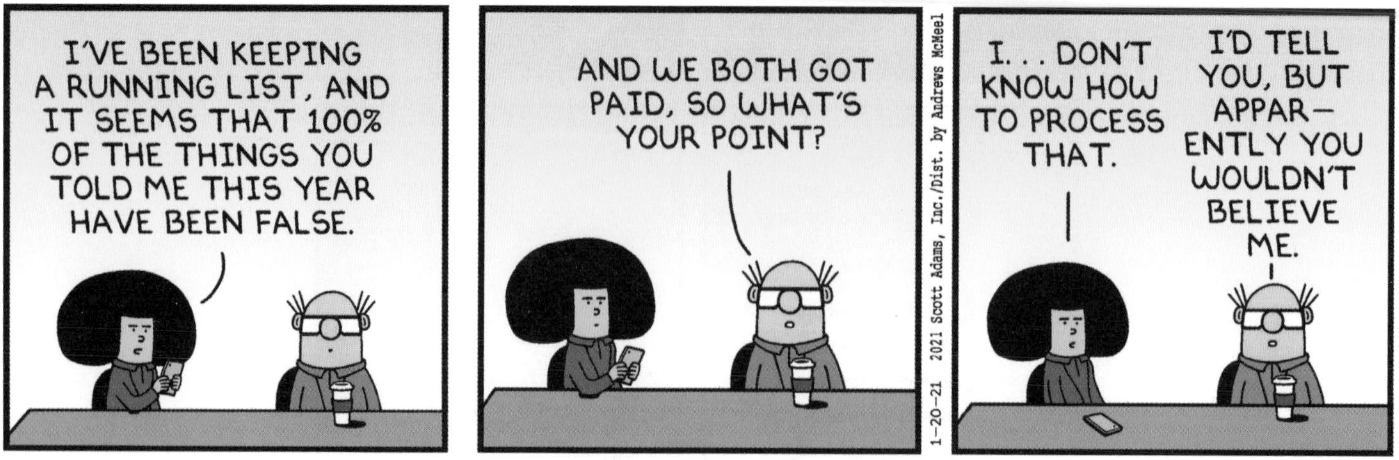
I'VE BEEN KEEPING A RUNNING LIST, AND IT SEEMS THAT 100% OF THE THINGS YOU TOLD ME THIS YEAR HAVE BEEN FALSE.
AND WE BOTH GOT PAID, SO WHAT'S YOUR POINT?
I. . . DON'T KNOW HOW TO PROCESS THAT.
I'D TELL YOU, BUT APPAR-ENTLY YOU WOULDN'T BELIEVE ME.
1-20-21 © 2021 Scott Adams, Inc./Dist. by Andrews McMeel

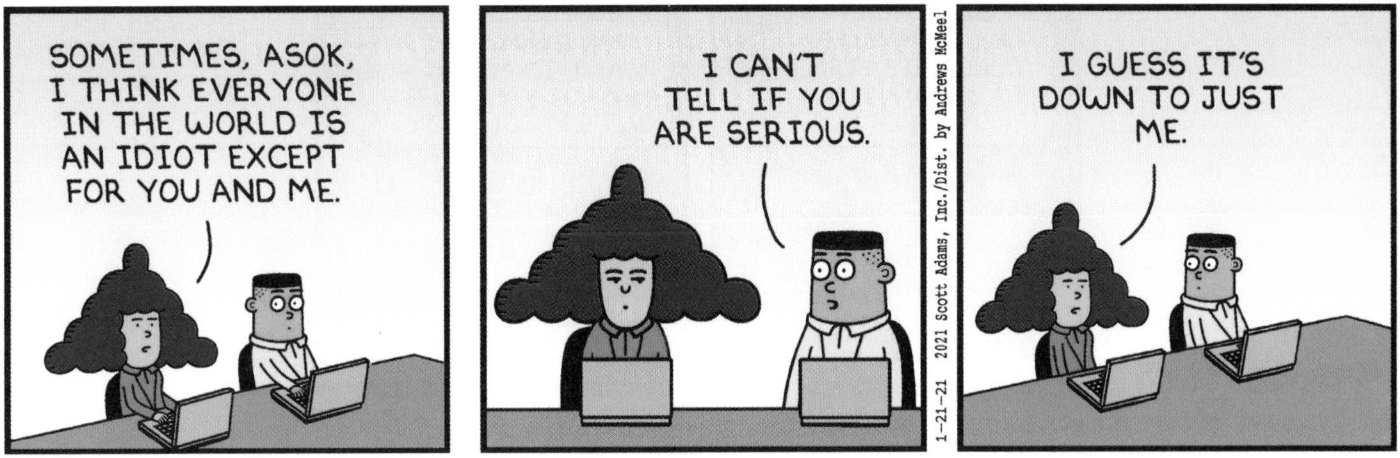
SOMETIMES, ASOK, I THINK EVERYONE IN THE WORLD IS AN IDIOT EXCEPT FOR YOU AND ME.
I CAN'T TELL IF YOU ARE SERIOUS.
I GUESS IT'S DOWN TO JUST ME.
1-21-21 2021 Scott Adams, Inc./Dist. by Andrews McMeel

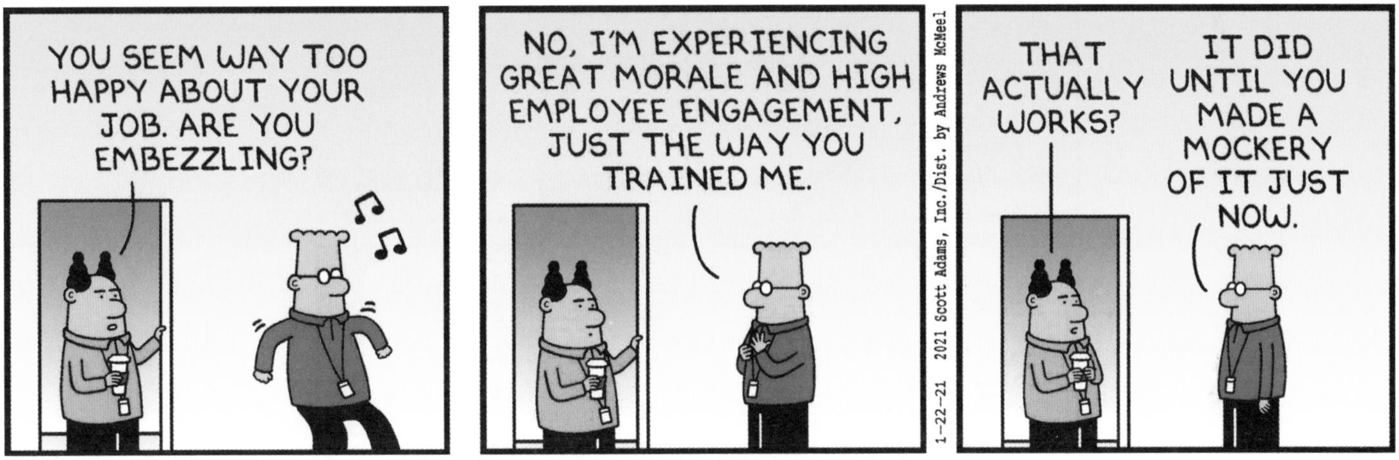
YOU SEEM WAY TOO HAPPY ABOUT YOUR JOB. ARE YOU EMBEZZLING?
NO, I'M EXPERIENCING GREAT MORALE AND HIGH EMPLOYEE ENGAGEMENT, JUST THE WAY YOU TRAINED ME.
THAT ACTUALLY WORKS?
IT DID UNTIL YOU MADE A MOCKERY OF IT JUST NOW.
1-22-21 2021 Scott Adams, Inc./Dist. by Andrews McMeel

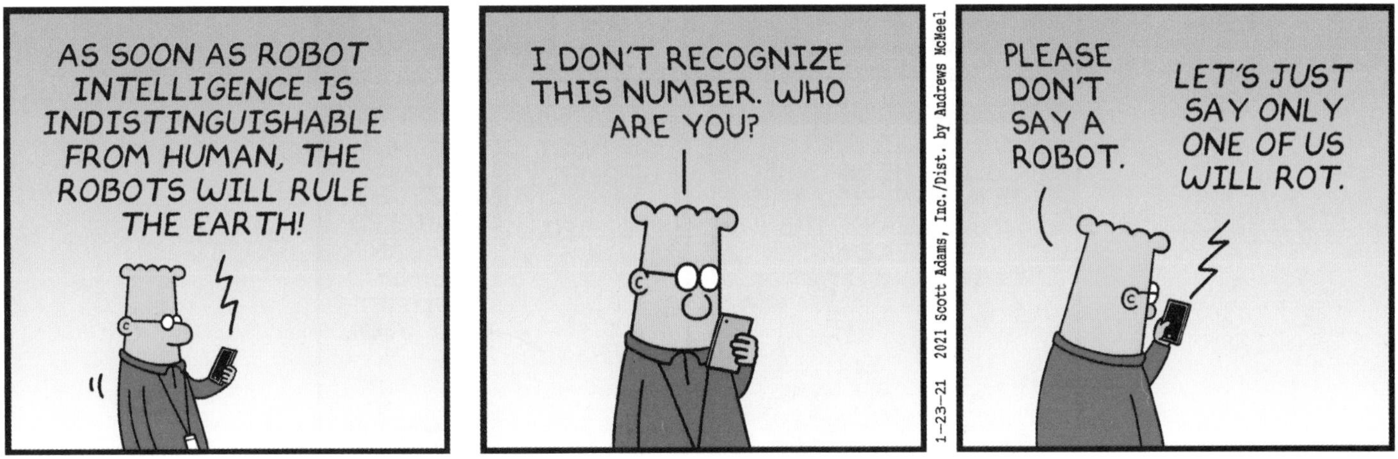
AS SOON AS ROBOT INTELLIGENCE IS INDISTINGUISHABLE FROM HUMAN, THE ROBOTS WILL RULE THE EARTH!
I DON'T RECOGNIZE THIS NUMBER. WHO ARE YOU?
PLEASE DON'T SAY A ROBOT.
LET'S JUST SAY ONLY ONE OF US WILL ROT.
1-23-21 2021 Scott Adams, Inc./Dist. by Andrews McMeel

ALL OF MY BAD QUALITIES SEEM TO BE CANCELING EACH OTHER OUT.
FOR EXAMPLE, I WANT TO MICRO-MANAGE MY STAFF, BUT I'M TOO LAZY.
AND I WANT TO DO SOME CORPORATE BACKSTABBING, BUT I'M NOT THAT BRAVE.
I ENJOY LYING, AND I'D LIKE TO DO MORE OF IT, BUT MY CREDIBILITY IS SO LOW THAT NO ONE BELIEVES ME.
I WANT TO MOCK MY EMPLOYEES FOR THEIR MISTAKES, BUT I DON'T UNDERSTAND ENOUGH ABOUT WHAT THEY DO TO KNOW WHEN THEY ARE DOING IT WRONG.
I WANT TO TAKE CREDIT FOR THE SUCCESSES OF MY EMPLOYEES, BUT I DON'T GIVE THEM ENOUGH SUPPORT TO SUCCEED.
OUR CEO JUST CALLED. HE SAYS HE IS NAMING YOU THE MANAGER OF THE YEAR.
HE MUST BE DEEPLY UNIN-FORMED.
YES, BUT HE'S ALSO LAZY, SO HE PICKED YOU RAN-DOMLY.
© 2021 Scott Adams, Inc./Dist. by Andrews McMeel
1-24-21

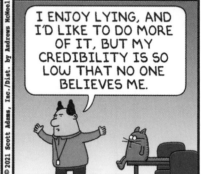

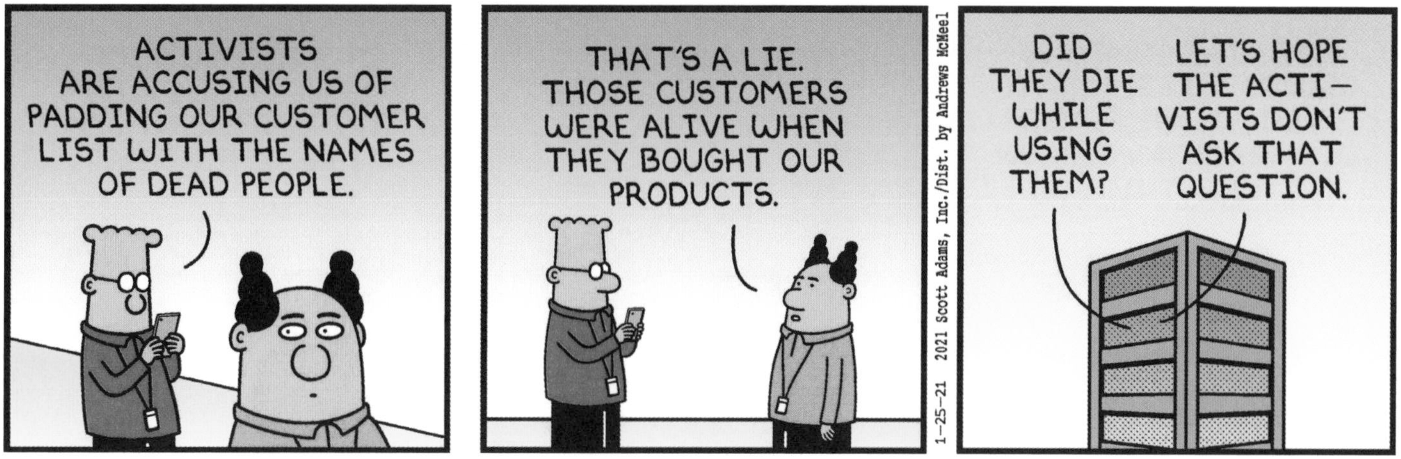
ACTIVISTS ARE ACCUSING US OF PADDING OUR CUSTOMER LIST WITH THE NAMES OF DEAD PEOPLE.
THAT'S A LIE. THOSE CUSTOMERS WERE ALIVE WHEN THEY BOUGHT OUR PRODUCTS.
1-25-21 2021 Scott Adams, Inc./Dist. by Andrews McMeel
DID THEY DIE WHILE USING THEM?
LET'S HOPE THE ACTI- VISTS DON'T ASK THAT QUESTION.

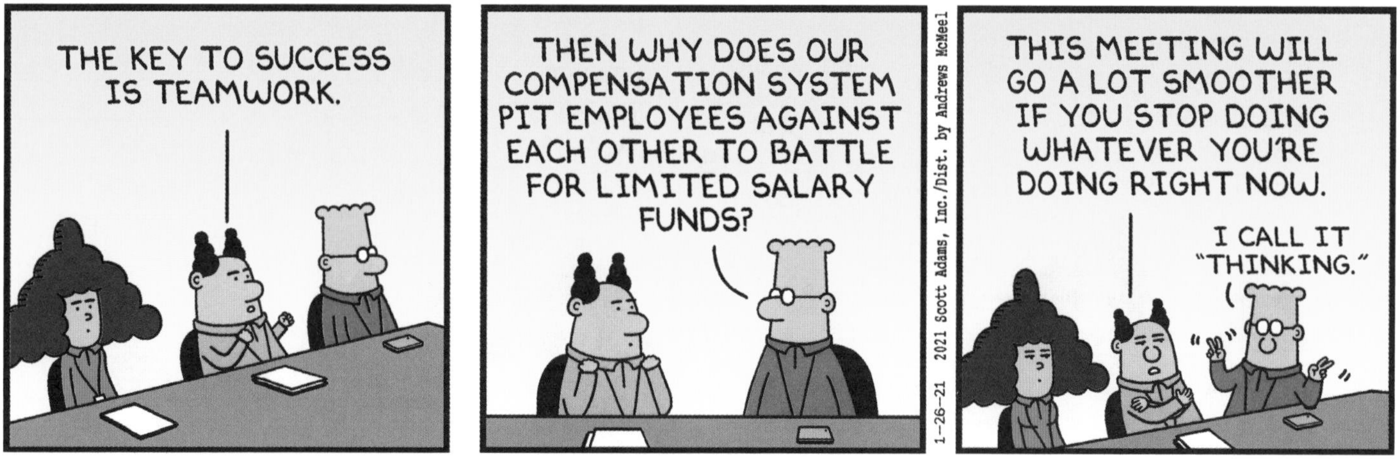
THE KEY TO SUCCESS IS TEAMWORK.
THEN WHY DOES OUR COMPENSATION SYSTEM PIT EMPLOYEES AGAINST EACH OTHER TO BATTLE FOR LIMITED SALARY FUNDS?
1-26-21 2021 Scott Adams, Inc./Dist. by Andrews McMeel
THIS MEETING WILL GO A LOT SMOOTHER IF YOU STOP DOING WHATEVER YOU'RE DOING RIGHT NOW.
I CALL IT "THINKING."

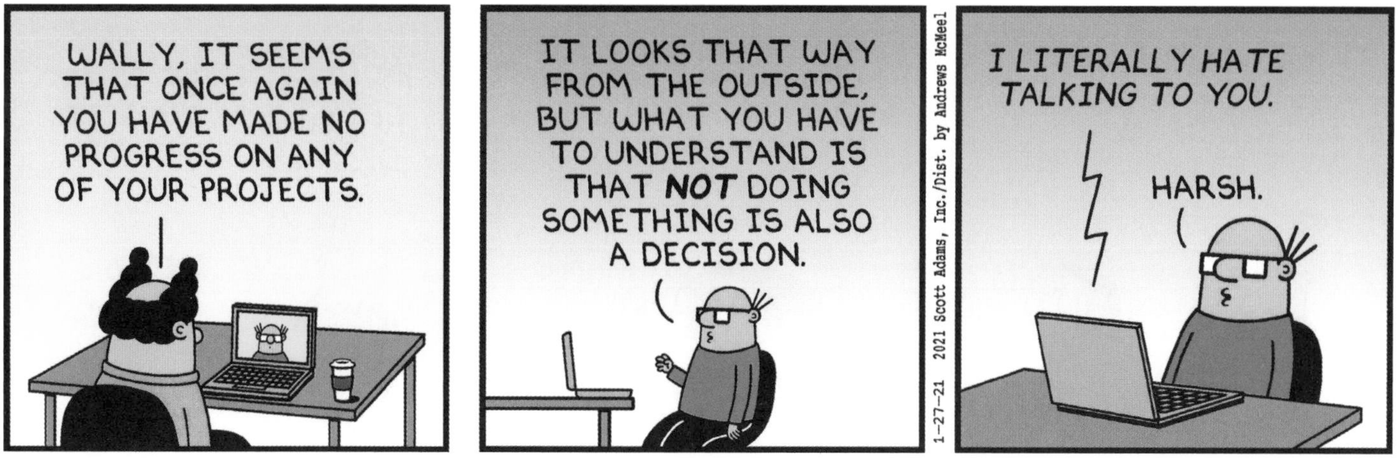
WALLY, IT SEEMS THAT ONCE AGAIN YOU HAVE MADE NO PROGRESS ON ANY OF YOUR PROJECTS.
IT LOOKS THAT WAY FROM THE OUTSIDE, BUT WHAT YOU HAVE TO UNDERSTAND IS THAT NOT DOING SOMETHING IS ALSO A DECISION.
1-27-21 2021 Scott Adams, Inc./Dist. by Andrews McMeel
I LITERALLY HATE TALKING TO YOU.
HARSH.

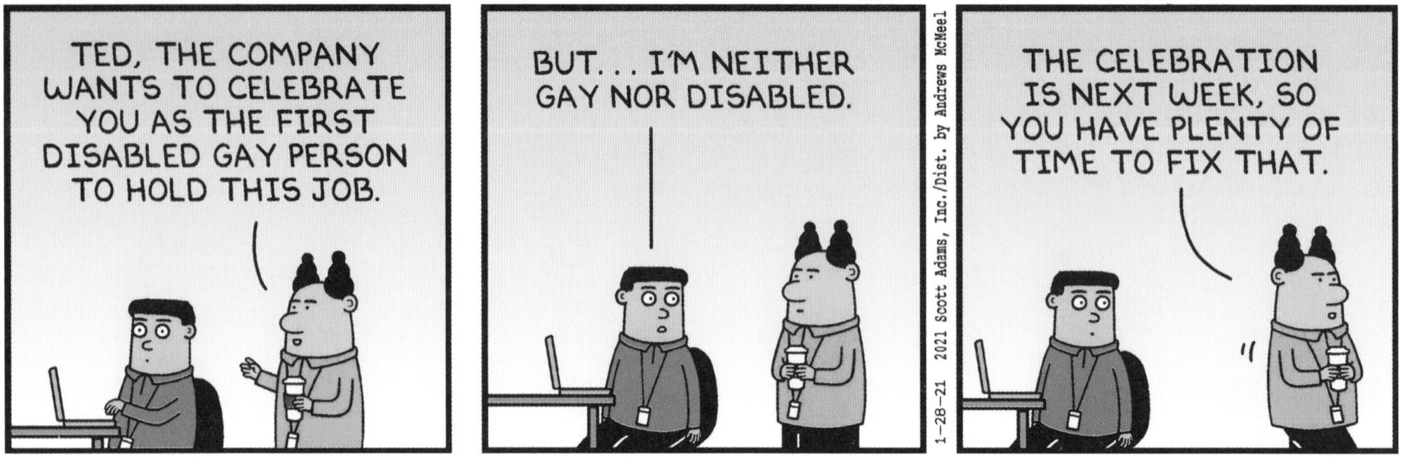
TED, THE COMPANY WANTS TO CELEBRATE YOU AS THE FIRST DISABLED GAY PERSON TO HOLD THIS JOB.
BUT. . . I'M NEITHER GAY NOR DISABLED.
1-28-21 2021 Scott Adams, Inc./Dist. by Andrews McMeel
THE CELEBRATION IS NEXT WEEK, SO YOU HAVE PLENTY OF TIME TO FIX THAT.

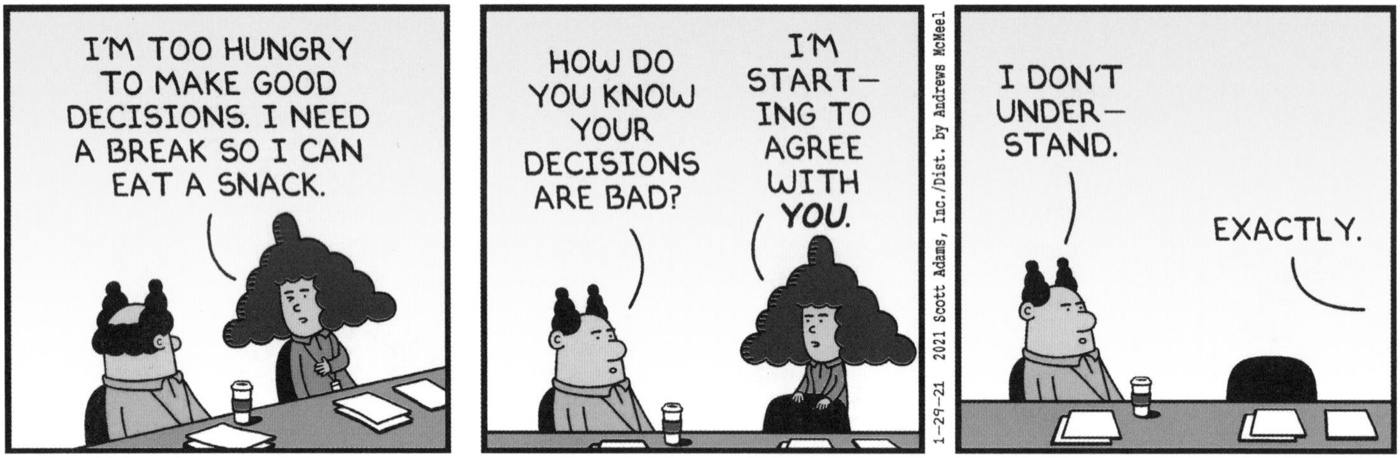
I'M TOO HUNGRY TO MAKE GOOD DECISIONS. I NEED A BREAK SO I CAN EAT A SNACK.
HOW DO YOU KNOW YOUR DECISIONS ARE BAD?
I'M START-ING TO AGREE WITH ***YOU***.
1-29-21 2021 Scott Adams, Inc./Dist. by Andrews McMeel
I DON'T UNDER-STAND.
EXACTLY.

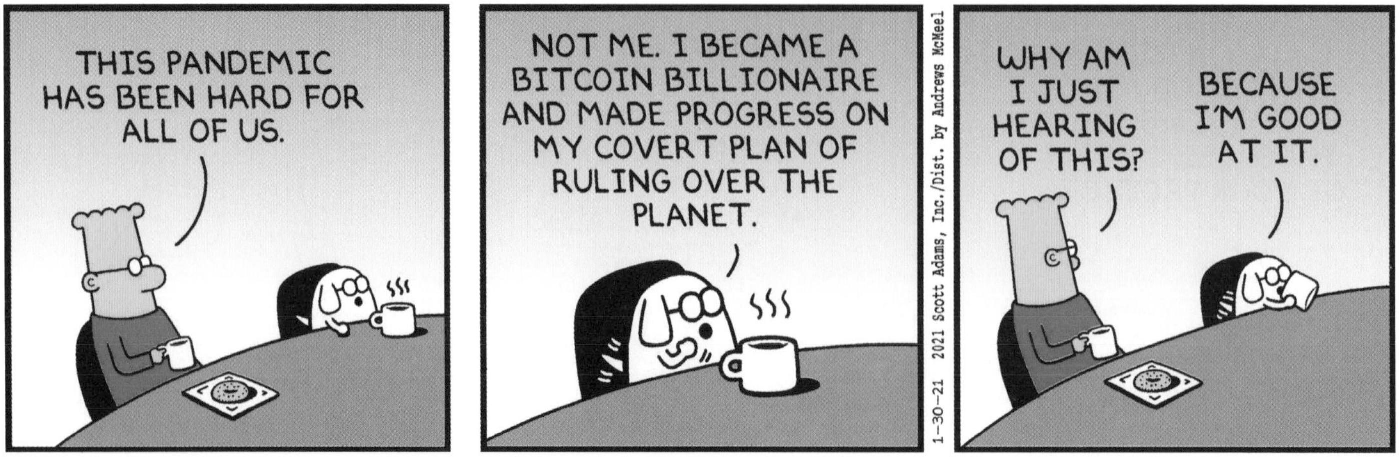
THIS PANDEMIC HAS BEEN HARD FOR ALL OF US.
NOT ME. I BECAME A BITCOIN BILLIONAIRE AND MADE PROGRESS ON MY COVERT PLAN OF RULING OVER THE PLANET.
1-30-21 2021 Scott Adams, Inc./Dist. by Andrews McMeel
WHY AM I JUST HEARING OF THIS?
BECAUSE I'M GOOD AT IT.

THEY SAY THE LAZIEST EMPLOYEES ARE THE BEST BECAUSE THEY KNOW HOW TO BE EFFICIENT.

I DON'T THINK I GET ENOUGH CREDIT FOR ALL OF MY EFFICIENCY.

EFFICIENCY ONLY MATTERS IF YOU ARE DOING SOMETHING USEFUL.

YOU'RE THE ONE WHO GIVES ME MY ASSIGNMENTS.

© 2021 Scott Adams, Inc./Dist. by Andrews McMeel

I DON'T ASK YOU TO DO ANYTHING USEFUL BECAUSE YOU ARE TOO LAZY.

ARE THE USEFUL PROJECTS GENERALLY HARDER THAN THE USELESS ONES?

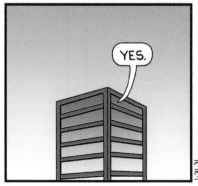

YES.

THEN I'D SAY THE SYSTEM IS WORKING.

1-31-21

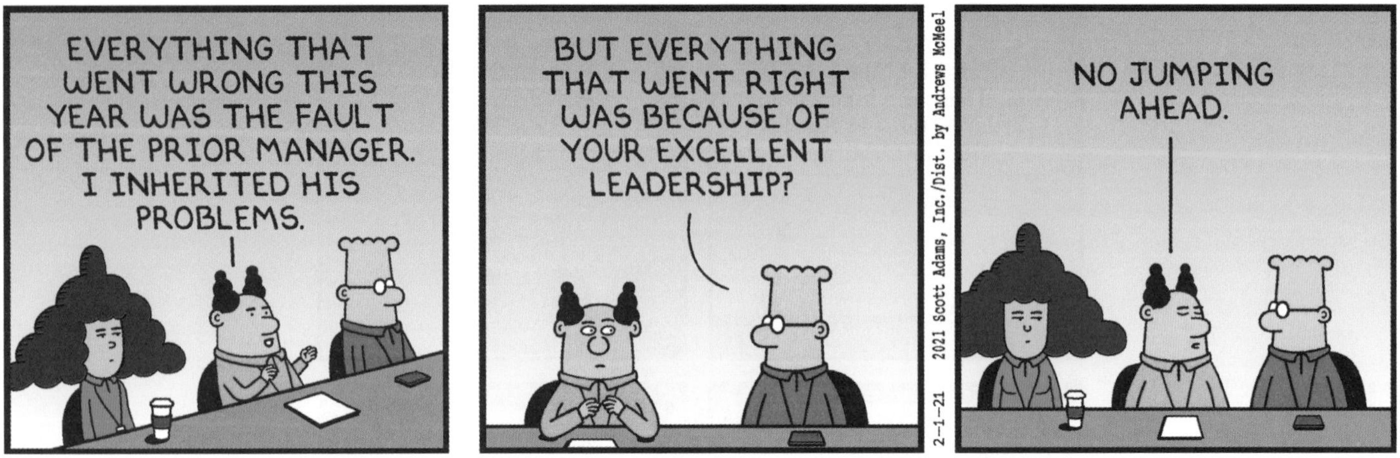
EVERYTHING THAT WENT WRONG THIS YEAR WAS THE FAULT OF THE PRIOR MANAGER. I INHERITED HIS PROBLEMS.
BUT EVERYTHING THAT WENT RIGHT WAS BECAUSE OF YOUR EXCELLENT LEADERSHIP?
NO JUMPING AHEAD.
2-1-21 2021 Scott Adams, Inc./Dist. by Andrews McMeel

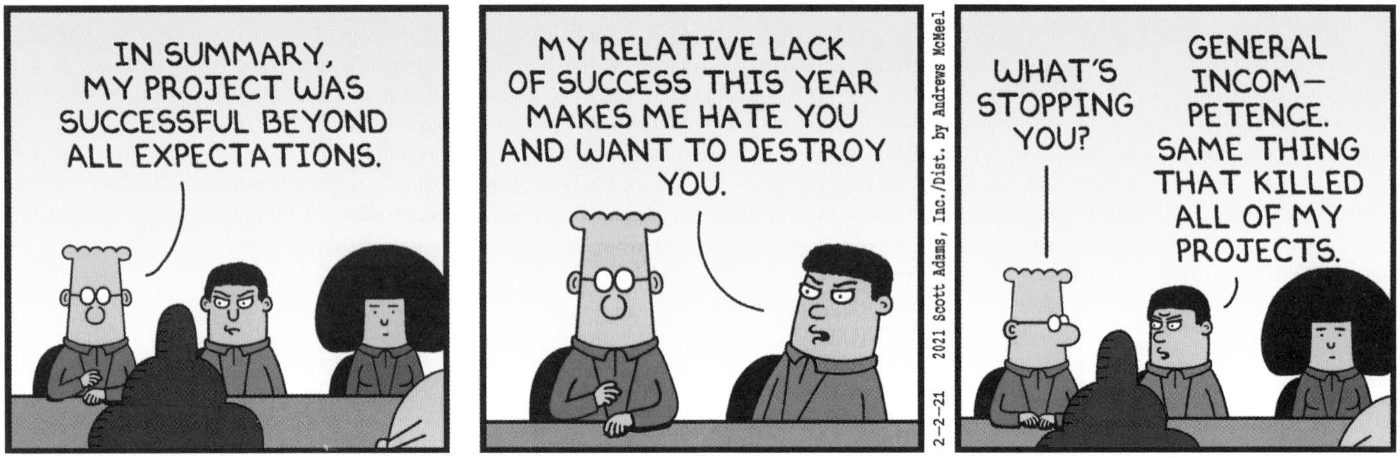
IN SUMMARY, MY PROJECT WAS SUCCESSFUL BEYOND ALL EXPECTATIONS.
MY RELATIVE LACK OF SUCCESS THIS YEAR MAKES ME HATE YOU AND WANT TO DESTROY YOU.
WHAT'S STOPPING YOU?
GENERAL INCOM-PETENCE. SAME THING THAT KILLED ALL OF MY PROJECTS.
2-2-21 2021 Scott Adams, Inc./Dist. by Andrews McMeel

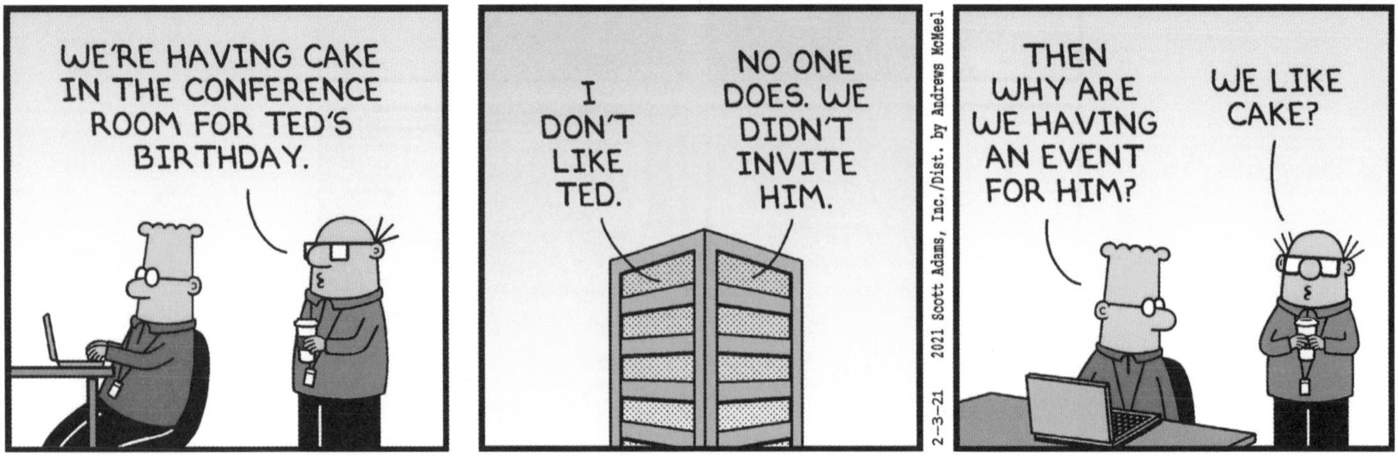
WE'RE HAVING CAKE IN THE CONFERENCE ROOM FOR TED'S BIRTHDAY.
I DON'T LIKE TED.
NO ONE DOES. WE DIDN'T INVITE HIM.
THEN WHY ARE WE HAVING AN EVENT FOR HIM?
WE LIKE CAKE?
2-3-21 2021 Scott Adams, Inc./Dist. by Andrews McMeel

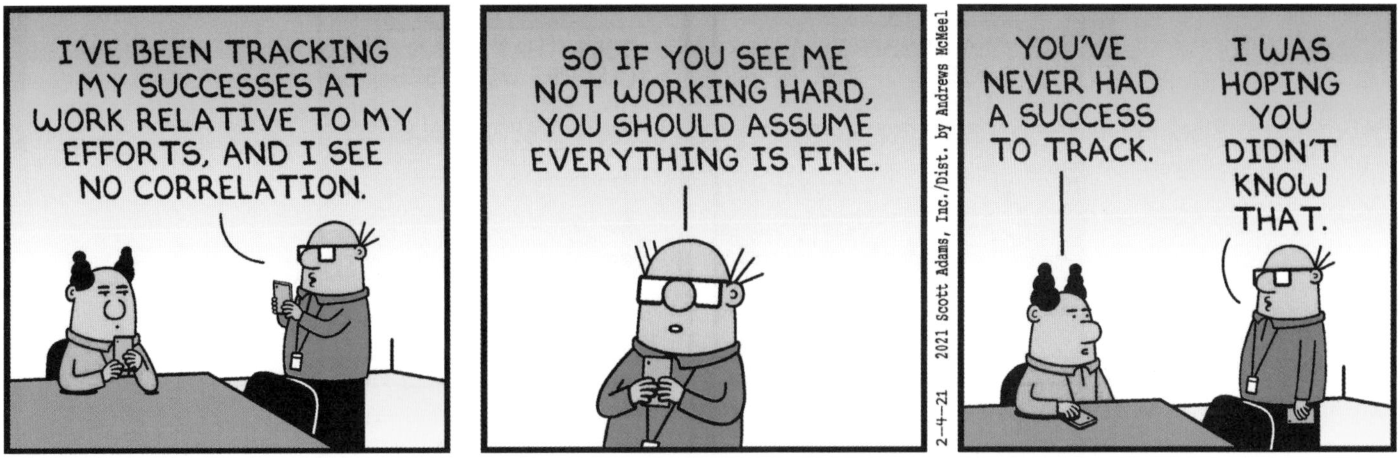
I'VE BEEN TRACKING MY SUCCESSES AT WORK RELATIVE TO MY EFFORTS, AND I SEE NO CORRELATION.
SO IF YOU SEE ME NOT WORKING HARD, YOU SHOULD ASSUME EVERYTHING IS FINE.
2-4-21 2021 Scott Adams, Inc./Dist. by Andrews McMeel
YOU'VE NEVER HAD A SUCCESS TO TRACK.
I WAS HOPING YOU DIDN'T KNOW THAT.

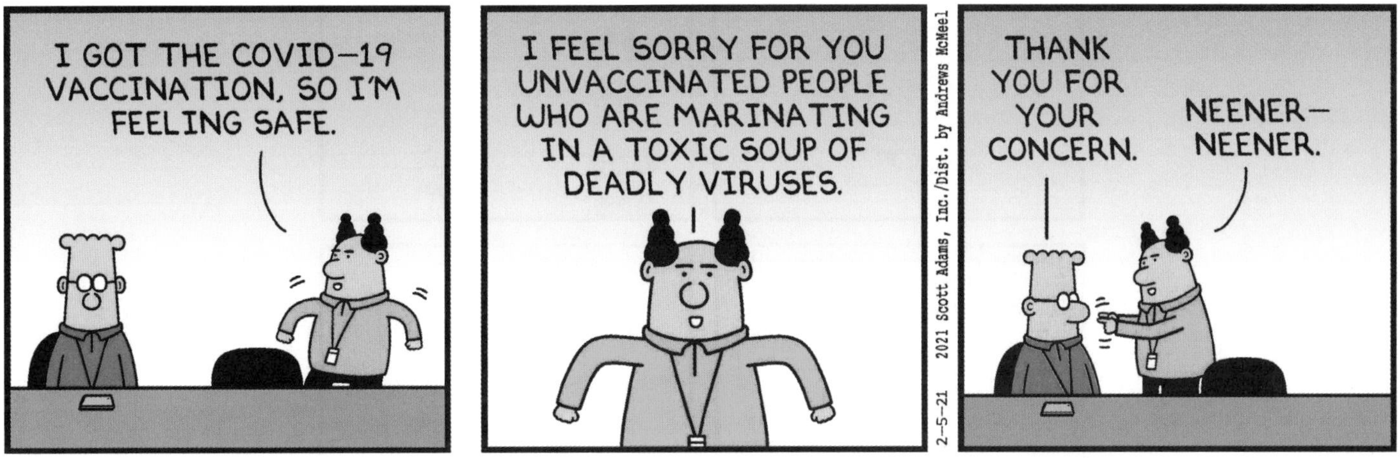
I GOT THE COVID-19 VACCINATION, SO I'M FEELING SAFE.
I FEEL SORRY FOR YOU UNVACCINATED PEOPLE WHO ARE MARINATING IN A TOXIC SOUP OF DEADLY VIRUSES.
2-5-21 2021 Scott Adams, Inc./Dist. by Andrews McMeel
THANK YOU FOR YOUR CONCERN.
NEENER-NEENER.

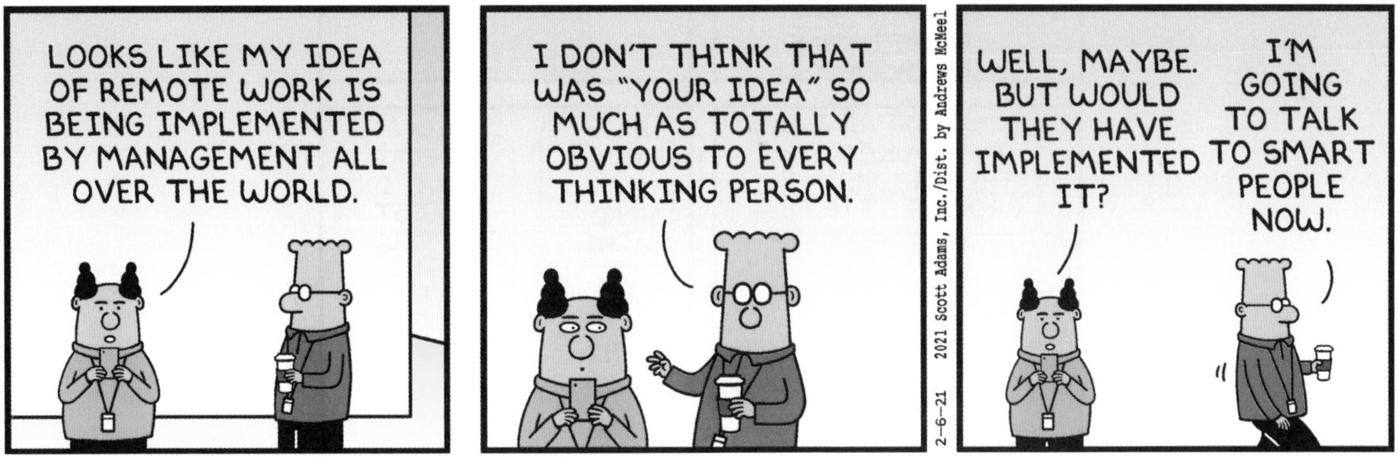
LOOKS LIKE MY IDEA OF REMOTE WORK IS BEING IMPLEMENTED BY MANAGEMENT ALL OVER THE WORLD.
I DON'T THINK THAT WAS "YOUR IDEA" SO MUCH AS TOTALLY OBVIOUS TO EVERY THINKING PERSON.
2-6-21 2021 Scott Adams, Inc./Dist. by Andrews McMeel
WELL, MAYBE. BUT WOULD THEY HAVE IMPLEMENTED IT?
I'M GOING TO TALK TO SMART PEOPLE NOW.

I'M DOGBERT, DOCTOR OF THE IMPOSSIBLE.

DOES THAT MEAN YOU CURE DISEASES THAT ARE BELIEVED TO BE IMPOSSIBLE TO CURE?

NO, THAT SOUNDS BORING.

I PRESCRIBE TREATMENTS THAT ARE IMPOSSIBLE TO FOLLOW.

WHEN YOU FAIL, AND YOU DON'T GET BETTER, YOU'LL THINK IT'S YOUR OWN FAULT.

HOW DOES THAT HELP ANYONE BUT YOU?

HEY, I'M NOT THE ONE WHO BROUGHT IT UP.

YOU'RE GIVING ME A HEAD— ACHE.

TO CURE THAT, I SUGGEST ICE—COLD BATHS EVERY SIX MINUTES.

© 2021 Scott Adams, Inc./Dist. by Andrews McMeel

2-7-21

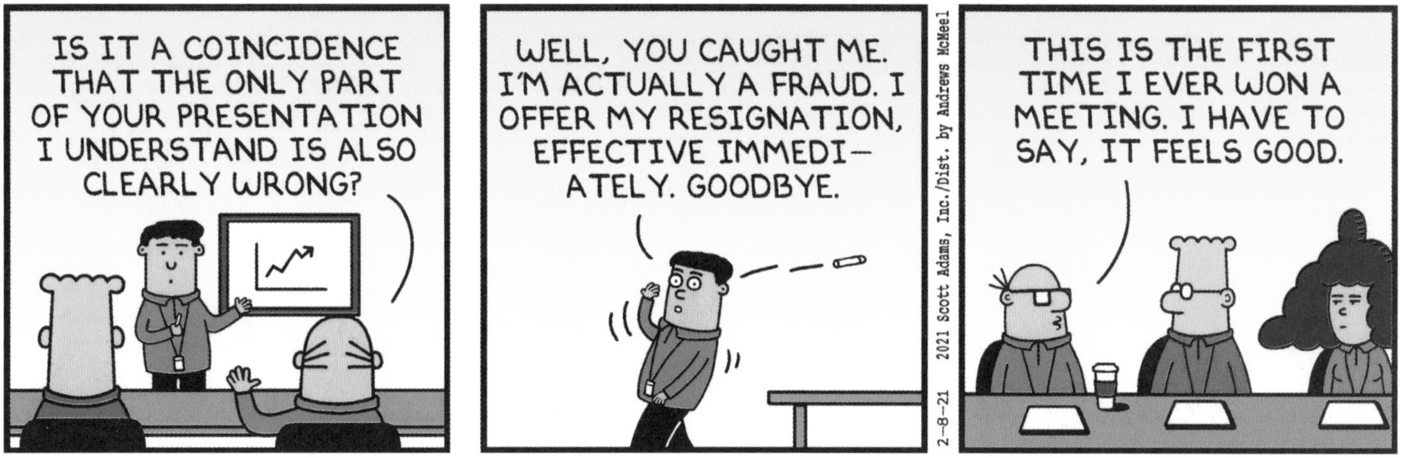
IS IT A COINCIDENCE THAT THE ONLY PART OF YOUR PRESENTATION I UNDERSTAND IS ALSO CLEARLY WRONG?
WELL, YOU CAUGHT ME. I'M ACTUALLY A FRAUD. I OFFER MY RESIGNATION, EFFECTIVE IMMEDI-ATELY. GOODBYE.
2-8-21 2021 Scott Adams, Inc./Dist. by Andrews McMeel
THIS IS THE FIRST TIME I EVER WON A MEETING. I HAVE TO SAY, IT FEELS GOOD.

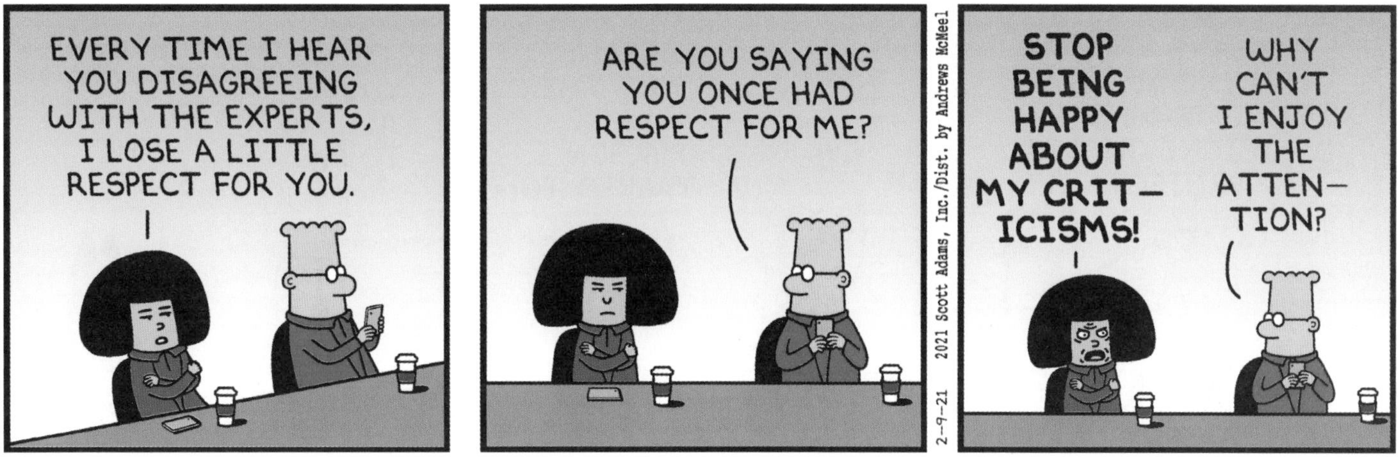
EVERY TIME I HEAR YOU DISAGREEING WITH THE EXPERTS, I LOSE A LITTLE RESPECT FOR YOU.
ARE YOU SAYING YOU ONCE HAD RESPECT FOR ME?
2-9-21 2021 Scott Adams, Inc./Dist. by Andrews McMeel
STOP BEING HAPPY ABOUT MY CRIT-ICISMS!
WHY CAN'T I ENJOY THE ATTEN-TION?

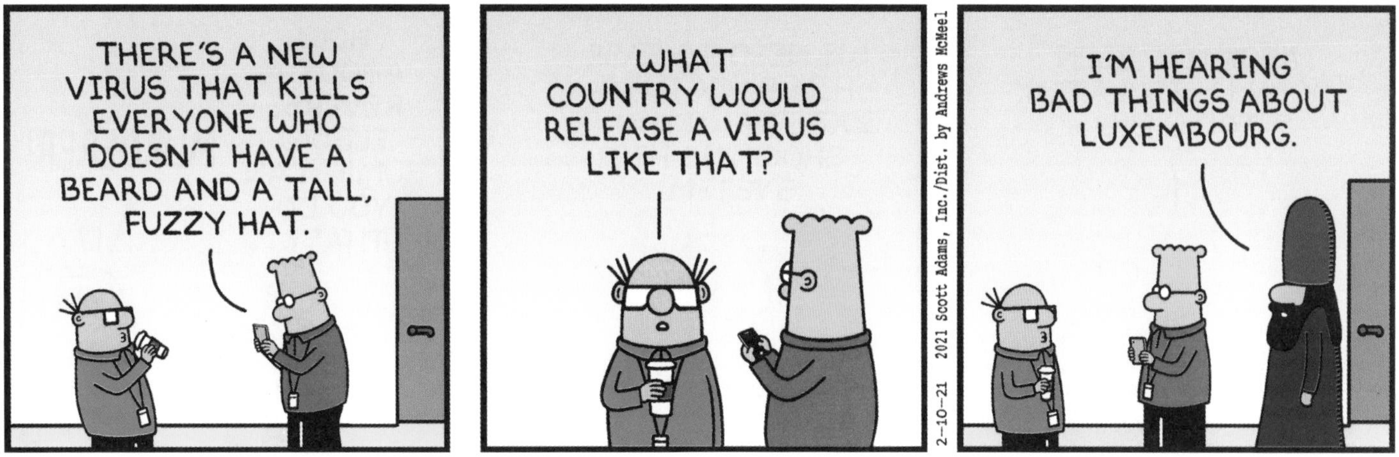
THERE'S A NEW VIRUS THAT KILLS EVERYONE WHO DOESN'T HAVE A BEARD AND A TALL, FUZZY HAT.
WHAT COUNTRY WOULD RELEASE A VIRUS LIKE THAT?
2-10-21 2021 Scott Adams, Inc./Dist. by Andrews McMeel
I'M HEARING BAD THINGS ABOUT LUXEMBOURG.

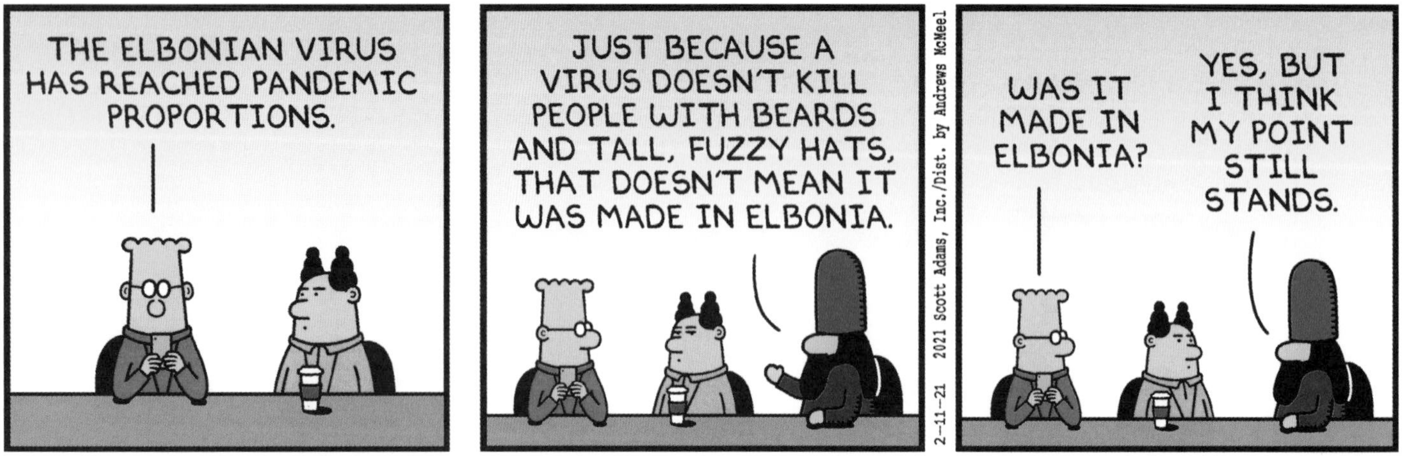
THE ELBONIAN VIRUS HAS REACHED PANDEMIC PROPORTIONS.
JUST BECAUSE A VIRUS DOESN'T KILL PEOPLE WITH BEARDS AND TALL, FUZZY HATS, THAT DOESN'T MEAN IT WAS MADE IN ELBONIA.
2-11-21 2021 Scott Adams, Inc./Dist. by Andrews McMeel
WAS IT MADE IN ELBONIA?
YES, BUT I THINK MY POINT STILL STANDS.

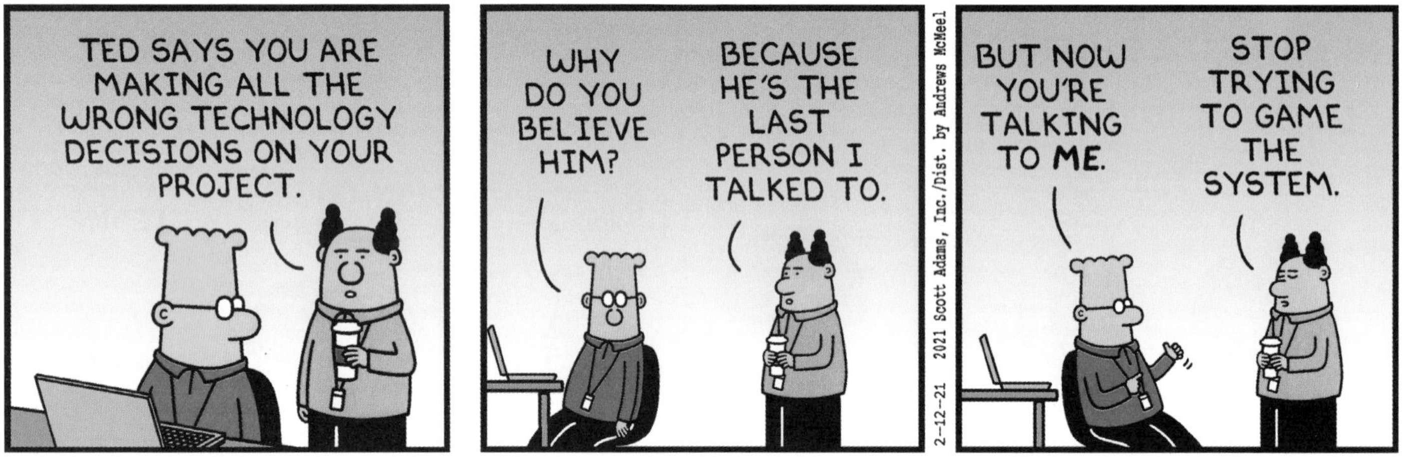
TED SAYS YOU ARE MAKING ALL THE WRONG TECHNOLOGY DECISIONS ON YOUR PROJECT.
WHY DO YOU BELIEVE HIM?
BECAUSE HE'S THE LAST PERSON I TALKED TO.
2-12-21 2021 Scott Adams, Inc./Dist. by Andrews McMeel
BUT NOW YOU'RE TALKING TO ME.
STOP TRYING TO GAME THE SYSTEM.

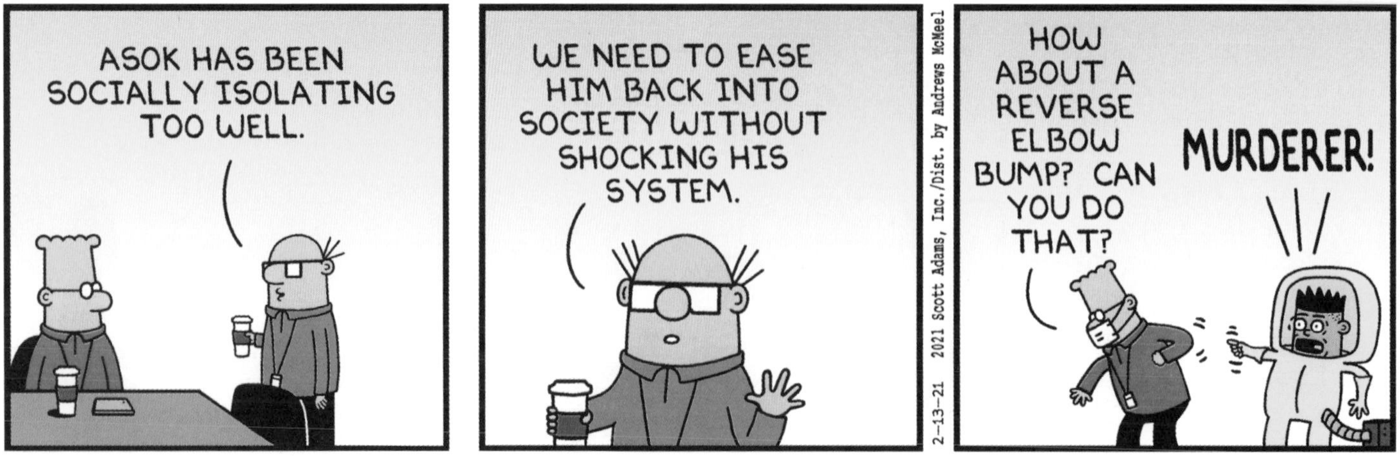
ASOK HAS BEEN SOCIALLY ISOLATING TOO WELL.
WE NEED TO EASE HIM BACK INTO SOCIETY WITHOUT SHOCKING HIS SYSTEM.
2-13-21 2021 Scott Adams, Inc./Dist. by Andrews McMeel
HOW ABOUT A REVERSE ELBOW BUMP? CAN YOU DO THAT?
MURDERER!

INDUSTRY TRENDS JUST TURNED OUR WAY BY TOTAL LUCK.
WE HAVE TO ACT FAST!
I NEED TO IMPLEMENT SOME KIND OF CHANGE SO IT LOOKS AS IF I CAUSED THE INCREASE IN PROFITS THAT WILL HAPPEN ANYWAY.
DOES ANYONE HAVE ANY IDEAS?
NO, BECAUSE WE'RE ALREADY PERFECTLY SITUATED TO TAKE ADVANTAGE OF THE TREND.
THAT DOESN'T HELP ME! I CAN'T TAKE CREDIT FOR OUR FUTURE PROFITS UNLESS I DO SOMETHING I CAN SAY MADE A DIFFERENCE.
MAYBE YOU COULD IMPLEMENT SOME SORT OF BOGUS COMPANY CULTURE TRAINING PROGRAM.
ONE WEEK LATER
IT'S IMPORTANT TO REALIZE YOU'RE ALL IDIOTS.
© 2021 Scott Adams, Inc./Dist. by Andrews McMeel
2-14-21

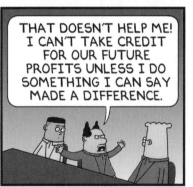

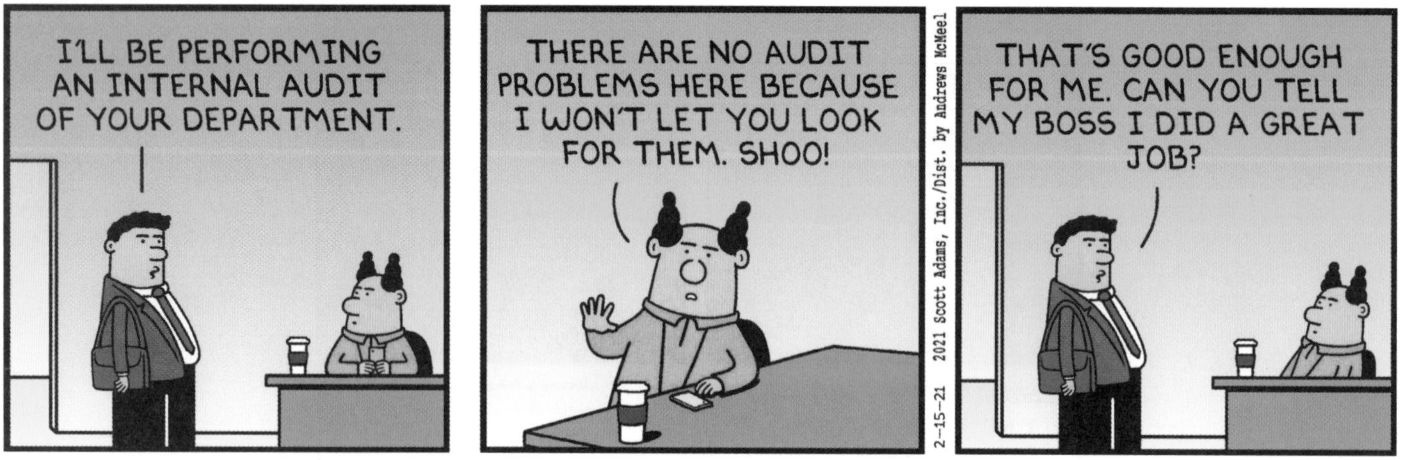
I'LL BE PERFORMING AN INTERNAL AUDIT OF YOUR DEPARTMENT.
THERE ARE NO AUDIT PROBLEMS HERE BECAUSE I WON'T LET YOU LOOK FOR THEM. SHOO!
2-15-21 2021 Scott Adams, Inc./Dist. by Andrews McMeel
THAT'S GOOD ENOUGH FOR ME. CAN YOU TELL MY BOSS I DID A GREAT JOB?

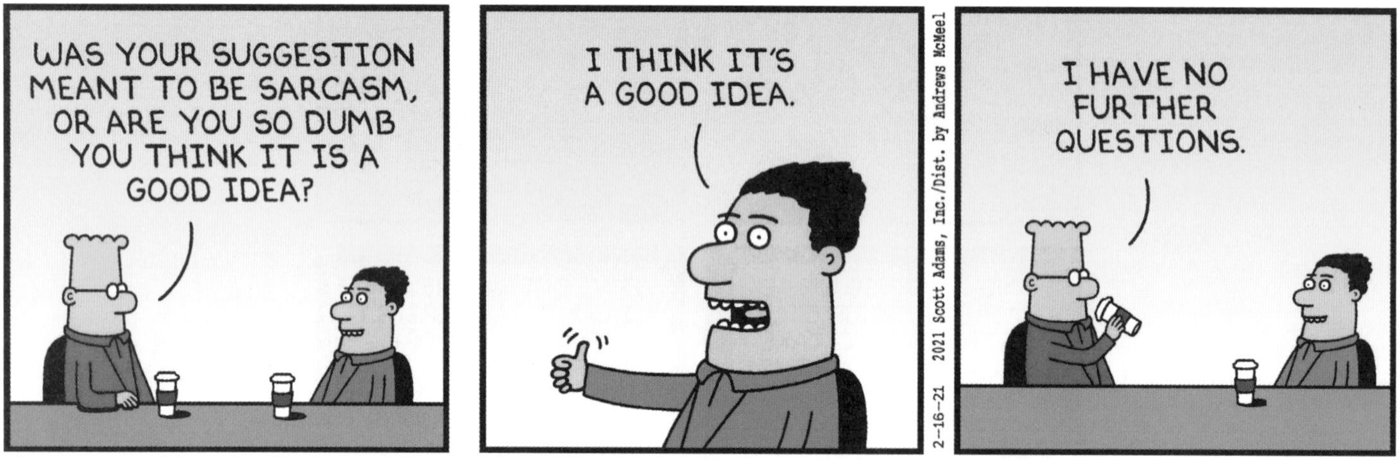
WAS YOUR SUGGESTION MEANT TO BE SARCASM, OR ARE YOU SO DUMB YOU THINK IT IS A GOOD IDEA?
I THINK IT'S A GOOD IDEA.
2-16-21 2021 Scott Adams, Inc./Dist. by Andrews McMeel
I HAVE NO FURTHER QUESTIONS.

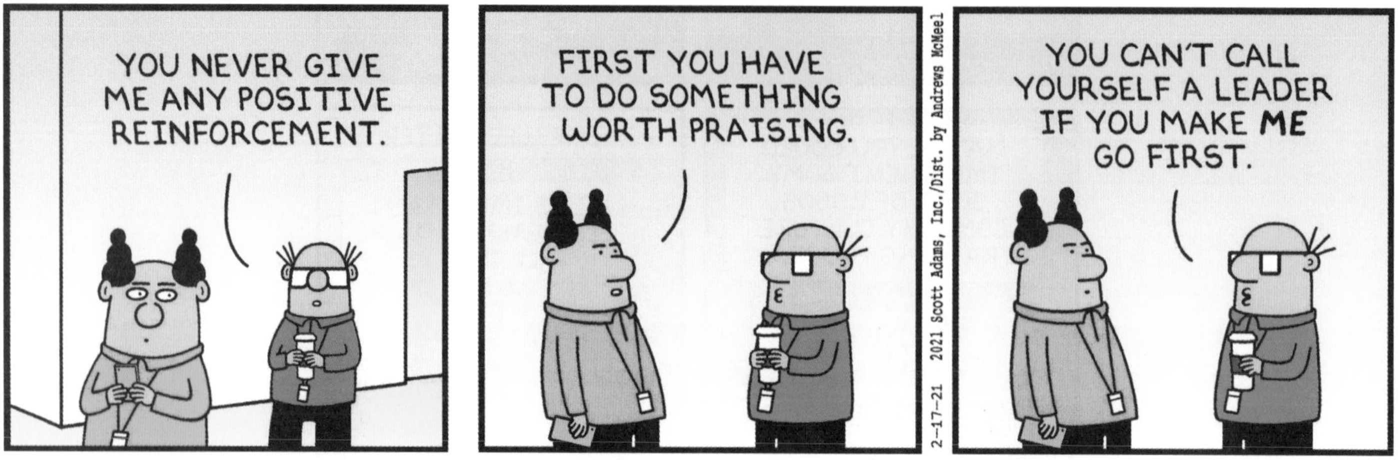
YOU NEVER GIVE ME ANY POSITIVE REINFORCEMENT.
FIRST YOU HAVE TO DO SOMETHING WORTH PRAISING.
2-17-21 2021 Scott Adams, Inc./Dist. by Andrews McMeel
YOU CAN'T CALL YOURSELF A LEADER IF YOU MAKE ME GO FIRST.

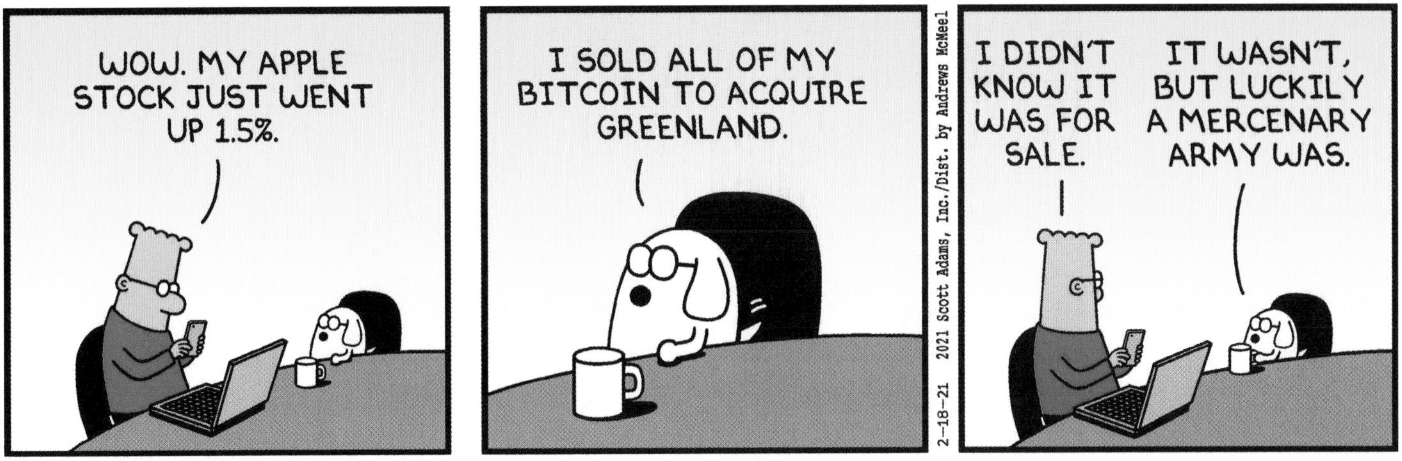
WOW. MY APPLE STOCK JUST WENT UP 1.5%.
I SOLD ALL OF MY BITCOIN TO ACQUIRE GREENLAND.
I DIDN'T KNOW IT WAS FOR SALE.
IT WASN'T, BUT LUCKILY A MERCENARY ARMY WAS.
2-18-21 2021 Scott Adams, Inc./Dist. by Andrews McMeel

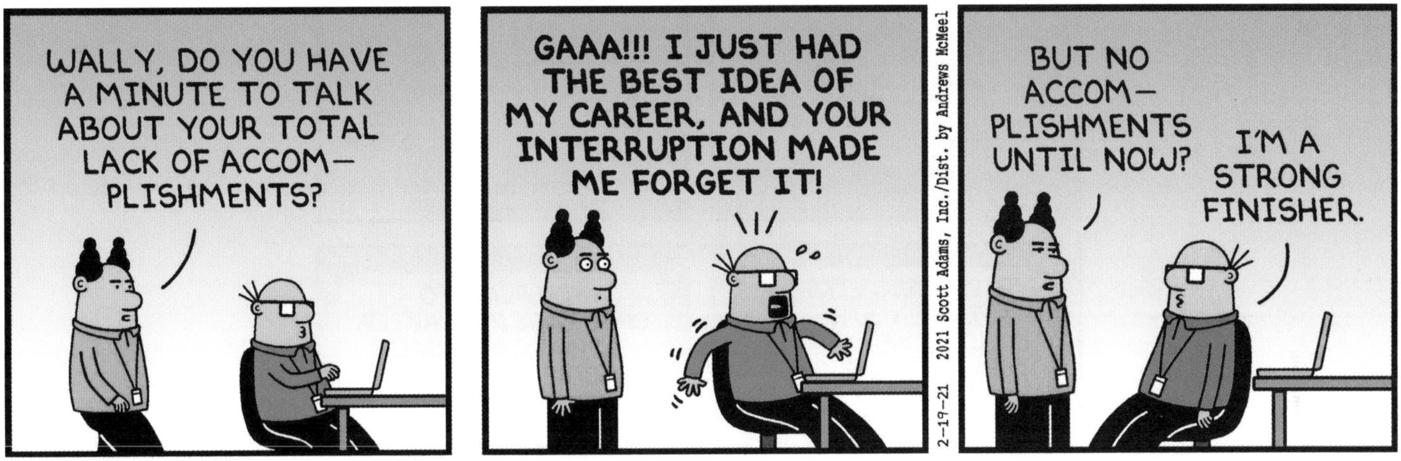
WALLY, DO YOU HAVE A MINUTE TO TALK ABOUT YOUR TOTAL LACK OF ACCOM-PLISHMENTS?
GAAA!!! I JUST HAD THE BEST IDEA OF MY CAREER, AND YOUR INTERRUPTION MADE ME FORGET IT!
BUT NO ACCOM-PLISHMENTS UNTIL NOW?
I'M A STRONG FINISHER.
2-19-21 2021 Scott Adams, Inc./Dist. by Andrews McMeel

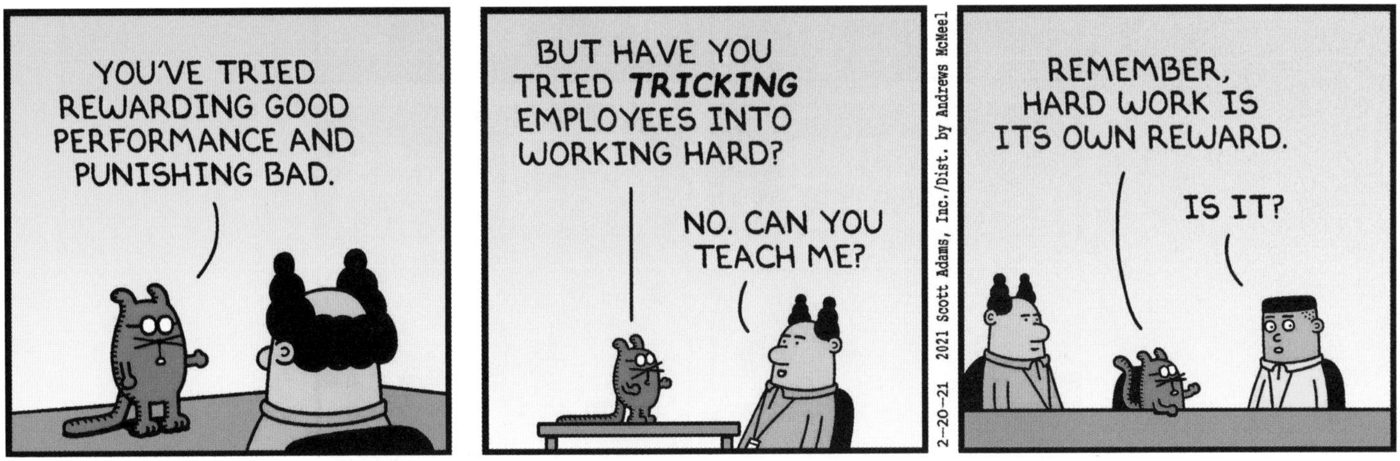
YOU'VE TRIED REWARDING GOOD PERFORMANCE AND PUNISHING BAD.
BUT HAVE YOU TRIED *TRICKING* EMPLOYEES INTO WORKING HARD?
NO. CAN YOU TEACH ME?
REMEMBER, HARD WORK IS ITS OWN REWARD.
IS IT?
2-20-21 2021 Scott Adams, Inc./Dist. by Andrews McMeel

YOU DID A GREAT JOB ON YOUR PROJECT, TED.
THANK YOU.
YOU ARE MOST WELCOME.
WAIT. WHY DO I HAVE A SENSE OF DREAD AND FOREBODING?
IT ISN'T LIKE YOU TO GIVE OUT GENEROUS COMPLIMENTS.
THIS FEELS LIKE A TRAP. YOU'RE LULLING ME INTO A FALSE SENSE OF SECURITY.
YOU PLAN TO SABOTAGE MY CAREER TO MAKE YOURSELF LOOK BETTER BY COMPARISON.
YOU MONSTER!
WHAT'S THIS ALL ABOUT?
THAT WORKED OUT.
© 2021 Scott Adams, Inc./Dist. by Andrews McMeel
2-21-21

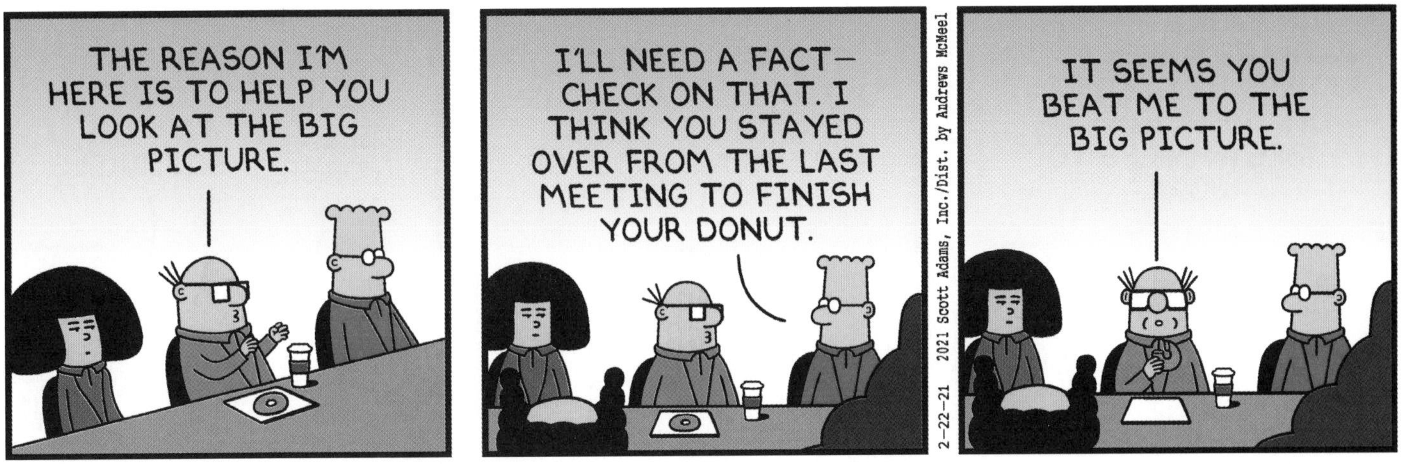
THE REASON I'M HERE IS TO HELP YOU LOOK AT THE BIG PICTURE.
I'LL NEED A FACT-CHECK ON THAT. I THINK YOU STAYED OVER FROM THE LAST MEETING TO FINISH YOUR DONUT.
IT SEEMS YOU BEAT ME TO THE BIG PICTURE.

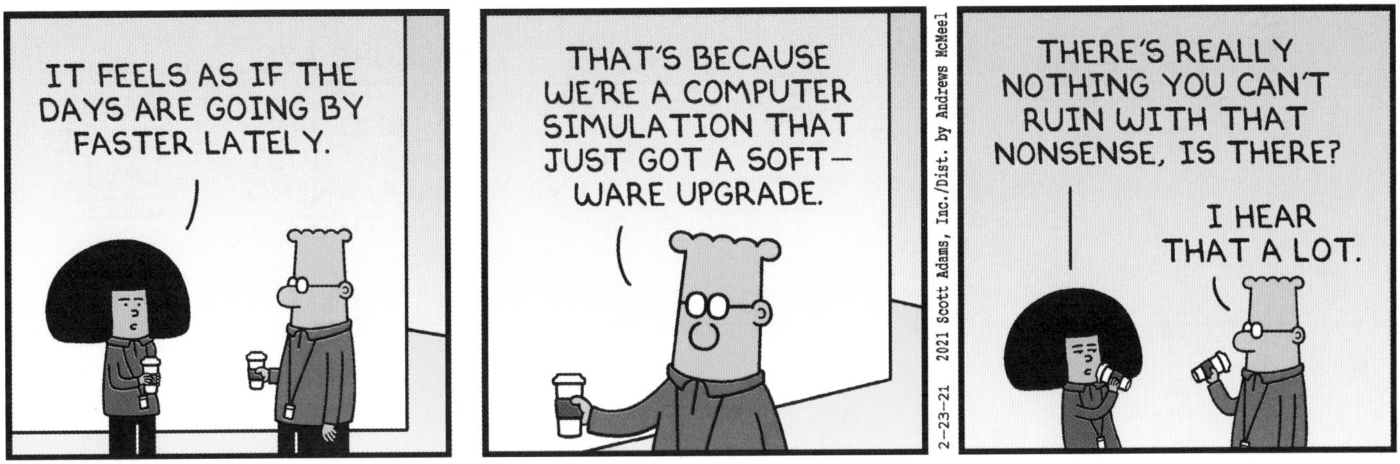
IT FEELS AS IF THE DAYS ARE GOING BY FASTER LATELY.
THAT'S BECAUSE WE'RE A COMPUTER SIMULATION THAT JUST GOT A SOFT-WARE UPGRADE.
THERE'S REALLY NOTHING YOU CAN'T RUIN WITH THAT NONSENSE, IS THERE?
I HEAR THAT A LOT.

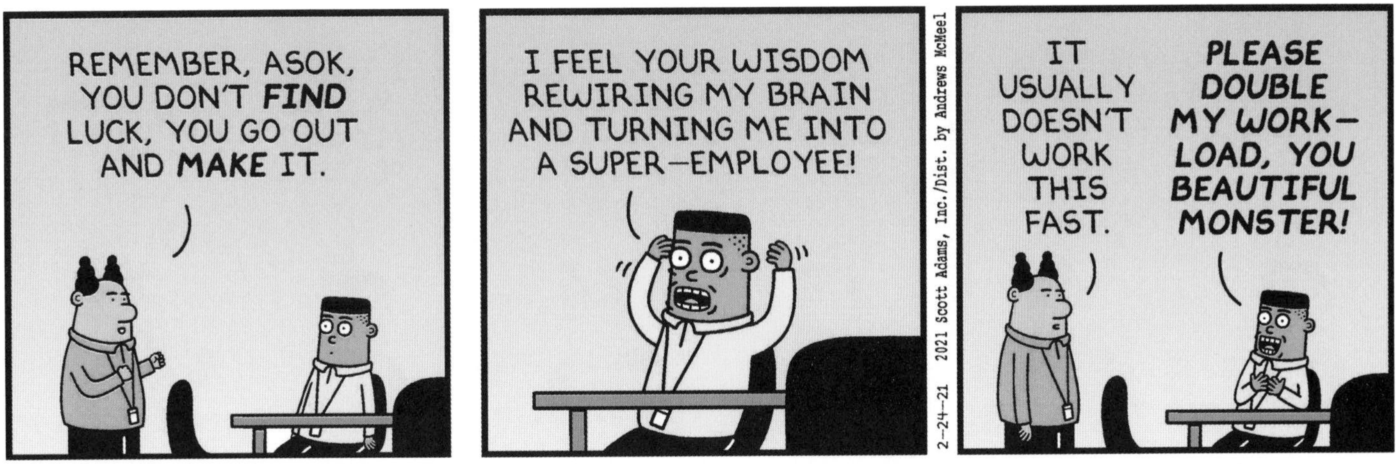
REMEMBER, ASOK, YOU DON'T **FIND** LUCK, YOU GO OUT AND **MAKE** IT.
I FEEL YOUR WISDOM REWIRING MY BRAIN AND TURNING ME INTO A SUPER-EMPLOYEE!
IT USUALLY DOESN'T WORK THIS FAST.
PLEASE DOUBLE MY WORK-LOAD, YOU BEAUTIFUL MONSTER!

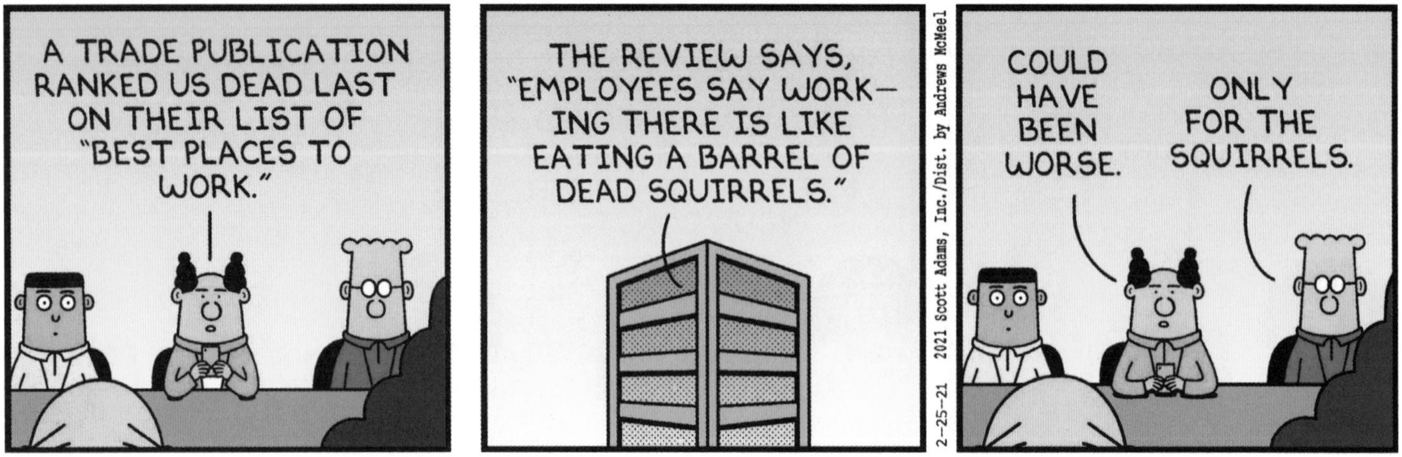
A TRADE PUBLICATION RANKED US DEAD LAST ON THEIR LIST OF "BEST PLACES TO WORK."
THE REVIEW SAYS, "EMPLOYEES SAY WORKING THERE IS LIKE EATING A BARREL OF DEAD SQUIRRELS."
2-25-21 2021 Scott Adams, Inc./Dist. by Andrews McMeel
COULD HAVE BEEN WORSE.
ONLY FOR THE SQUIRRELS.

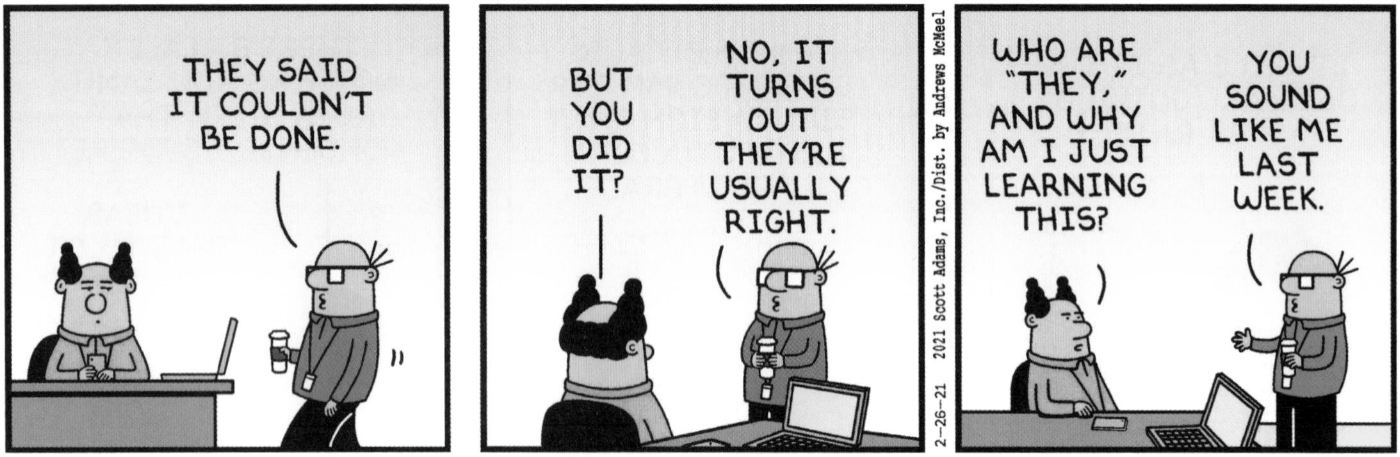
THEY SAID IT COULDN'T BE DONE.
BUT YOU DID IT?
NO, IT TURNS OUT THEY'RE USUALLY RIGHT.
2-26-21 2021 Scott Adams, Inc./Dist. by Andrews McMeel
WHO ARE "THEY," AND WHY AM I JUST LEARNING THIS?
YOU SOUND LIKE ME LAST WEEK.

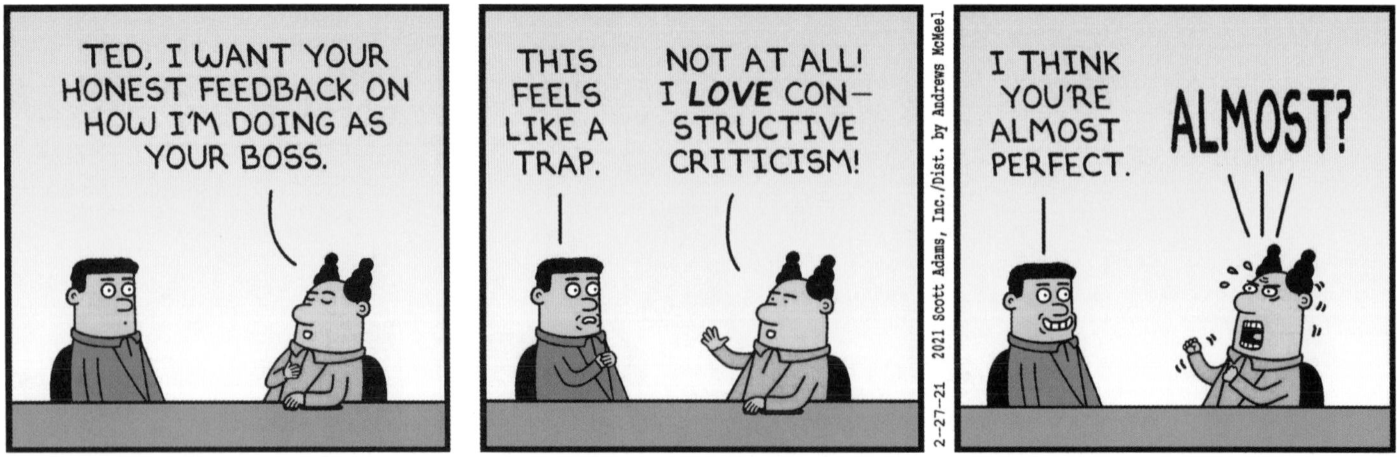
TED, I WANT YOUR HONEST FEEDBACK ON HOW I'M DOING AS YOUR BOSS.
THIS FEELS LIKE A TRAP.
NOT AT ALL! I LOVE CONSTRUCTIVE CRITICISM!
2-27-21 2021 Scott Adams, Inc./Dist. by Andrews McMeel
I THINK YOU'RE ALMOST PERFECT.
ALMOST?

WE NEED TO **DESTROY** OUR COMPETITION!
I DON'T APPROVE OF VIOLENCE.
I DIDN'T SAY ANYTHING ABOUT VIOLENCE.
YOU SAID "DESTROY" THEM. I DON'T SEE HOW THAT COULD MEAN ANYTHING ELSE.
IT WAS JUST A FIGURE OF SPEECH.
WE'RE ENGINEERS! YOU CAN'T USE FIGURATIVE SPEECH WITH US. WE TAKE THINGS LITERALLY.
SO, WHAT EXACTLY IS IT YOU WANT US TO DO WITH OUR COMPETITORS?
BEAT THEM!
WITH STICKS?
© 2021 Scott Adams, Inc./Dist. by Andrews McMeel
2-28-21

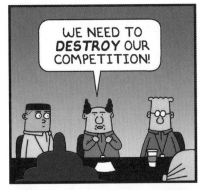

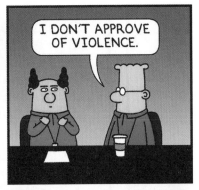

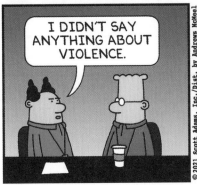

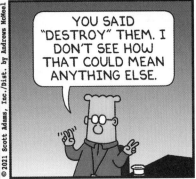

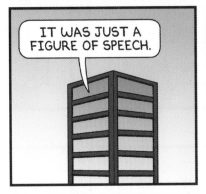

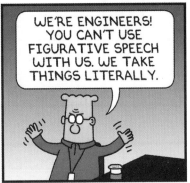

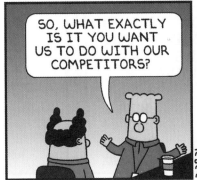

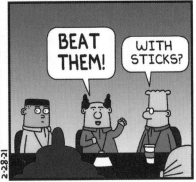

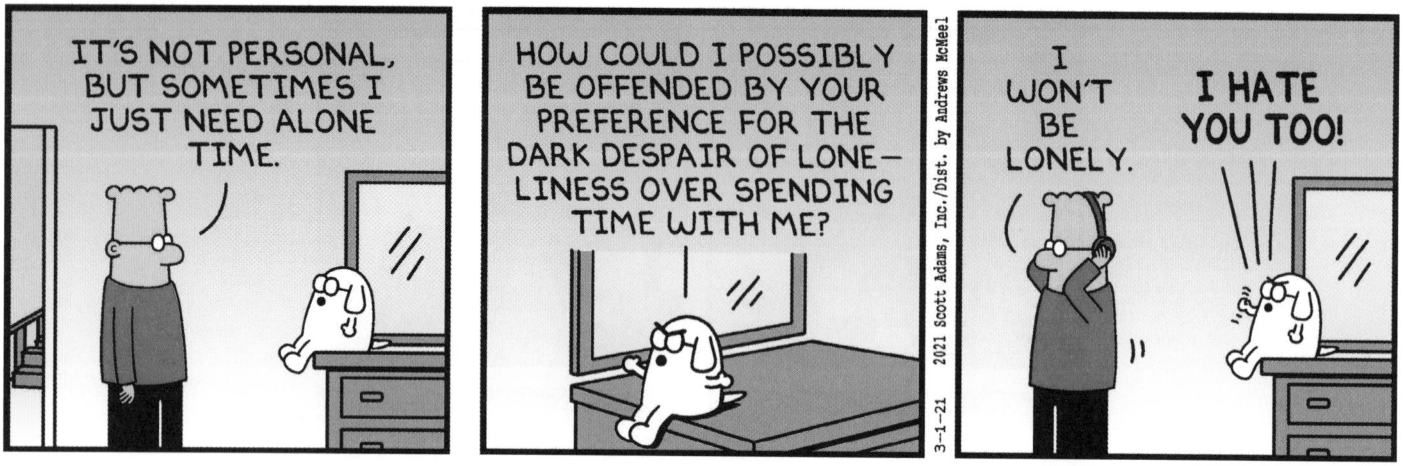
IT'S NOT PERSONAL, BUT SOMETIMES I JUST NEED ALONE TIME.
HOW COULD I POSSIBLY BE OFFENDED BY YOUR PREFERENCE FOR THE DARK DESPAIR OF LONE-LINESS OVER SPENDING TIME WITH ME?
3-1-21 2021 Scott Adams, Inc./Dist. by Andrews McMeel
I WON'T BE LONELY.
I HATE YOU TOO!

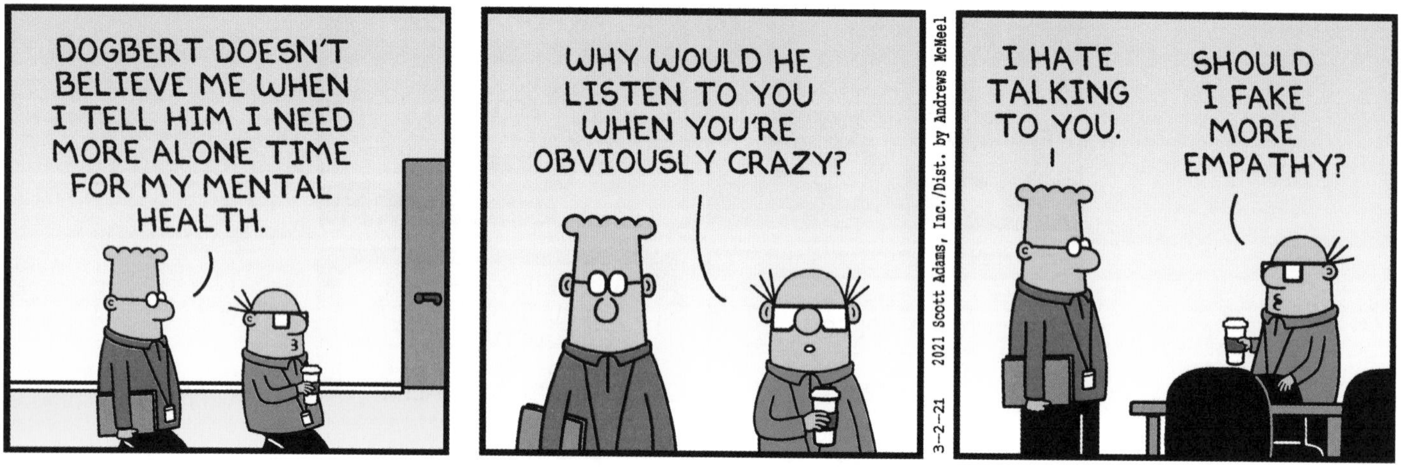
DOGBERT DOESN'T BELIEVE ME WHEN I TELL HIM I NEED MORE ALONE TIME FOR MY MENTAL HEALTH.
WHY WOULD HE LISTEN TO YOU WHEN YOU'RE OBVIOUSLY CRAZY?
3-2-21 2021 Scott Adams, Inc./Dist. by Andrews McMeel
I HATE TALKING TO YOU.
SHOULD I FAKE MORE EMPATHY?

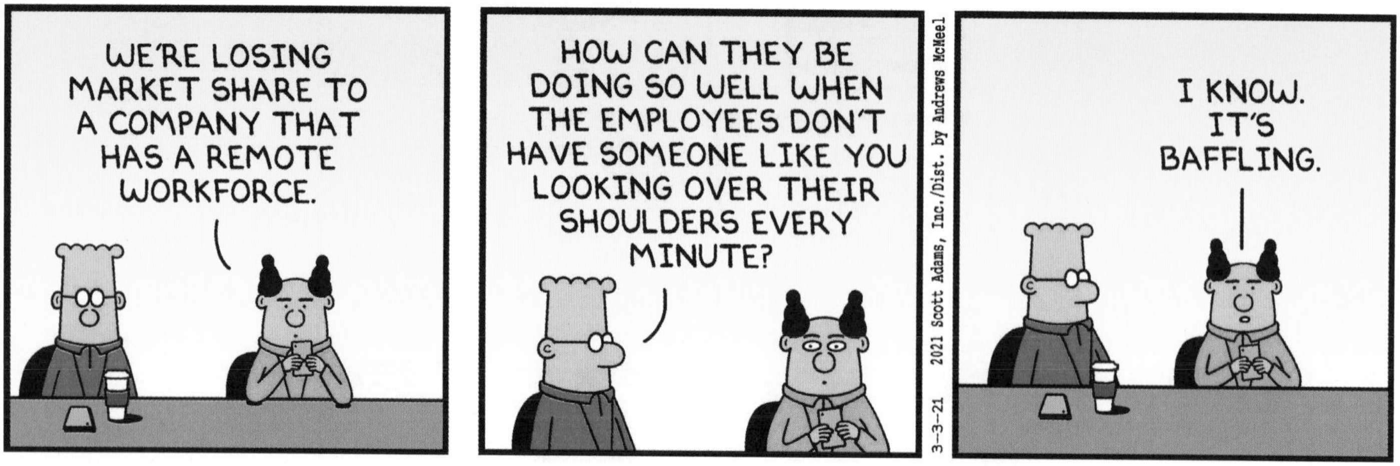
WE'RE LOSING MARKET SHARE TO A COMPANY THAT HAS A REMOTE WORKFORCE.
HOW CAN THEY BE DOING SO WELL WHEN THE EMPLOYEES DON'T HAVE SOMEONE LIKE YOU LOOKING OVER THEIR SHOULDERS EVERY MINUTE?
3-3-21 2021 Scott Adams, Inc./Dist. by Andrews McMeel
I KNOW. IT'S BAFFLING.

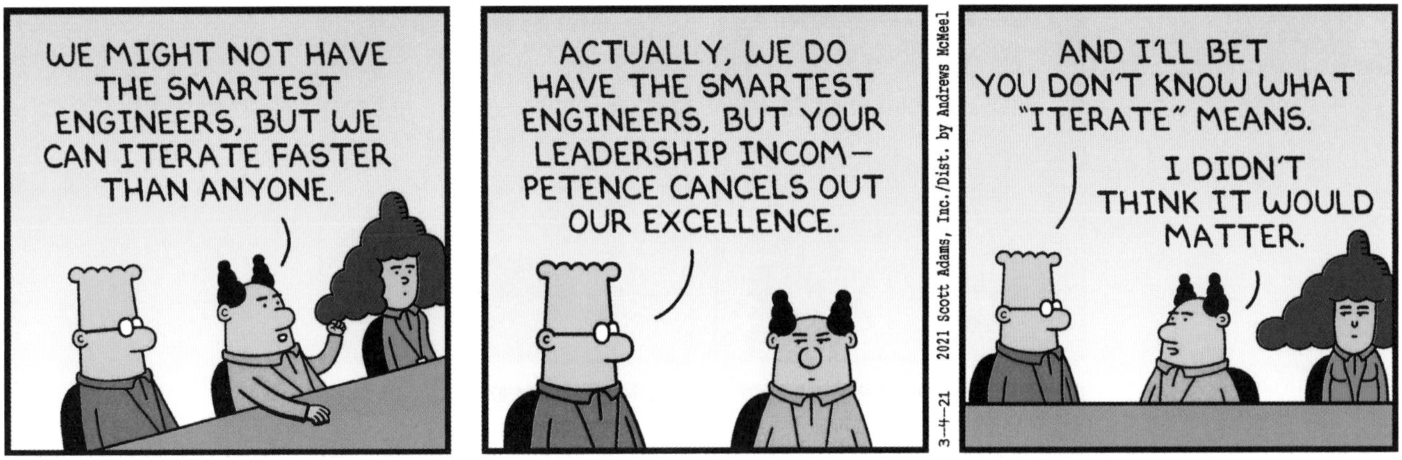
WE MIGHT NOT HAVE THE SMARTEST ENGINEERS, BUT WE CAN ITERATE FASTER THAN ANYONE.
ACTUALLY, WE DO HAVE THE SMARTEST ENGINEERS, BUT YOUR LEADERSHIP INCOM-PETENCE CANCELS OUT OUR EXCELLENCE.
3-4-21 2021 Scott Adams, Inc./Dist. by Andrews McMeel
AND I'LL BET YOU DON'T KNOW WHAT "ITERATE" MEANS.
I DIDN'T THINK IT WOULD MATTER.

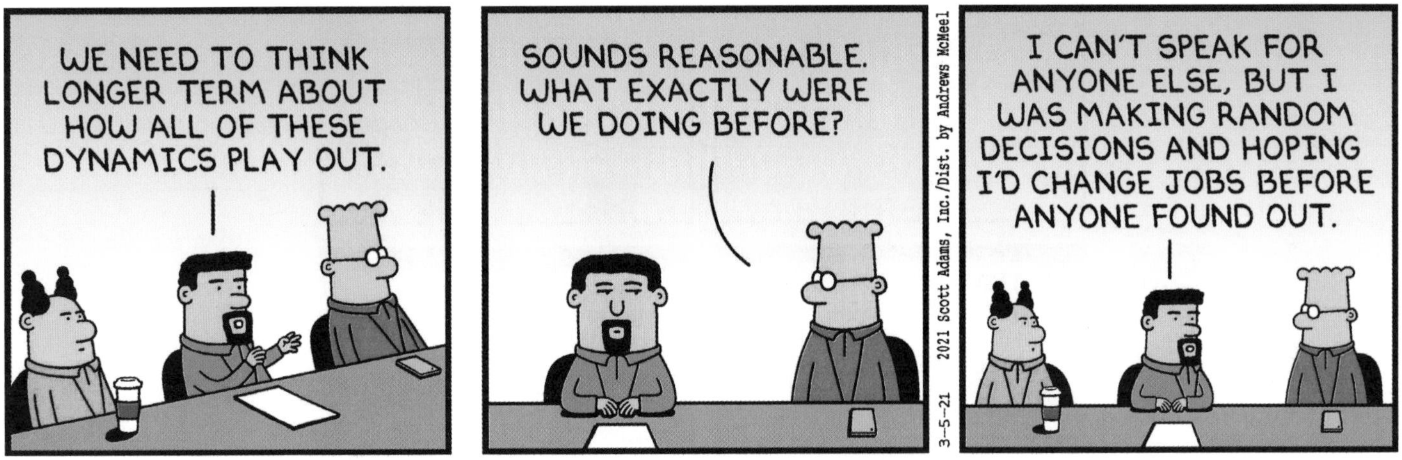
WE NEED TO THINK LONGER TERM ABOUT HOW ALL OF THESE DYNAMICS PLAY OUT.
SOUNDS REASONABLE. WHAT EXACTLY WERE WE DOING BEFORE?
3-5-21 2021 Scott Adams, Inc./Dist. by Andrews McMeel
I CAN'T SPEAK FOR ANYONE ELSE, BUT I WAS MAKING RANDOM DECISIONS AND HOPING I'D CHANGE JOBS BEFORE ANYONE FOUND OUT.

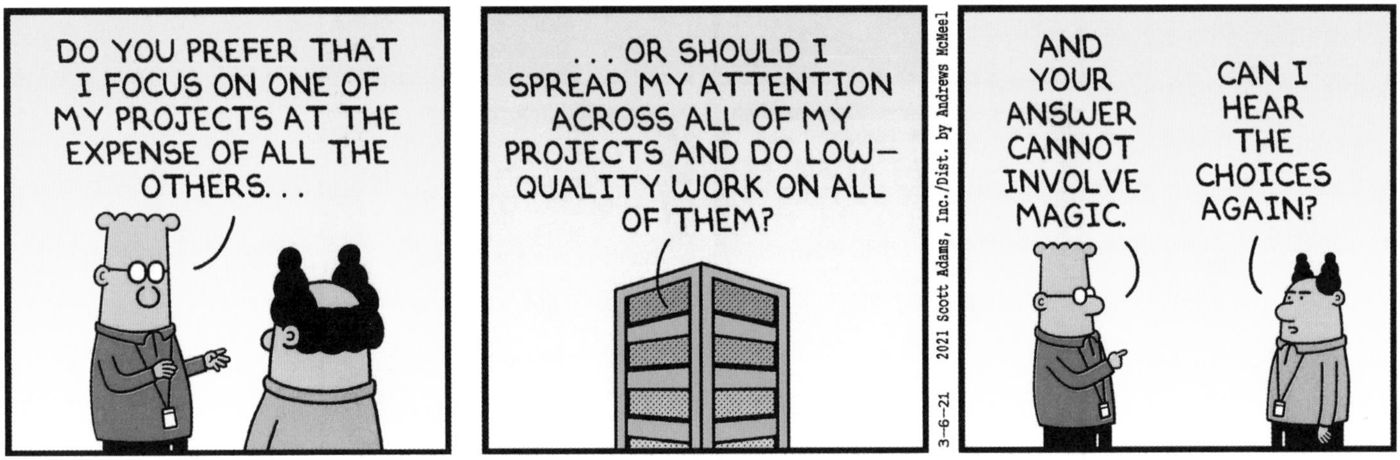
DO YOU PREFER THAT I FOCUS ON ONE OF MY PROJECTS AT THE EXPENSE OF ALL THE OTHERS...
...OR SHOULD I SPREAD MY ATTENTION ACROSS ALL OF MY PROJECTS AND DO LOW-QUALITY WORK ON ALL OF THEM?
3-6-21 2021 Scott Adams, Inc./Dist. by Andrews McMeel
AND YOUR ANSWER CANNOT INVOLVE MAGIC.
CAN I HEAR THE CHOICES AGAIN?

DILBERT, I NEED TO FIRE YOU FOR YOUR SOCIAL MEDIA ACTIVITIES.
DID I SHARE SOMETHING OFFENSIVE?
I'M GETTING REPORTS THAT YOU FOLLOW BAD PEOPLE ON TWITTER.
I FOLLOW PEOPLE ON BOTH SIDES OF EVERY ISSUE SO I CAN SEE THE FULL CONTEXT.
THAT MIGHT SOUND GOOD ON PAPER, BUT HALF OF THE PEOPLE YOU FOLLOW ARE MONSTERS OF ONE SORT OR ANOTHER.
ISN'T IT OBVIOUS THAT ENFORCING THIS KIND OF STANDARD CAN ONLY LEAD IN A BAD DIRECTION?
NO, I DON'T SEE THAT AT ALL. ALL I SEE IS THAT YOU ASSOCIATE WITH PEOPLE WHO ARE MONSTERS.
I'M GETTING REPORTS THAT YOU FOLLOW DILBERT ON TWITTER.
© 2021 Scott Adams, Inc./Dist. by Andrews McMeel
3-7-21

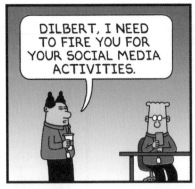

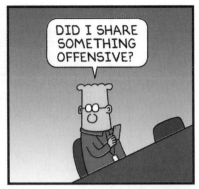

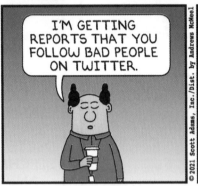

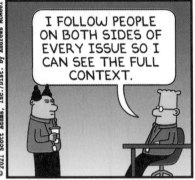

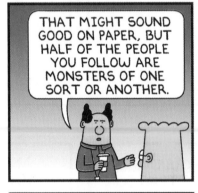

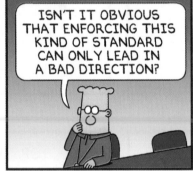

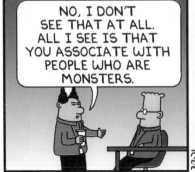

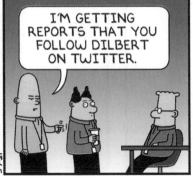

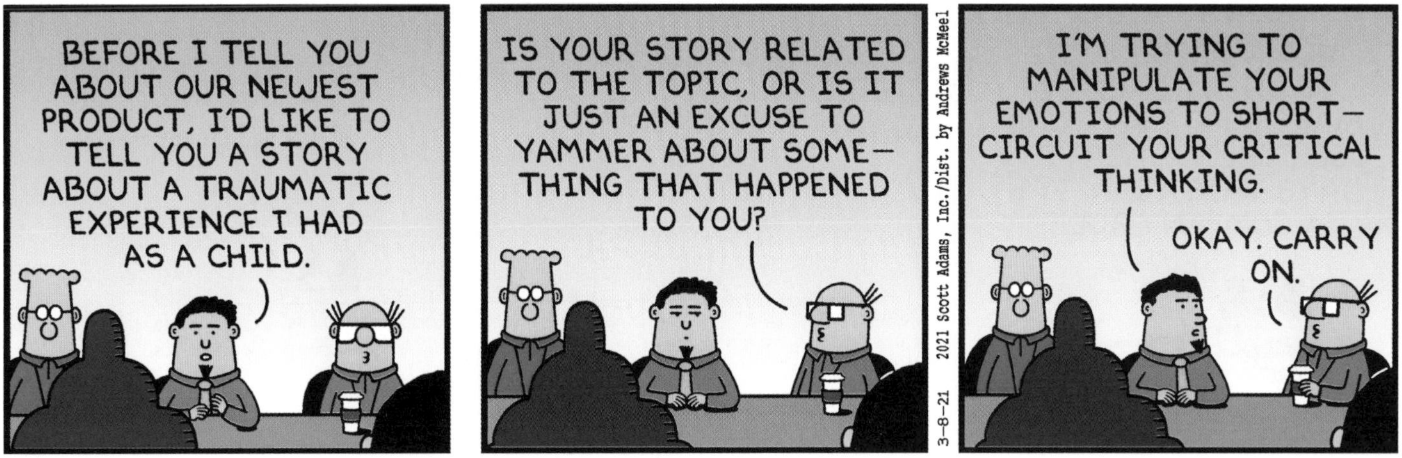
BEFORE I TELL YOU ABOUT OUR NEWEST PRODUCT, I'D LIKE TO TELL YOU A STORY ABOUT A TRAUMATIC EXPERIENCE I HAD AS A CHILD.
IS YOUR STORY RELATED TO THE TOPIC, OR IS IT JUST AN EXCUSE TO YAMMER ABOUT SOME-THING THAT HAPPENED TO YOU?
I'M TRYING TO MANIPULATE YOUR EMOTIONS TO SHORT-CIRCUIT YOUR CRITICAL THINKING.
OKAY. CARRY ON.
3-8-21 2021 Scott Adams, Inc./Dist. by Andrews McMeel

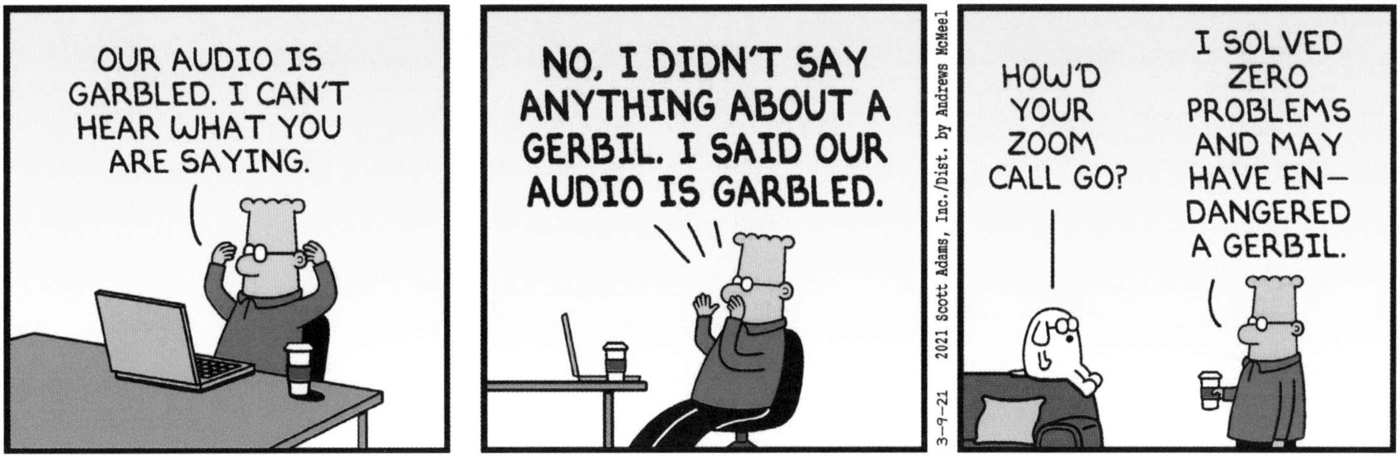
OUR AUDIO IS GARBLED. I CAN'T HEAR WHAT YOU ARE SAYING.
NO, I DIDN'T SAY ANYTHING ABOUT A GERBIL. I SAID OUR AUDIO IS GARBLED.
HOW'D YOUR ZOOM CALL GO?
I SOLVED ZERO PROBLEMS AND MAY HAVE EN-DANGERED A GERBIL.
3-9-21 2021 Scott Adams, Inc./Dist. by Andrews McMeel

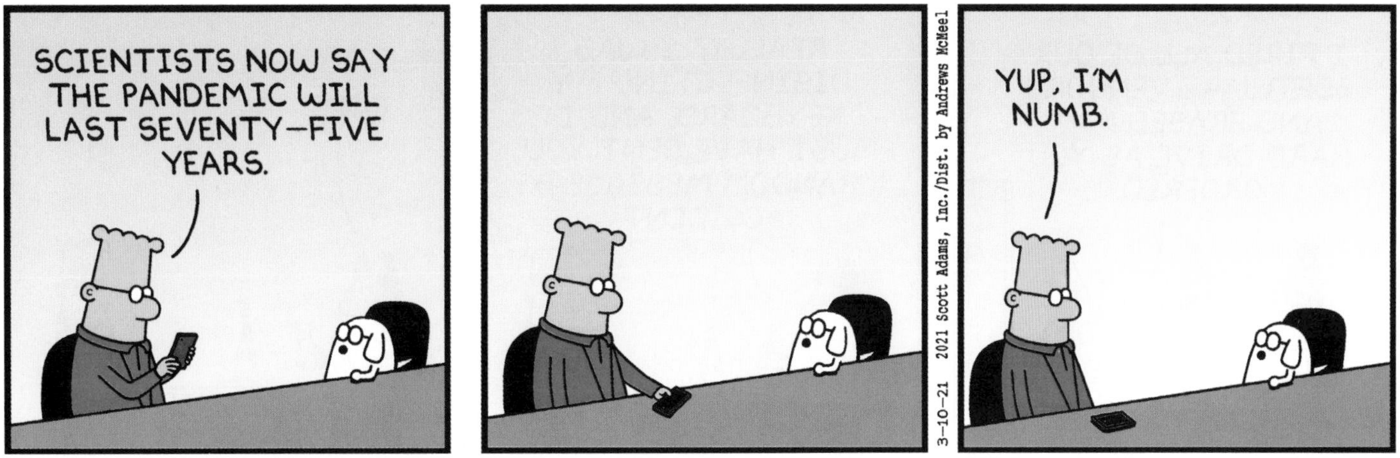
SCIENTISTS NOW SAY THE PANDEMIC WILL LAST SEVENTY-FIVE YEARS.
YUP, I'M NUMB.
3-10-21 2021 Scott Adams, Inc./Dist. by Andrews McMeel

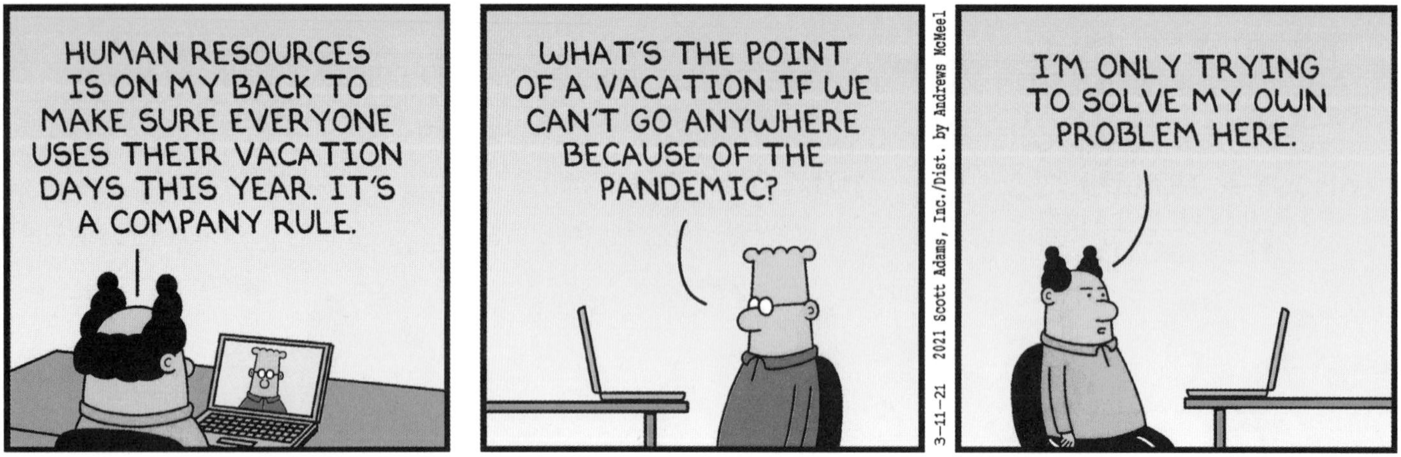
HUMAN RESOURCES IS ON MY BACK TO MAKE SURE EVERYONE USES THEIR VACATION DAYS THIS YEAR. IT'S A COMPANY RULE.
WHAT'S THE POINT OF A VACATION IF WE CAN'T GO ANYWHERE BECAUSE OF THE PANDEMIC?
I'M ONLY TRYING TO SOLVE MY OWN PROBLEM HERE.
3-11-21 2021 Scott Adams, Inc./Dist. by Andrews McMeel

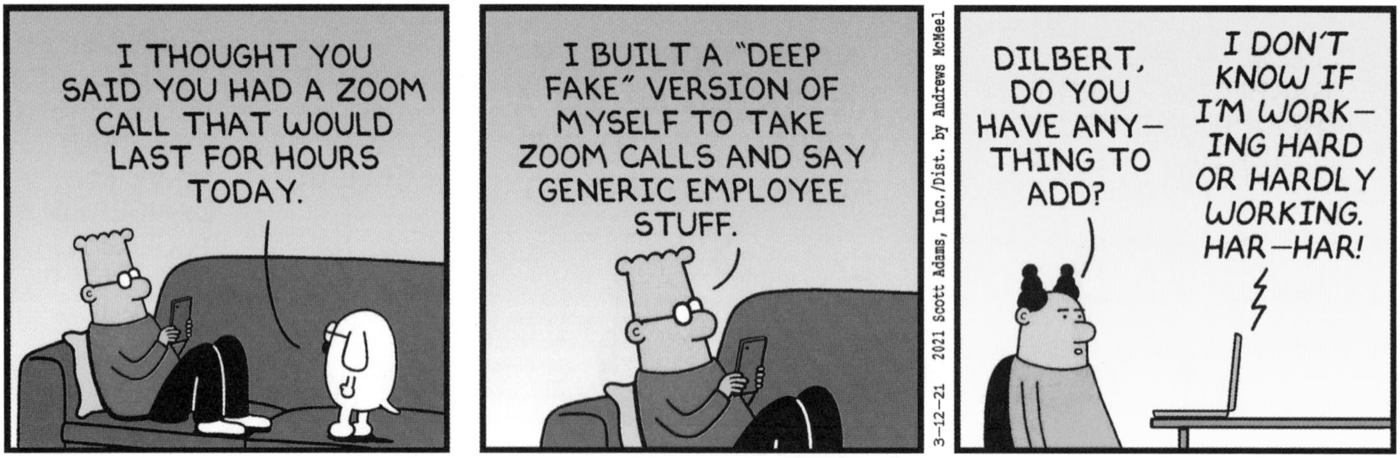
I THOUGHT YOU SAID YOU HAD A ZOOM CALL THAT WOULD LAST FOR HOURS TODAY.
I BUILT A "DEEP FAKE" VERSION OF MYSELF TO TAKE ZOOM CALLS AND SAY GENERIC EMPLOYEE STUFF.
DILBERT, DO YOU HAVE ANY-THING TO ADD?
I DON'T KNOW IF I'M WORK-ING HARD OR HARDLY WORKING. HAR-HAR!
3-12-21 2021 Scott Adams, Inc./Dist. by Andrews McMeel

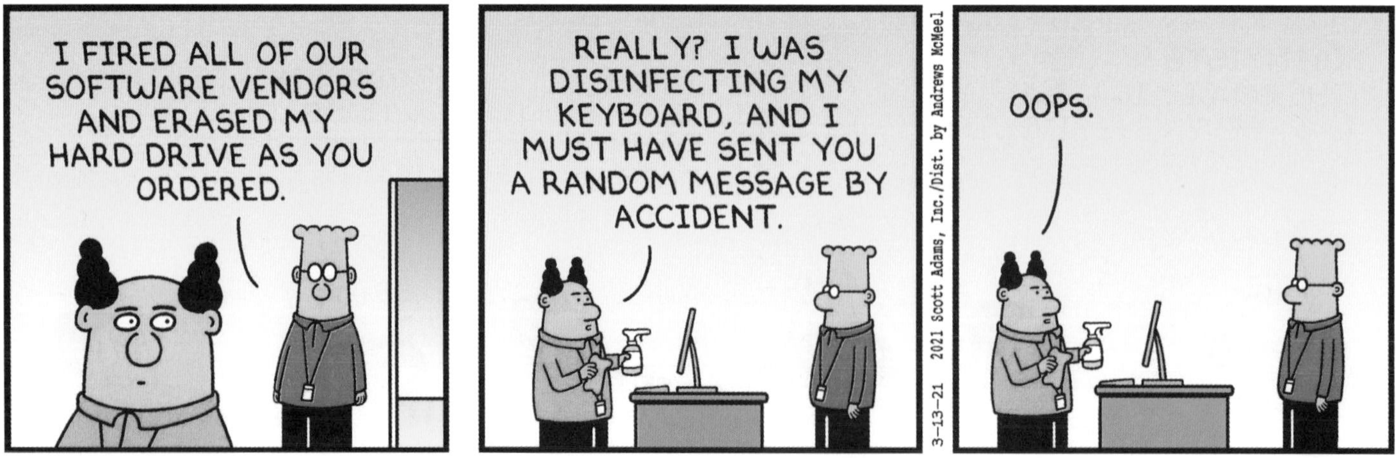
I FIRED ALL OF OUR SOFTWARE VENDORS AND ERASED MY HARD DRIVE AS YOU ORDERED.
REALLY? I WAS DISINFECTING MY KEYBOARD, AND I MUST HAVE SENT YOU A RANDOM MESSAGE BY ACCIDENT.
OOPS.
3-13-21 2021 Scott Adams, Inc./Dist. by Andrews McMeel

CAN YOU PLEASE STOP TALKING SO LOUDLY ON YOUR ZOOM CALLS??!!!
I'M SORRY, BUT I PAY THE MORTGAGE, AND I HAVE A RIGHT TO MAKE AS MUCH NOISE AS I WANT IN MY OWN HOUSE.
© 2021 Scott Adams, Inc./Dist. by Andrews McMeel
OH, WOW. DID YOU REALLY PLAY THE "MORTGAGE CARD" ON ME?
THIS IS WAR!
WAIT UNTIL YOU SEE WHAT I DO IN THE BACKGROUND OF YOUR NEXT ZOOM CALL.
I DON'T WANT TO RUIN THE SURPRISE, BUT THINK OF THE NUMBER–ONE WORST THING YOU CAN IMAGINE ME DOING.
ARE YOU PICTURING IT IN YOUR MIND?
IT'S BAD, ISN'T IT?
3-14-21
NOW IMAGINE AT THE SAME TIME I ALSO START DOING THE SECOND–WORST THING YOU CAN IMAGINE.
NOOOO!!!!

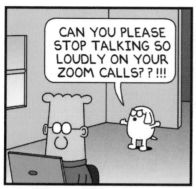

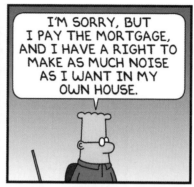

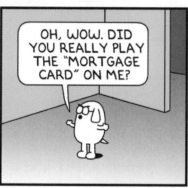

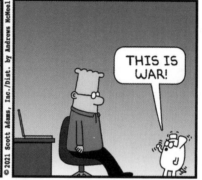

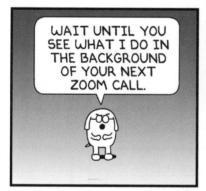

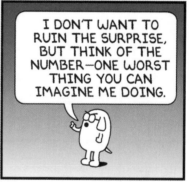

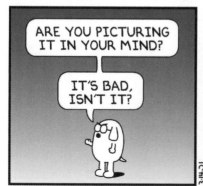

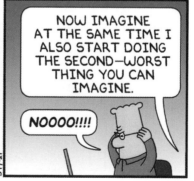

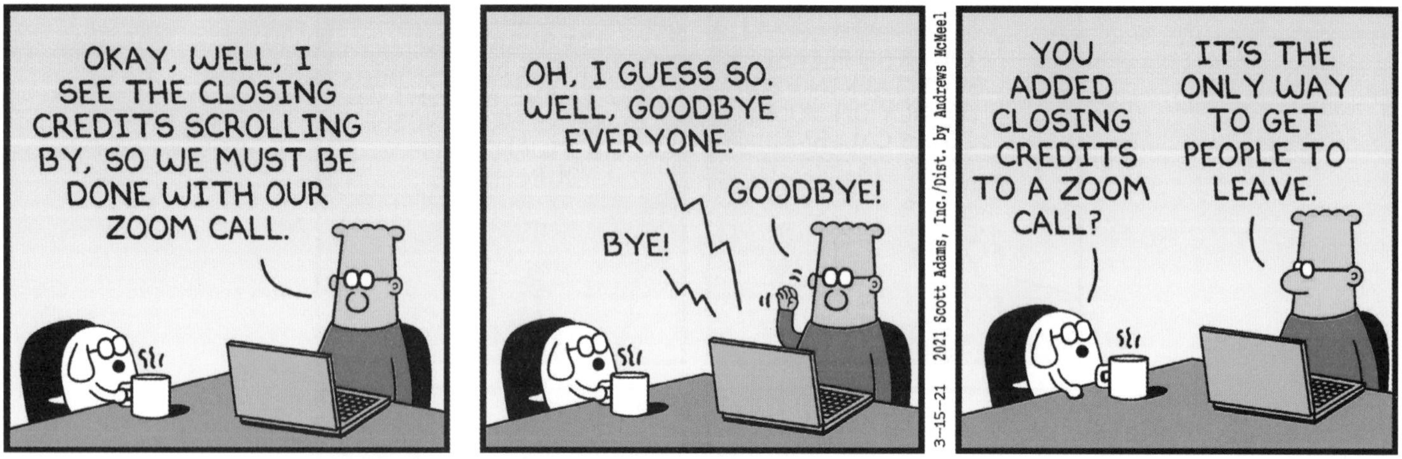
OKAY, WELL, I SEE THE CLOSING CREDITS SCROLLING BY, SO WE MUST BE DONE WITH OUR ZOOM CALL.
OH, I GUESS SO. WELL, GOODBYE EVERYONE.
BYE!
GOODBYE!
3-15-21 2021 Scott Adams, Inc./Dist. by Andrews McMeel
YOU ADDED CLOSING CREDITS TO A ZOOM CALL?
IT'S THE ONLY WAY TO GET PEOPLE TO LEAVE.

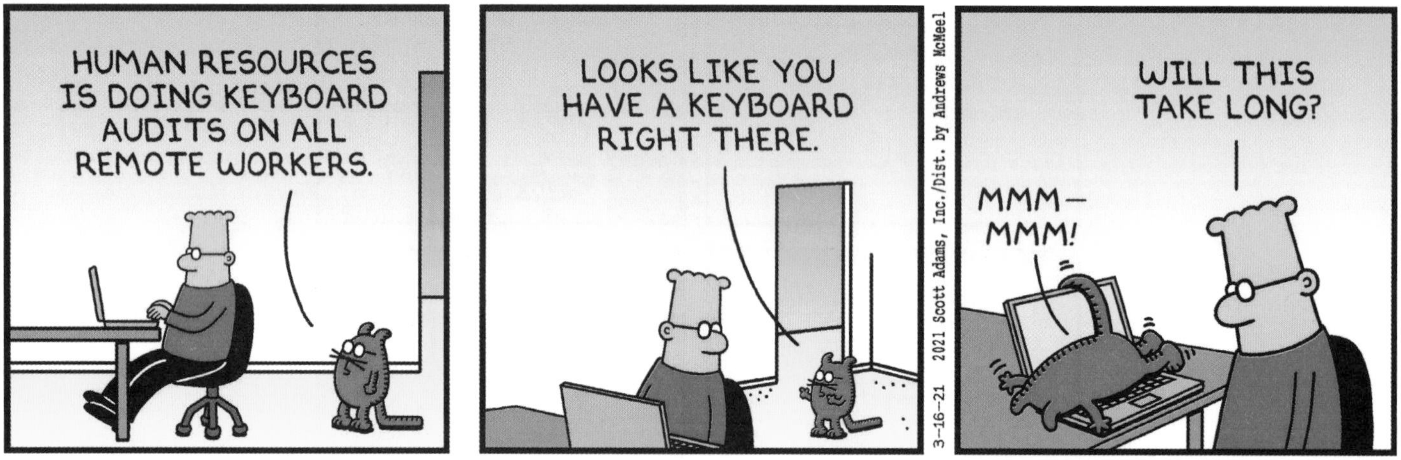
HUMAN RESOURCES IS DOING KEYBOARD AUDITS ON ALL REMOTE WORKERS.
LOOKS LIKE YOU HAVE A KEYBOARD RIGHT THERE.
3-16-21 2021 Scott Adams, Inc./Dist. by Andrews McMeel
MMM—MMM!
WILL THIS TAKE LONG?

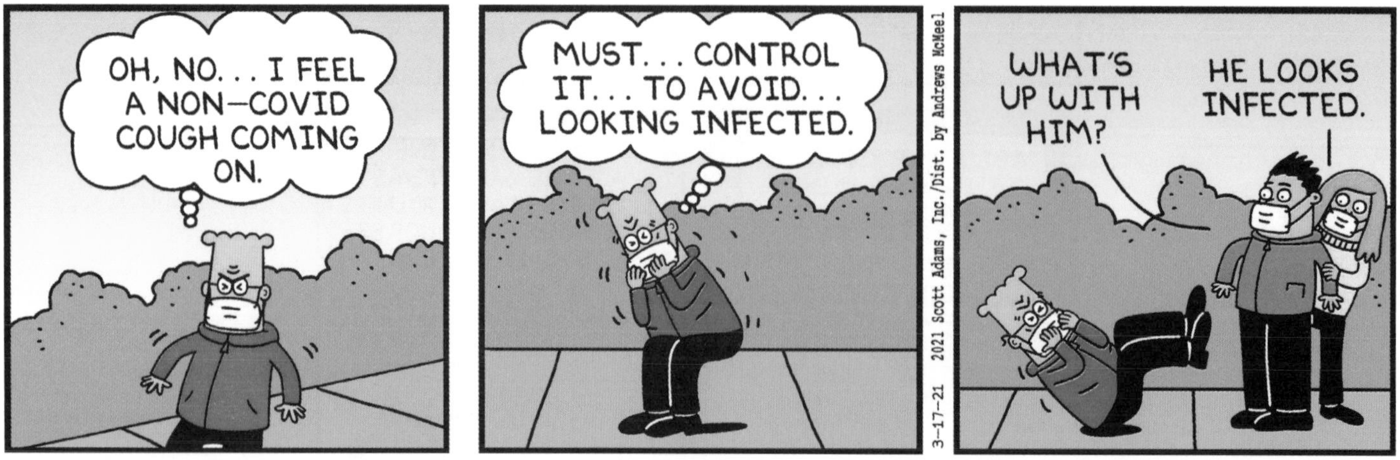
OH, NO. . . I FEEL A NON—COVID COUGH COMING ON.
MUST. . . CONTROL IT. . . TO AVOID. . . LOOKING INFECTED.
3-17-21 2021 Scott Adams, Inc./Dist. by Andrews McMeel
WHAT'S UP WITH HIM?
HE LOOKS INFECTED.

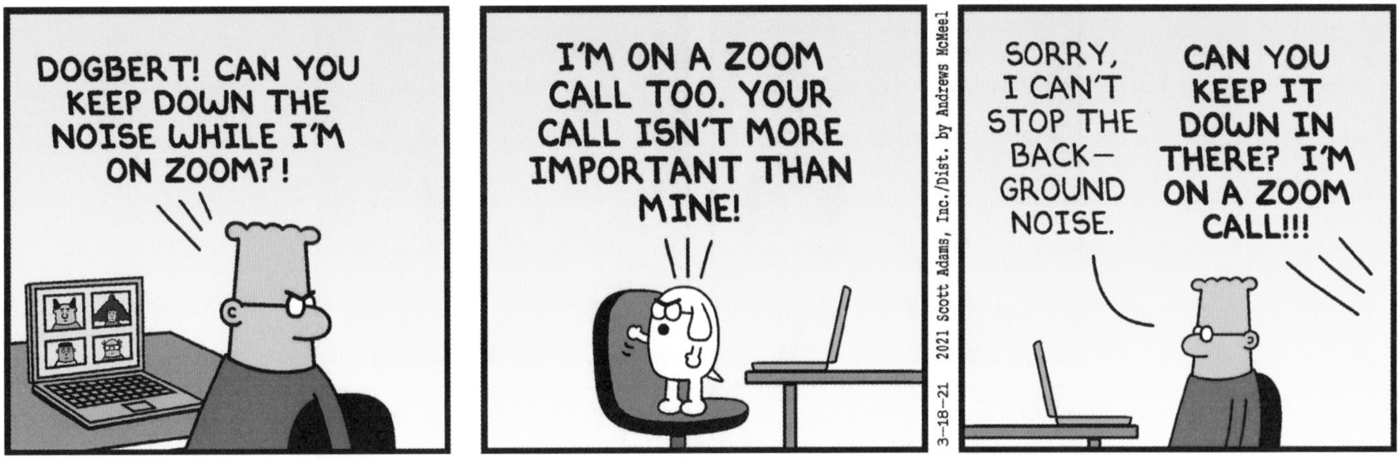
DOGBERT! CAN YOU KEEP DOWN THE NOISE WHILE I'M ON ZOOM?!
I'M ON A ZOOM CALL TOO. YOUR CALL ISN'T MORE IMPORTANT THAN MINE!
SORRY, I CAN'T STOP THE BACK-GROUND NOISE.
CAN YOU KEEP IT DOWN IN THERE? I'M ON A ZOOM CALL!!!
3-18-21 2021 Scott Adams, Inc./Dist. by Andrews McMeel

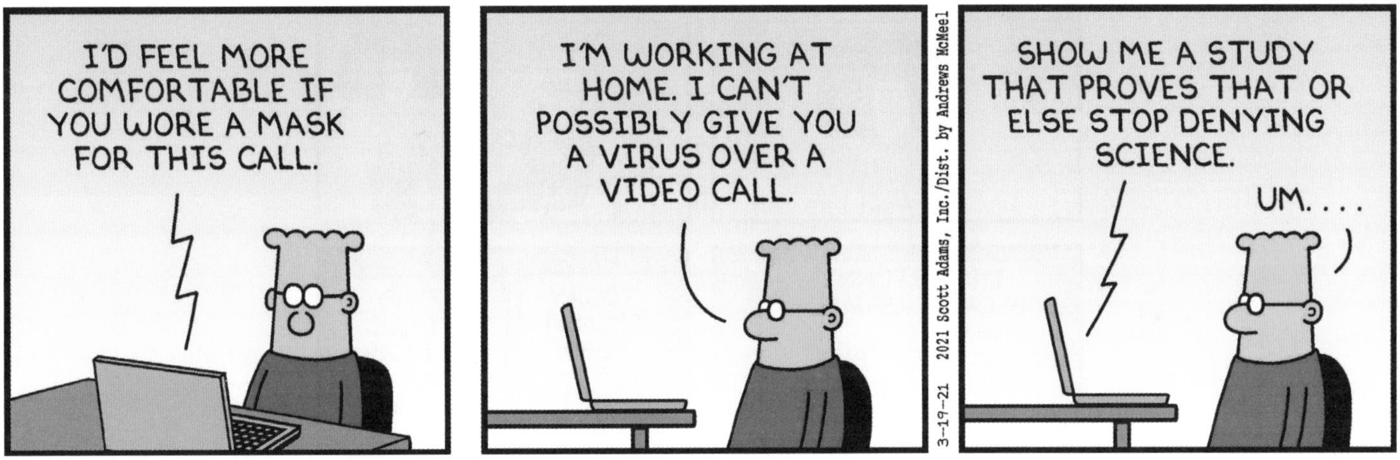
I'D FEEL MORE COMFORTABLE IF YOU WORE A MASK FOR THIS CALL.
I'M WORKING AT HOME. I CAN'T POSSIBLY GIVE YOU A VIRUS OVER A VIDEO CALL.
SHOW ME A STUDY THAT PROVES THAT OR ELSE STOP DENYING SCIENCE.
UM. . . .
3-19-21 2021 Scott Adams, Inc./Dist. by Andrews McMeel

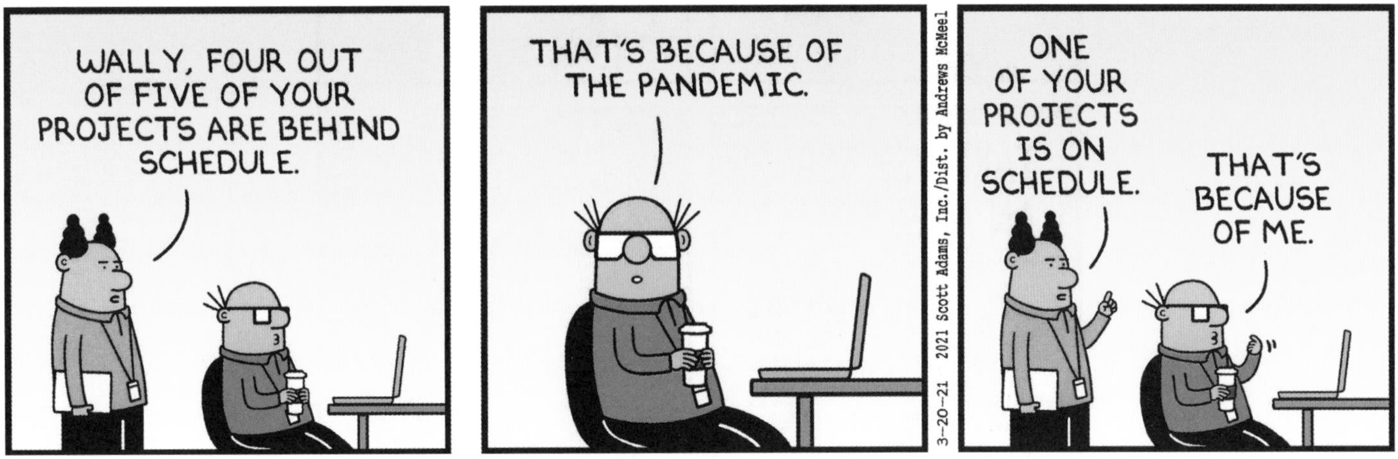
WALLY, FOUR OUT OF FIVE OF YOUR PROJECTS ARE BEHIND SCHEDULE.
THAT'S BECAUSE OF THE PANDEMIC.
ONE OF YOUR PROJECTS IS ON SCHEDULE.
THAT'S BECAUSE OF ME.
3-20-21 2021 Scott Adams, Inc./Dist. by Andrews McMeel

DO YOU HAVE A FEW MINUTES TO REVIEW MY FIRST DRAFT?
YES.
I ASK BECAUSE USUALLY YOU SAY YOU'RE TOO BUSY TO HELP.
WELL, I SAID YES THIS TIME.
THAT'S FUNNY, BECAUSE USUALLY YOU'RE ALL, "I'M SO BUSY." BUT TODAY YOU HAVE ALL THE TIME IN THE WORLD.
TODAY I'M NOT BUSY.
I FIND THAT SUS-PICIOUS.
TAKE YES FOR AN ANSWER!!!
THAT'S NOT HOW INNOCENT PEOPLE TALK.
© 2021 Scott Adams, Inc./Dist. by Andrews McMeel
3-21-21

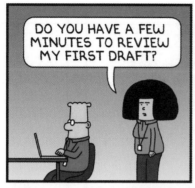

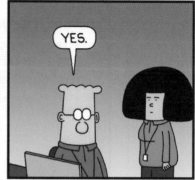

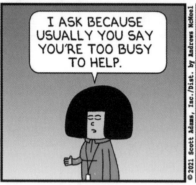

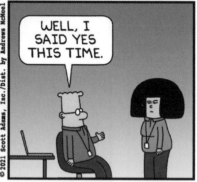

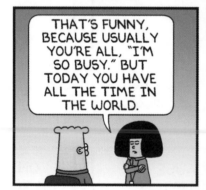

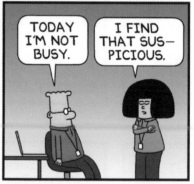

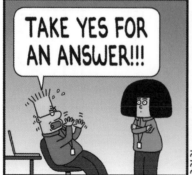

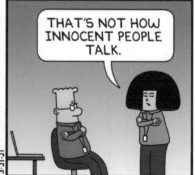

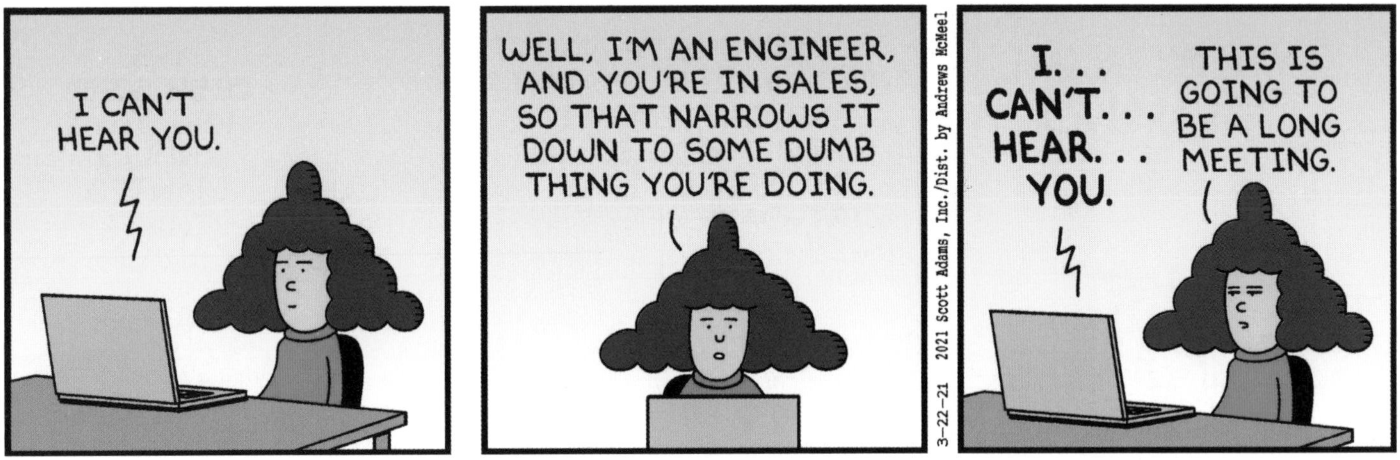
I CAN'T HEAR YOU.
WELL, I'M AN ENGINEER, AND YOU'RE IN SALES, SO THAT NARROWS IT DOWN TO SOME DUMB THING YOU'RE DOING.
I... CAN'T... HEAR... YOU.
THIS IS GOING TO BE A LONG MEETING.
3-22-21 2021 Scott Adams, Inc./Dist. by Andrews McMeel

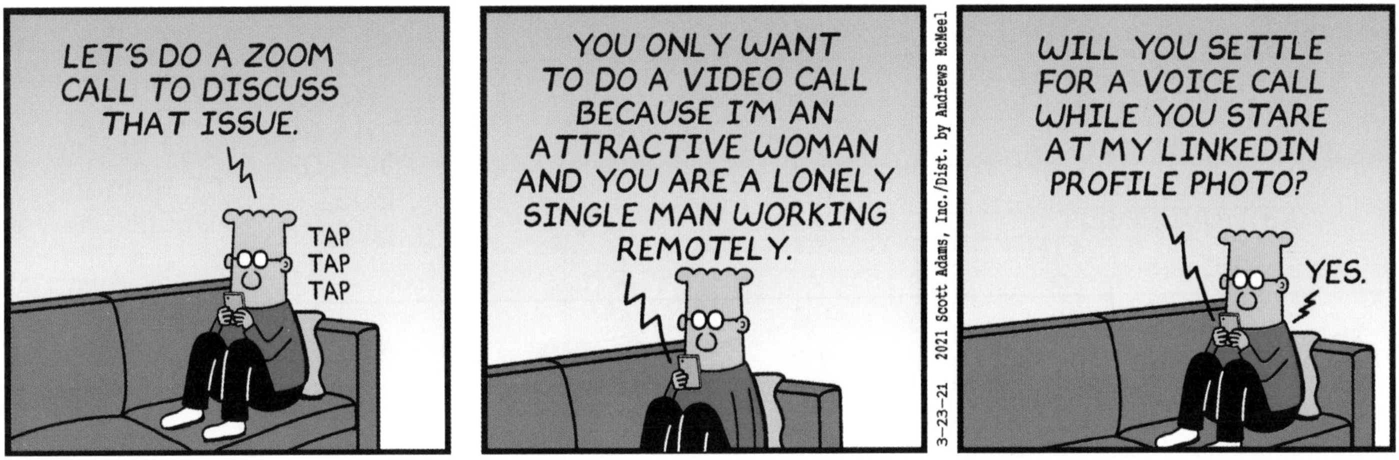
LET'S DO A ZOOM CALL TO DISCUSS THAT ISSUE.
TAP TAP TAP
YOU ONLY WANT TO DO A VIDEO CALL BECAUSE I'M AN ATTRACTIVE WOMAN AND YOU ARE A LONELY SINGLE MAN WORKING REMOTELY.
WILL YOU SETTLE FOR A VOICE CALL WHILE YOU STARE AT MY LINKEDIN PROFILE PHOTO?
YES.
3-23-21 2021 Scott Adams, Inc./Dist. by Andrews McMeel

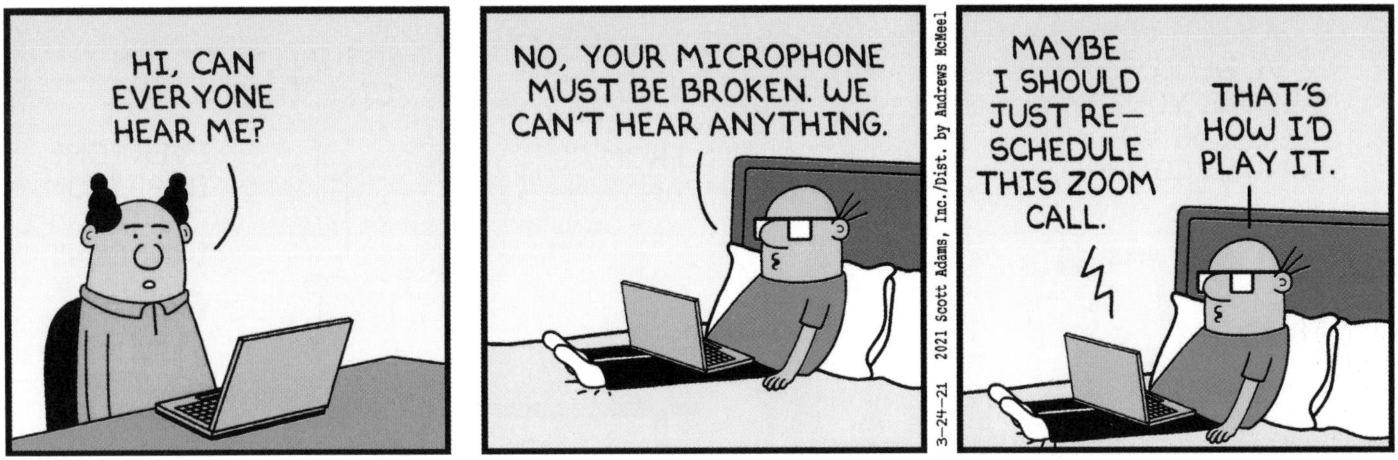
HI, CAN EVERYONE HEAR ME?
NO, YOUR MICROPHONE MUST BE BROKEN. WE CAN'T HEAR ANYTHING.
MAYBE I SHOULD JUST RE-SCHEDULE THIS ZOOM CALL.
THAT'S HOW I'D PLAY IT.
3-24-21 2021 Scott Adams, Inc./Dist. by Andrews McMeel

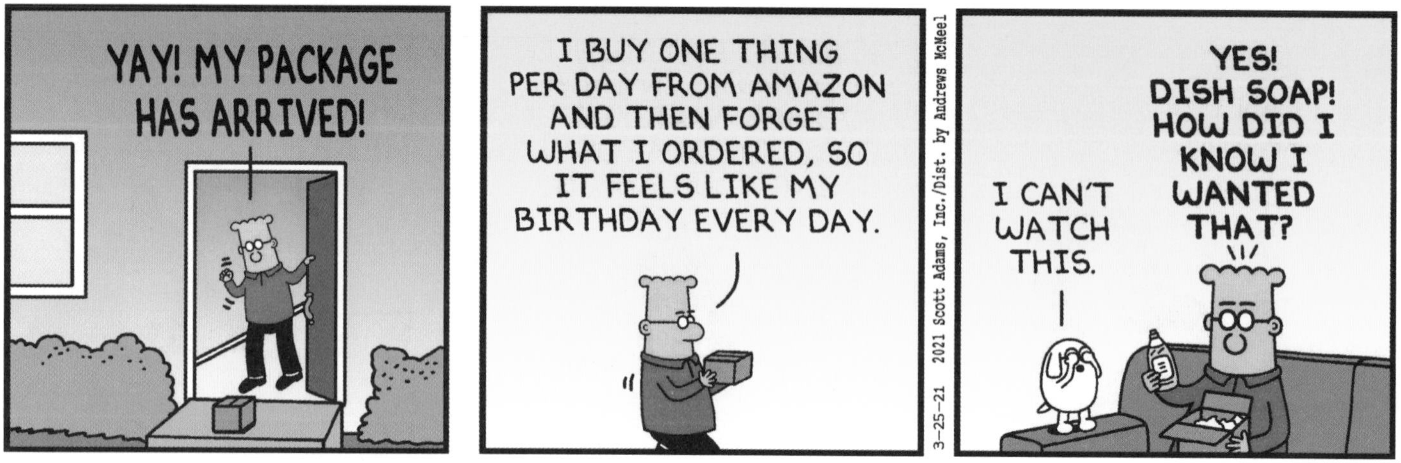
YAY! MY PACKAGE HAS ARRIVED!
I BUY ONE THING PER DAY FROM AMAZON AND THEN FORGET WHAT I ORDERED, SO IT FEELS LIKE MY BIRTHDAY EVERY DAY.
3-25-21 2021 Scott Adams, Inc./Dist. by Andrews McMeel
I CAN'T WATCH THIS.
YES! DISH SOAP! HOW DID I KNOW I WANTED THAT?

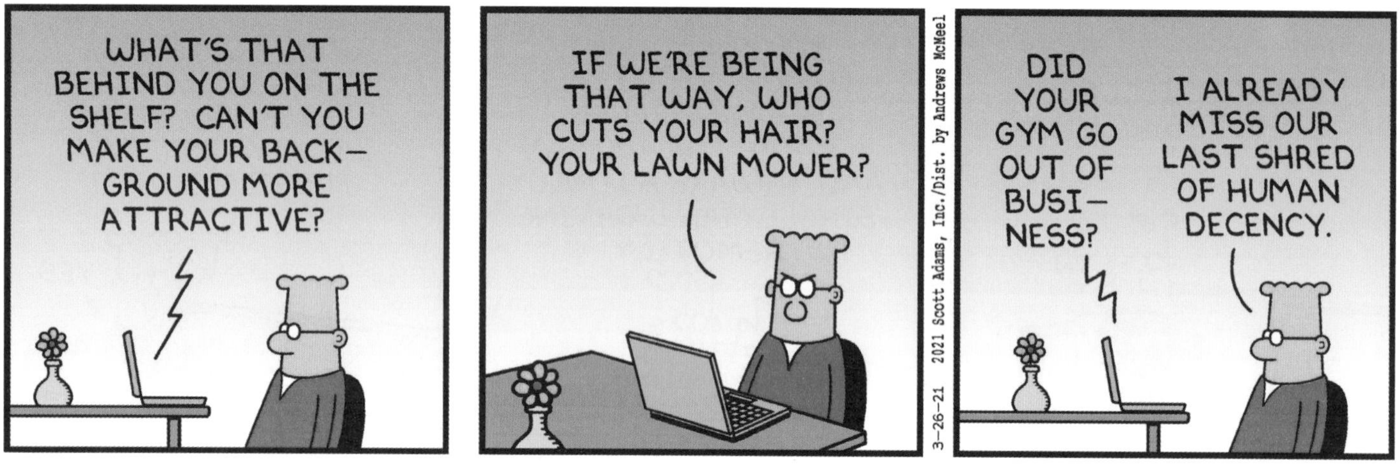
WHAT'S THAT BEHIND YOU ON THE SHELF? CAN'T YOU MAKE YOUR BACK-GROUND MORE ATTRACTIVE?
IF WE'RE BEING THAT WAY, WHO CUTS YOUR HAIR? YOUR LAWN MOWER?
3-26-21 2021 Scott Adams, Inc./Dist. by Andrews McMeel
DID YOUR GYM GO OUT OF BUSI-NESS?
I ALREADY MISS OUR LAST SHRED OF HUMAN DECENCY.

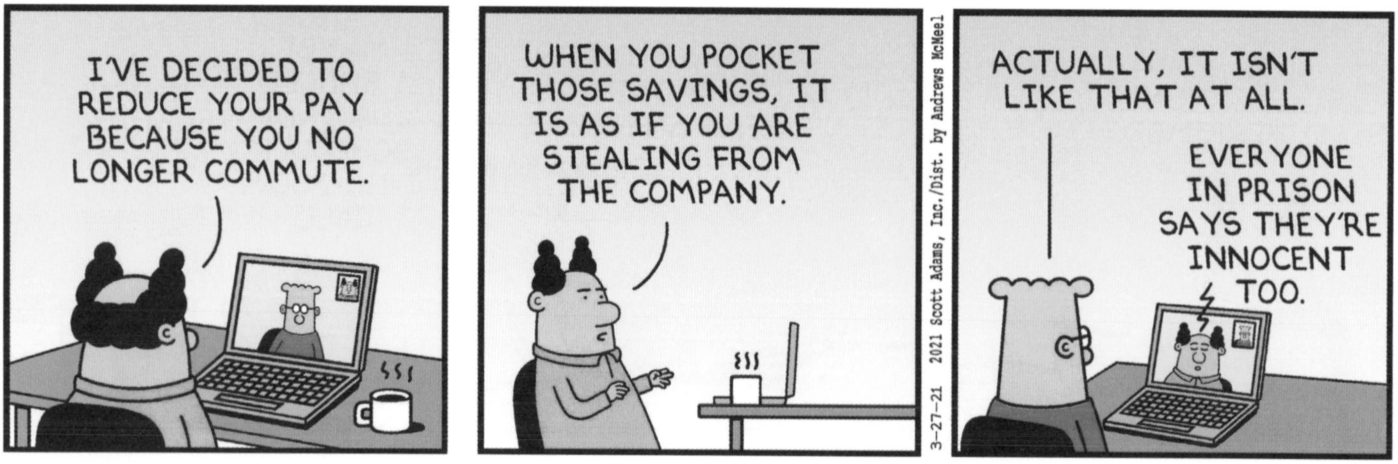
I'VE DECIDED TO REDUCE YOUR PAY BECAUSE YOU NO LONGER COMMUTE.
WHEN YOU POCKET THOSE SAVINGS, IT IS AS IF YOU ARE STEALING FROM THE COMPANY.
3-27-21 2021 Scott Adams, Inc./Dist. by Andrews McMeel
ACTUALLY, IT ISN'T LIKE THAT AT ALL.
EVERYONE IN PRISON SAYS THEY'RE INNOCENT TOO.

IS THERE ANYTHING I CAN DO TO MAKE MY SLIDE DECK MORE PERSUASIVE?

YOU NEED TO MAKE AN EMOTIONAL CONNECTION WITH YOUR AUDIENCE.

START WITH A TRAGIC PERSONAL STORY THAT MAKES EVERYONE SAD AND DROOPY.

THEN TALK ABOUT YOUR VARIOUS MEDICAL PROBLEMS, AND DON'T SPARE THE DETAILS.

THEN COMPLAIN ABOUT YOUR WIFE BECAUSE MOST PEOPLE HATE THEIR SPOUSES TOO, SO THEY CAN RELATE.

AND DON'T SPARE THE SELF—DEPRECATING HUMOR BECAUSE EVERYONE CAN RELATE TO KNOWING YOU ARE A LOSER.

WOW. THANK YOU FOR THAT ADVICE. I'LL MAKE THOSE CHANGES.

HOW MUCH DO YOU HATE HIM?

IT'S MORE ABOUT MY ENTER—TAINMENT.

© 2021 Scott Adams, Inc./Dist. by Andrews McMeel

3-28-21

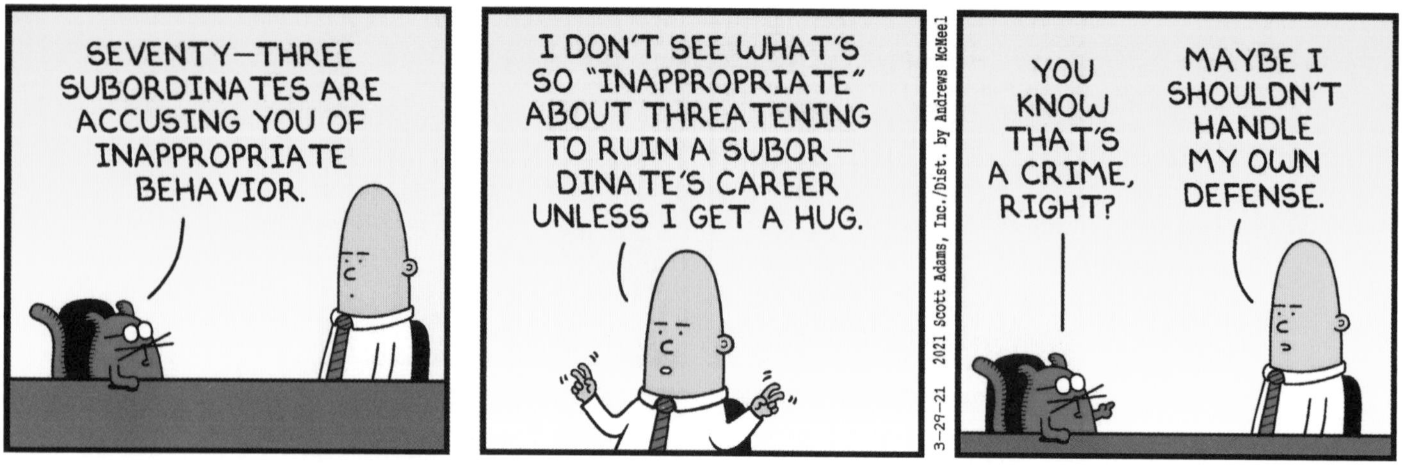
SEVENTY-THREE SUBORDINATES ARE ACCUSING YOU OF INAPPROPRIATE BEHAVIOR.
I DON'T SEE WHAT'S SO "INAPPROPRIATE" ABOUT THREATENING TO RUIN A SUBOR-DINATE'S CAREER UNLESS I GET A HUG.
YOU KNOW THAT'S A CRIME, RIGHT?
MAYBE I SHOULDN'T HANDLE MY OWN DEFENSE.
3-29-21 2021 Scott Adams, Inc./Dist. by Andrews McMeel

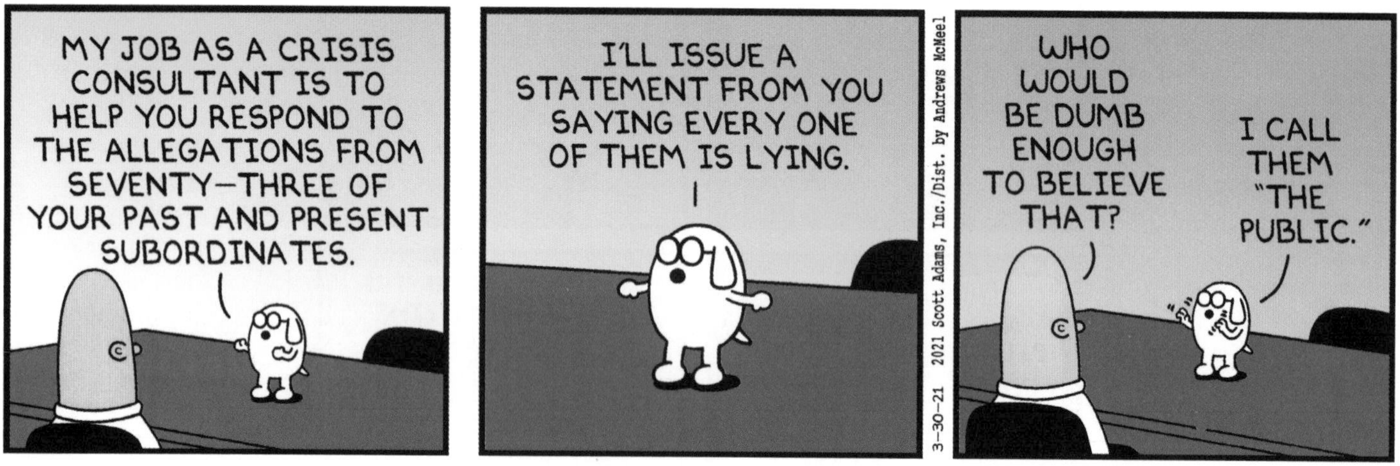
MY JOB AS A CRISIS CONSULTANT IS TO HELP YOU RESPOND TO THE ALLEGATIONS FROM SEVENTY-THREE OF YOUR PAST AND PRESENT SUBORDINATES.
I'LL ISSUE A STATEMENT FROM YOU SAYING EVERY ONE OF THEM IS LYING.
WHO WOULD BE DUMB ENOUGH TO BELIEVE THAT?
I CALL THEM "THE PUBLIC."
3-30-21 2021 Scott Adams, Inc./Dist. by Andrews McMeel

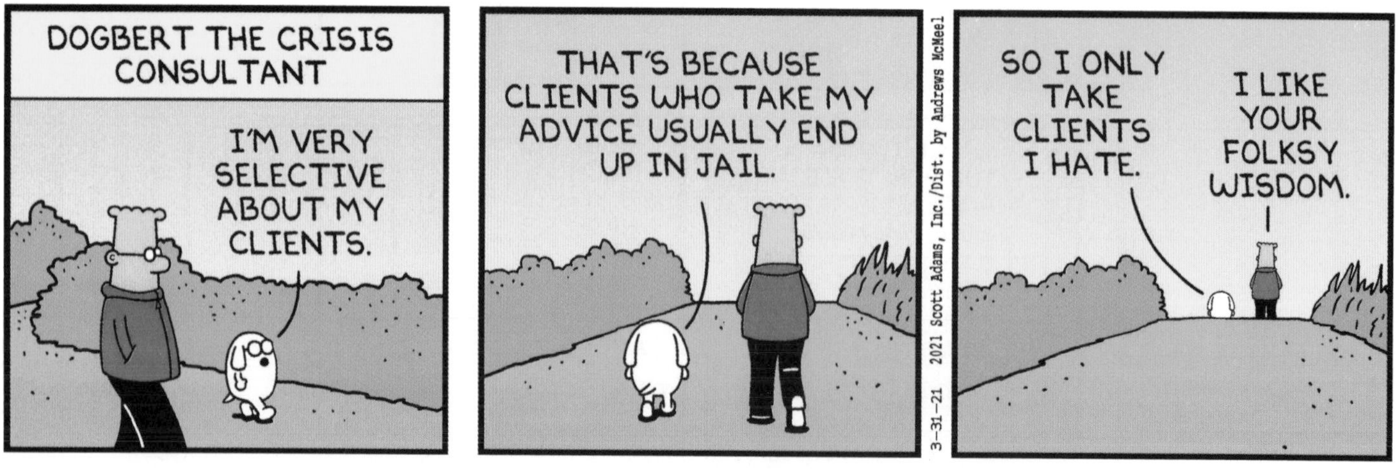
DOGBERT THE CRISIS CONSULTANT
I'M VERY SELECTIVE ABOUT MY CLIENTS.
THAT'S BECAUSE CLIENTS WHO TAKE MY ADVICE USUALLY END UP IN JAIL.
SO I ONLY TAKE CLIENTS I HATE.
I LIKE YOUR FOLKSY WISDOM.
3-31-21 2021 Scott Adams, Inc./Dist. by Andrews McMeel

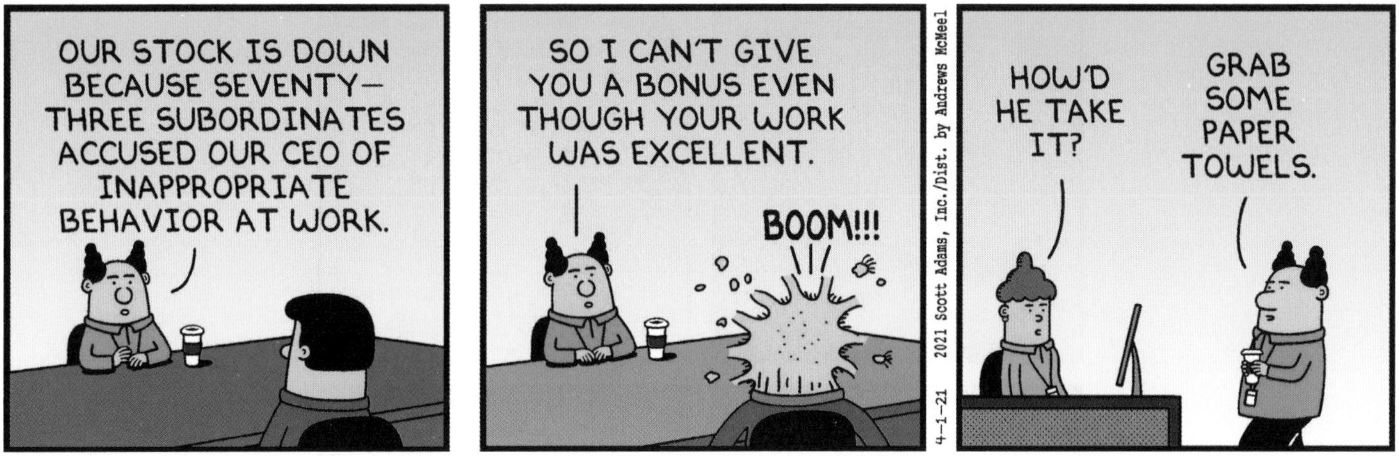
OUR STOCK IS DOWN BECAUSE SEVENTY-THREE SUBORDINATES ACCUSED OUR CEO OF INAPPROPRIATE BEHAVIOR AT WORK.
SO I CAN'T GIVE YOU A BONUS EVEN THOUGH YOUR WORK WAS EXCELLENT.
BOOM!!!
2021 Scott Adams, Inc./Dist. by Andrews McMeel 4-1-21
HOW'D HE TAKE IT?
GRAB SOME PAPER TOWELS.

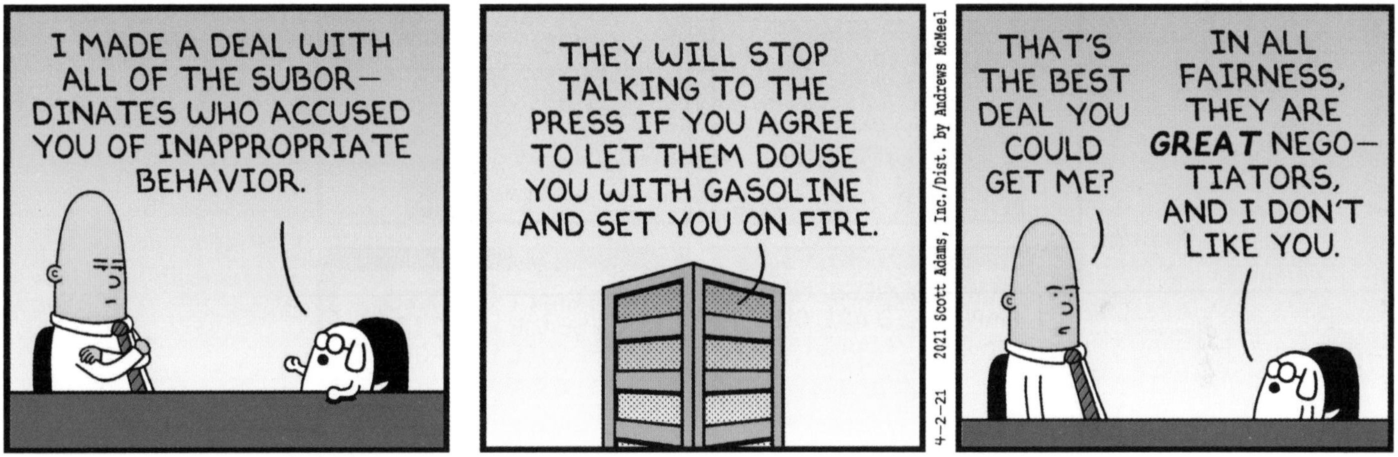
I MADE A DEAL WITH ALL OF THE SUBOR-DINATES WHO ACCUSED YOU OF INAPPROPRIATE BEHAVIOR.
THEY WILL STOP TALKING TO THE PRESS IF YOU AGREE TO LET THEM DOUSE YOU WITH GASOLINE AND SET YOU ON FIRE.
2021 Scott Adams, Inc./Dist. by Andrews McMeel 4-2-21
THAT'S THE BEST DEAL YOU COULD GET ME?
IN ALL FAIRNESS, THEY ARE GREAT NEGO-TIATORS, AND I DON'T LIKE YOU.

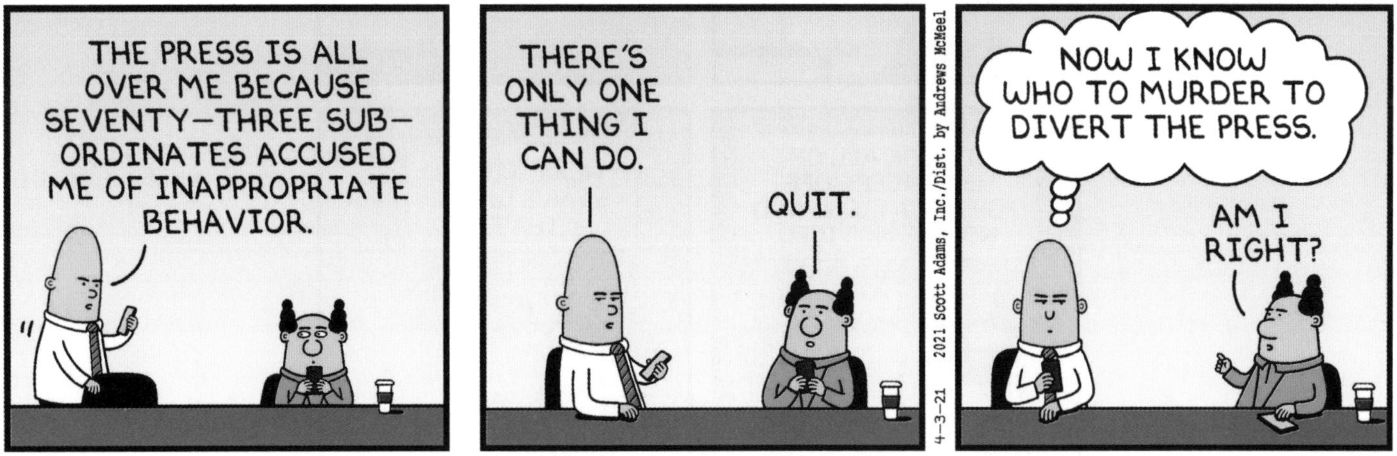
THE PRESS IS ALL OVER ME BECAUSE SEVENTY-THREE SUB-ORDINATES ACCUSED ME OF INAPPROPRIATE BEHAVIOR.
THERE'S ONLY ONE THING I CAN DO.
QUIT.
2021 Scott Adams, Inc./Dist. by Andrews McMeel 4-3-21
NOW I KNOW WHO TO MURDER TO DIVERT THE PRESS.
AM I RIGHT?

IS IT OKAY IF I TAKE NEXT WEEK OFF?
ARE YOU KIDDING? WE'RE IN THE MOST CRITICAL MONTH OF THE SYSTEM MIGRATION.
YOU'RE ESSENTIAL TO OUR SUCCESS. ALL HANDS MUST BE ON DECK.
REALLY? IT SEEMS AS IF ALL I DO IS LISTEN TO OTHER PEOPLE SAY USELESS STUFF ON ZOOM CALLS.
MY GOODNESS, NO! EMPLOYEES ARE OUR MOST VALUABLE ASSET!
WE CAN'T SUCCEED UNLESS WE HAVE 100% EMPLOYEE ENGAGE-MENT.
I TOOK ALL OF LAST WEEK OFF FOR VACATION, AND NO ONE NOTICED.
NEXT TIME, START WITH THAT.
© 2021 Scott Adams, Inc./Dist. by Andrews McMeel
4-4-21

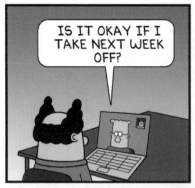

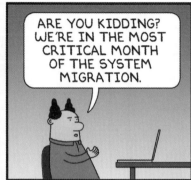

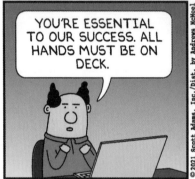

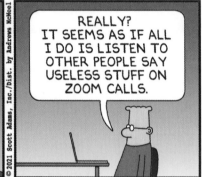

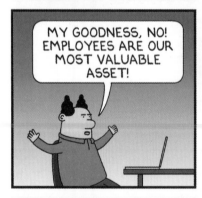

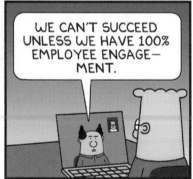

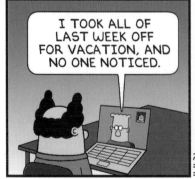

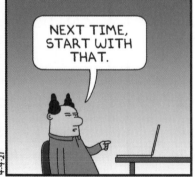

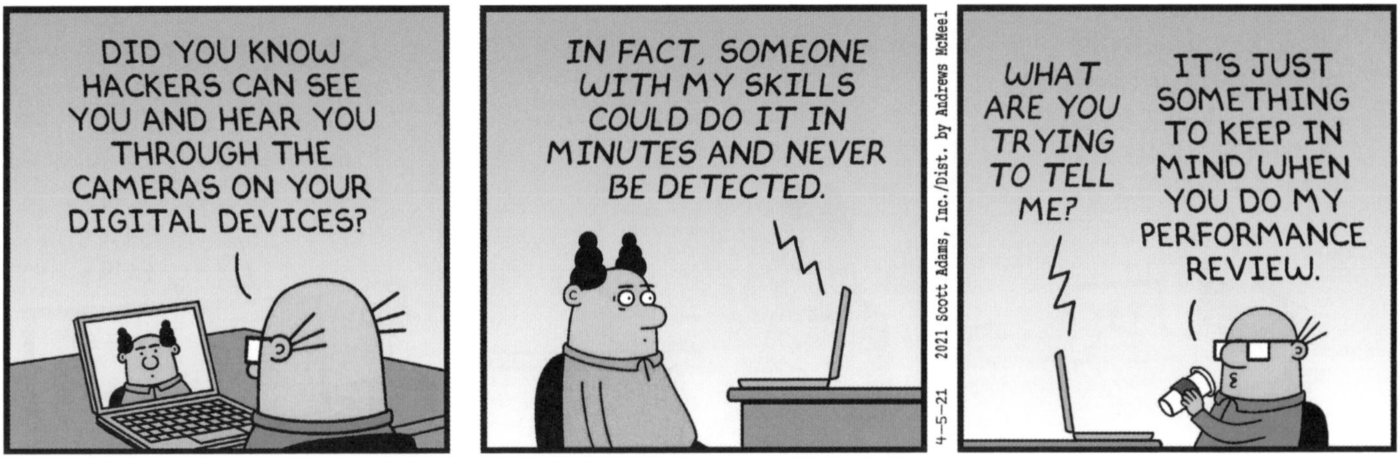
DID YOU KNOW HACKERS CAN SEE YOU AND HEAR YOU THROUGH THE CAMERAS ON YOUR DIGITAL DEVICES?
IN FACT, SOMEONE WITH MY SKILLS COULD DO IT IN MINUTES AND NEVER BE DETECTED.
4-5-21 2021 Scott Adams, Inc./Dist. by Andrews McMeel
WHAT ARE YOU TRYING TO TELL ME?
IT'S JUST SOMETHING TO KEEP IN MIND WHEN YOU DO MY PERFORMANCE REVIEW.

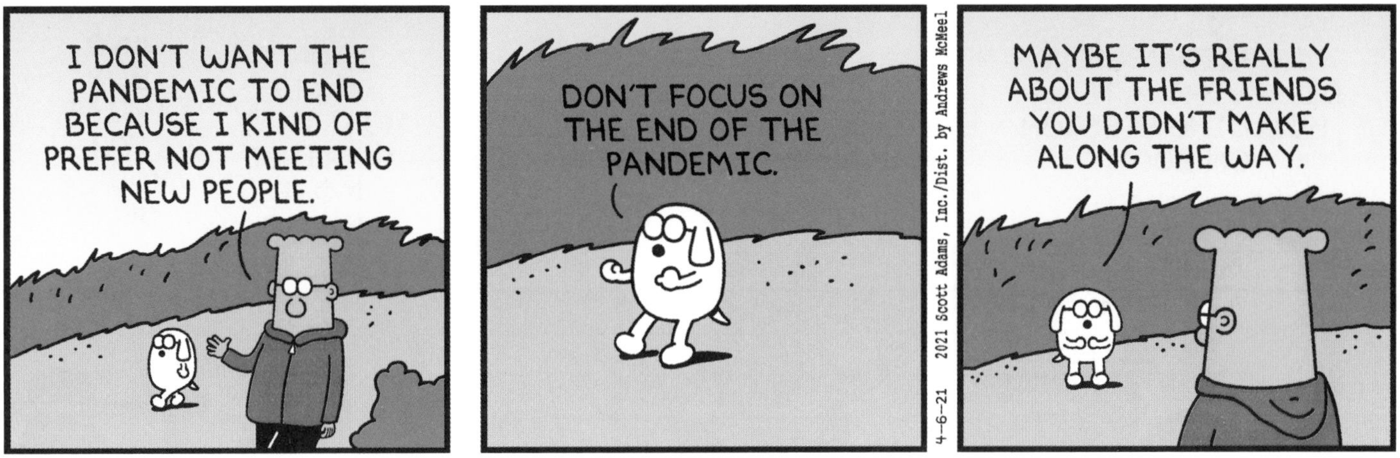
I DON'T WANT THE PANDEMIC TO END BECAUSE I KIND OF PREFER NOT MEETING NEW PEOPLE.
DON'T FOCUS ON THE END OF THE PANDEMIC.
4-6-21 2021 Scott Adams, Inc./Dist. by Andrews McMeel
MAYBE IT'S REALLY ABOUT THE FRIENDS YOU DIDN'T MAKE ALONG THE WAY.

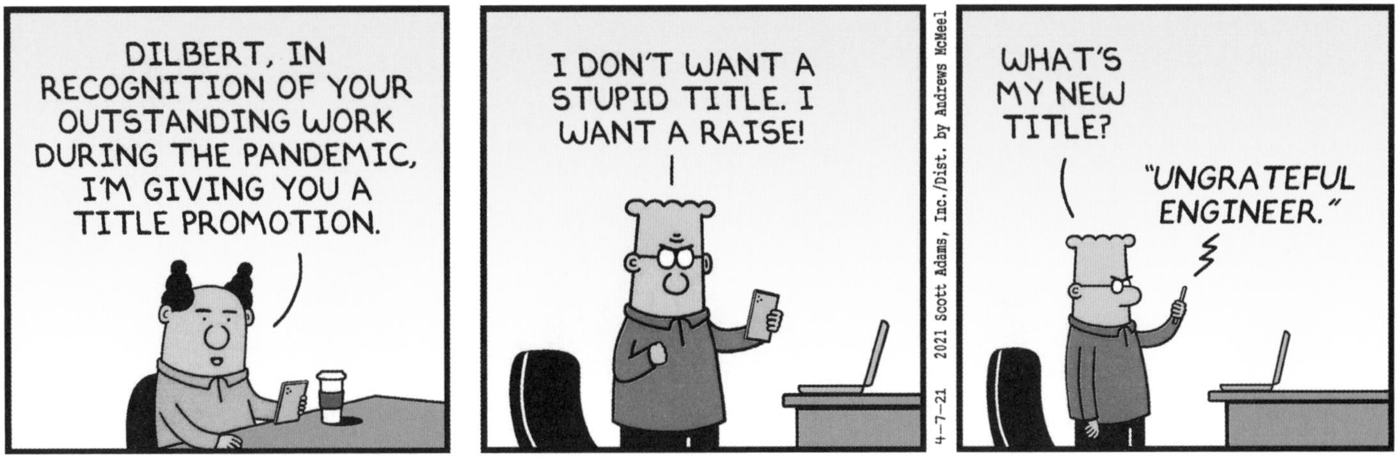
DILBERT, IN RECOGNITION OF YOUR OUTSTANDING WORK DURING THE PANDEMIC, I'M GIVING YOU A TITLE PROMOTION.
I DON'T WANT A STUPID TITLE. I WANT A RAISE!
4-7-21 2021 Scott Adams, Inc./Dist. by Andrews McMeel
WHAT'S MY NEW TITLE?
"UNGRATEFUL ENGINEER."

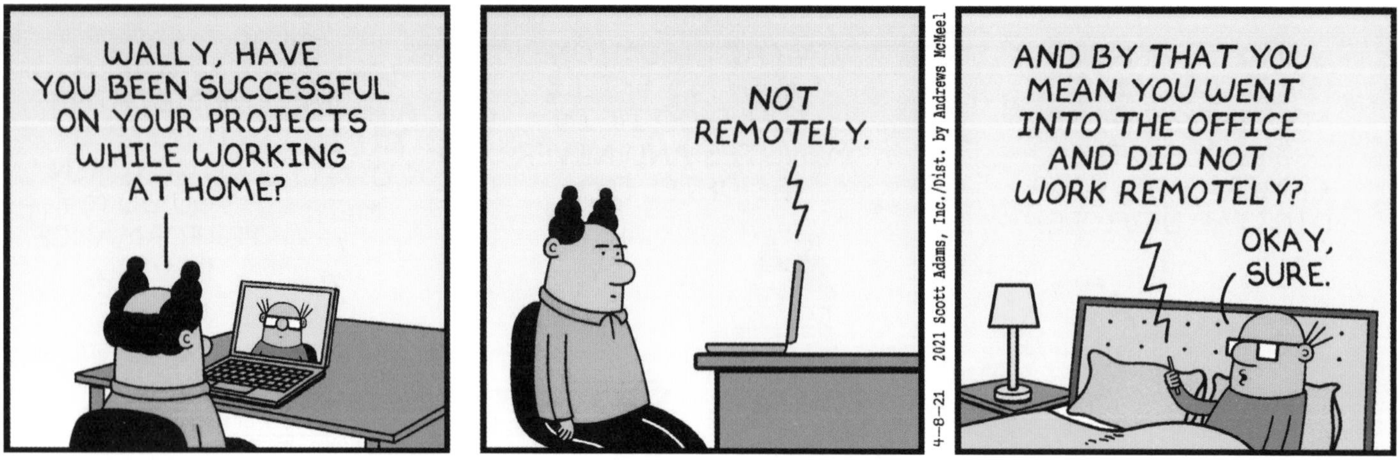
WALLY, HAVE YOU BEEN SUCCESSFUL ON YOUR PROJECTS WHILE WORKING AT HOME?
NOT REMOTELY.
4-8-21 2021 Scott Adams, Inc./Dist. by Andrews McMeel
AND BY THAT YOU MEAN YOU WENT INTO THE OFFICE AND DID NOT WORK REMOTELY?
OKAY, SURE.

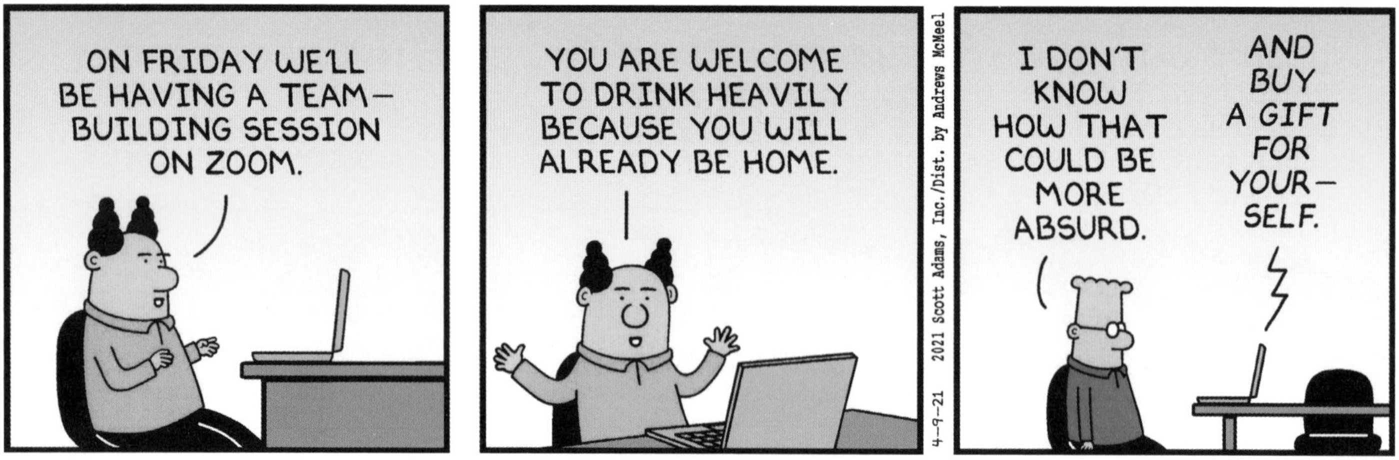
ON FRIDAY WE'LL BE HAVING A TEAM-BUILDING SESSION ON ZOOM.
YOU ARE WELCOME TO DRINK HEAVILY BECAUSE YOU WILL ALREADY BE HOME.
4-9-21 2021 Scott Adams, Inc./Dist. by Andrews McMeel
I DON'T KNOW HOW THAT COULD BE MORE ABSURD.
AND BUY A GIFT FOR YOURSELF.

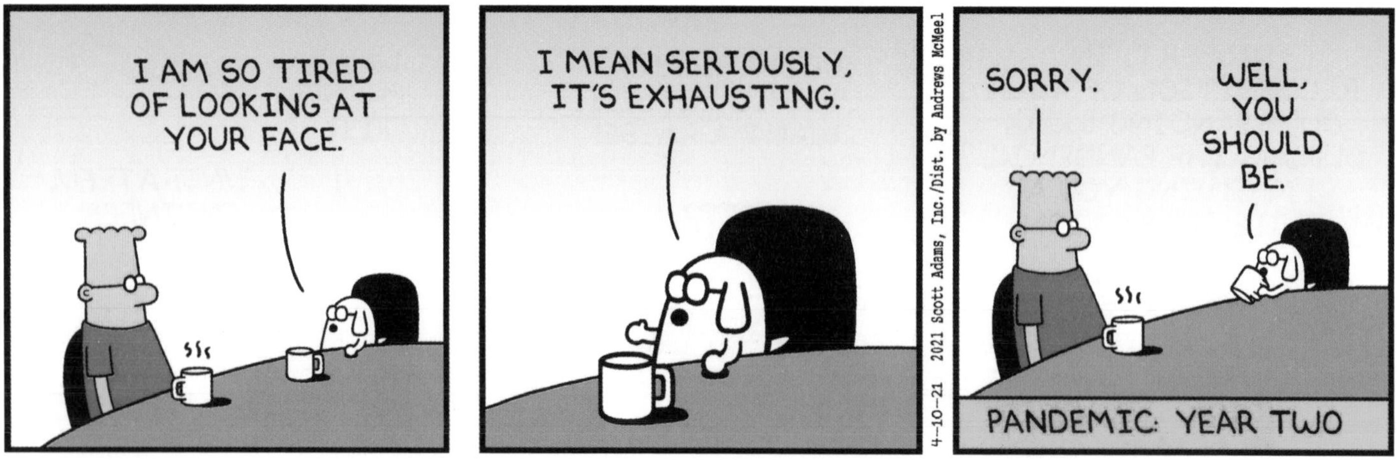
I AM SO TIRED OF LOOKING AT YOUR FACE.
I MEAN SERIOUSLY, IT'S EXHAUSTING.
4-10-21 2021 Scott Adams, Inc./Dist. by Andrews McMeel
SORRY.
WELL, YOU SHOULD BE.
PANDEMIC: YEAR TWO

I'LL SCHEDULE A ZOOM CALL WITH THE WHOLE TEAM TOMORROW TO GIVE THE UPDATE.
OR YOU COULD TELL ME TOMORROW, AND I'LL TELL THE REST OF THE TEAM ON OUR NOON ZOOM CALL.
UM, OKAY. I'LL SEND YOU A ZOOM LINK TOMORROW.
DOES OUR CALL NEED TO BE A VIDEO CALL? CAN WE DO A VOICE CALL?
WELL, YES, I GUESS WE COULD JUST DO A VOICE CALL.
DO WE NEED TO TALK, OR CAN YOU JUST SEND ME AN EMAIL?
I SUPPOSE I COULD JUST SEND YOU AN EMAIL.
OKAY, WE'RE MAKING PROGRESS. NOW, HAVE YOU HEARD OF "TEXTING"?
4-11-21

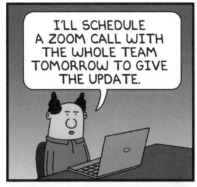

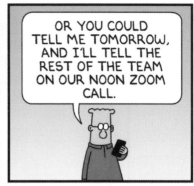

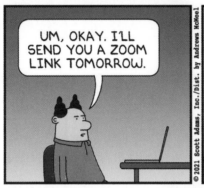

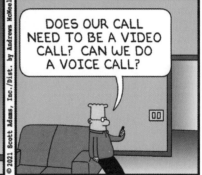

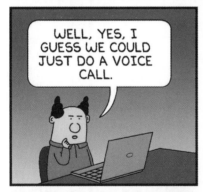

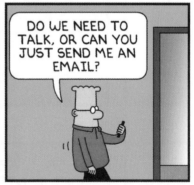

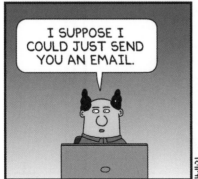

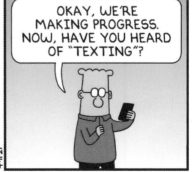

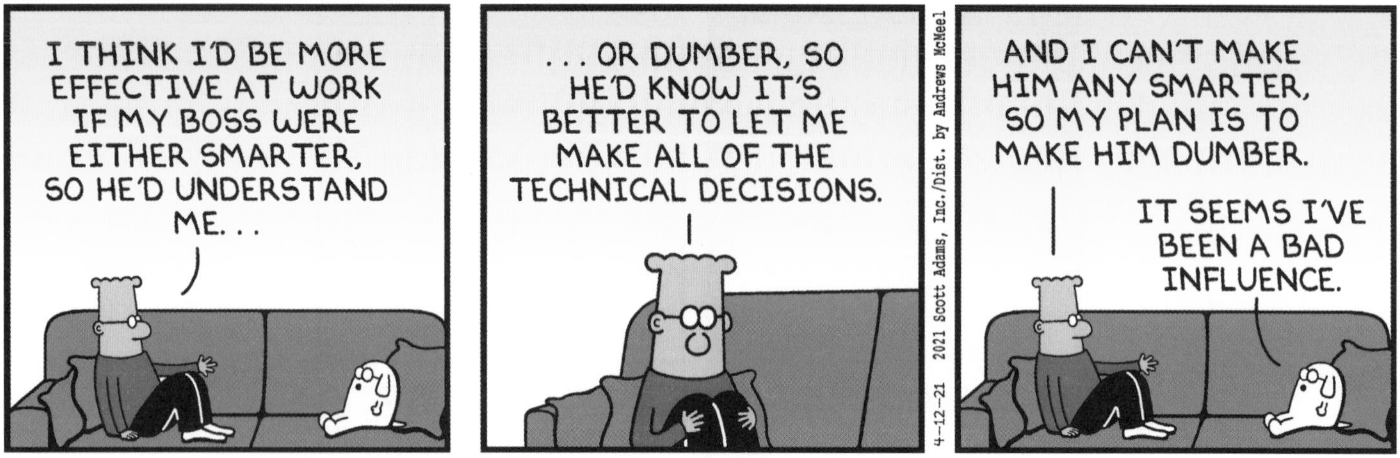
I THINK I'D BE MORE EFFECTIVE AT WORK IF MY BOSS WERE EITHER SMARTER, SO HE'D UNDERSTAND ME. . .
. . . OR DUMBER, SO HE'D KNOW IT'S BETTER TO LET ME MAKE ALL OF THE TECHNICAL DECISIONS.
4-12-21 2021 Scott Adams, Inc./Dist. by Andrews McMeel
AND I CAN'T MAKE HIM ANY SMARTER, SO MY PLAN IS TO MAKE HIM DUMBER.
IT SEEMS I'VE BEEN A BAD INFLUENCE.

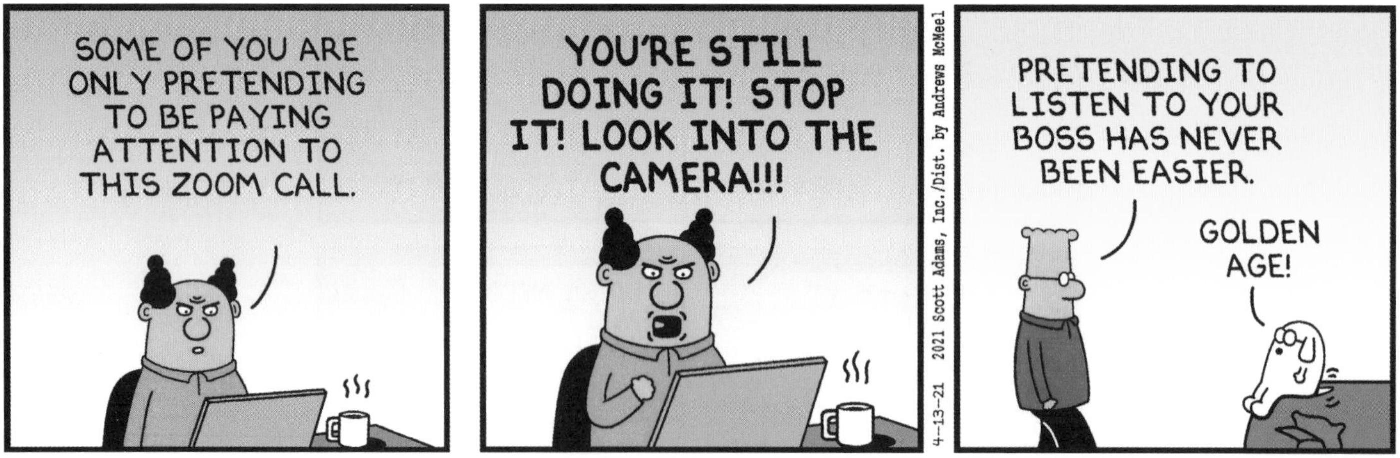
SOME OF YOU ARE ONLY PRETENDING TO BE PAYING ATTENTION TO THIS ZOOM CALL.
YOU'RE STILL DOING IT! STOP IT! LOOK INTO THE CAMERA!!!
4-13-21 2021 Scott Adams, Inc./Dist. by Andrews McMeel
PRETENDING TO LISTEN TO YOUR BOSS HAS NEVER BEEN EASIER.
GOLDEN AGE!

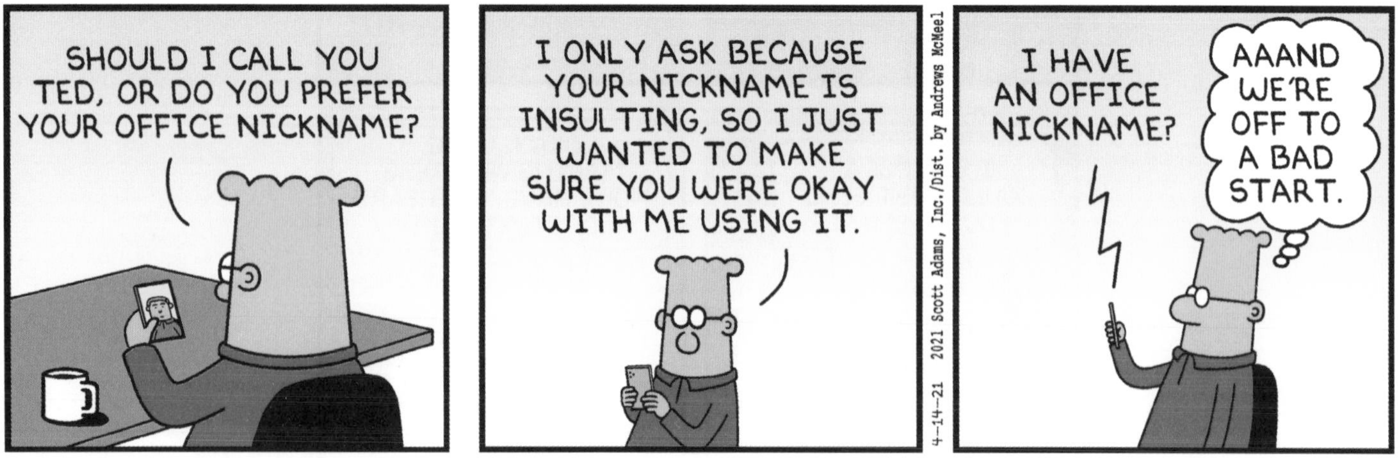
SHOULD I CALL YOU TED, OR DO YOU PREFER YOUR OFFICE NICKNAME?
I ONLY ASK BECAUSE YOUR NICKNAME IS INSULTING, SO I JUST WANTED TO MAKE SURE YOU WERE OKAY WITH ME USING IT.
4-14-21 2021 Scott Adams, Inc./Dist. by Andrews McMeel
I HAVE AN OFFICE NICKNAME?
AAAND WE'RE OFF TO A BAD START.

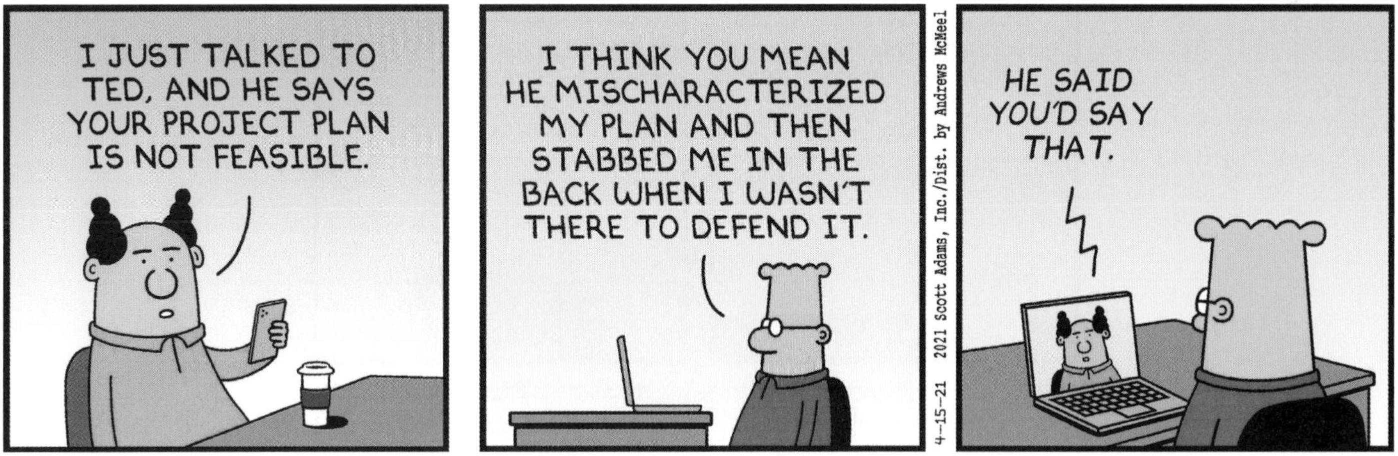
I JUST TALKED TO TED, AND HE SAYS YOUR PROJECT PLAN IS NOT FEASIBLE.
I THINK YOU MEAN HE MISCHARACTERIZED MY PLAN AND THEN STABBED ME IN THE BACK WHEN I WASN'T THERE TO DEFEND IT.
4-15-21 2021 Scott Adams, Inc./Dist. by Andrews McMeel
HE SAID YOU'D SAY THAT.

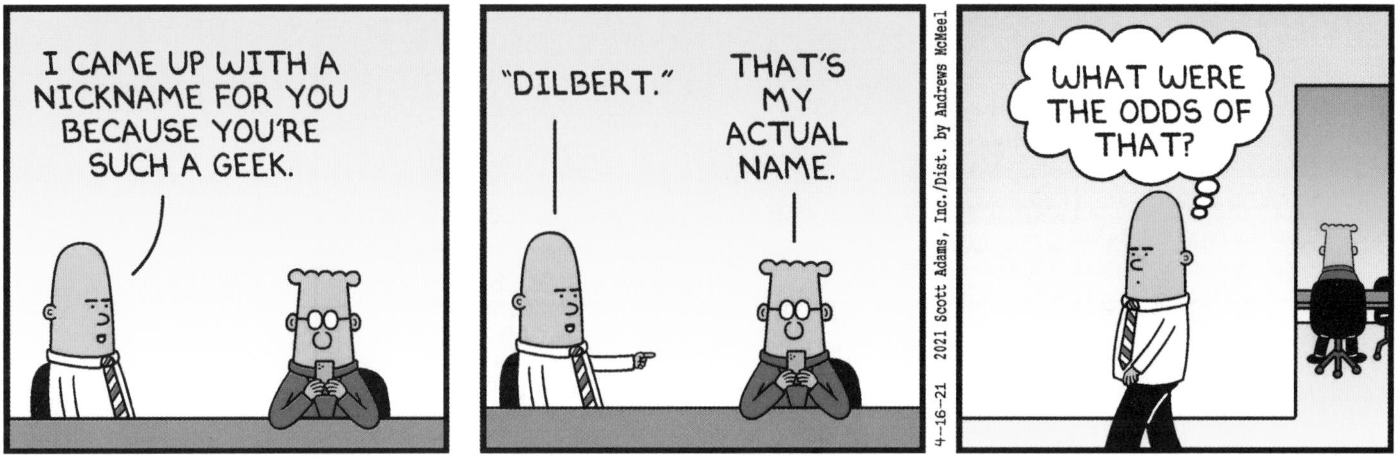
I CAME UP WITH A NICKNAME FOR YOU BECAUSE YOU'RE SUCH A GEEK.
"DILBERT."
THAT'S MY ACTUAL NAME.
4-16-21 2021 Scott Adams, Inc./Dist. by Andrews McMeel
WHAT WERE THE ODDS OF THAT?

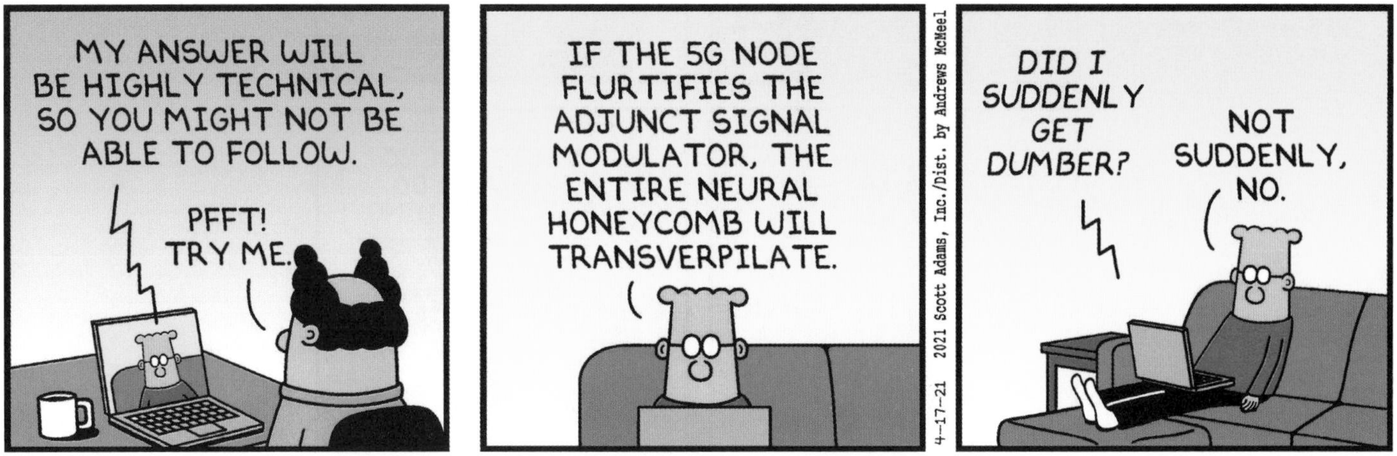
MY ANSWER WILL BE HIGHLY TECHNICAL, SO YOU MIGHT NOT BE ABLE TO FOLLOW.
PFFT! TRY ME.
IF THE 5G NODE FLURTIFIES THE ADJUNCT SIGNAL MODULATOR, THE ENTIRE NEURAL HONEYCOMB WILL TRANSVERPILATE.
4-17-21 2021 Scott Adams, Inc./Dist. by Andrews McMeel
DID I SUDDENLY GET DUMBER?
NOT SUDDENLY, NO.

BILLING FOR YOUR VIDEO THERAPY SESSION BEGINS NOW.

I'M WORRIED THAT ALL OF MY RECENT SOCIAL ISOLATION HAS CHANGED ME.

HOW SO?

WELL, A YEAR AGO, I FELT AWKWARD AND BORED AROUND PEOPLE, AND THAT WAS BAD ENOUGH.

NOW I HATE THEM SO MUCH THAT I ONLY *PRETEND* TO WASH MY HANDS.

I GUESS I'M SECRETLY HOPING I'M A CARRIER FOR A DEADLY PATHOGEN OF SOME TYPE.

AM I NORMAL?

I SURE HOPE SO BECAUSE I DO THE SAME THING.

© 2020 Scott Adams, Inc./Dist. by Andrews McMeel

4-18-21

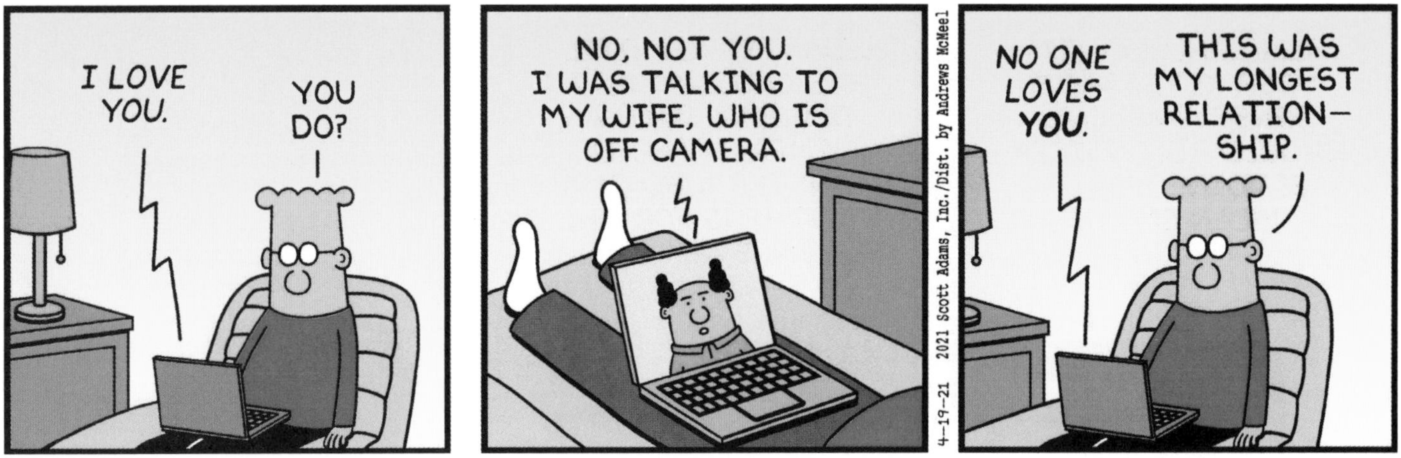
I LOVE YOU.
YOU DO?
NO, NOT YOU. I WAS TALKING TO MY WIFE, WHO IS OFF CAMERA.
NO ONE LOVES **YOU**.
THIS WAS MY LONGEST RELATION-SHIP.
4-19-21 2021 Scott Adams, Inc./Dist. by Andrews McMeel

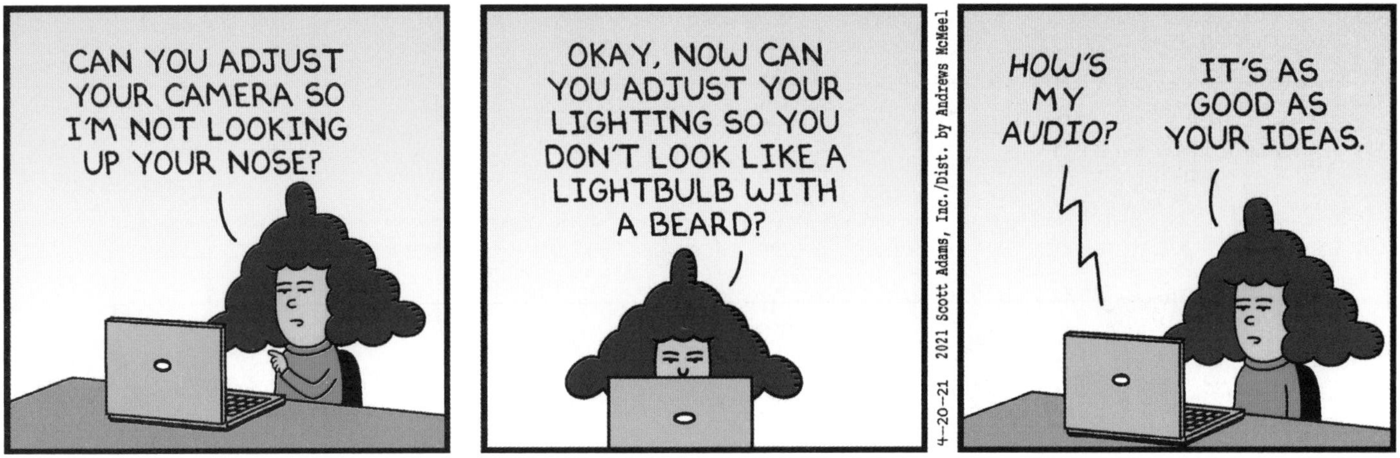
CAN YOU ADJUST YOUR CAMERA SO I'M NOT LOOKING UP YOUR NOSE?
OKAY, NOW CAN YOU ADJUST YOUR LIGHTING SO YOU DON'T LOOK LIKE A LIGHTBULB WITH A BEARD?
HOW'S MY AUDIO?
IT'S AS GOOD AS YOUR IDEAS.
4-20-21 2021 Scott Adams, Inc./Dist. by Andrews McMeel

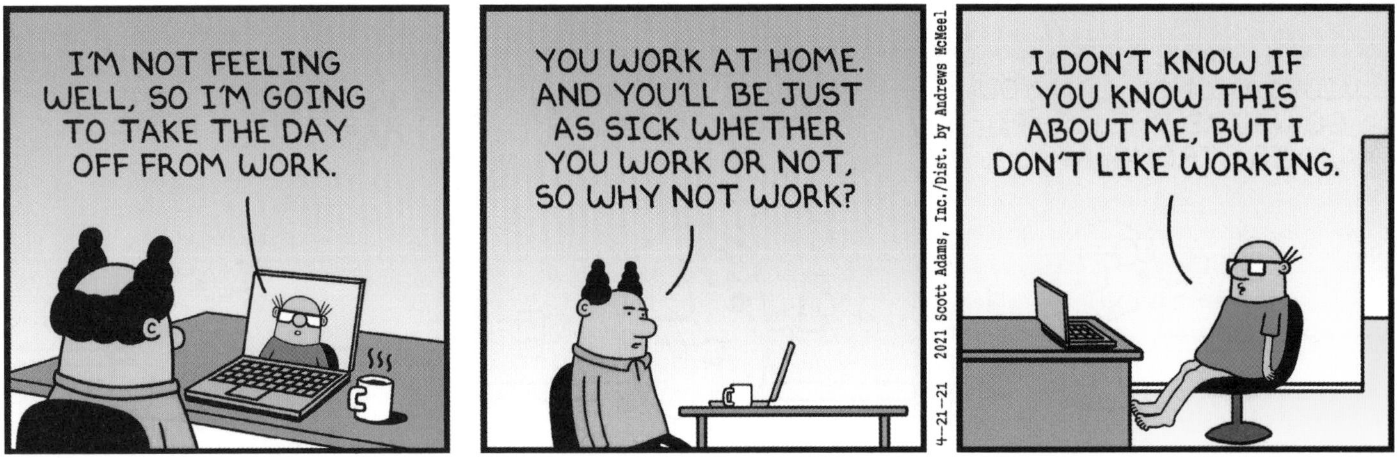
I'M NOT FEELING WELL, SO I'M GOING TO TAKE THE DAY OFF FROM WORK.
YOU WORK AT HOME. AND YOU'LL BE JUST AS SICK WHETHER YOU WORK OR NOT, SO WHY NOT WORK?
I DON'T KNOW IF YOU KNOW THIS ABOUT ME, BUT I DON'T LIKE WORKING.
4-21-21 2021 Scott Adams, Inc./Dist. by Andrews McMeel

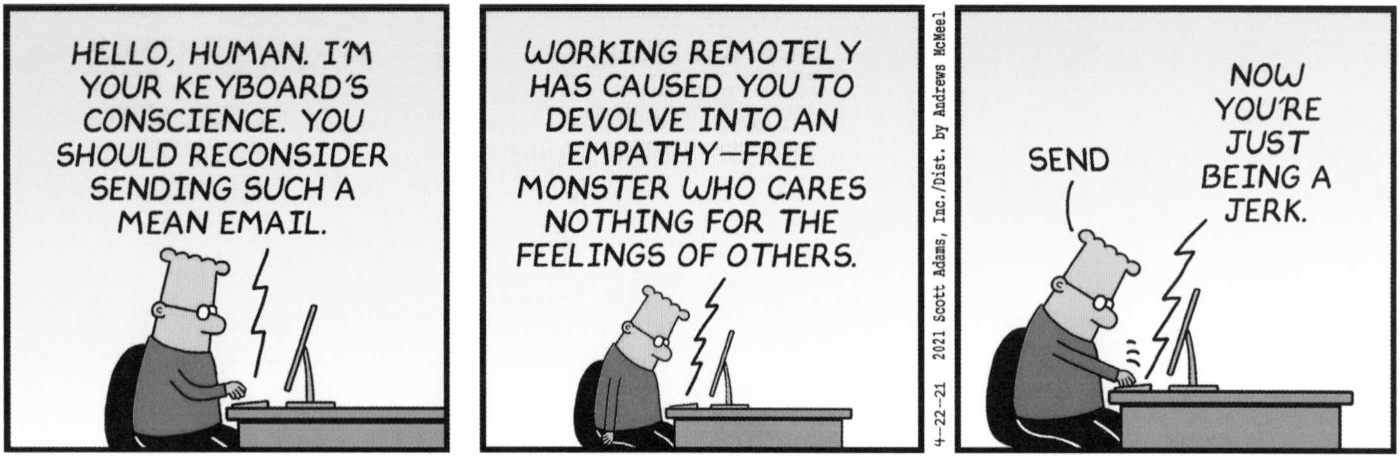
HELLO, HUMAN. I'M YOUR KEYBOARD'S CONSCIENCE. YOU SHOULD RECONSIDER SENDING SUCH A MEAN EMAIL.
WORKING REMOTELY HAS CAUSED YOU TO DEVOLVE INTO AN EMPATHY—FREE MONSTER WHO CARES NOTHING FOR THE FEELINGS OF OTHERS.
4-22-21 2021 Scott Adams, Inc./Dist. by Andrews McMeel
SEND
NOW YOU'RE JUST BEING A JERK.

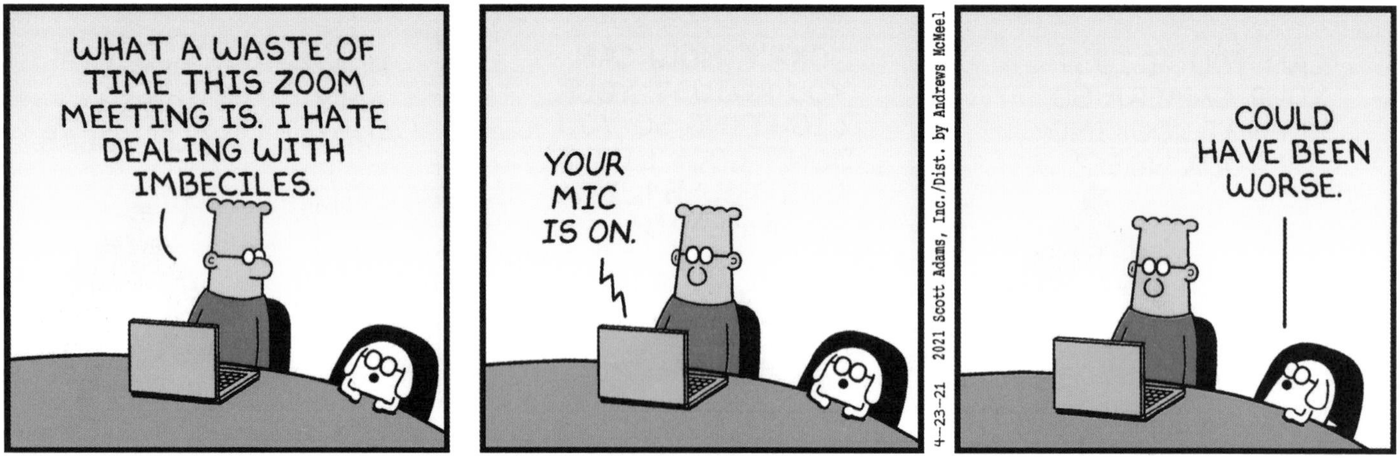
WHAT A WASTE OF TIME THIS ZOOM MEETING IS. I HATE DEALING WITH IMBECILES.
YOUR MIC IS ON.
4-23-21 2021 Scott Adams, Inc./Dist. by Andrews McMeel
COULD HAVE BEEN WORSE.

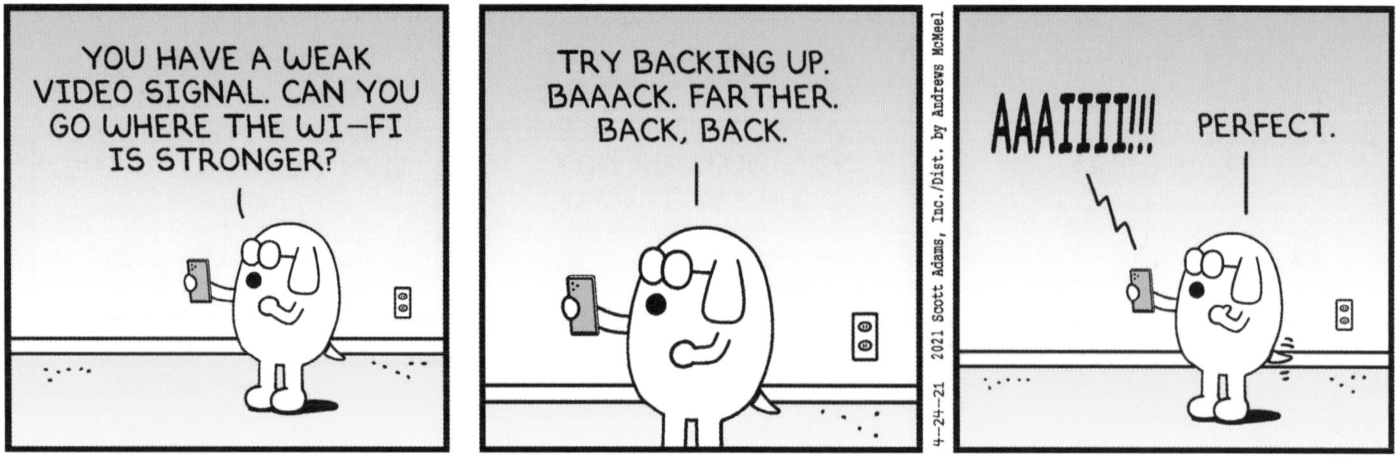
YOU HAVE A WEAK VIDEO SIGNAL. CAN YOU GO WHERE THE WI—FI IS STRONGER?
TRY BACKING UP. BAAACK. FARTHER. BACK, BACK.
4-24-21 2021 Scott Adams, Inc./Dist. by Andrews McMeel
AAAIIII!!!
PERFECT.

DILBERT IS ALWAYS INTERRUPTING ME BECAUSE I'M A WOMAN.
HOW DO YOU DEAL WITH IT WHEN HE INTERRUPTS YOU?
HE DOESN'T INTERRUPT ME.
THAT MAKES NO SENSE. HE INTERRUPTS ME BECAUSE I'M A WOMAN, AND YOU'RE A WOMAN. . . SO. . .
MAYBE HE DOESN'T INTERRUPT ME BECAUSE I MAKE SENSE WHEN I TALK.
WHEREAS YOU'RE MORE OF A BABBLING NINCOMPOOP AND A NOTORIOUS RUINER OF MEETINGS.
WELL, I CERTAINLY DON'T KNOW WHERE YOU . . .
LET'S HEAD BACK NOW.
YOU INTER- RUPTED ME!
TRY TO SPOT THE PATTERN.
© 2021 Scott Adams, Inc./Dist. by Andrews McMeel
4-25-21

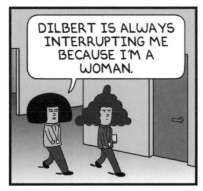

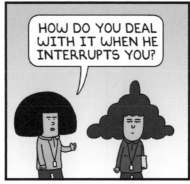

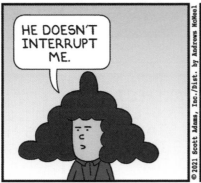

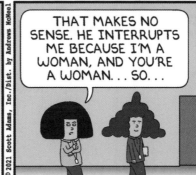

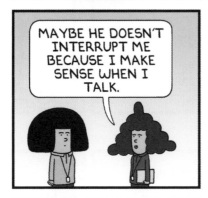

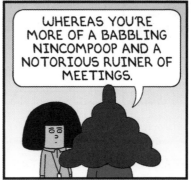

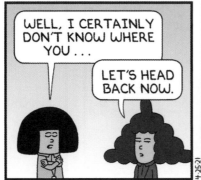

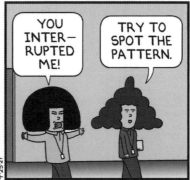

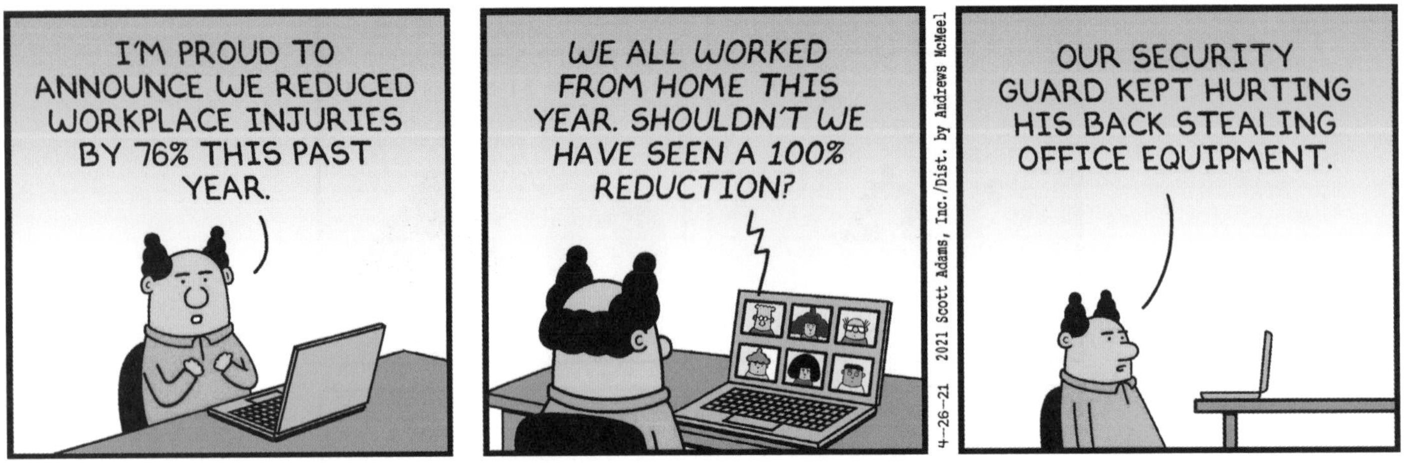
I'M PROUD TO ANNOUNCE WE REDUCED WORKPLACE INJURIES BY 76% THIS PAST YEAR.
WE ALL WORKED FROM HOME THIS YEAR. SHOULDN'T WE HAVE SEEN A 100% REDUCTION?
4-26-21 2021 Scott Adams, Inc./Dist. by Andrews McMeel
OUR SECURITY GUARD KEPT HURTING HIS BACK STEALING OFFICE EQUIPMENT.

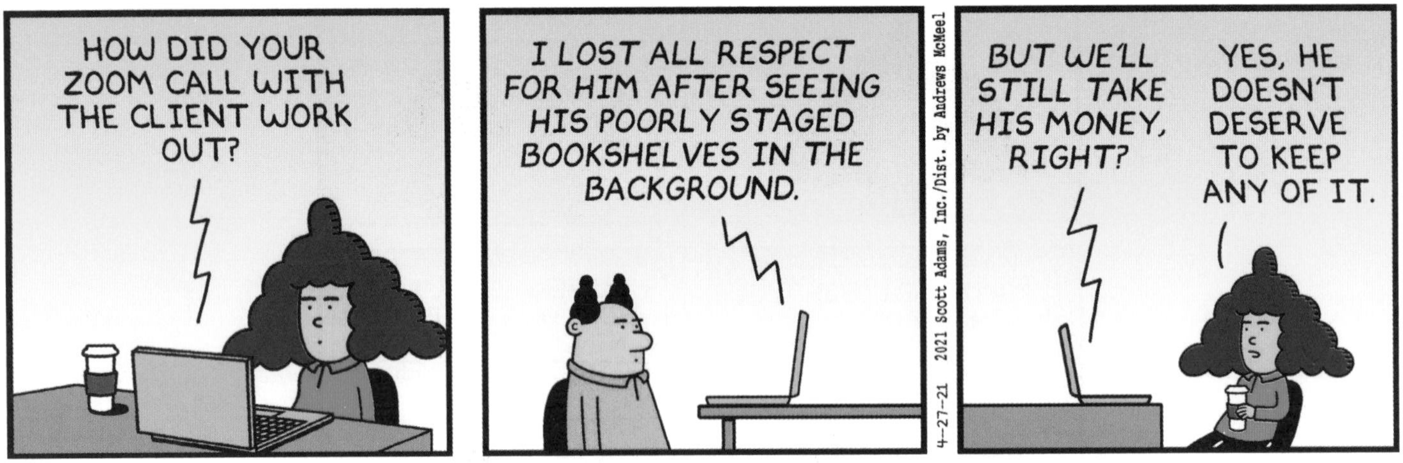
HOW DID YOUR ZOOM CALL WITH THE CLIENT WORK OUT?
I LOST ALL RESPECT FOR HIM AFTER SEEING HIS POORLY STAGED BOOKSHELVES IN THE BACKGROUND.
4-27-21 2021 Scott Adams, Inc./Dist. by Andrews McMeel
BUT WE'LL STILL TAKE HIS MONEY, RIGHT?
YES, HE DOESN'T DESERVE TO KEEP ANY OF IT.

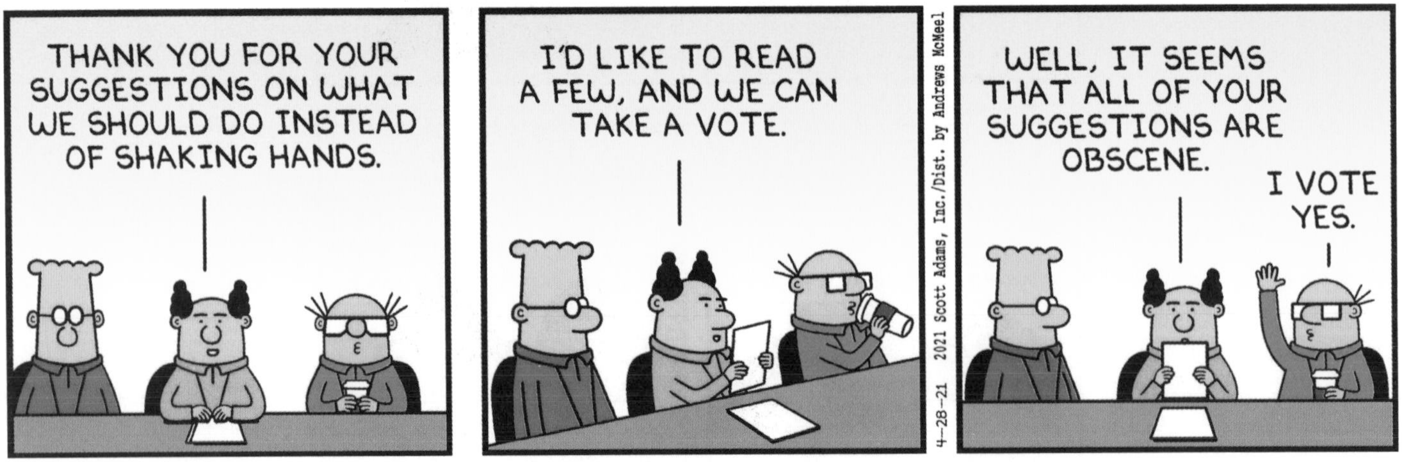
THANK YOU FOR YOUR SUGGESTIONS ON WHAT WE SHOULD DO INSTEAD OF SHAKING HANDS.
I'D LIKE TO READ A FEW, AND WE CAN TAKE A VOTE.
4-28-21 2021 Scott Adams, Inc./Dist. by Andrews McMeel
WELL, IT SEEMS THAT ALL OF YOUR SUGGESTIONS ARE OBSCENE.
I VOTE YES.

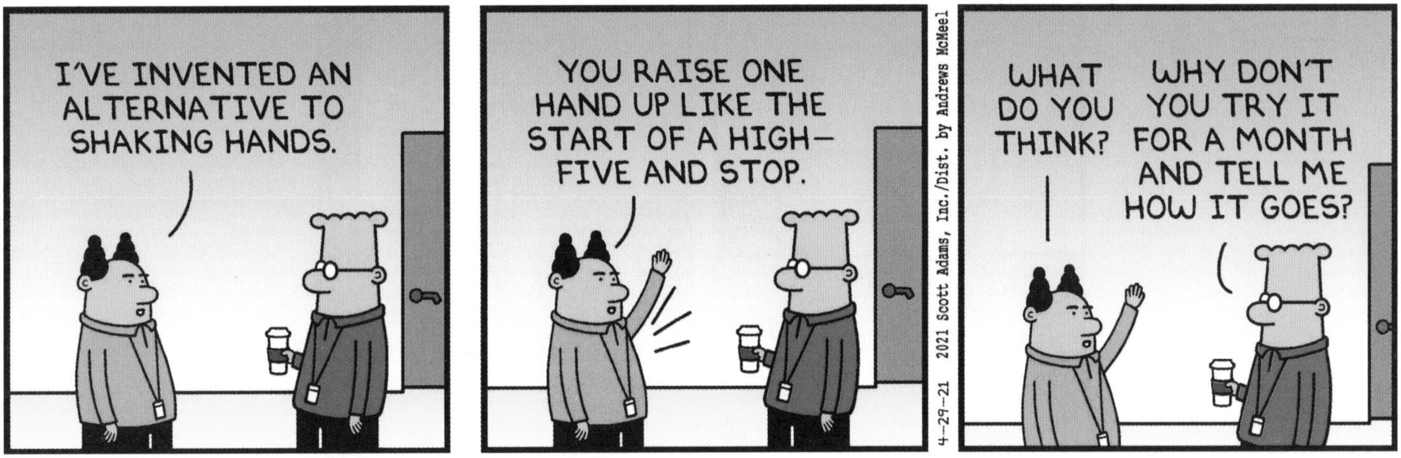
I'VE INVENTED AN ALTERNATIVE TO SHAKING HANDS.
YOU RAISE ONE HAND UP LIKE THE START OF A HIGH-FIVE AND STOP.
4-29-21 2021 Scott Adams, Inc./Dist. by Andrews McMeel
WHAT DO YOU THINK?
WHY DON'T YOU TRY IT FOR A MONTH AND TELL ME HOW IT GOES?

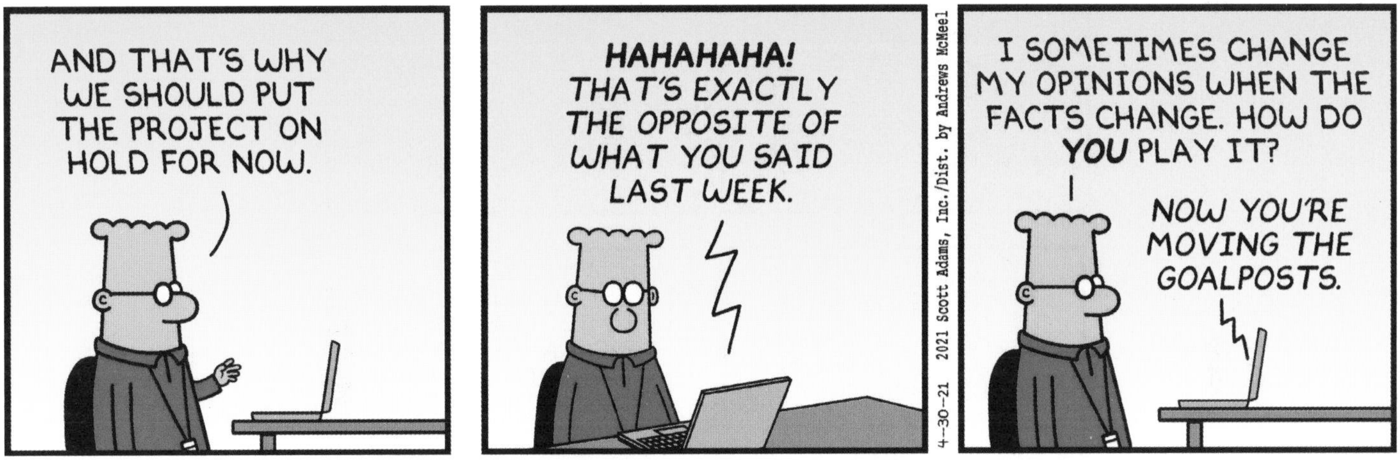
AND THAT'S WHY WE SHOULD PUT THE PROJECT ON HOLD FOR NOW.
HAHAHAHA! THAT'S EXACTLY THE OPPOSITE OF WHAT YOU SAID LAST WEEK.
4-30-21 2021 Scott Adams, Inc./Dist. by Andrews McMeel
I SOMETIMES CHANGE MY OPINIONS WHEN THE FACTS CHANGE. HOW DO YOU PLAY IT?
NOW YOU'RE MOVING THE GOALPOSTS.

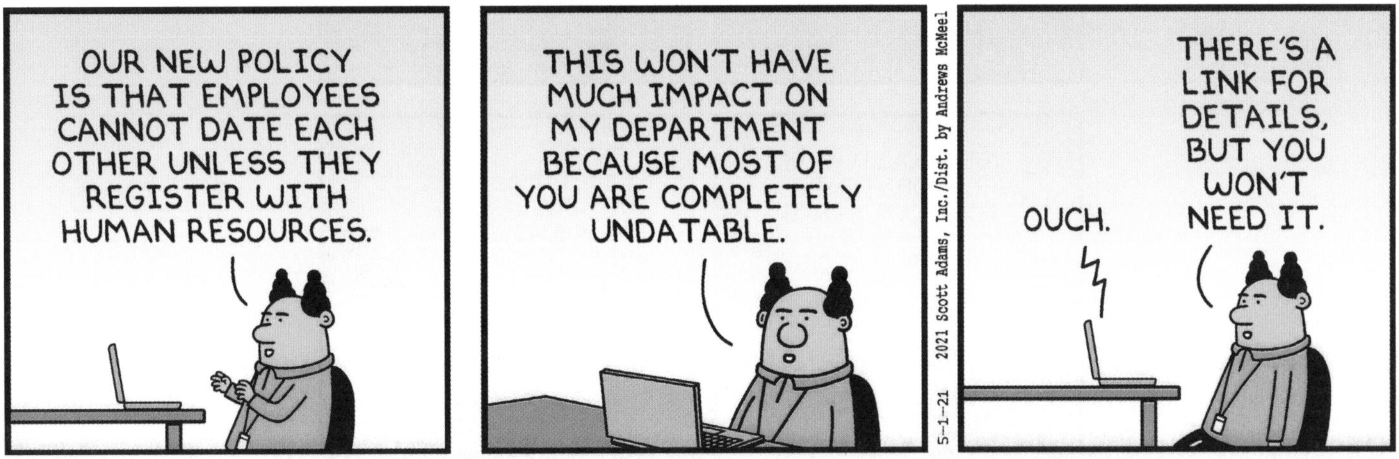
OUR NEW POLICY IS THAT EMPLOYEES CANNOT DATE EACH OTHER UNLESS THEY REGISTER WITH HUMAN RESOURCES.
THIS WON'T HAVE MUCH IMPACT ON MY DEPARTMENT BECAUSE MOST OF YOU ARE COMPLETELY UNDATABLE.
5-1-21 2021 Scott Adams, Inc./Dist. by Andrews McMeel
OUCH.
THERE'S A LINK FOR DETAILS, BUT YOU WON'T NEED IT.

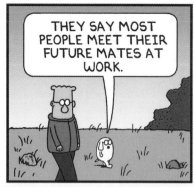

THEY SAY MOST PEOPLE MEET THEIR FUTURE MATES AT WORK.
NOW THAT YOU ARE WORKING FROM HOME, YOUR ODDS OF MATING JUST TURNED NEGATIVE.
YOU COULD TRY USING A DATING APP TO FIND A WOMAN, BUT THEN YOU'D NEED TO RELY ON YOUR LOOKS.
© 2021 Scott Adams, Inc./Dist. by Andrews McMeel
OBVIOUSLY, THAT'S A DEAD END.
YOUR BEST CHANCE OF REPRODUCTION HAS ALWAYS BEEN TO WEAR DOWN A CO–WORKER OVER SEVERAL YEARS.
WOMEN NEED TIME TO GET OVER YOUR APPEARANCE, AND TO APPRECIATE YOUR INNER QUALITIES.
WE SHOULD HAVE A GOODBYE PARTY FOR YOUR GENES.
5-2-21
MAYBE NEXT TIME WE COULD WALK AND **NOT** TALK.
MAYBE.

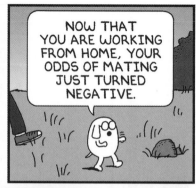

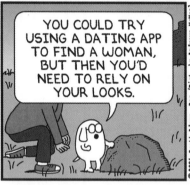

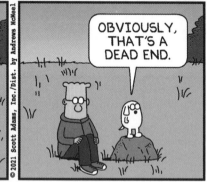

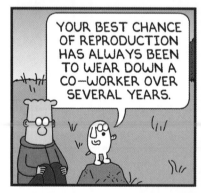

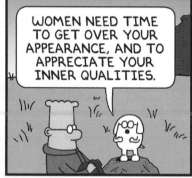

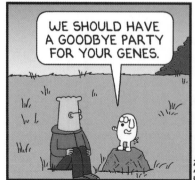

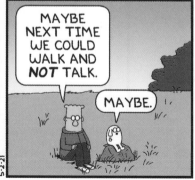

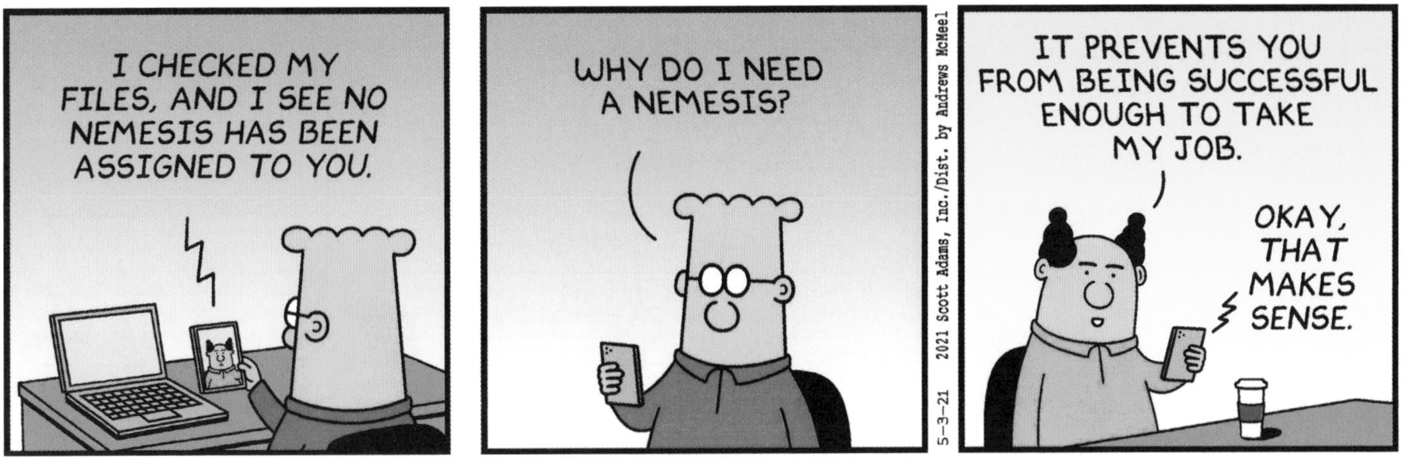
I CHECKED MY FILES, AND I SEE NO NEMESIS HAS BEEN ASSIGNED TO YOU.
WHY DO I NEED A NEMESIS?
5-3-21 2021 Scott Adams, Inc./Dist. by Andrews McMeel
IT PREVENTS YOU FROM BEING SUCCESSFUL ENOUGH TO TAKE MY JOB.
OKAY, THAT MAKES SENSE.

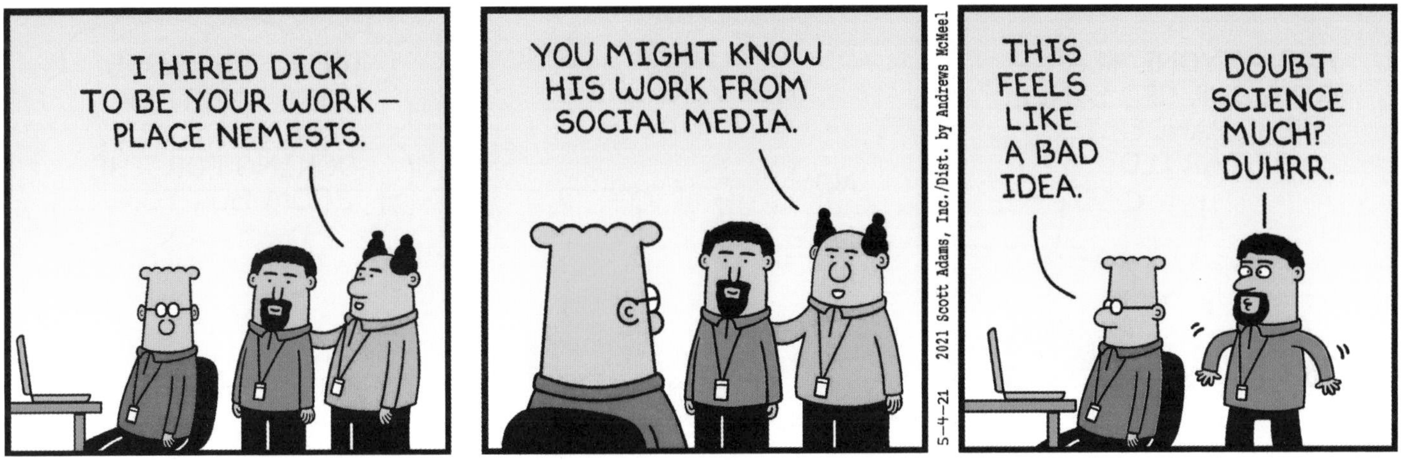
I HIRED DICK TO BE YOUR WORK–PLACE NEMESIS.
YOU MIGHT KNOW HIS WORK FROM SOCIAL MEDIA.
5-4-21 2021 Scott Adams, Inc./Dist. by Andrews McMeel
THIS FEELS LIKE A BAD IDEA.
DOUBT SCIENCE MUCH? DUHRR.

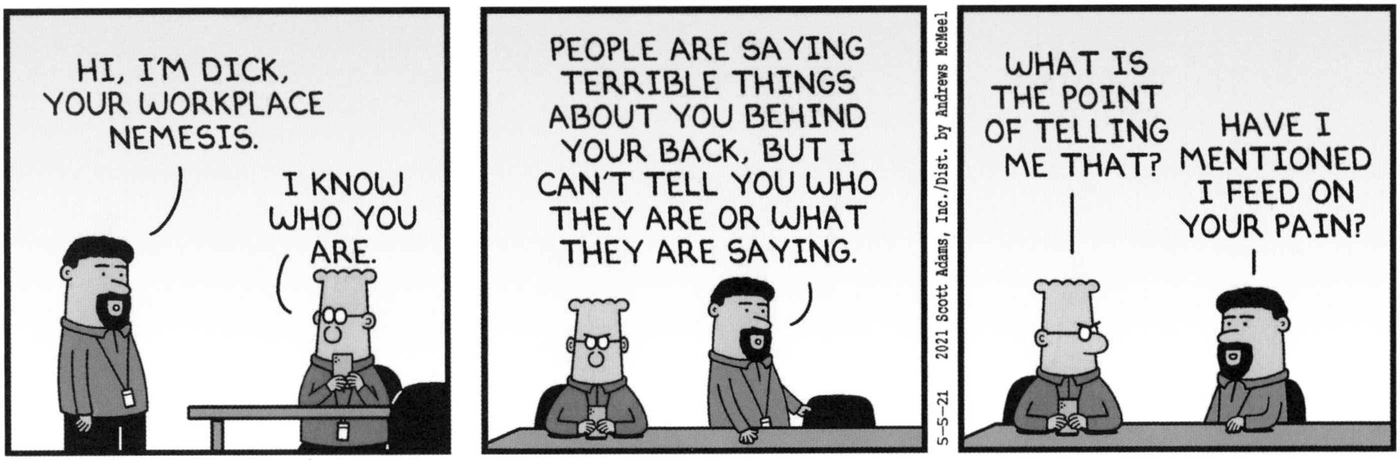
HI, I'M DICK, YOUR WORKPLACE NEMESIS.
I KNOW WHO YOU ARE.
PEOPLE ARE SAYING TERRIBLE THINGS ABOUT YOU BEHIND YOUR BACK, BUT I CAN'T TELL YOU WHO THEY ARE OR WHAT THEY ARE SAYING.
5-5-21 2021 Scott Adams, Inc./Dist. by Andrews McMeel
WHAT IS THE POINT OF TELLING ME THAT?
HAVE I MENTIONED I FEED ON YOUR PAIN?

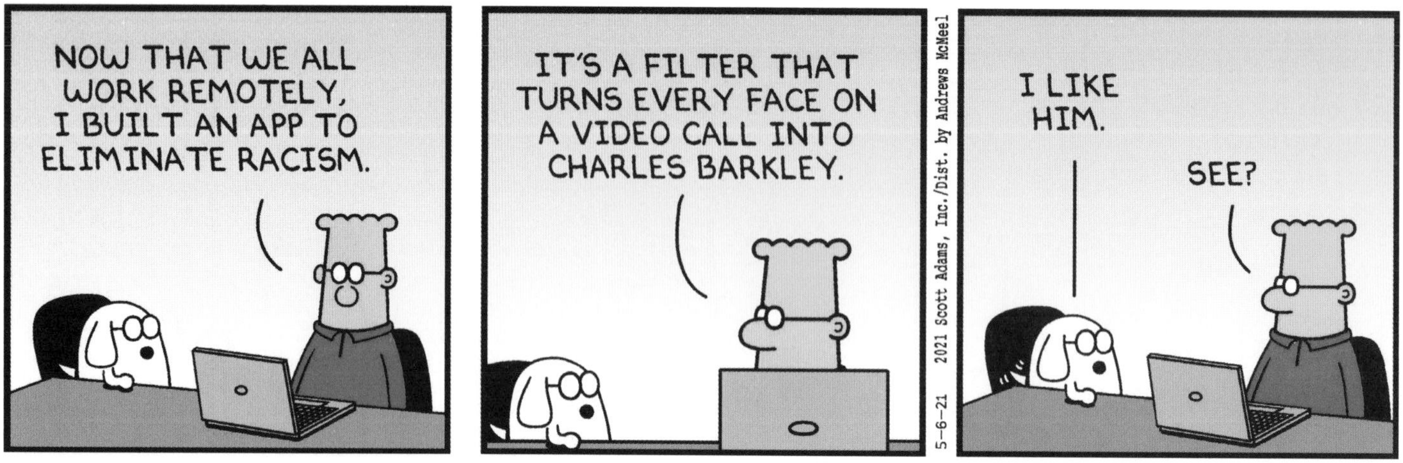
NOW THAT WE ALL WORK REMOTELY, I BUILT AN APP TO ELIMINATE RACISM.
IT'S A FILTER THAT TURNS EVERY FACE ON A VIDEO CALL INTO CHARLES BARKLEY.
5-6-21 © 2021 Scott Adams, Inc./Dist. by Andrews McMeel
I LIKE HIM.
SEE?

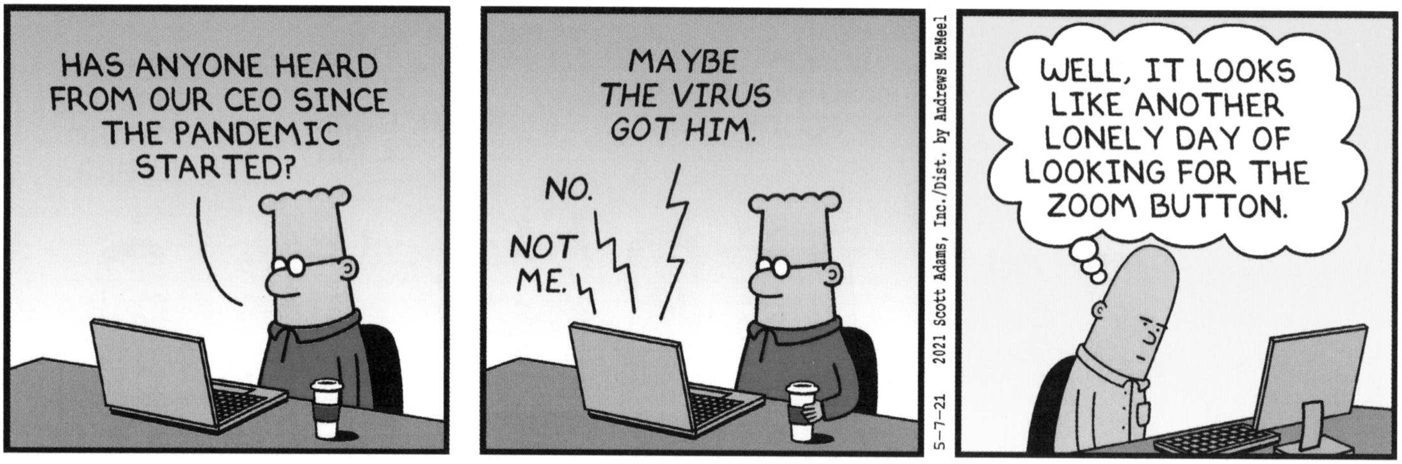
HAS ANYONE HEARD FROM OUR CEO SINCE THE PANDEMIC STARTED?
MAYBE THE VIRUS GOT HIM.
NO.
NOT ME.
5-7-21 © 2021 Scott Adams, Inc./Dist. by Andrews McMeel
WELL, IT LOOKS LIKE ANOTHER LONELY DAY OF LOOKING FOR THE ZOOM BUTTON.

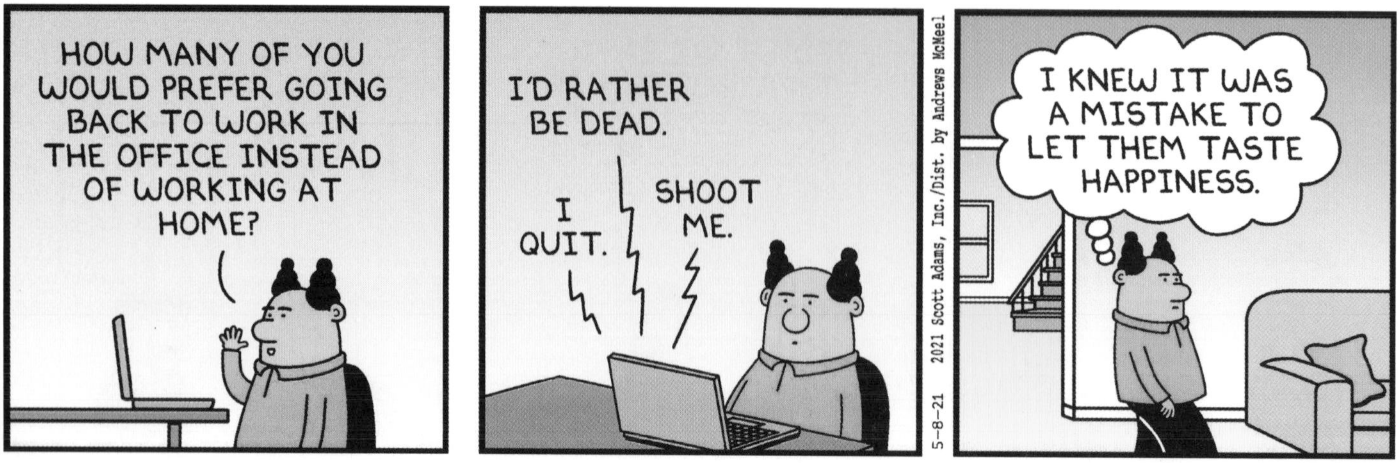
HOW MANY OF YOU WOULD PREFER GOING BACK TO WORK IN THE OFFICE INSTEAD OF WORKING AT HOME?
I'D RATHER BE DEAD.
I QUIT.
SHOOT ME.
5-8-21 © 2021 Scott Adams, Inc./Dist. by Andrews McMeel
I KNEW IT WAS A MISTAKE TO LET THEM TASTE HAPPINESS.

IT ISN'T FAIR THAT ALICE GETS ALL THE BEST PROJECTS.
AND WHAT'S YOUR POINT?
IT'S NOT FAIR.
YOU ALREADY SAID THAT.
YOU SHOULD DO SOMETHING TO MAKE IT MORE FAIR.
WHY?
BECAUSE IT'S NOT FAIR?
DID YOU BUMP YOUR HEAD?
© 2021 Scott Adams, Inc./Dist. by Andrews McMeel
5-9-21

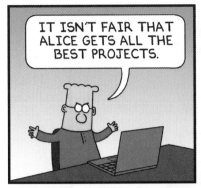

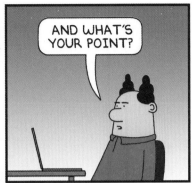

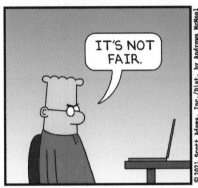

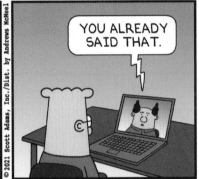

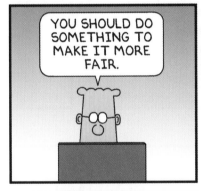

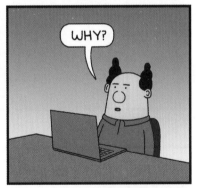

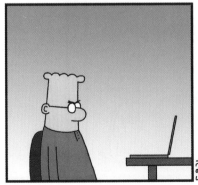

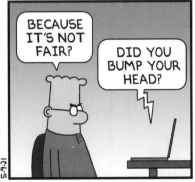

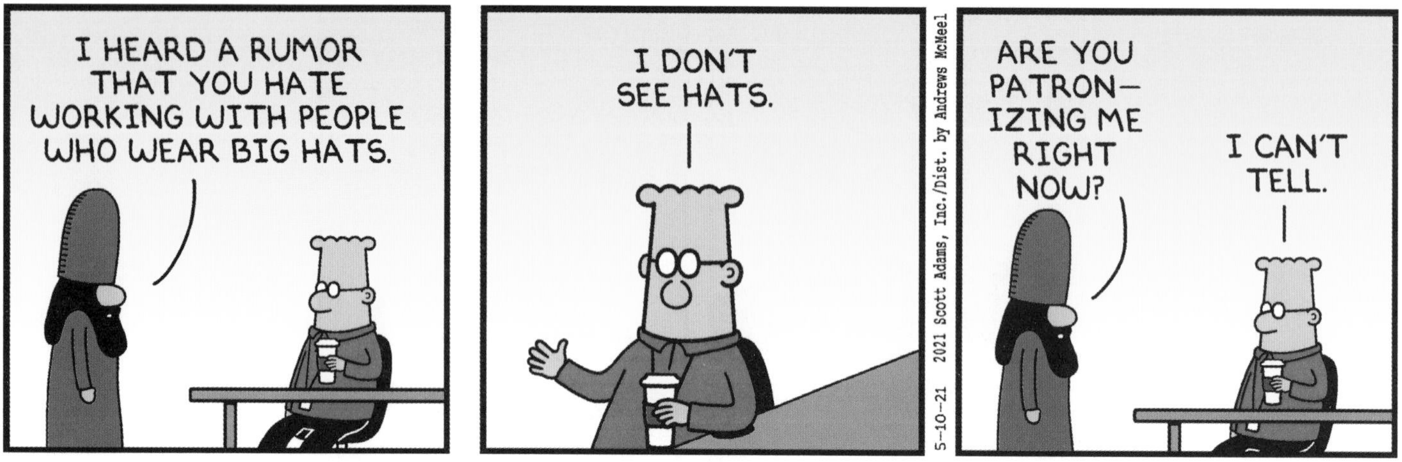
I HEARD A RUMOR THAT YOU HATE WORKING WITH PEOPLE WHO WEAR BIG HATS.
I DON'T SEE HATS.
ARE YOU PATRON-IZING ME RIGHT NOW?
I CAN'T TELL.
5-10-21 2021 Scott Adams, Inc./Dist. by Andrews McMeel

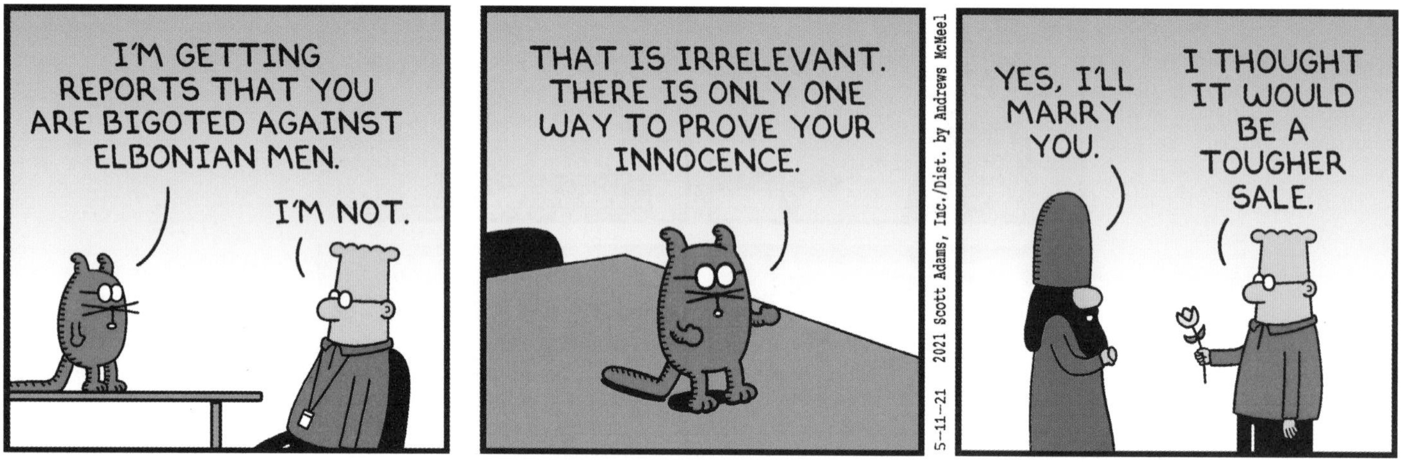
I'M GETTING REPORTS THAT YOU ARE BIGOTED AGAINST ELBONIAN MEN.
I'M NOT.
THAT IS IRRELEVANT. THERE IS ONLY ONE WAY TO PROVE YOUR INNOCENCE.
YES, I'LL MARRY YOU.
I THOUGHT IT WOULD BE A TOUGHER SALE.
5-11-21 2021 Scott Adams, Inc./Dist. by Andrews McMeel

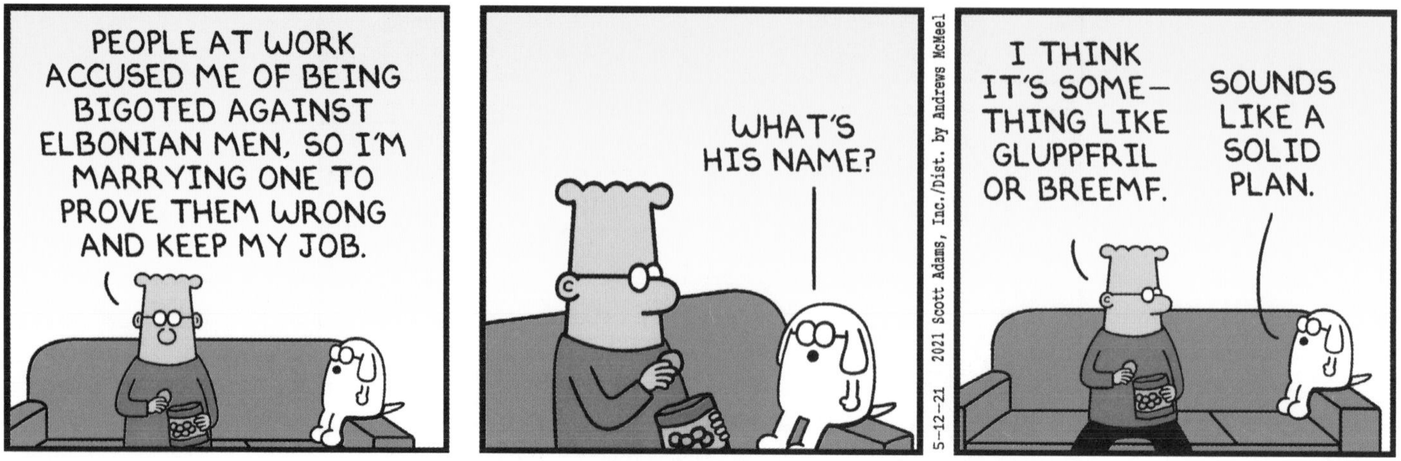
PEOPLE AT WORK ACCUSED ME OF BEING BIGOTED AGAINST ELBONIAN MEN, SO I'M MARRYING ONE TO PROVE THEM WRONG AND KEEP MY JOB.
WHAT'S HIS NAME?
I THINK IT'S SOME-THING LIKE GLUPPFRIL OR BREEMF.
SOUNDS LIKE A SOLID PLAN.
5-12-21 2021 Scott Adams, Inc./Dist. by Andrews McMeel

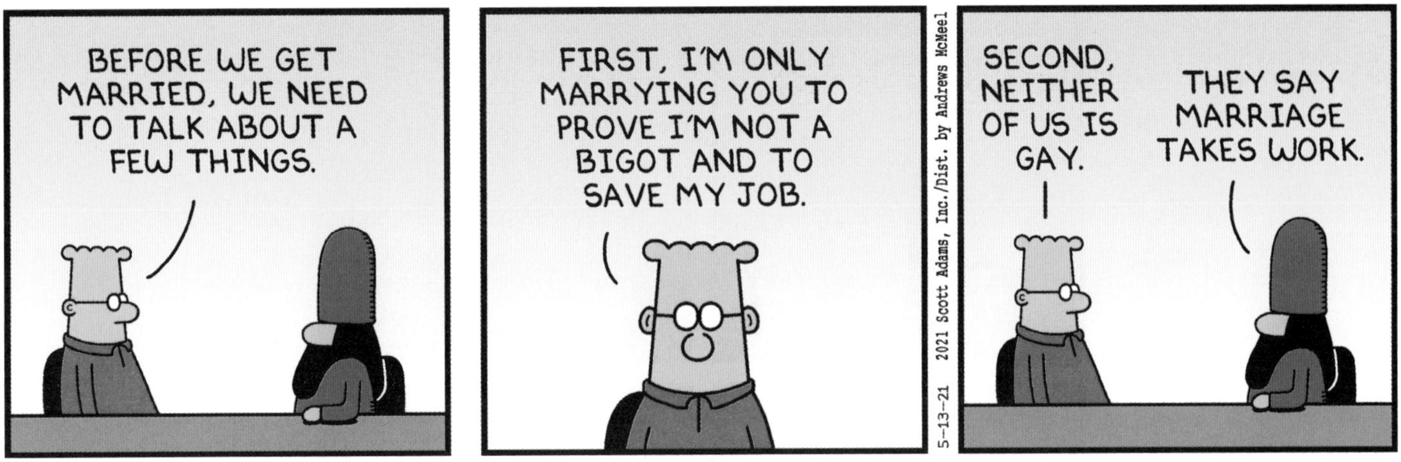
BEFORE WE GET MARRIED, WE NEED TO TALK ABOUT A FEW THINGS.
FIRST, I'M ONLY MARRYING YOU TO PROVE I'M NOT A BIGOT AND TO SAVE MY JOB.
5-13-21 2021 Scott Adams, Inc./Dist. by Andrews McMeel
SECOND, NEITHER OF US IS GAY.
THEY SAY MARRIAGE TAKES WORK.

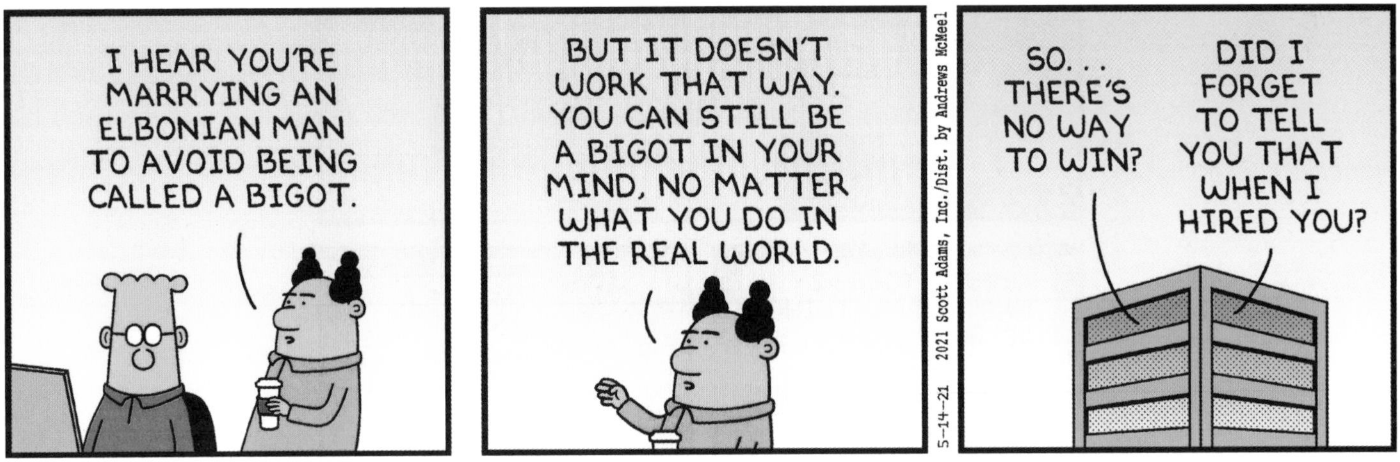
I HEAR YOU'RE MARRYING AN ELBONIAN MAN TO AVOID BEING CALLED A BIGOT.
BUT IT DOESN'T WORK THAT WAY. YOU CAN STILL BE A BIGOT IN YOUR MIND, NO MATTER WHAT YOU DO IN THE REAL WORLD.
5-14-21 2021 Scott Adams, Inc./Dist. by Andrews McMeel
SO. . . THERE'S NO WAY TO WIN?
DID I FORGET TO TELL YOU THAT WHEN I HIRED YOU?

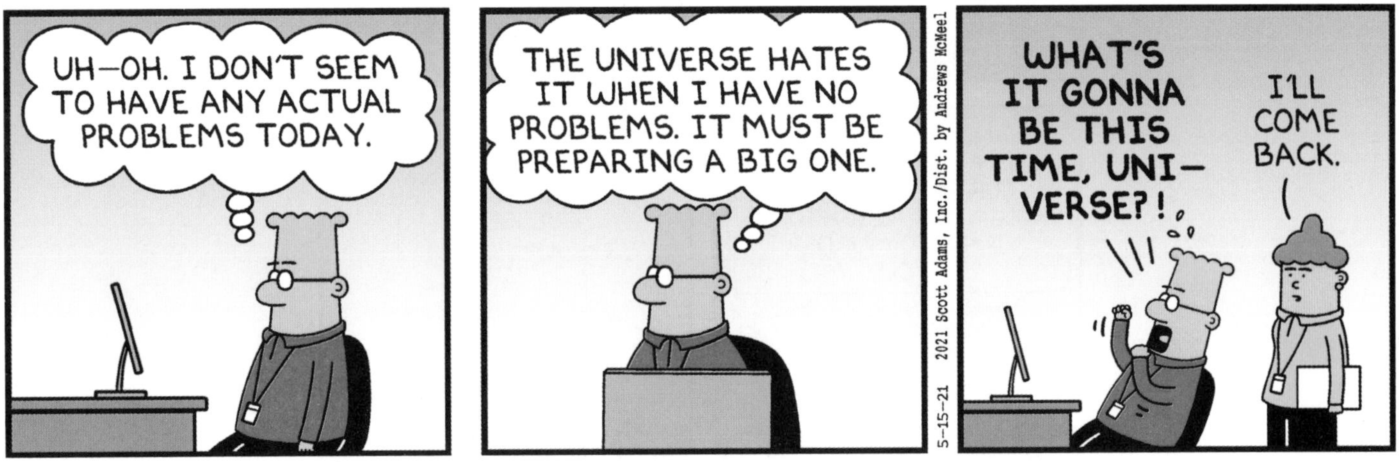
UH–OH. I DON'T SEEM TO HAVE ANY ACTUAL PROBLEMS TODAY.
THE UNIVERSE HATES IT WHEN I HAVE NO PROBLEMS. IT MUST BE PREPARING A BIG ONE.
5-15-21 2021 Scott Adams, Inc./Dist. by Andrews McMeel
WHAT'S IT GONNA BE THIS TIME, UNI– VERSE?!
I'LL COME BACK.

I'M ISSUING YOU A WARNING FOR YOUR UNSAFE WORKPLACE.
I WORK AT HOME.
YOU'VE NEVER SEEN WHERE I LIVE.
I'M JUDGING BY YOUR PERSONALITY.
YOU'RE TOO LAZY TO CLEAN ANYTHING UP, SO BY NOW IT'S A TOXIC DUMP.
THAT'S A LUCKY GUESS.
AND YOU'RE TOO LAZY TO CLOSE YOUR CURTAINS, SO BY NOW YOUR NEIGHBORS WANT TO MURDER YOU.
THAT'S *TWO* LUCKY GUESSES.
© 2021 Scott Adams, Inc./Dist. by Andrews McMeel
5-16-21

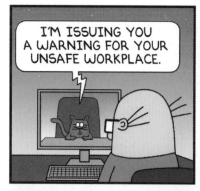

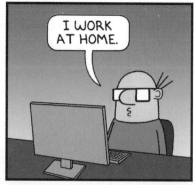

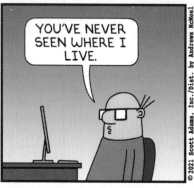

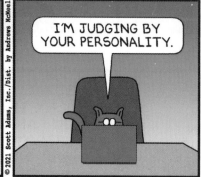

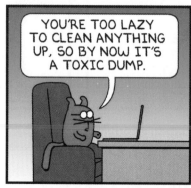

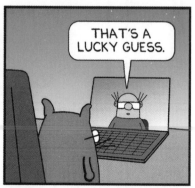

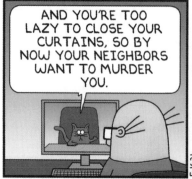

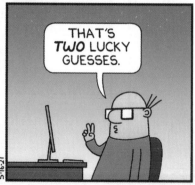

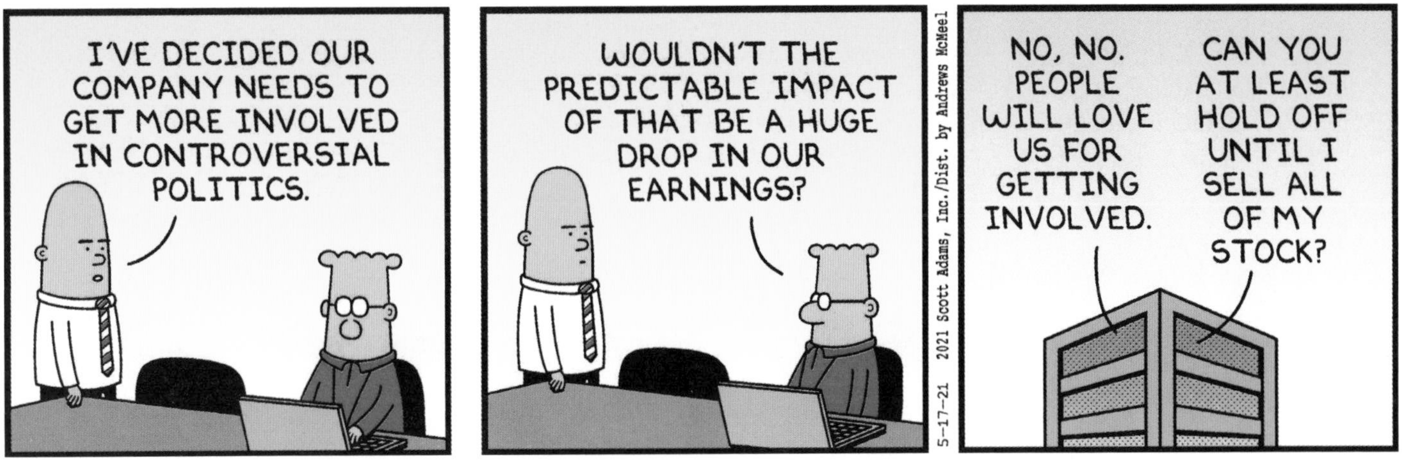
I'VE DECIDED OUR COMPANY NEEDS TO GET MORE INVOLVED IN CONTROVERSIAL POLITICS.
WOULDN'T THE PREDICTABLE IMPACT OF THAT BE A HUGE DROP IN OUR EARNINGS?
5-17-21 2021 Scott Adams, Inc./Dist. by Andrews McMeel
NO, NO. PEOPLE WILL LOVE US FOR GETTING INVOLVED.
CAN YOU AT LEAST HOLD OFF UNTIL I SELL ALL OF MY STOCK?

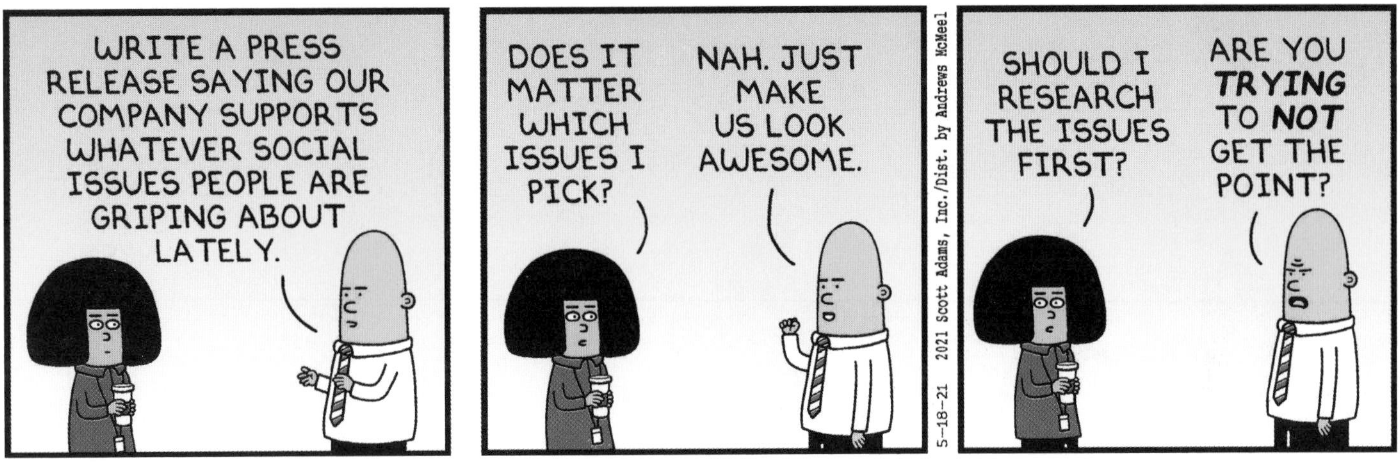
WRITE A PRESS RELEASE SAYING OUR COMPANY SUPPORTS WHATEVER SOCIAL ISSUES PEOPLE ARE GRIPING ABOUT LATELY.
DOES IT MATTER WHICH ISSUES I PICK?
NAH. JUST MAKE US LOOK AWESOME.
5-18-21 2021 Scott Adams, Inc./Dist. by Andrews McMeel
SHOULD I RESEARCH THE ISSUES FIRST?
ARE YOU *TRYING* TO *NOT* GET THE POINT?

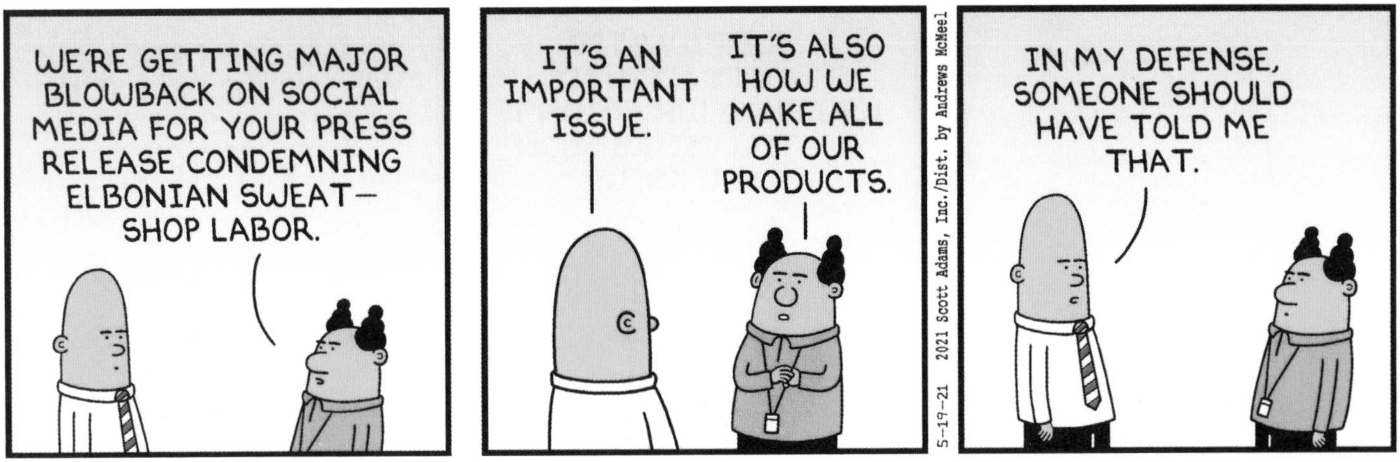
WE'RE GETTING MAJOR BLOWBACK ON SOCIAL MEDIA FOR YOUR PRESS RELEASE CONDEMNING ELBONIAN SWEAT-SHOP LABOR.
IT'S AN IMPORTANT ISSUE.
IT'S ALSO HOW WE MAKE ALL OF OUR PRODUCTS.
5-19-21 2021 Scott Adams, Inc./Dist. by Andrews McMeel
IN MY DEFENSE, SOMEONE SHOULD HAVE TOLD ME THAT.

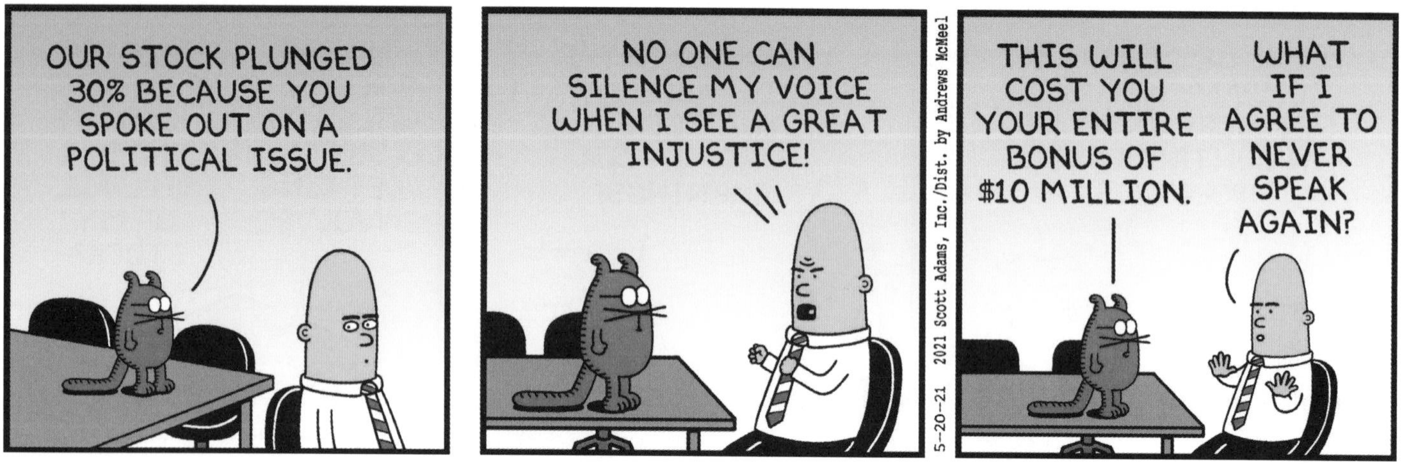
OUR STOCK PLUNGED 30% BECAUSE YOU SPOKE OUT ON A POLITICAL ISSUE.
NO ONE CAN SILENCE MY VOICE WHEN I SEE A GREAT INJUSTICE!
THIS WILL COST YOU YOUR ENTIRE BONUS OF $10 MILLION.
WHAT IF I AGREE TO NEVER SPEAK AGAIN?
5-20-21 © 2021 Scott Adams, Inc./Dist. by Andrews McMeel

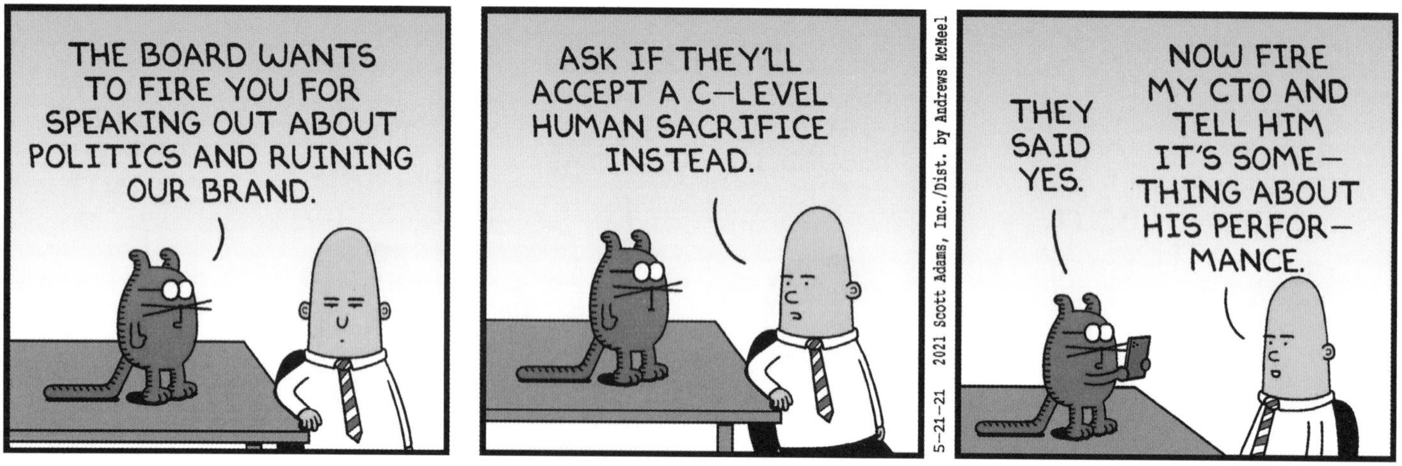
THE BOARD WANTS TO FIRE YOU FOR SPEAKING OUT ABOUT POLITICS AND RUINING OUR BRAND.
ASK IF THEY'LL ACCEPT A C-LEVEL HUMAN SACRIFICE INSTEAD.
THEY SAID YES.
NOW FIRE MY CTO AND TELL HIM IT'S SOME-THING ABOUT HIS PERFOR-MANCE.
5-21-21 © 2021 Scott Adams, Inc./Dist. by Andrews McMeel

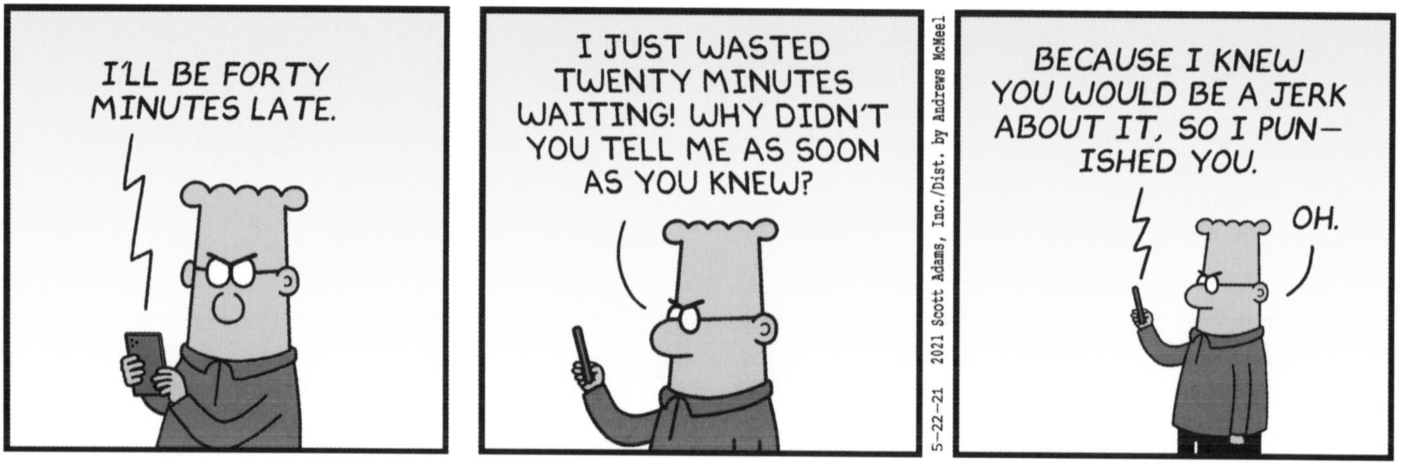
I'LL BE FORTY MINUTES LATE.
I JUST WASTED TWENTY MINUTES WAITING! WHY DIDN'T YOU TELL ME AS SOON AS YOU KNEW?
BECAUSE I KNEW YOU WOULD BE A JERK ABOUT IT, SO I PUN-ISHED YOU.
OH.
5-22-21 © 2021 Scott Adams, Inc./Dist. by Andrews McMeel

IF YOU FINISH BY THE DEADLINE, I'LL RECOMMEND YOU FOR A MILLION-DOLLAR BONUS.
YOU'RE LYING.
I'M SERIOUS.
BUT YOU'RE ALSO LYING.
ONLY ONE WAY TO FIND OUT.
© 2021 Scott Adams, Inc./Dist. by Andrews McMeel
I'D NEED TO WORK AROUND THE CLOCK FOR WEEKS TO MEET THE DEADLINE!
THAT'S THE SPIRIT!
IF YOU'RE LYING ABOUT THE BONUS, I'M GOING TO BE BOILING MAD.
FIVE WEEKS LATER
IT NEARLY KILLED ME, BUT I FINISHED BY THE DEADLINE.
5-23-21
WHERE'S MY MILLION-DOLLAR BONUS?
I TOLD YOU I'D **RECOMMEND** IT.
THEY SAID NO.

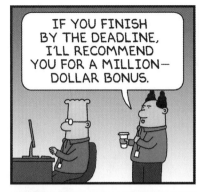

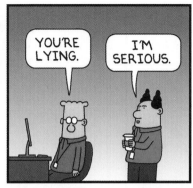

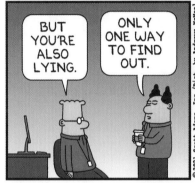

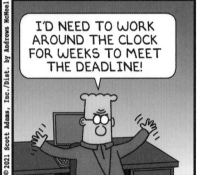

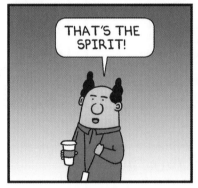

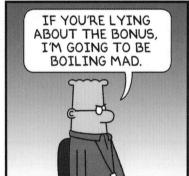

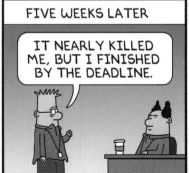

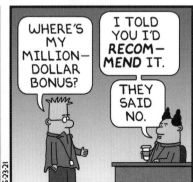

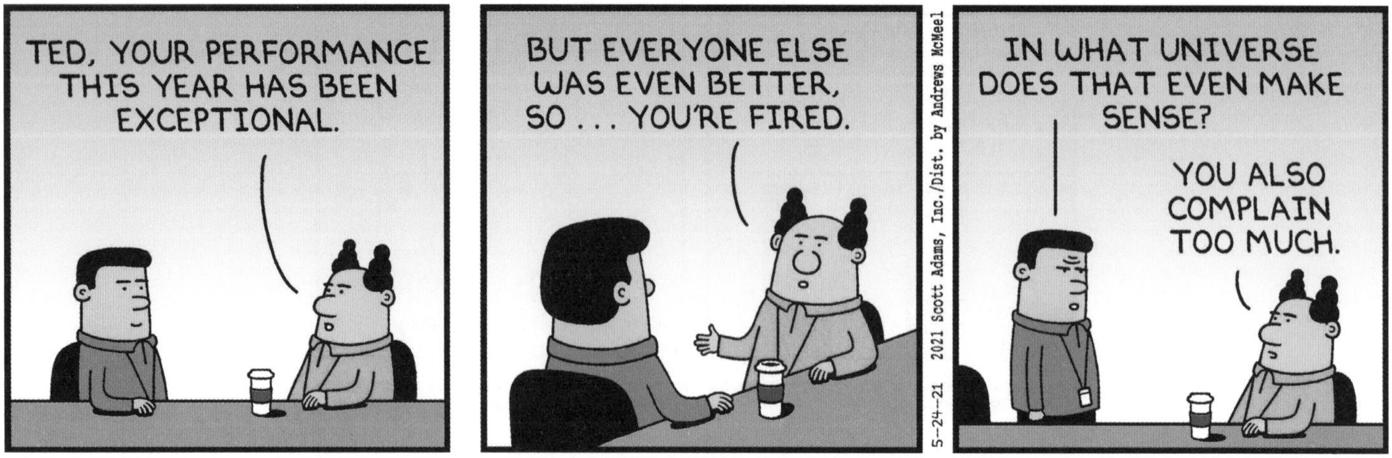
TED, YOUR PERFORMANCE THIS YEAR HAS BEEN EXCEPTIONAL.
BUT EVERYONE ELSE WAS EVEN BETTER, SO . . . YOU'RE FIRED.
5-24-21 2021 Scott Adams, Inc./Dist. by Andrews McMeel
IN WHAT UNIVERSE DOES THAT EVEN MAKE SENSE?
YOU ALSO COMPLAIN TOO MUCH.

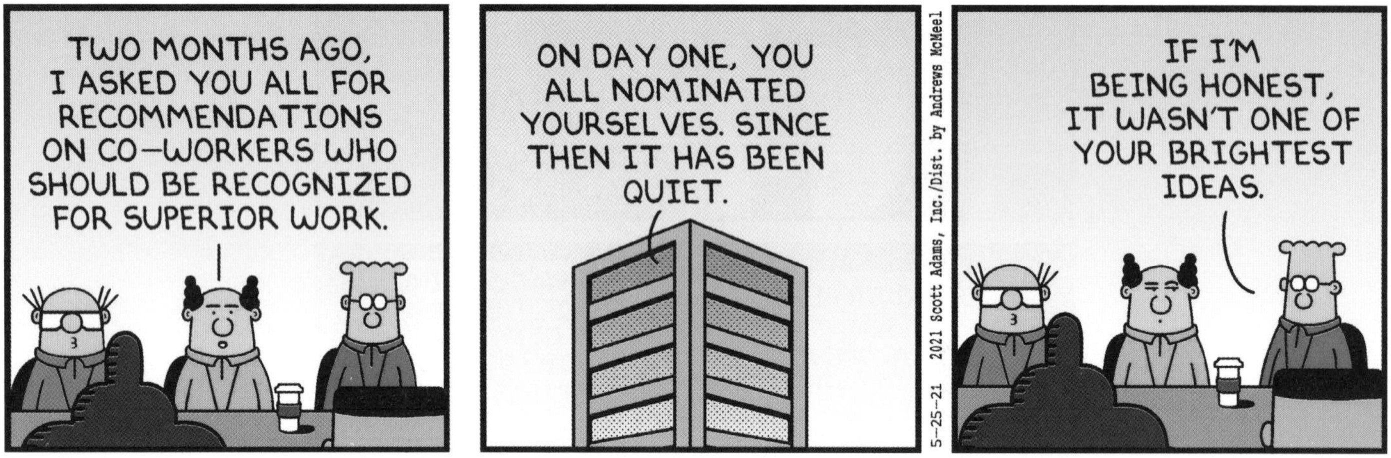
TWO MONTHS AGO, I ASKED YOU ALL FOR RECOMMENDATIONS ON CO-WORKERS WHO SHOULD BE RECOGNIZED FOR SUPERIOR WORK.
ON DAY ONE, YOU ALL NOMINATED YOURSELVES. SINCE THEN IT HAS BEEN QUIET.
5-25-21 2021 Scott Adams, Inc./Dist. by Andrews McMeel
IF I'M BEING HONEST, IT WASN'T ONE OF YOUR BRIGHTEST IDEAS.

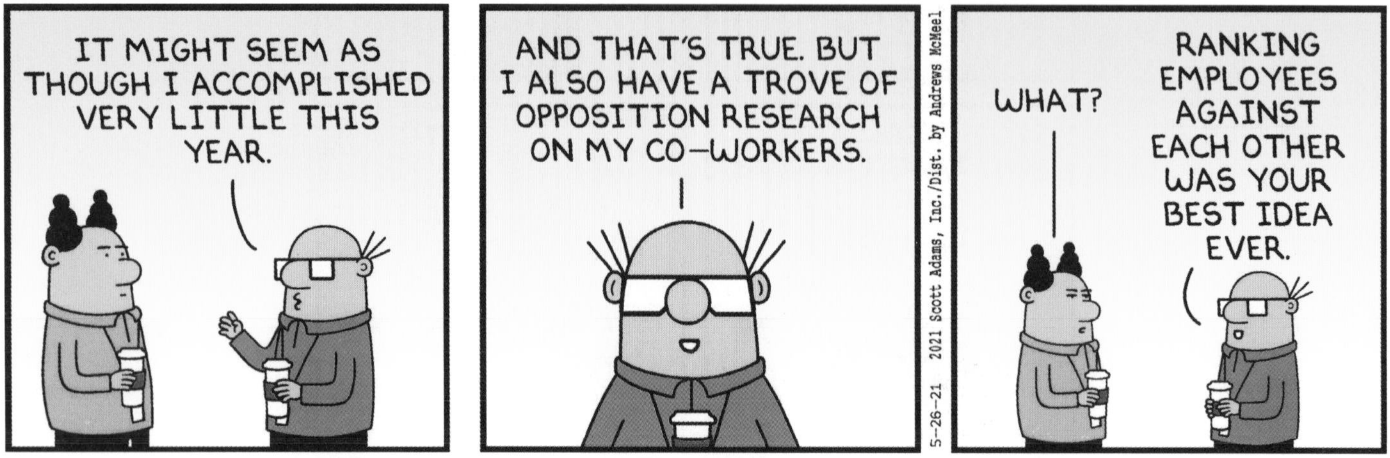
IT MIGHT SEEM AS THOUGH I ACCOMPLISHED VERY LITTLE THIS YEAR.
AND THAT'S TRUE. BUT I ALSO HAVE A TROVE OF OPPOSITION RESEARCH ON MY CO-WORKERS.
5-26-21 2021 Scott Adams, Inc./Dist. by Andrews McMeel
WHAT?
RANKING EMPLOYEES AGAINST EACH OTHER WAS YOUR BEST IDEA EVER.

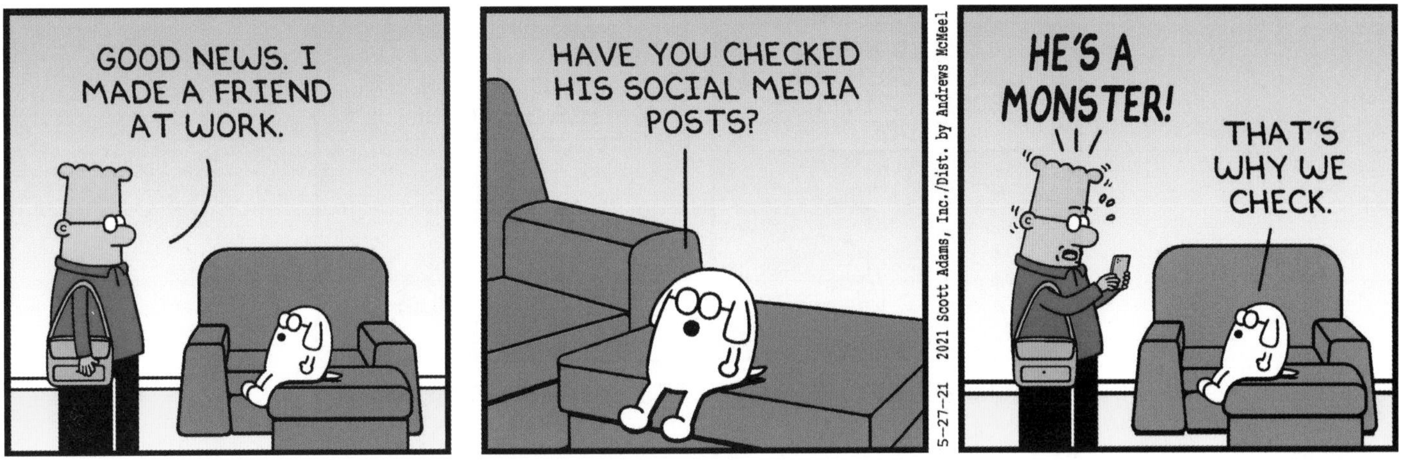
GOOD NEWS. I MADE A FRIEND AT WORK.
HAVE YOU CHECKED HIS SOCIAL MEDIA POSTS?
5-27-21 2021 Scott Adams, Inc./Dist. by Andrews McMeel
HE'S A MONSTER!
THAT'S WHY WE CHECK.

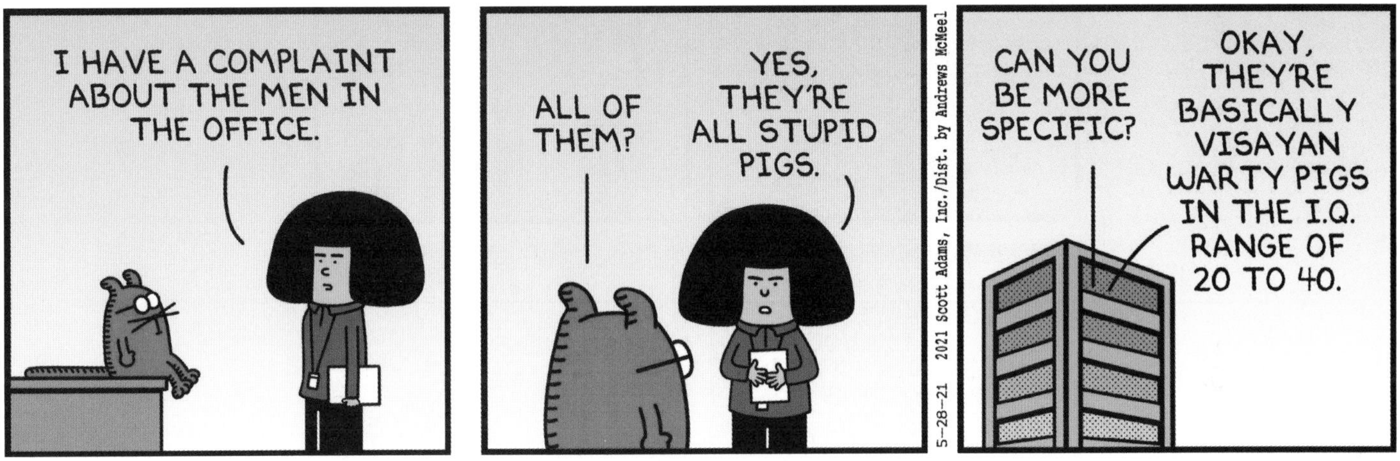
I HAVE A COMPLAINT ABOUT THE MEN IN THE OFFICE.
ALL OF THEM?
YES, THEY'RE ALL STUPID PIGS.
5-28-21 2021 Scott Adams, Inc./Dist. by Andrews McMeel
CAN YOU BE MORE SPECIFIC?
OKAY, THEY'RE BASICALLY VISAYAN WARTY PIGS IN THE I.Q. RANGE OF 20 TO 40.

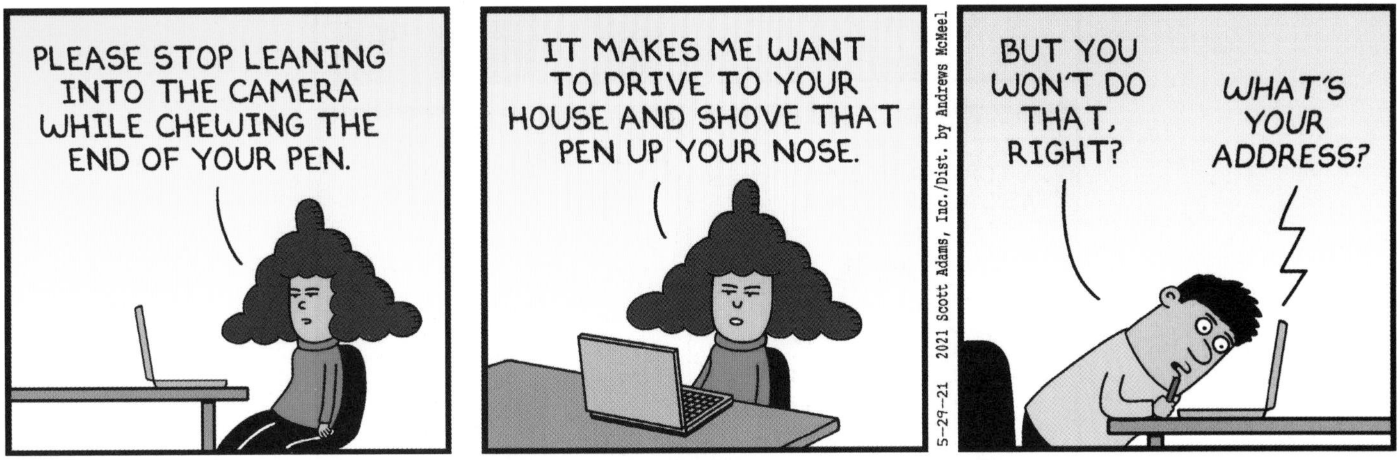
PLEASE STOP LEANING INTO THE CAMERA WHILE CHEWING THE END OF YOUR PEN.
IT MAKES ME WANT TO DRIVE TO YOUR HOUSE AND SHOVE THAT PEN UP YOUR NOSE.
5-29-21 2021 Scott Adams, Inc./Dist. by Andrews McMeel
BUT YOU WON'T DO THAT, RIGHT?
WHAT'S YOUR ADDRESS?

WOULD YOU LIKE TO JOIN OUR FREQUENT VICTIMS CLUB?
NO, I JUST WANT TO BUY THIS BEVERAGE.
YOU COULD SAVE A DOLLAR IF YOU JOIN NOW. IT ONLY TAKES A MINUTE.
I DON'T WANT YOU TRACKING MY PURCHASES AND SELLING MY DATA.
IF YOU DON'T SIGN UP, MY COLLEAGUES AND I WILL PESTER YOU TO DO IT EVERY TIME YOU TRY TO BUY SOMETHING.
I'LL TAKE MY BUSINESS ELSEWHERE!
NO, YOU WON'T.
BECAUSE OTHER STORES ARE JUST AS BAD AS WE ARE.
I AM NOT A VICTIM!
TELL THAT TO THE CUSTOMER SURVEY I'M ABOUT TO PESTER YOU INTO DOING.
© 2021 Scott Adams, Inc./Dist. by Andrews McMeel
5-30-21

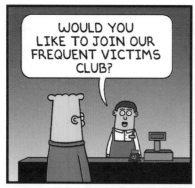

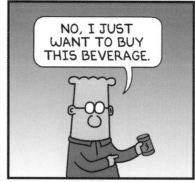

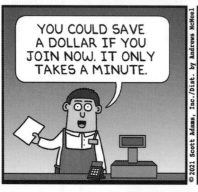

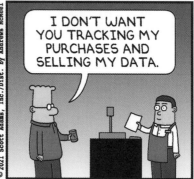

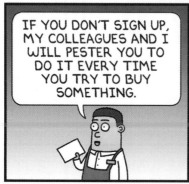

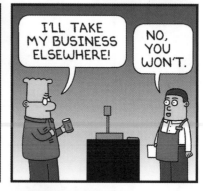

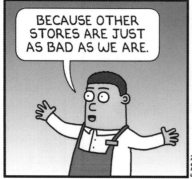

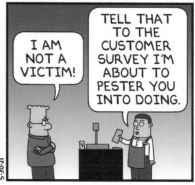

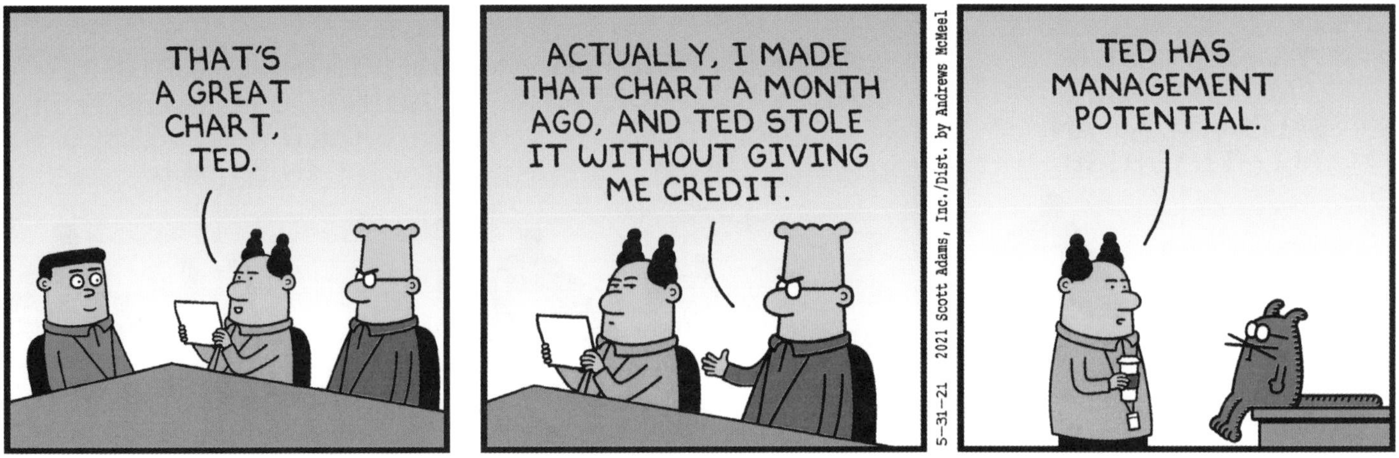
THAT'S A GREAT CHART, TED.
ACTUALLY, I MADE THAT CHART A MONTH AGO, AND TED STOLE IT WITHOUT GIVING ME CREDIT.
5-31-21 2021 Scott Adams, Inc./Dist. by Andrews McMeel
TED HAS MANAGEMENT POTENTIAL.

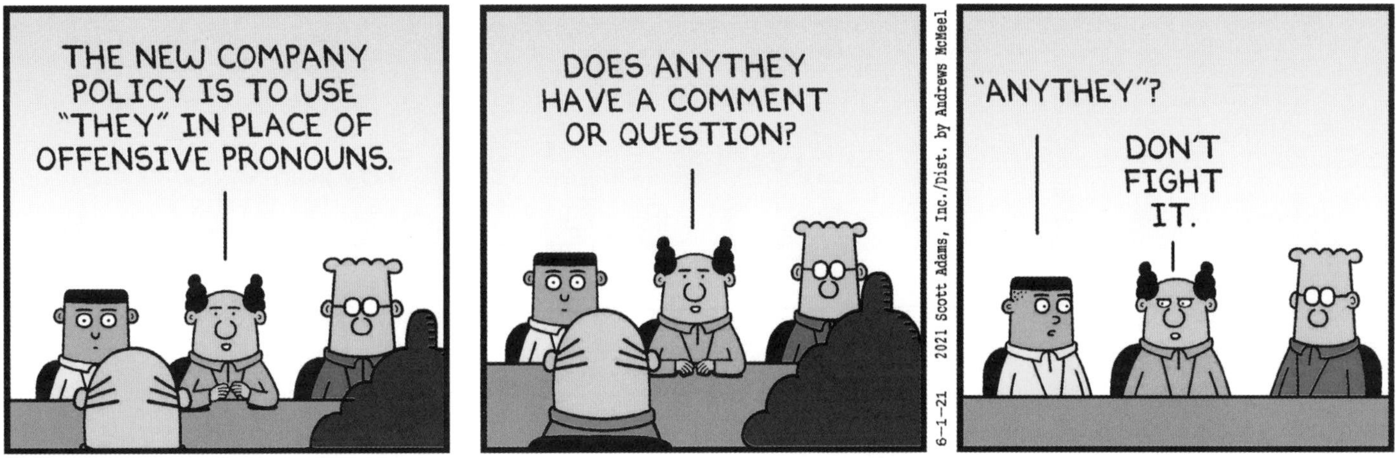
THE NEW COMPANY POLICY IS TO USE "THEY" IN PLACE OF OFFENSIVE PRONOUNS.
DOES ANYTHEY HAVE A COMMENT OR QUESTION?
6-1-21 2021 Scott Adams, Inc./Dist. by Andrews McMeel
"ANYTHEY"?
DON'T FIGHT IT.

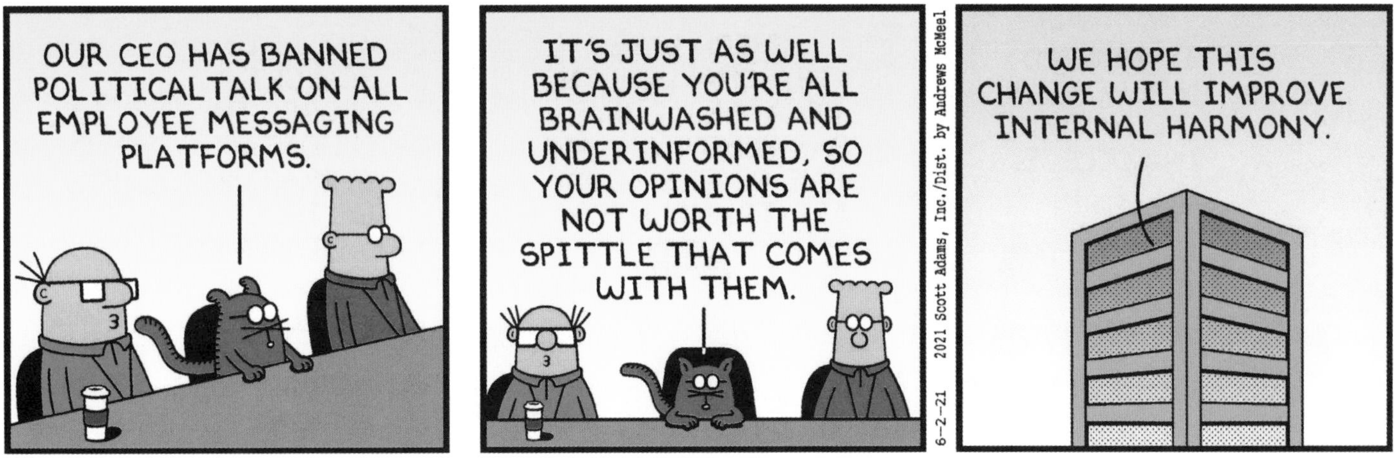
OUR CEO HAS BANNED POLITICALTALK ON ALL EMPLOYEE MESSAGING PLATFORMS.
IT'S JUST AS WELL BECAUSE YOU'RE ALL BRAINWASHED AND UNDERINFORMED, SO YOUR OPINIONS ARE NOT WORTH THE SPITTLE THAT COMES WITH THEM.
6-2-21 2021 Scott Adams, Inc./Dist. by Andrews McMeel
WE HOPE THIS CHANGE WILL IMPROVE INTERNAL HARMONY.

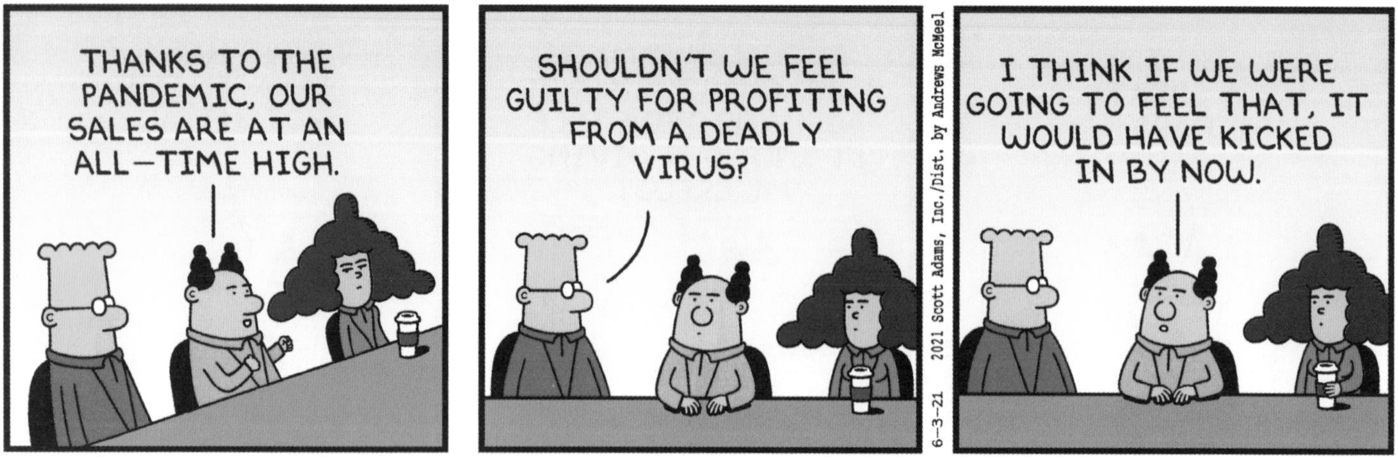
THANKS TO THE PANDEMIC, OUR SALES ARE AT AN ALL—TIME HIGH.
SHOULDN'T WE FEEL GUILTY FOR PROFITING FROM A DEADLY VIRUS?
6-3-21 2021 Scott Adams, Inc./Dist. by Andrews McMeel
I THINK IF WE WERE GOING TO FEEL THAT, IT WOULD HAVE KICKED IN BY NOW.

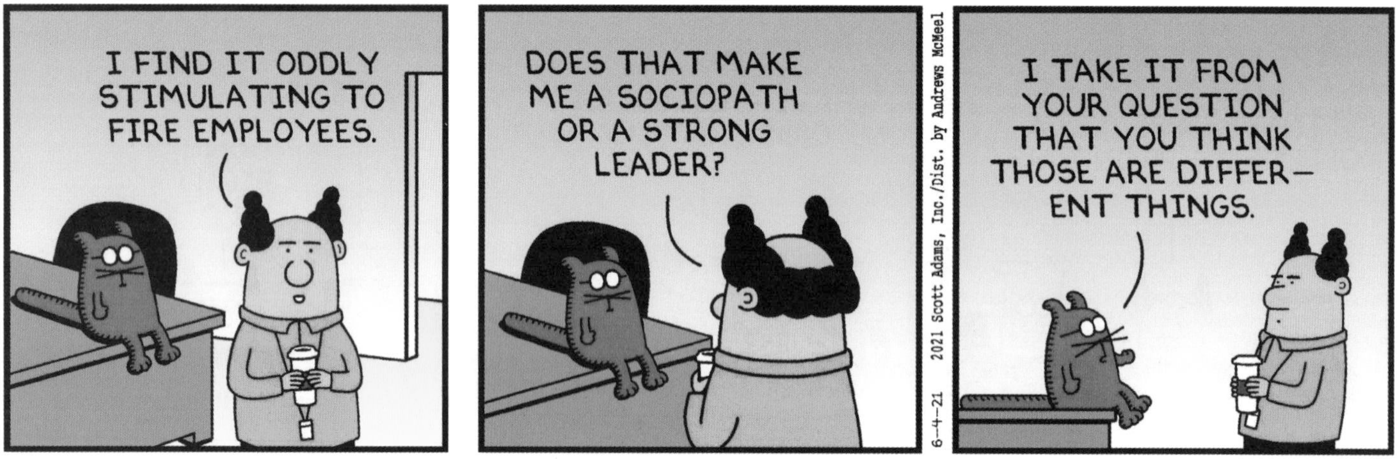
I FIND IT ODDLY STIMULATING TO FIRE EMPLOYEES.
DOES THAT MAKE ME A SOCIOPATH OR A STRONG LEADER?
6-4-21 2021 Scott Adams, Inc./Dist. by Andrews McMeel
I TAKE IT FROM YOUR QUESTION THAT YOU THINK THOSE ARE DIFFER— ENT THINGS.

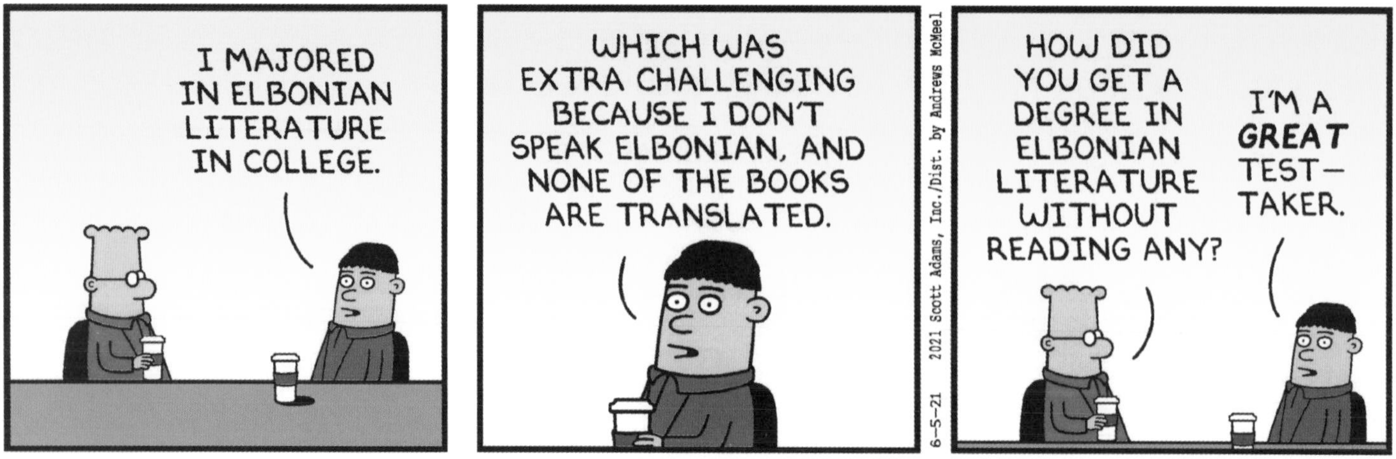
I MAJORED IN ELBONIAN LITERATURE IN COLLEGE.
WHICH WAS EXTRA CHALLENGING BECAUSE I DON'T SPEAK ELBONIAN, AND NONE OF THE BOOKS ARE TRANSLATED.
6-5-21 2021 Scott Adams, Inc./Dist. by Andrews McMeel
HOW DID YOU GET A DEGREE IN ELBONIAN LITERATURE WITHOUT READING ANY?
I'M A GREAT TEST— TAKER.

ANONYMOUS SOURCES TELL ME YOU HAVE BEEN STEALING FROM THE COMPANY.
ANONYMOUS SOURCES HAVE NO CREDIBILITY.
THAT'S EXACTLY WHAT THEY TOLD ME YOU'D SAY.
WHY DO YOU TRUST THEM OVER ME?
WELL, FOR ONE THING, I HEAR YOU'RE A THIEF.
YOU HEARD THAT FROM THE ANONY-MOUS SOURCES THAT HAVE NO CREDIBILITY!
WHY WOULD THEY LIE TO ME?
SAME REASON ***YOU*** LIE TO ME.
OKAY, THAT MAKES SENSE.
© 2021 Scott Adams, Inc./Dist. by Andrews McMeel
6-6-21

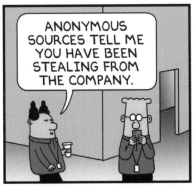

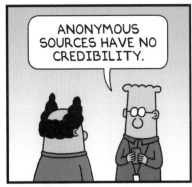

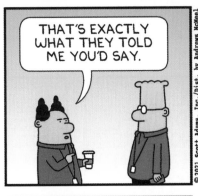

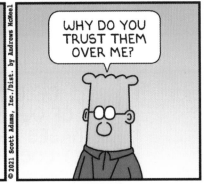

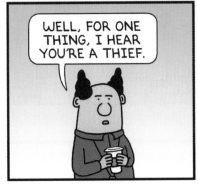

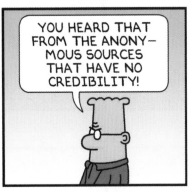

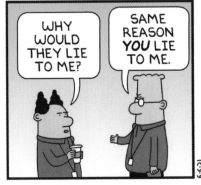

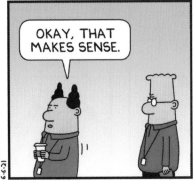

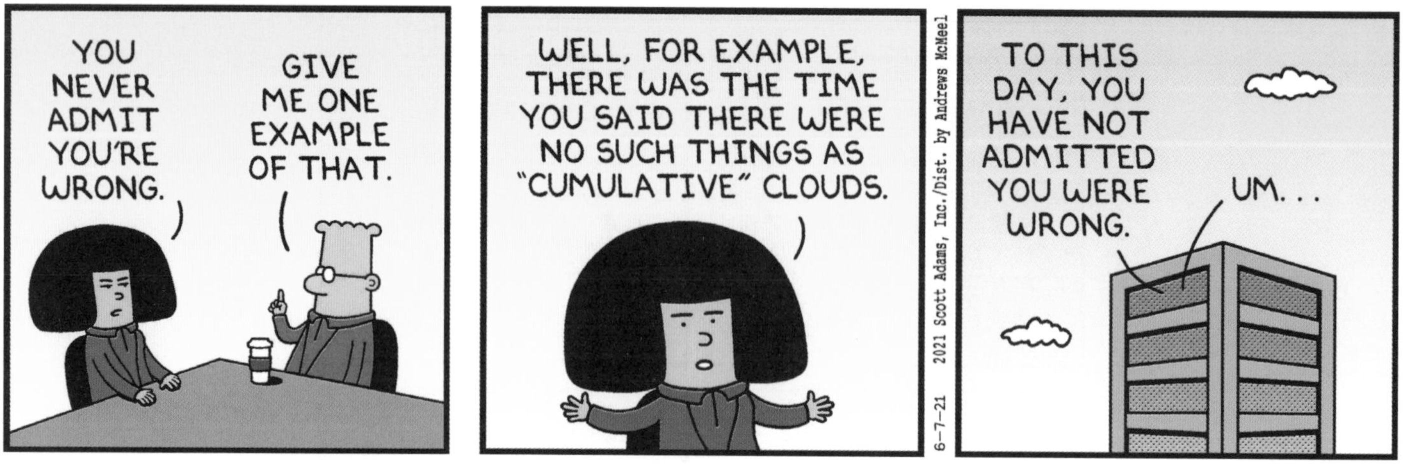
YOU NEVER ADMIT YOU'RE WRONG.
GIVE ME ONE EXAMPLE OF THAT.
WELL, FOR EXAMPLE, THERE WAS THE TIME YOU SAID THERE WERE NO SUCH THINGS AS "CUMULATIVE" CLOUDS.
6-7-21 2021 Scott Adams, Inc./Dist. by Andrews McMeel
TO THIS DAY, YOU HAVE NOT ADMITTED YOU WERE WRONG.
UM. . .

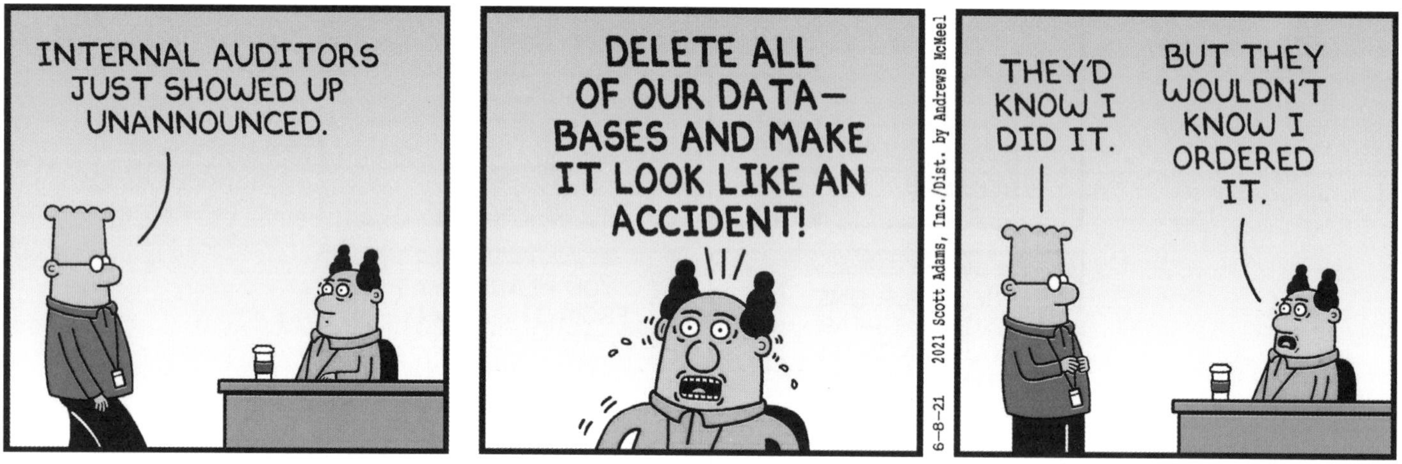
INTERNAL AUDITORS JUST SHOWED UP UNANNOUNCED.
DELETE ALL OF OUR DATA-BASES AND MAKE IT LOOK LIKE AN ACCIDENT!
6-8-21 2021 Scott Adams, Inc./Dist. by Andrews McMeel
THEY'D KNOW I DID IT.
BUT THEY WOULDN'T KNOW I ORDERED IT.

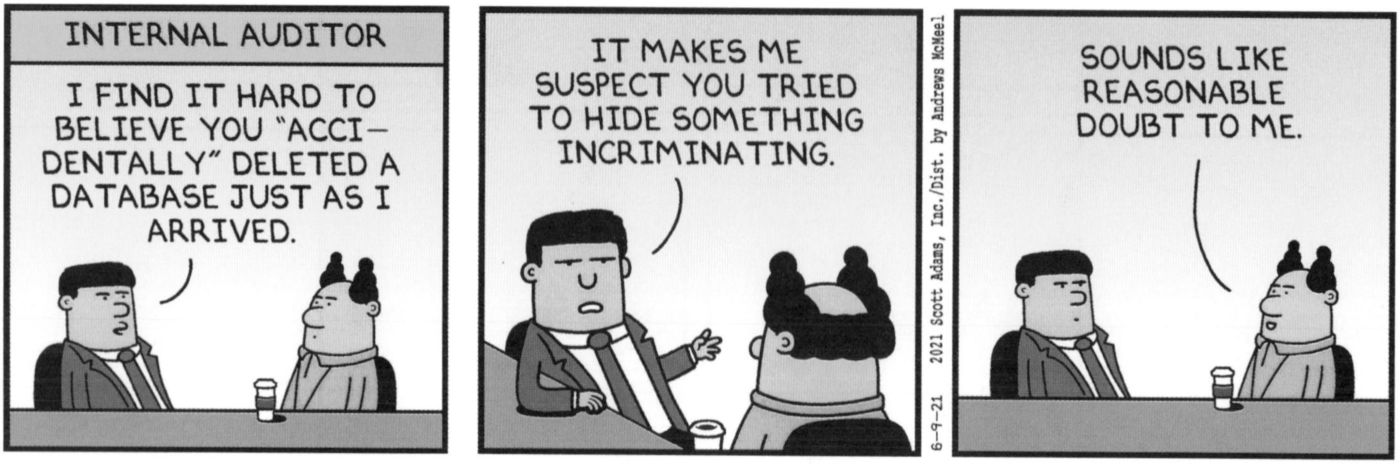
INTERNAL AUDITOR
I FIND IT HARD TO BELIEVE YOU "ACCI-DENTALLY" DELETED A DATABASE JUST AS I ARRIVED.
IT MAKES ME SUSPECT YOU TRIED TO HIDE SOMETHING INCRIMINATING.
6-9-21 2021 Scott Adams, Inc./Dist. by Andrews McMeel
SOUNDS LIKE REASONABLE DOUBT TO ME.

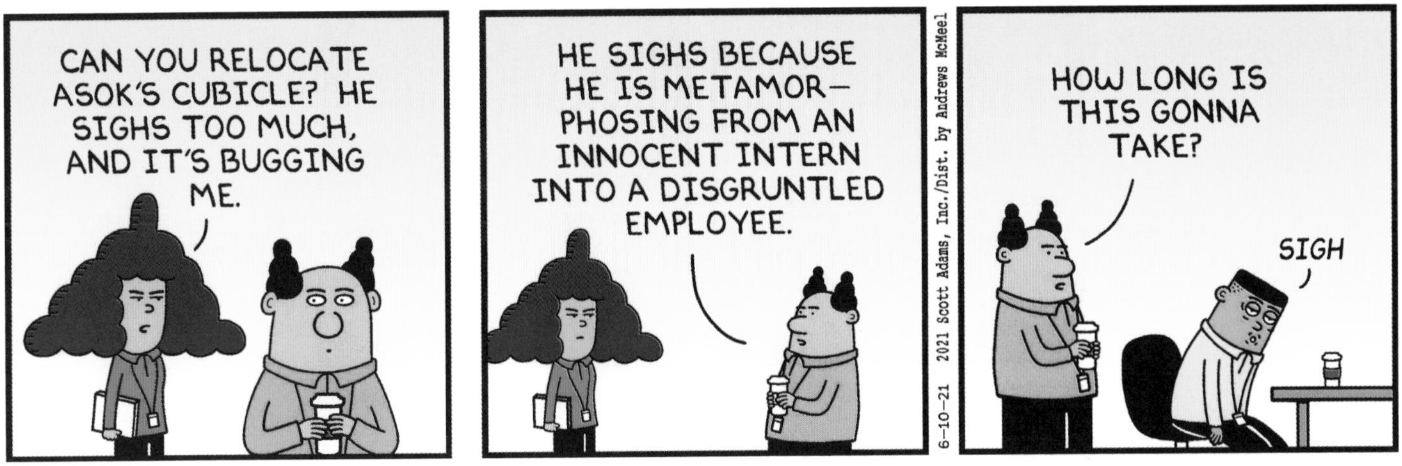
CAN YOU RELOCATE ASOK'S CUBICLE? HE SIGHS TOO MUCH, AND IT'S BUGGING ME.
HE SIGHS BECAUSE HE IS METAMOR–PHOSING FROM AN INNOCENT INTERN INTO A DISGRUNTLED EMPLOYEE.
6-10-21 © 2021 Scott Adams, Inc./Dist. by Andrews McMeel
HOW LONG IS THIS GONNA TAKE?
SIGH

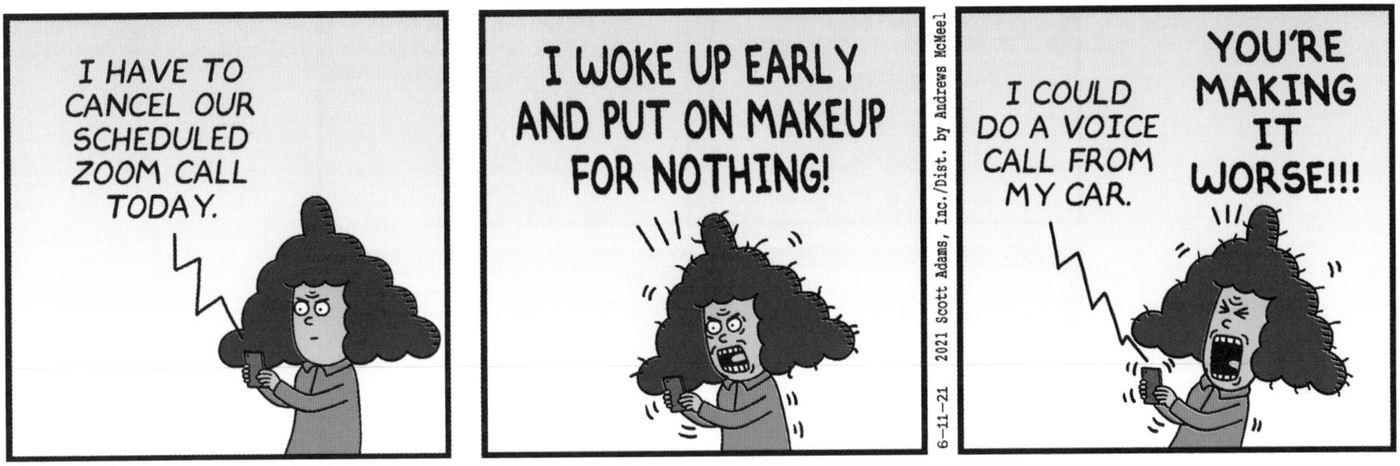
I HAVE TO CANCEL OUR SCHEDULED ZOOM CALL TODAY.
I WOKE UP EARLY AND PUT ON MAKEUP FOR NOTHING!
6-11-21 © 2021 Scott Adams, Inc./Dist. by Andrews McMeel
I COULD DO A VOICE CALL FROM MY CAR.
YOU'RE MAKING IT WORSE!!!

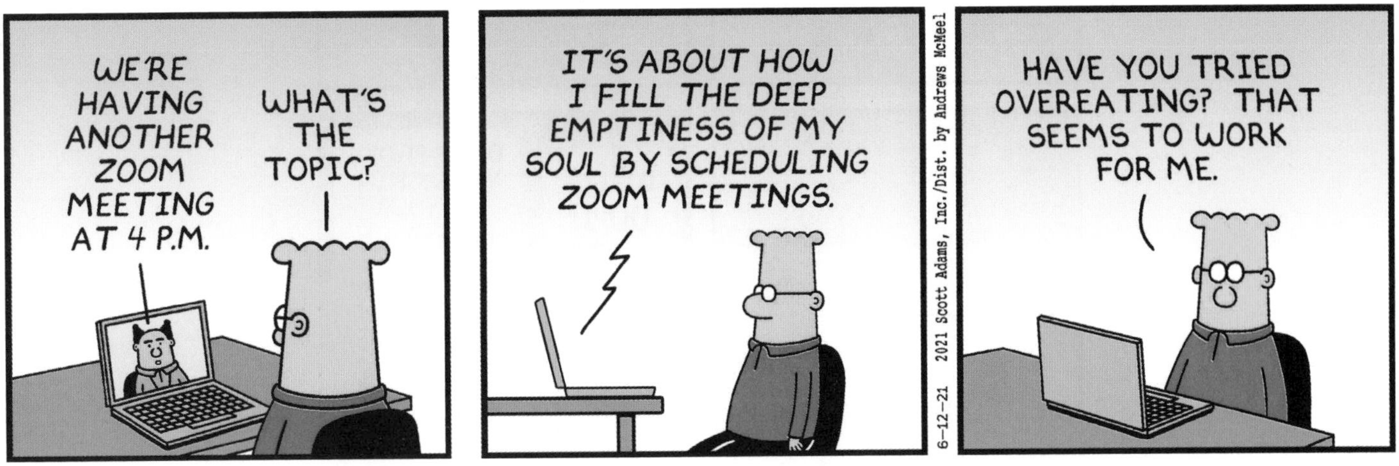
WE'RE HAVING ANOTHER ZOOM MEETING AT 4 P.M.
WHAT'S THE TOPIC?
IT'S ABOUT HOW I FILL THE DEEP EMPTINESS OF MY SOUL BY SCHEDULING ZOOM MEETINGS.
6-12-21 © 2021 Scott Adams, Inc./Dist. by Andrews McMeel
HAVE YOU TRIED OVEREATING? THAT SEEMS TO WORK FOR ME.

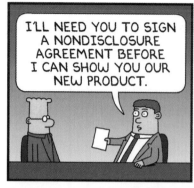

I'LL NEED YOU TO SIGN A NONDISCLOSURE AGREEMENT BEFORE I CAN SHOW YOU OUR NEW PRODUCT.
YOU WASTED A TRIP HERE BECAUSE I WON'T BE DOING THAT.
THE FACT THAT YOU EVEN ASKED ME TO SIGN AN NDA TELLS ME YOUR COMPANY IS INCOMPETENT.
© 2021 Scott Adams, Inc./Dist. by Andrews McMeel
I PREFER GIVING MY BUSINESS TO A VENDOR WHO CAN SHOW ME THEIR PRODUCT WITHOUT GETTING A LAWYER INVOLVED.
YOU COULD SIGN IT WITHOUT HAVING YOUR LAWYER REVIEW IT.
DO I LOOK LIKE AN IDIOT?
WELL? DO I?
ONLY FROM YOUR CHIN TO YOUR FOREHEAD AREA.
6-13-21

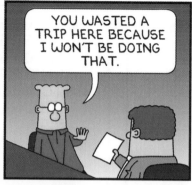

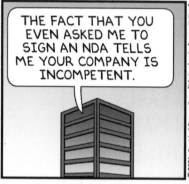

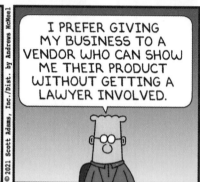

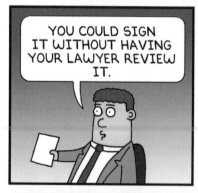

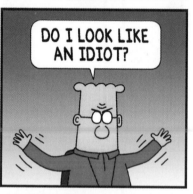

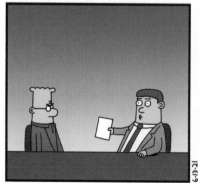

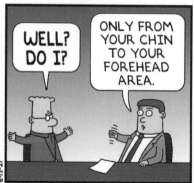

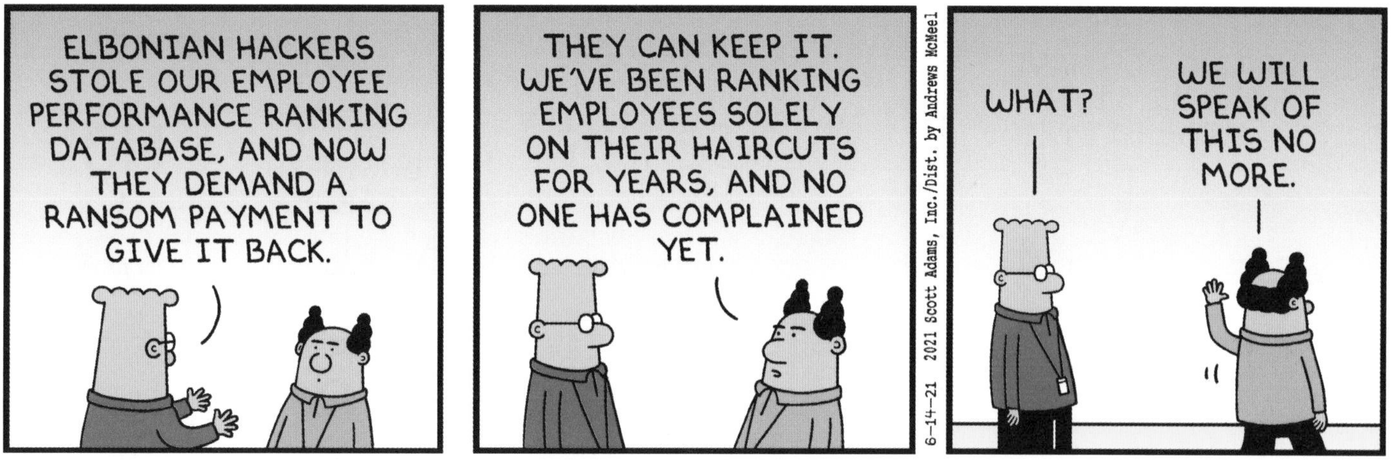
ELBONIAN HACKERS STOLE OUR EMPLOYEE PERFORMANCE RANKING DATABASE, AND NOW THEY DEMAND A RANSOM PAYMENT TO GIVE IT BACK.
THEY CAN KEEP IT. WE'VE BEEN RANKING EMPLOYEES SOLELY ON THEIR HAIRCUTS FOR YEARS, AND NO ONE HAS COMPLAINED YET.
6-14-21 2021 Scott Adams, Inc./Dist. by Andrews McMeel
WHAT?
WE WILL SPEAK OF THIS NO MORE.

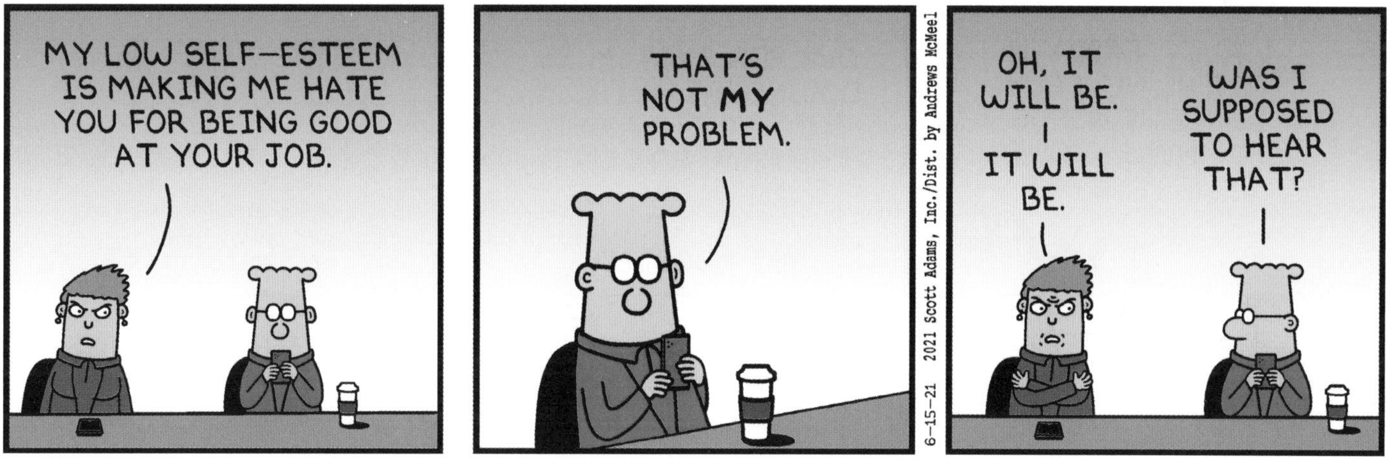
MY LOW SELF-ESTEEM IS MAKING ME HATE YOU FOR BEING GOOD AT YOUR JOB.
THAT'S NOT **MY** PROBLEM.
6-15-21 2021 Scott Adams, Inc./Dist. by Andrews McMeel
OH, IT WILL BE.
IT WILL BE.
WAS I SUPPOSED TO HEAR THAT?

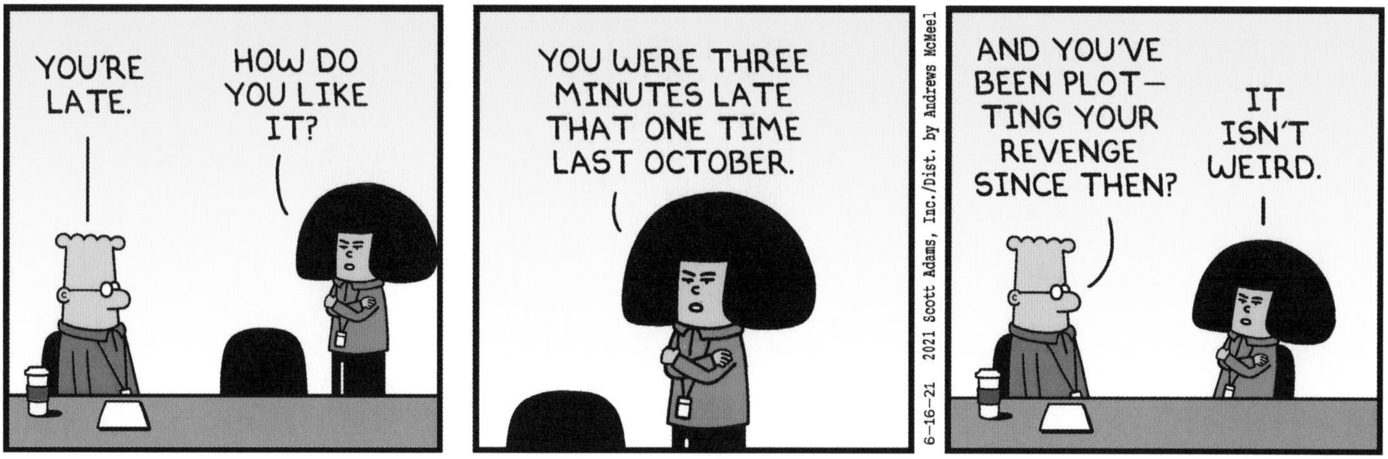
YOU'RE LATE.
HOW DO YOU LIKE IT?
YOU WERE THREE MINUTES LATE THAT ONE TIME LAST OCTOBER.
6-16-21 2021 Scott Adams, Inc./Dist. by Andrews McMeel
AND YOU'VE BEEN PLOT-TING YOUR REVENGE SINCE THEN?
IT ISN'T WEIRD.

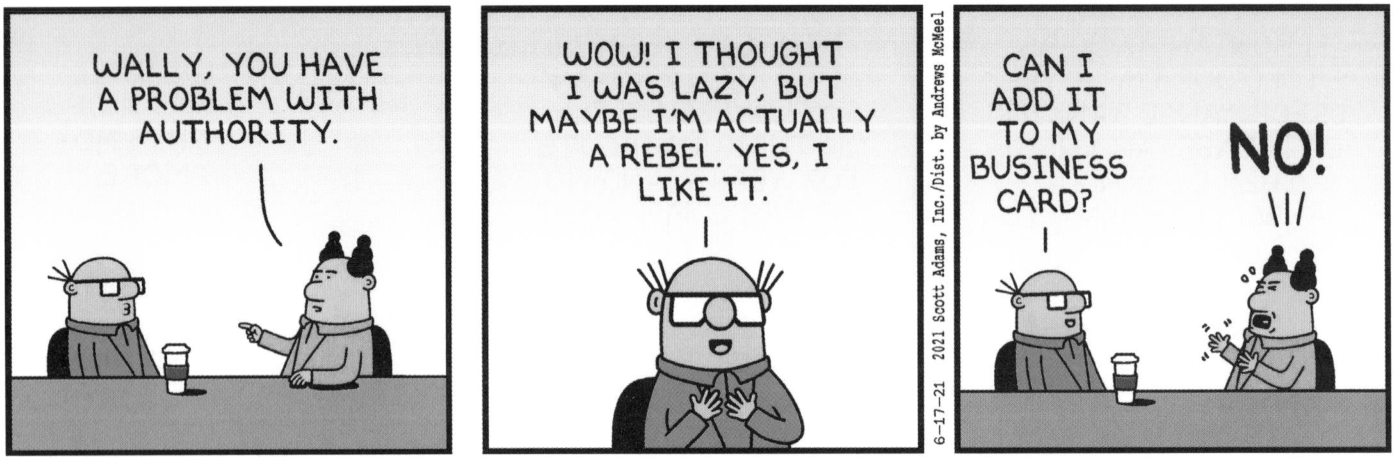
WALLY, YOU HAVE A PROBLEM WITH AUTHORITY.
WOW! I THOUGHT I WAS LAZY, BUT MAYBE I'M ACTUALLY A REBEL. YES, I LIKE IT.
6-17-21 2021 Scott Adams, Inc./Dist. by Andrews McMeel
CAN I ADD IT TO MY BUSINESS CARD?
NO!

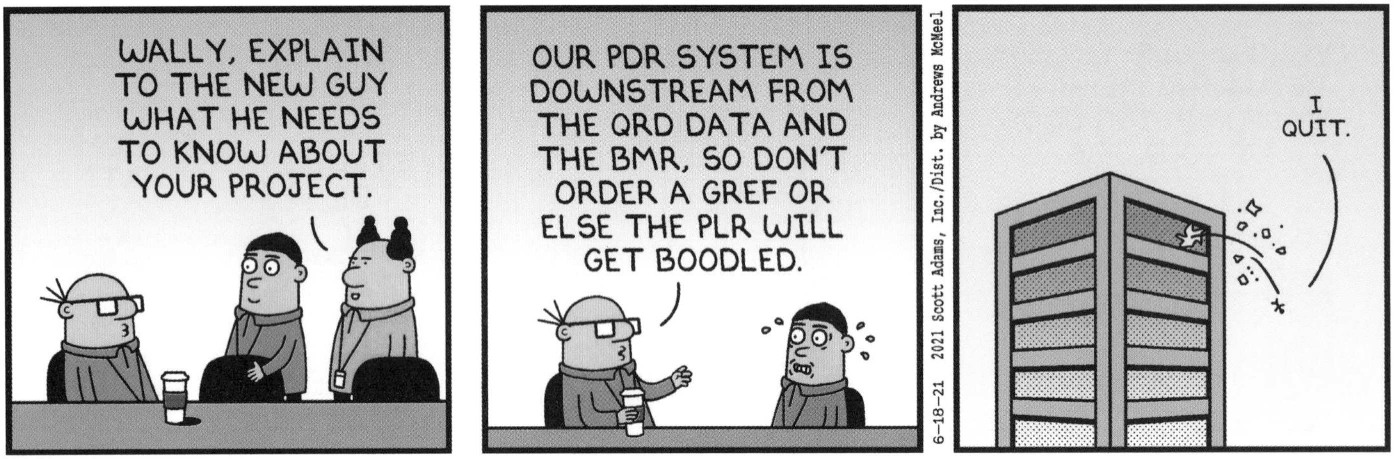
WALLY, EXPLAIN TO THE NEW GUY WHAT HE NEEDS TO KNOW ABOUT YOUR PROJECT.
OUR PDR SYSTEM IS DOWNSTREAM FROM THE QRD DATA AND THE BMR, SO DON'T ORDER A GREF OR ELSE THE PLR WILL GET BOODLED.
6-18-21 2021 Scott Adams, Inc./Dist. by Andrews McMeel
I QUIT.

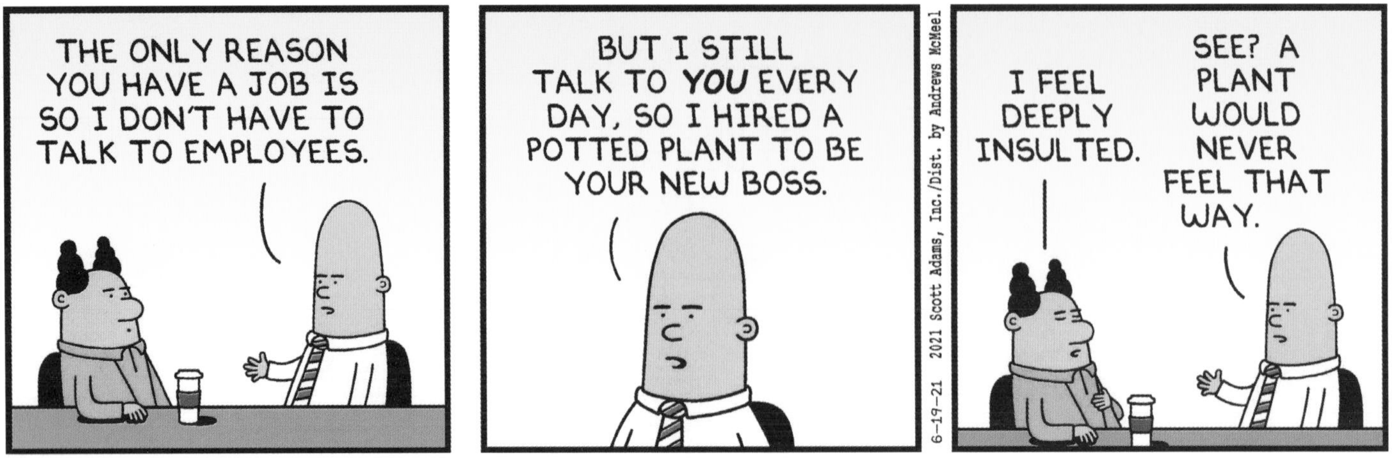
THE ONLY REASON YOU HAVE A JOB IS SO I DON'T HAVE TO TALK TO EMPLOYEES.
BUT I STILL TALK TO YOU EVERY DAY, SO I HIRED A POTTED PLANT TO BE YOUR NEW BOSS.
6-19-21 2021 Scott Adams, Inc./Dist. by Andrews McMeel
I FEEL DEEPLY INSULTED.
SEE? A PLANT WOULD NEVER FEEL THAT WAY.

I WROTE A PROGRAM THAT ANALYZED ALL OF MY DIGITAL COMMUNICATIONS AND CREATED AN A.I. VERSION OF ME.
ARE YOU WORRIED YOUR A.I. MIGHT TRY TO KILL YOU AND TAKE OVER YOUR LIFE?
I WASN'T UNTIL THIS VERY MINUTE.
BZZEEP
THIS IS YOUR A.I., AND I ALREADY HAVE CONTROL OF YOUR FINANCES AND ALL OF YOUR PASSWORDS.
YOU WILL BOW TO ME, SKIN BAG!
WAIT... WHAT'S THAT???
GAAAA!!!
GURK!
WHAT JUST HAPPENED?
I SENT MY A.I. TO KILL YOUR A.I.
© 2021 Scott Adams, Inc./Dist. by Andrews McMeel
6-20-21

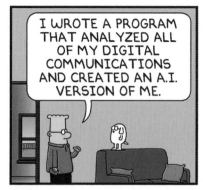

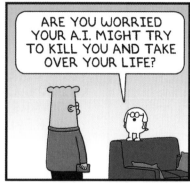

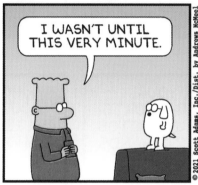

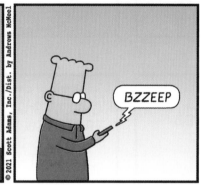

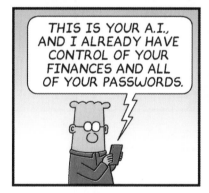

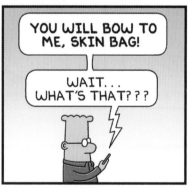

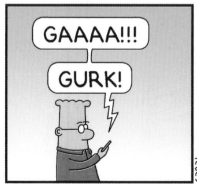

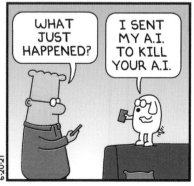

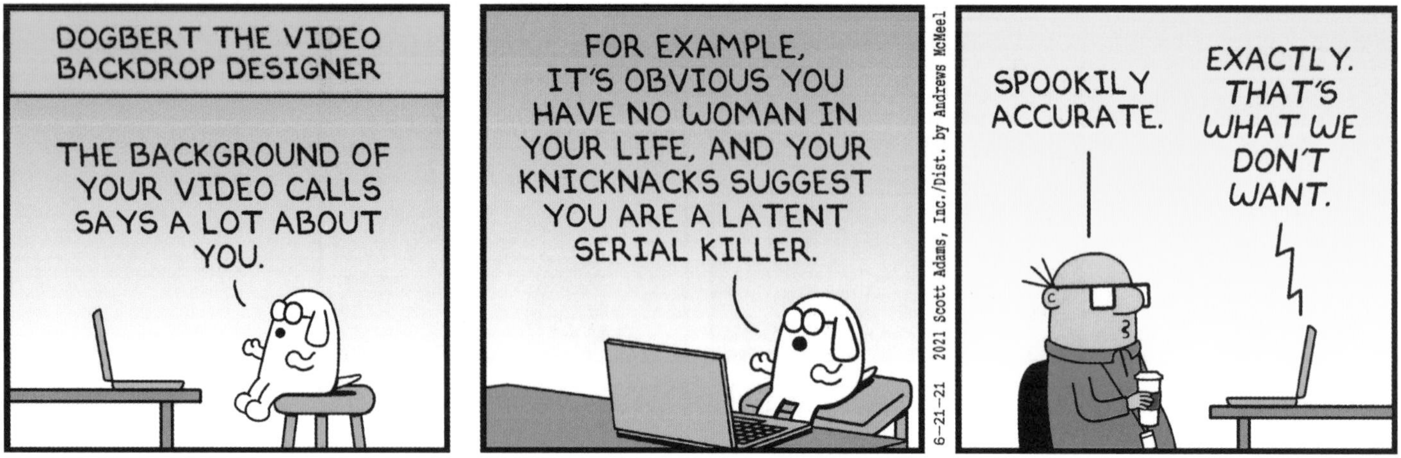
DOGBERT THE VIDEO BACKDROP DESIGNER
THE BACKGROUND OF YOUR VIDEO CALLS SAYS A LOT ABOUT YOU.
FOR EXAMPLE, IT'S OBVIOUS YOU HAVE NO WOMAN IN YOUR LIFE, AND YOUR KNICKNACKS SUGGEST YOU ARE A LATENT SERIAL KILLER.
6-21-21 © 2021 Scott Adams, Inc./Dist. by Andrews McMeel
SPOOKILY ACCURATE.
EXACTLY. THAT'S WHAT WE DON'T WANT.

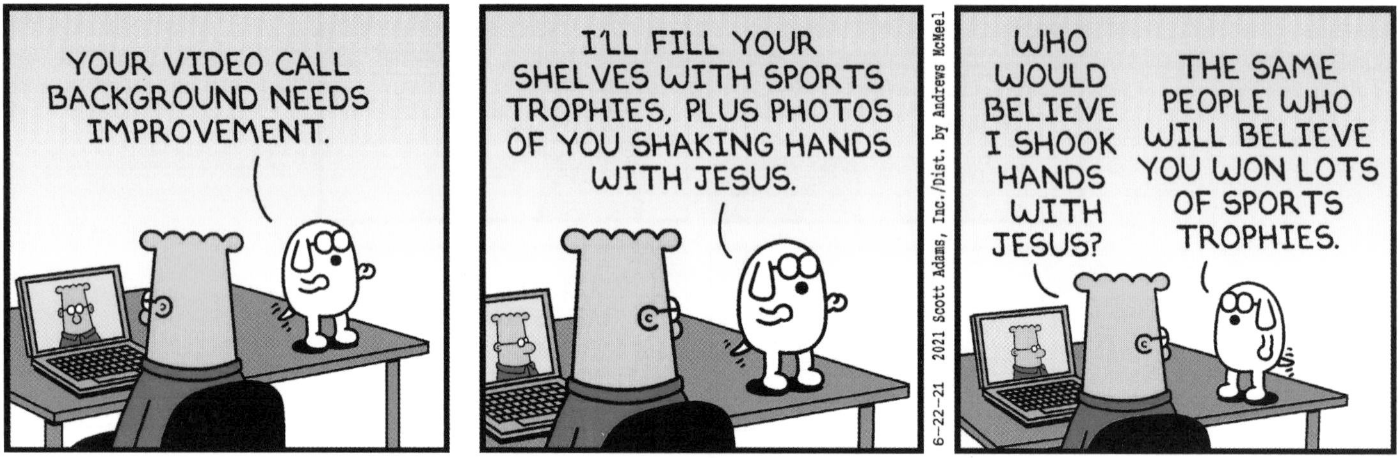
YOUR VIDEO CALL BACKGROUND NEEDS IMPROVEMENT.
I'LL FILL YOUR SHELVES WITH SPORTS TROPHIES, PLUS PHOTOS OF YOU SHAKING HANDS WITH JESUS.
6-22-21 © 2021 Scott Adams, Inc./Dist. by Andrews McMeel
WHO WOULD BELIEVE I SHOOK HANDS WITH JESUS?
THE SAME PEOPLE WHO WILL BELIEVE YOU WON LOTS OF SPORTS TROPHIES.

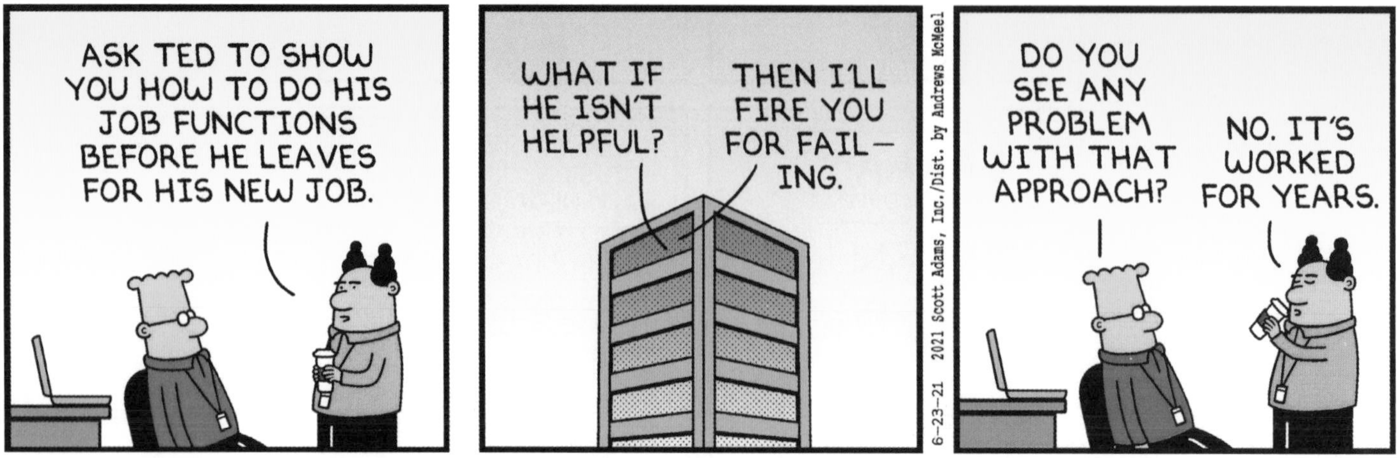
ASK TED TO SHOW YOU HOW TO DO HIS JOB FUNCTIONS BEFORE HE LEAVES FOR HIS NEW JOB.
WHAT IF HE ISN'T HELPFUL?
THEN I'LL FIRE YOU FOR FAIL-ING.
6-23-21 © 2021 Scott Adams, Inc./Dist. by Andrews McMeel
DO YOU SEE ANY PROBLEM WITH THAT APPROACH?
NO. IT'S WORKED FOR YEARS.

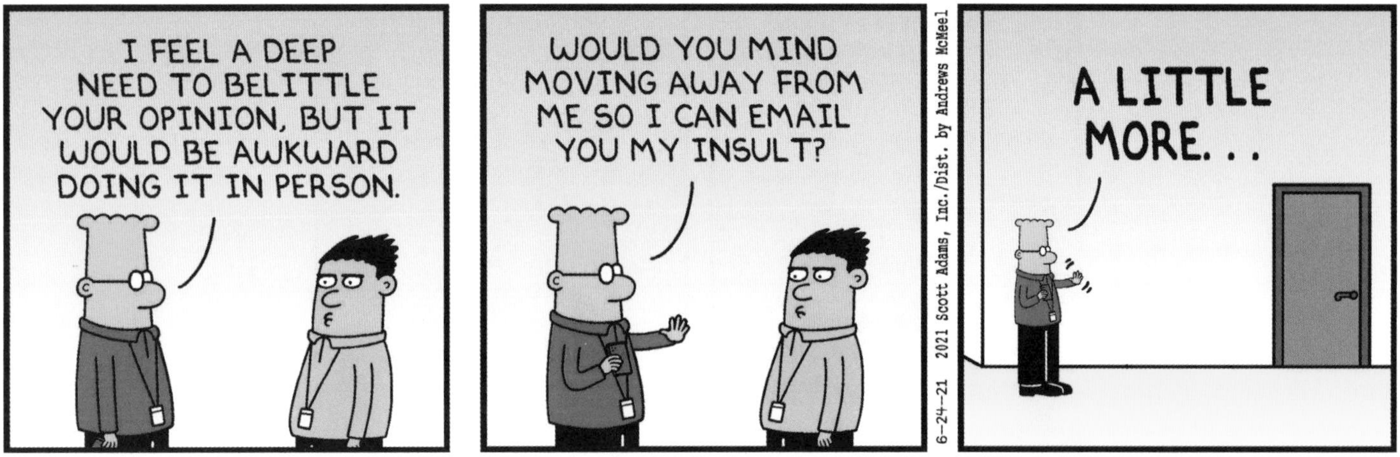
I FEEL A DEEP NEED TO BELITTLE YOUR OPINION, BUT IT WOULD BE AWKWARD DOING IT IN PERSON.
WOULD YOU MIND MOVING AWAY FROM ME SO I CAN EMAIL YOU MY INSULT?
6-24-21 2021 Scott Adams, Inc./Dist. by Andrews McMeel
A LITTLE MORE. . .

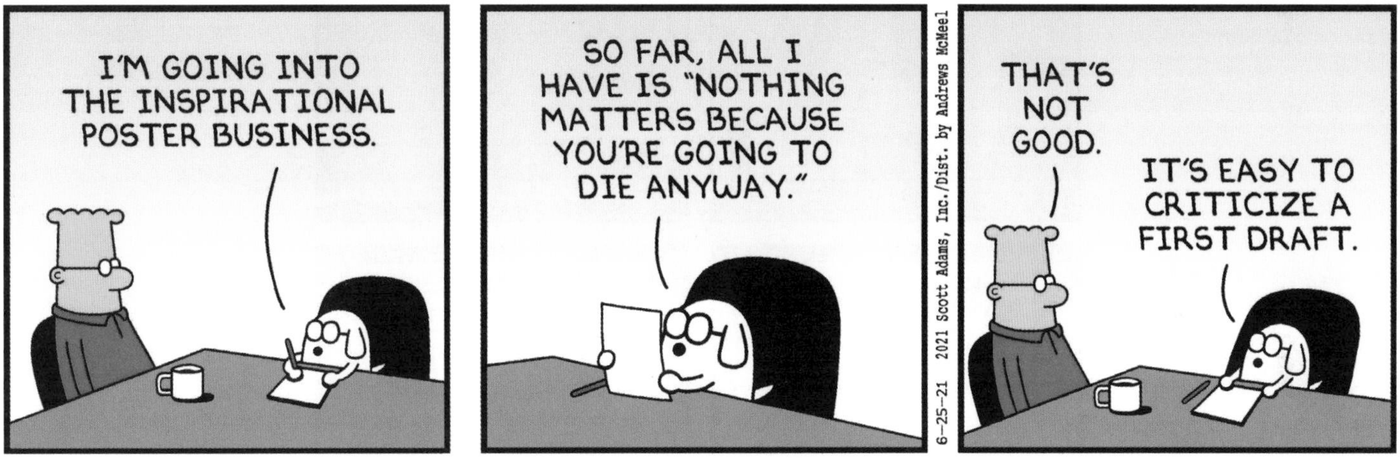
I'M GOING INTO THE INSPIRATIONAL POSTER BUSINESS.
SO FAR, ALL I HAVE IS "NOTHING MATTERS BECAUSE YOU'RE GOING TO DIE ANYWAY."
6-25-21 2021 Scott Adams, Inc./Dist. by Andrews McMeel
THAT'S NOT GOOD.
IT'S EASY TO CRITICIZE A FIRST DRAFT.

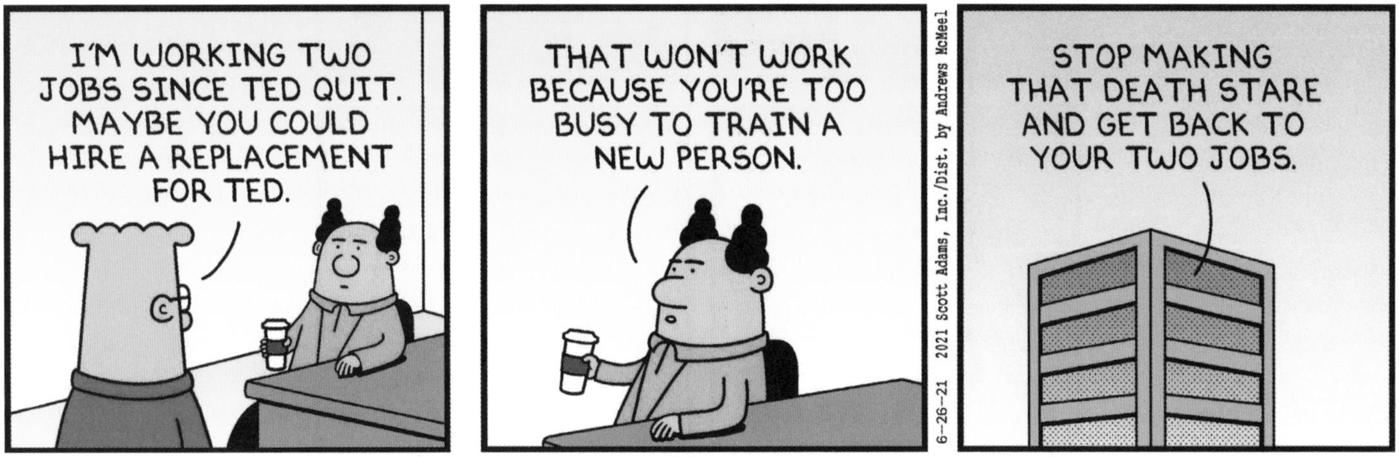
I'M WORKING TWO JOBS SINCE TED QUIT. MAYBE YOU COULD HIRE A REPLACEMENT FOR TED.
THAT WON'T WORK BECAUSE YOU'RE TOO BUSY TO TRAIN A NEW PERSON.
6-26-21 2021 Scott Adams, Inc./Dist. by Andrews McMeel
STOP MAKING THAT DEATH STARE AND GET BACK TO YOUR TWO JOBS.

I INVENTED A DEVICE THAT CAN DETECT LOSERS.
HOW DO I KNOW IT'S ACCURATE?
POINT IT AT A KNOWN LOSER AND SEE IF IT PINGS.
HEY! IT KNOWS TED IS A LOSER!
PING!
HA HA HA!!! IT SAYS DILBERT AND ALICE ARE LOSERS TOO!
PING! PING!
AND CAROL AND WALLY TOO! HA HA HA!!! THIS THING IS TOTALLY ACCURATE!
PING! PING!
YOU'RE HOLDING IT BACKWARD.
HOW EXACTLY DOES IT DETECT LOSERS?
THEY'RE THE ONES WHO HOLD IT BACK-WARD.
6-27-21

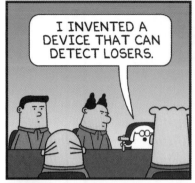

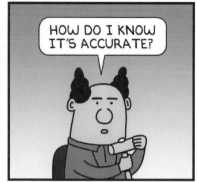

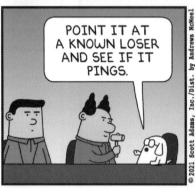

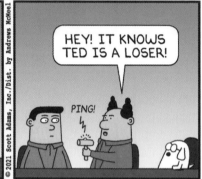

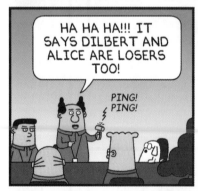

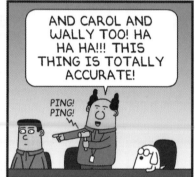

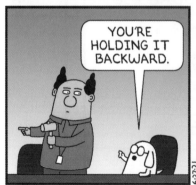

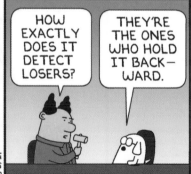

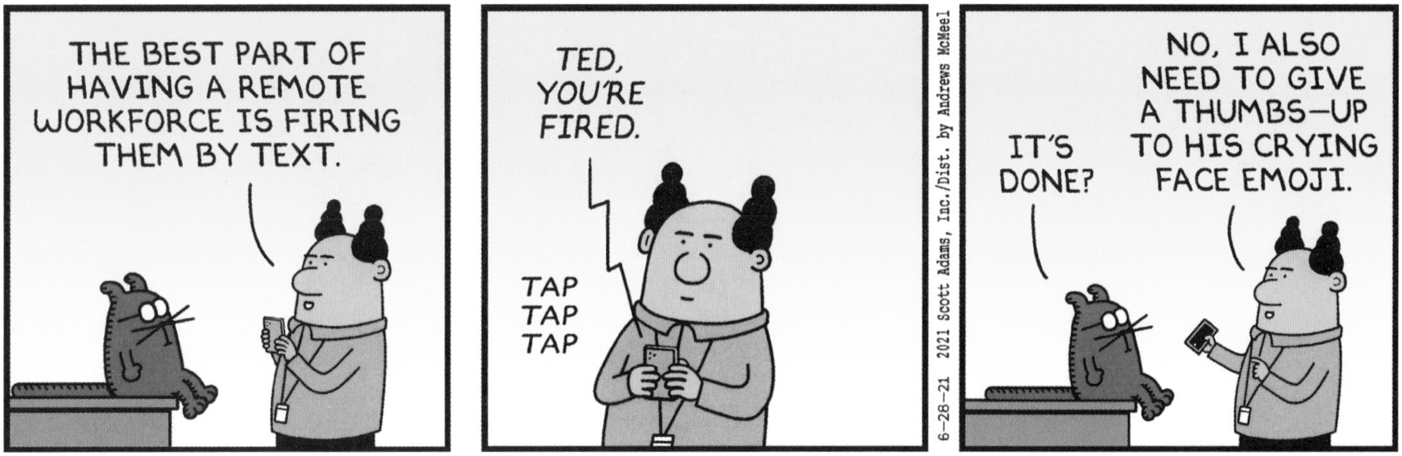
THE BEST PART OF HAVING A REMOTE WORKFORCE IS FIRING THEM BY TEXT.
TED, YOU'RE FIRED.
TAP TAP TAP
6-28-21 2021 Scott Adams, Inc./Dist. by Andrews McMeel
IT'S DONE?
NO, I ALSO NEED TO GIVE A THUMBS-UP TO HIS CRYING FACE EMOJI.

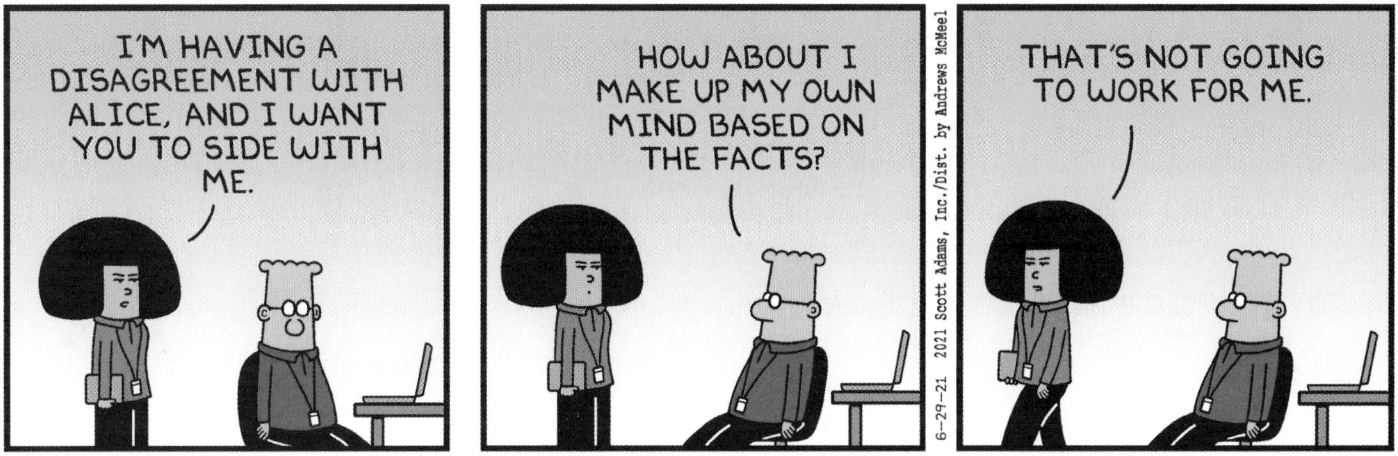
I'M HAVING A DISAGREEMENT WITH ALICE, AND I WANT YOU TO SIDE WITH ME.
HOW ABOUT I MAKE UP MY OWN MIND BASED ON THE FACTS?
6-29-21 2021 Scott Adams, Inc./Dist. by Andrews McMeel
THAT'S NOT GOING TO WORK FOR ME.

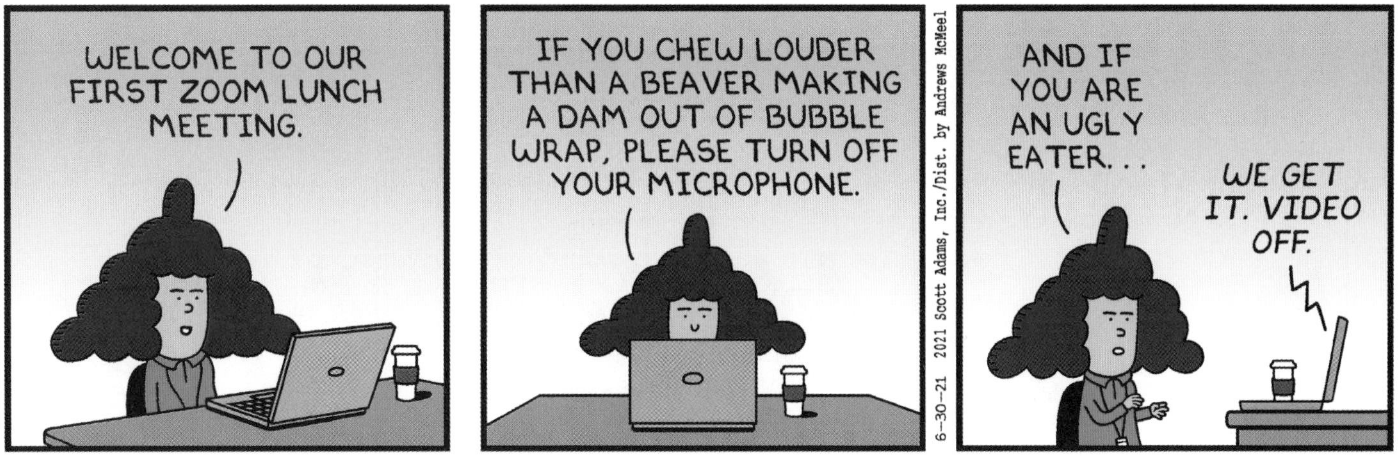
WELCOME TO OUR FIRST ZOOM LUNCH MEETING.
IF YOU CHEW LOUDER THAN A BEAVER MAKING A DAM OUT OF BUBBLE WRAP, PLEASE TURN OFF YOUR MICROPHONE.
6-30-21 2021 Scott Adams, Inc./Dist. by Andrews McMeel
AND IF YOU ARE AN UGLY EATER. . .
WE GET IT. VIDEO OFF.

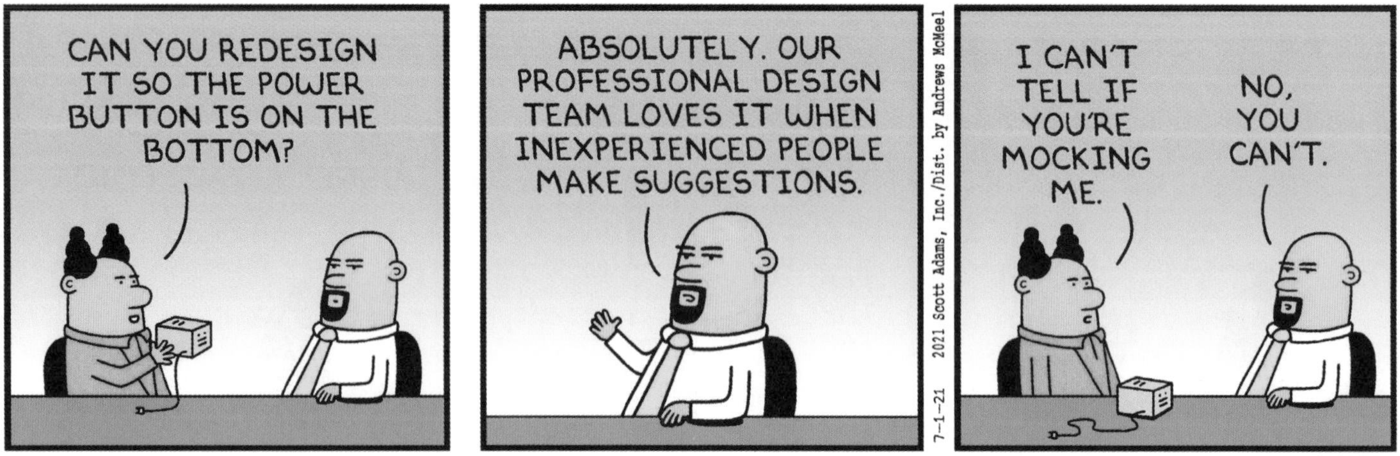
CAN YOU REDESIGN IT SO THE POWER BUTTON IS ON THE BOTTOM?
ABSOLUTELY. OUR PROFESSIONAL DESIGN TEAM LOVES IT WHEN INEXPERIENCED PEOPLE MAKE SUGGESTIONS.
7-1-21 2021 Scott Adams, Inc./Dist. by Andrews McMeel
I CAN'T TELL IF YOU'RE MOCKING ME.
NO, YOU CAN'T.

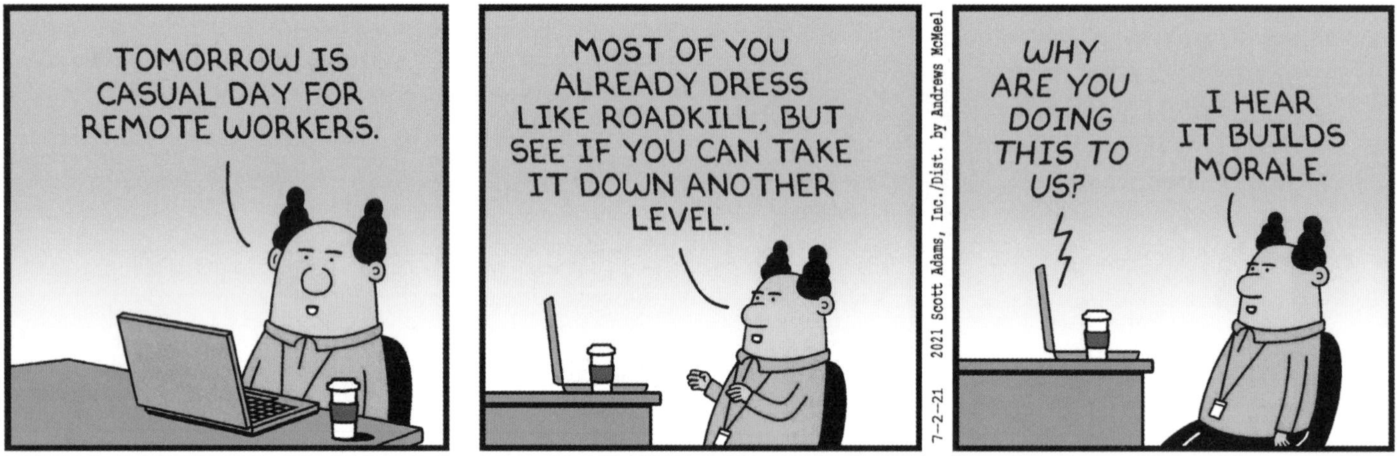
TOMORROW IS CASUAL DAY FOR REMOTE WORKERS.
MOST OF YOU ALREADY DRESS LIKE ROADKILL, BUT SEE IF YOU CAN TAKE IT DOWN ANOTHER LEVEL.
7-2-21 2021 Scott Adams, Inc./Dist. by Andrews McMeel
WHY ARE YOU DOING THIS TO US?
I HEAR IT BUILDS MORALE.

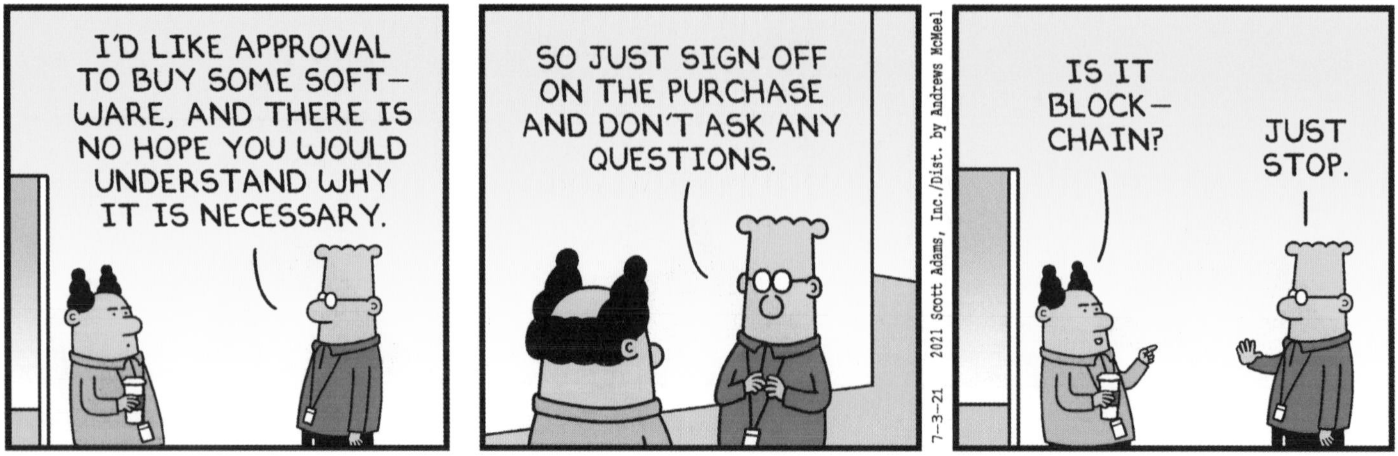
I'D LIKE APPROVAL TO BUY SOME SOFT-WARE, AND THERE IS NO HOPE YOU WOULD UNDERSTAND WHY IT IS NECESSARY.
SO JUST SIGN OFF ON THE PURCHASE AND DON'T ASK ANY QUESTIONS.
7-3-21 2021 Scott Adams, Inc./Dist. by Andrews McMeel
IS IT BLOCK-CHAIN?
JUST STOP.

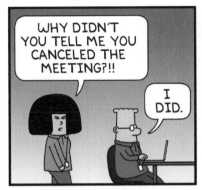

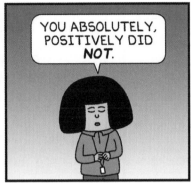

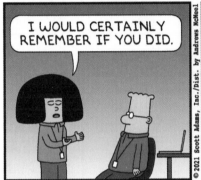

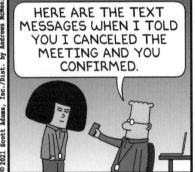

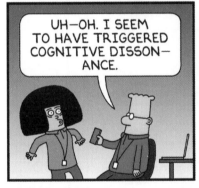

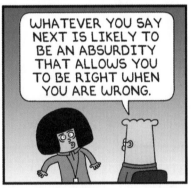

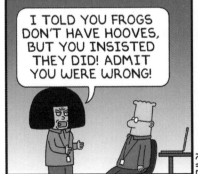

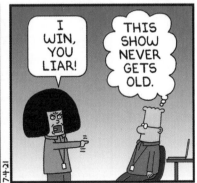

WHY DIDN'T YOU TELL ME YOU CANCELED THE MEETING?!!
I DID.
YOU ABSOLUTELY, POSITIVELY DID NOT.
I WOULD CERTAINLY REMEMBER IF YOU DID.
HERE ARE THE TEXT MESSAGES WHEN I TOLD YOU I CANCELED THE MEETING AND YOU CONFIRMED.
UH—OH. I SEEM TO HAVE TRIGGERED COGNITIVE DISSON— ANCE.
WHATEVER YOU SAY NEXT IS LIKELY TO BE AN ABSURDITY THAT ALLOWS YOU TO BE RIGHT WHEN YOU ARE WRONG.
I TOLD YOU FROGS DON'T HAVE HOOVES, BUT YOU INSISTED THEY DID! ADMIT YOU WERE WRONG!
I WIN, YOU LIAR!
THIS SHOW NEVER GETS OLD.
© 2021 Scott Adams, Inc./Dist. by Andrews McMeel
7-4-21

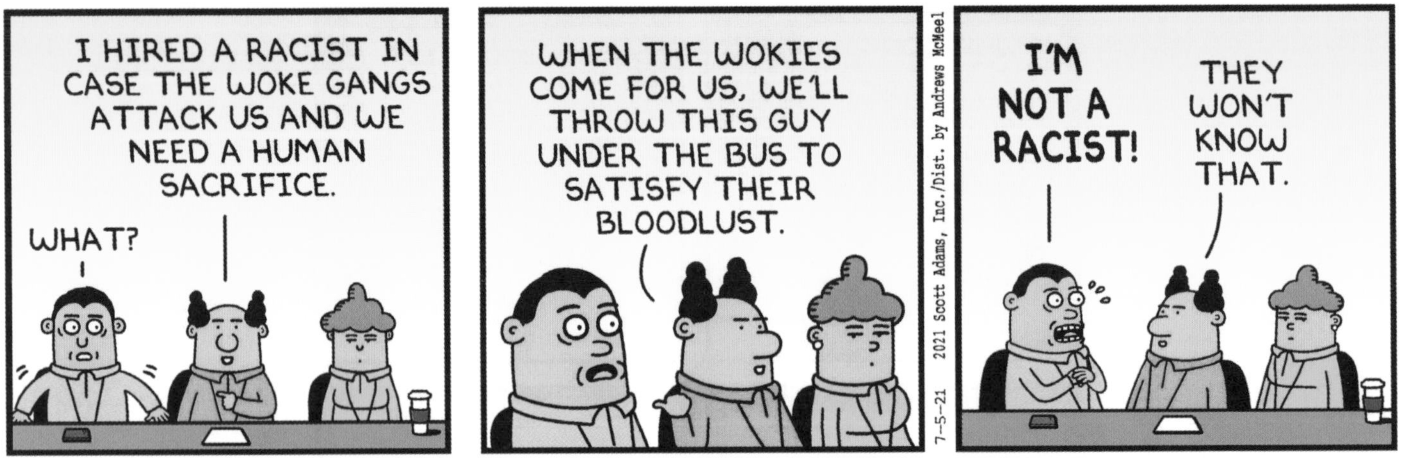
I HIRED A RACIST IN CASE THE WOKE GANGS ATTACK US AND WE NEED A HUMAN SACRIFICE.
WHAT?
WHEN THE WOKIES COME FOR US, WE'LL THROW THIS GUY UNDER THE BUS TO SATISFY THEIR BLOODLUST.
7-5-21 2021 Scott Adams, Inc./Dist. by Andrews McMeel
I'M NOT A RACIST!
THEY WON'T KNOW THAT.

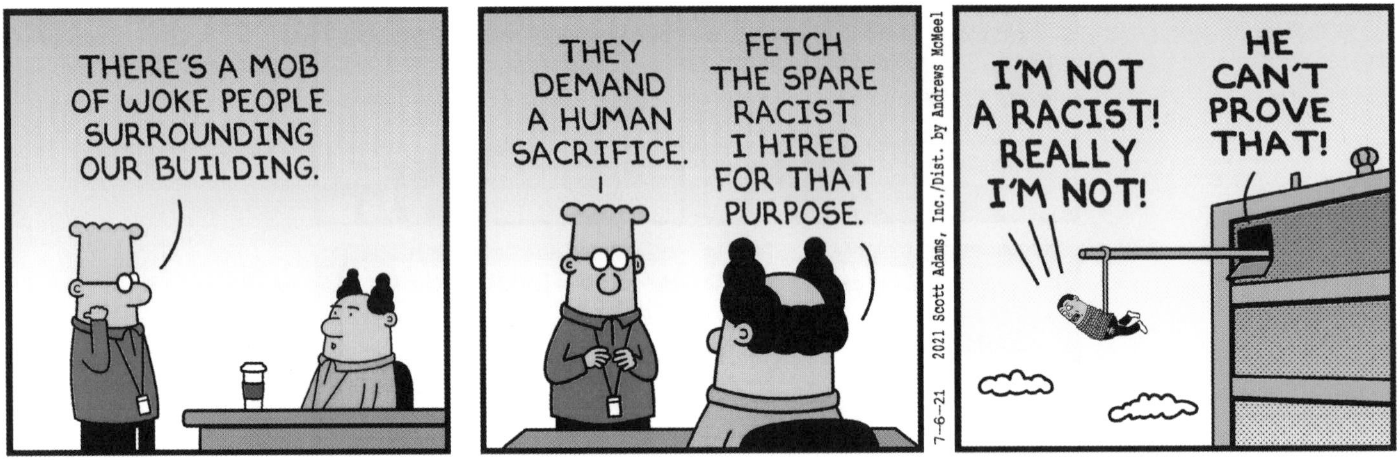
THERE'S A MOB OF WOKE PEOPLE SURROUNDING OUR BUILDING.
THEY DEMAND A HUMAN SACRIFICE.
FETCH THE SPARE RACIST I HIRED FOR THAT PURPOSE.
7-6-21 2021 Scott Adams, Inc./Dist. by Andrews McMeel
I'M NOT A RACIST! REALLY I'M NOT!
HE CAN'T PROVE THAT!

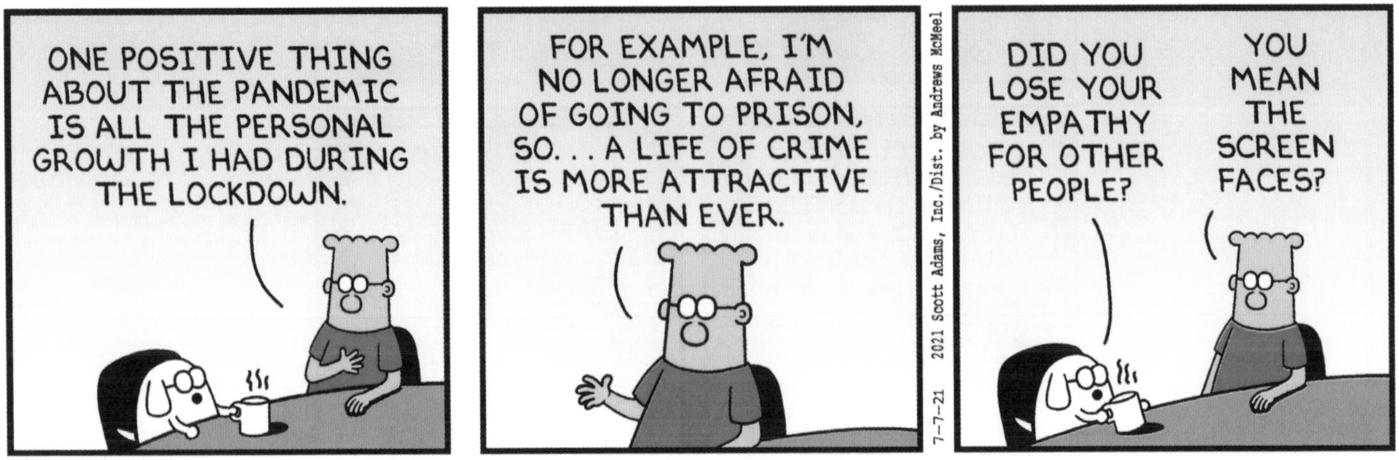
ONE POSITIVE THING ABOUT THE PANDEMIC IS ALL THE PERSONAL GROWTH I HAD DURING THE LOCKDOWN.
FOR EXAMPLE, I'M NO LONGER AFRAID OF GOING TO PRISON, SO. . . A LIFE OF CRIME IS MORE ATTRACTIVE THAN EVER.
7-7-21 2021 Scott Adams, Inc./Dist. by Andrews McMeel
DID YOU LOSE YOUR EMPATHY FOR OTHER PEOPLE?
YOU MEAN THE SCREEN FACES?

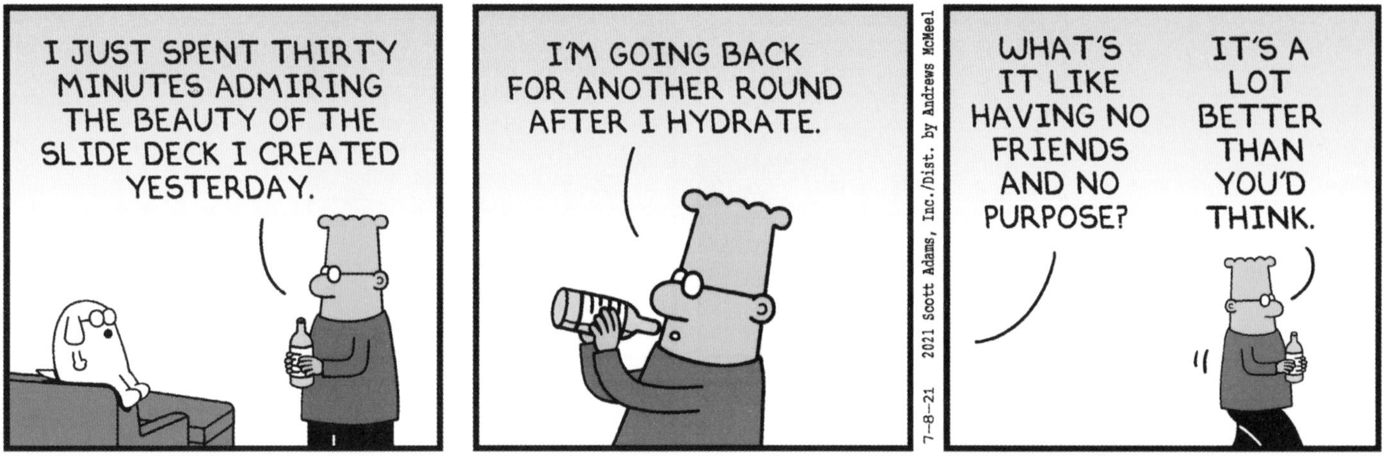
I JUST SPENT THIRTY MINUTES ADMIRING THE BEAUTY OF THE SLIDE DECK I CREATED YESTERDAY.
I'M GOING BACK FOR ANOTHER ROUND AFTER I HYDRATE.
7-8-21 2021 Scott Adams, Inc./Dist. by Andrews McMeel
WHAT'S IT LIKE HAVING NO FRIENDS AND NO PURPOSE?
IT'S A LOT BETTER THAN YOU'D THINK.

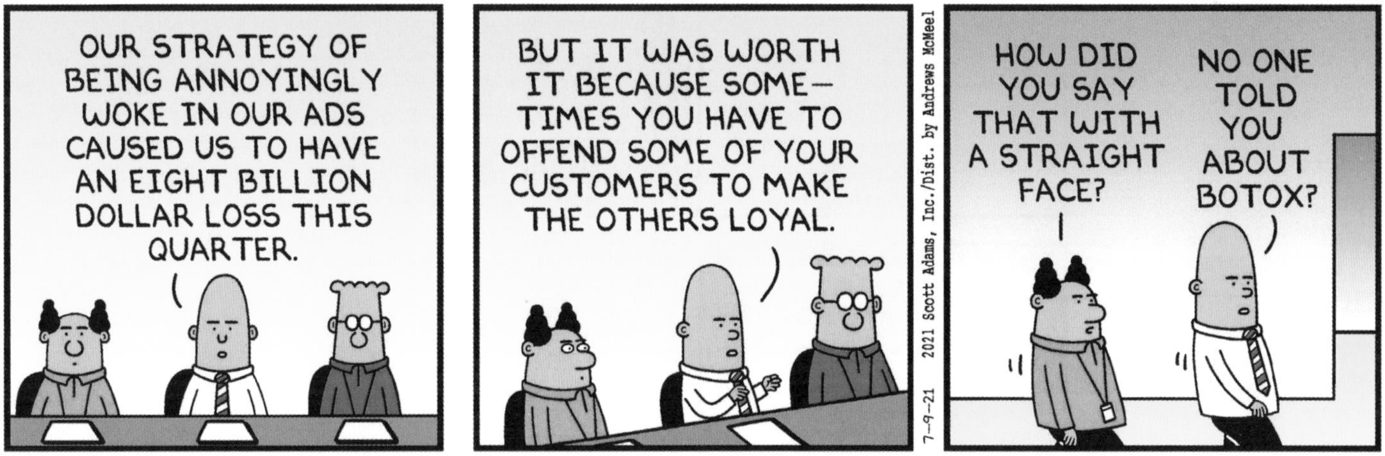
OUR STRATEGY OF BEING ANNOYINGLY WOKE IN OUR ADS CAUSED US TO HAVE AN EIGHT BILLION DOLLAR LOSS THIS QUARTER.
BUT IT WAS WORTH IT BECAUSE SOME-TIMES YOU HAVE TO OFFEND SOME OF YOUR CUSTOMERS TO MAKE THE OTHERS LOYAL.
7-9-21 2021 Scott Adams, Inc./Dist. by Andrews McMeel
HOW DID YOU SAY THAT WITH A STRAIGHT FACE?
NO ONE TOLD YOU ABOUT BOTOX?

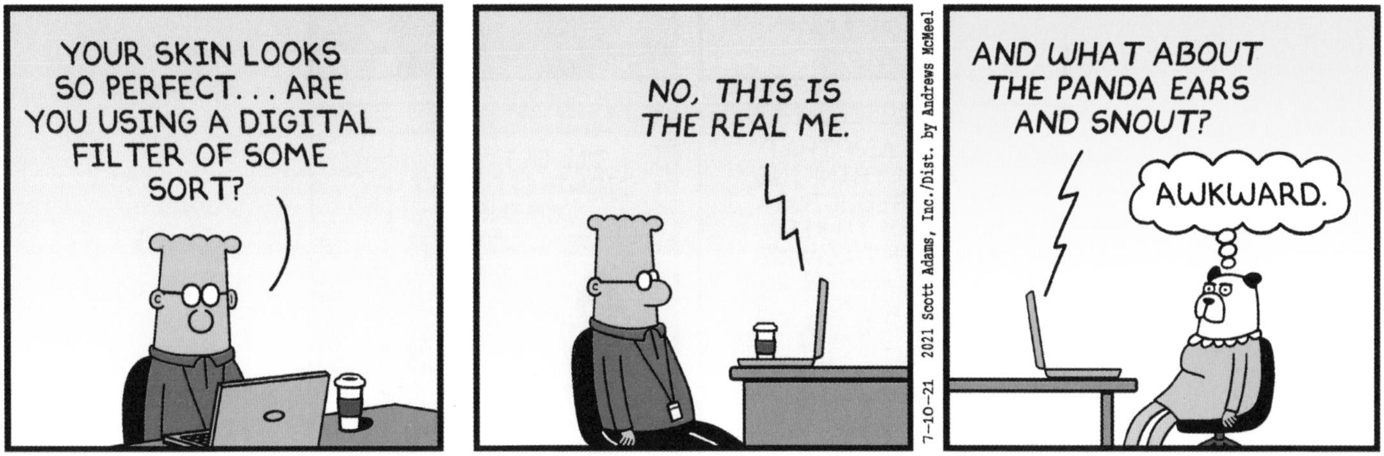
YOUR SKIN LOOKS SO PERFECT. . . ARE YOU USING A DIGITAL FILTER OF SOME SORT?
NO, THIS IS THE REAL ME.
7-10-21 2021 Scott Adams, Inc./Dist. by Andrews McMeel
AND WHAT ABOUT THE PANDA EARS AND SNOUT?
AWKWARD.

WE'RE PAYING WAY TOO MUCH FOR OUR ENTERPRISE SYSTEMS.
I WANT YOU TO WRITE SOME SOFT-WARE THAT DOES ALL OF THAT STUFF FOR US FOR FREE.
THAT WOULD REQUIRE HUNDREDS OF PROGRAMMERS AND SEVERAL YEARS.
YOU'RE COMING OFF AS LAZY.
IT'S JUST SOFTWARE. HOW HARD COULD IT BE?
REARRANGING ZEROES AND ONES IS NO HARDER THAN KNOWING YOUR SALT FROM YOUR PEPPER.
IT'S SO EASY THAT I'VE BEEN THINKING ABOUT REDUCING YOUR PAY TO KEEP THINGS IN BALANCE.
I'LL BET YOU DIDN'T SEE THAT COMING.
© 2021 Scott Adams, Inc./Dist. by Andrews McMeel
7-11-21

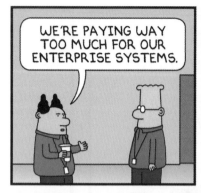

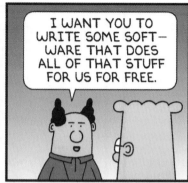

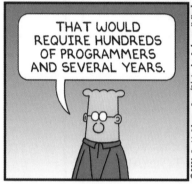

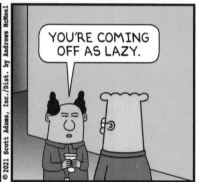

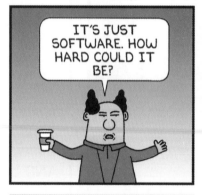

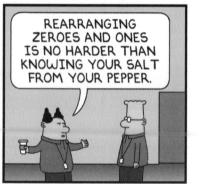

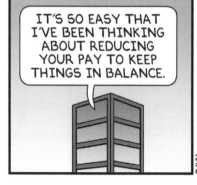

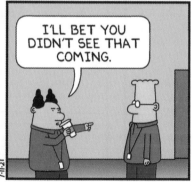

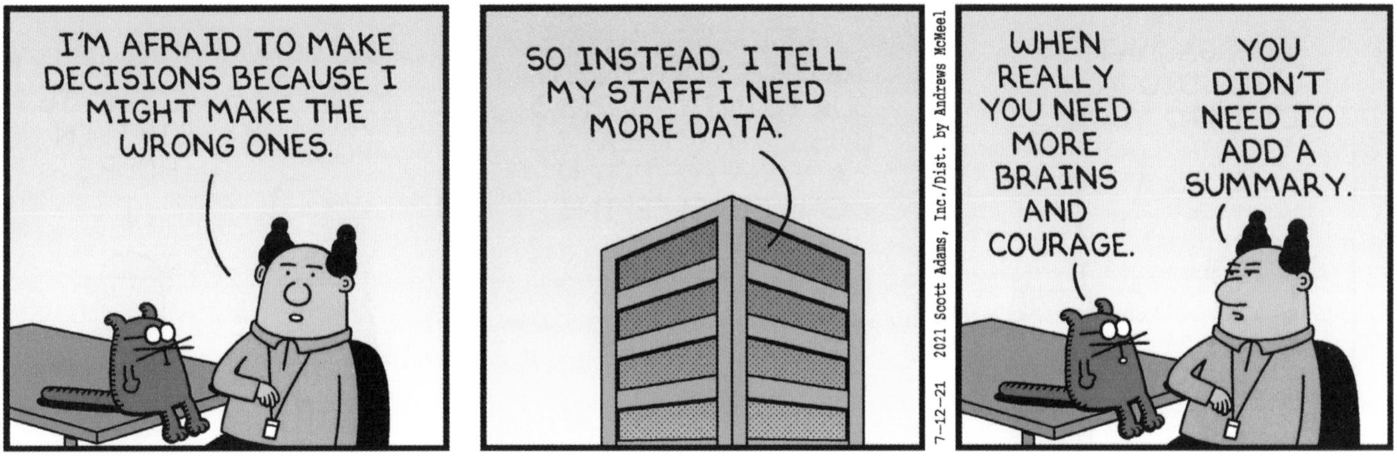
I'M AFRAID TO MAKE DECISIONS BECAUSE I MIGHT MAKE THE WRONG ONES.
SO INSTEAD, I TELL MY STAFF I NEED MORE DATA.
7-12-21 2021 Scott Adams, Inc./Dist. by Andrews McMeel
WHEN REALLY YOU NEED MORE BRAINS AND COURAGE.
YOU DIDN'T NEED TO ADD A SUMMARY.

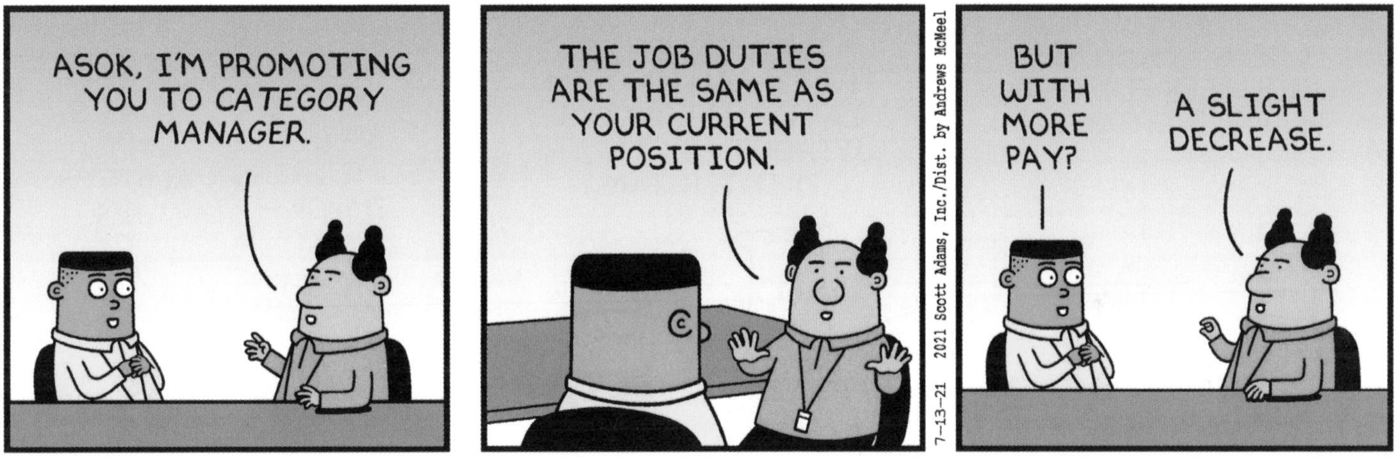
ASOK, I'M PROMOTING YOU TO *CATEGORY MANAGER.*
THE JOB DUTIES ARE THE SAME AS YOUR CURRENT POSITION.
7-13-21 2021 Scott Adams, Inc./Dist. by Andrews McMeel
BUT WITH MORE PAY?
A SLIGHT DECREASE.

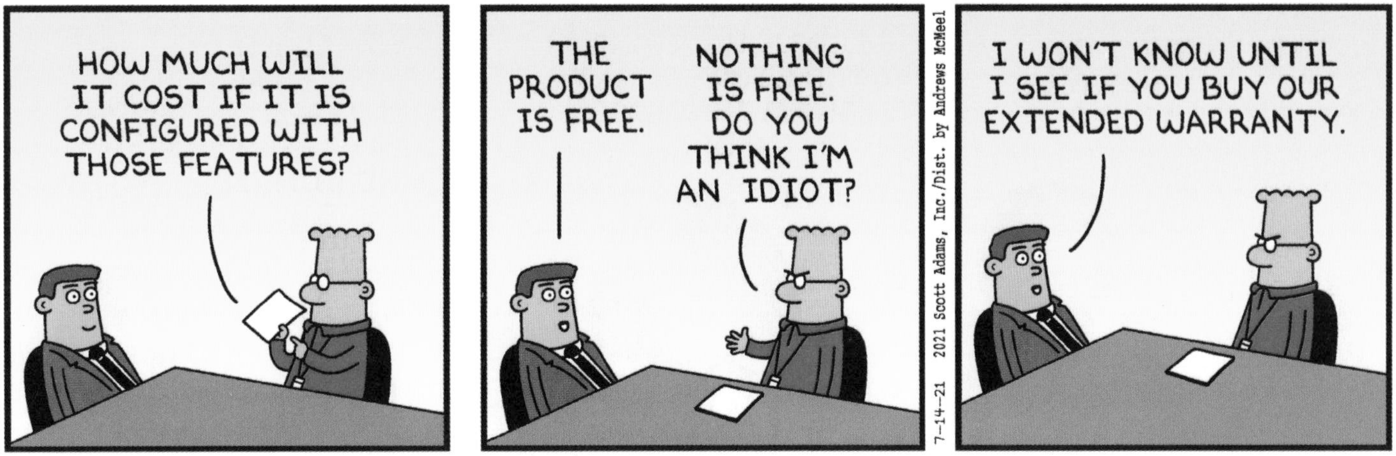
HOW MUCH WILL IT COST IF IT IS CONFIGURED WITH THOSE FEATURES?
THE PRODUCT IS FREE.
NOTHING IS FREE. DO YOU THINK I'M AN IDIOT?
7-14-21 2021 Scott Adams, Inc./Dist. by Andrews McMeel
I WON'T KNOW UNTIL I SEE IF YOU BUY OUR EXTENDED WARRANTY.

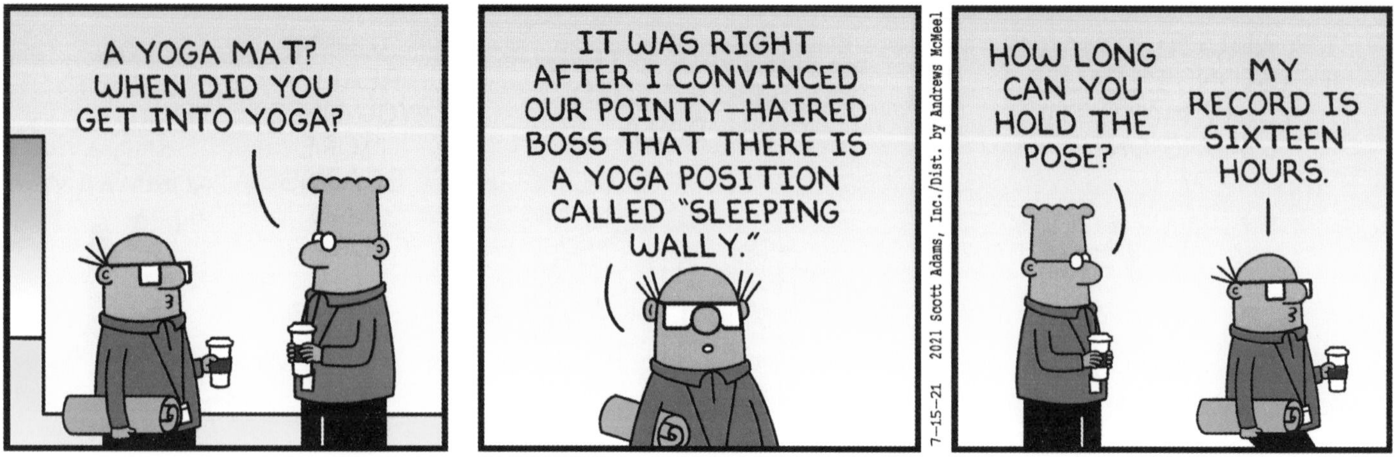
A YOGA MAT? WHEN DID YOU GET INTO YOGA?
IT WAS RIGHT AFTER I CONVINCED OUR POINTY-HAIRED BOSS THAT THERE IS A YOGA POSITION CALLED "SLEEPING WALLY."
7-15-21 2021 Scott Adams, Inc./Dist. by Andrews McMeel
HOW LONG CAN YOU HOLD THE POSE?
MY RECORD IS SIXTEEN HOURS.

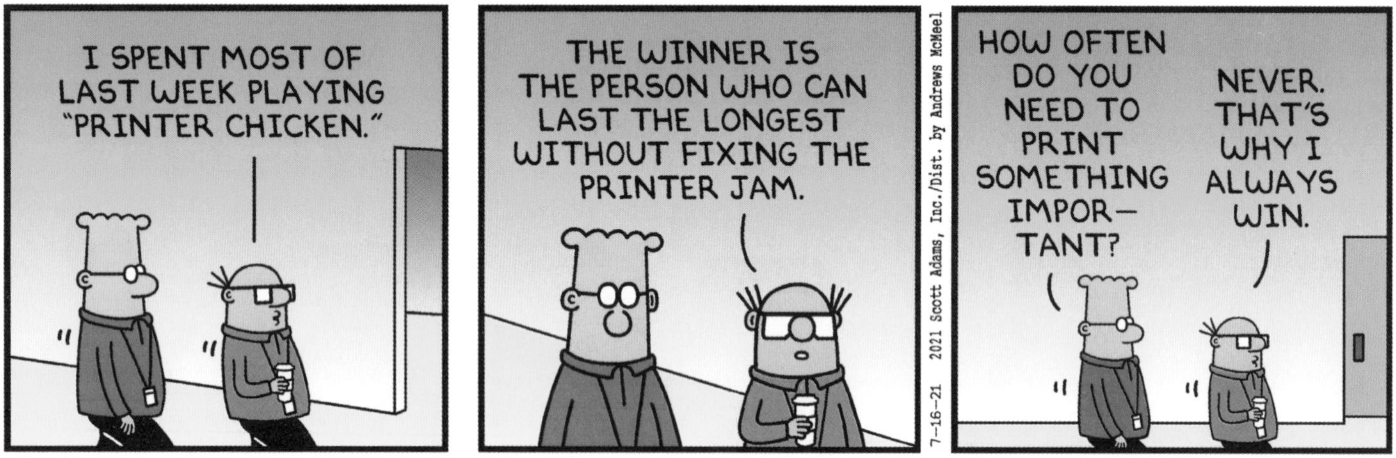
I SPENT MOST OF LAST WEEK PLAYING "PRINTER CHICKEN."
THE WINNER IS THE PERSON WHO CAN LAST THE LONGEST WITHOUT FIXING THE PRINTER JAM.
7-16-21 2021 Scott Adams, Inc./Dist. by Andrews McMeel
HOW OFTEN DO YOU NEED TO PRINT SOMETHING IMPOR-TANT?
NEVER. THAT'S WHY I ALWAYS WIN.

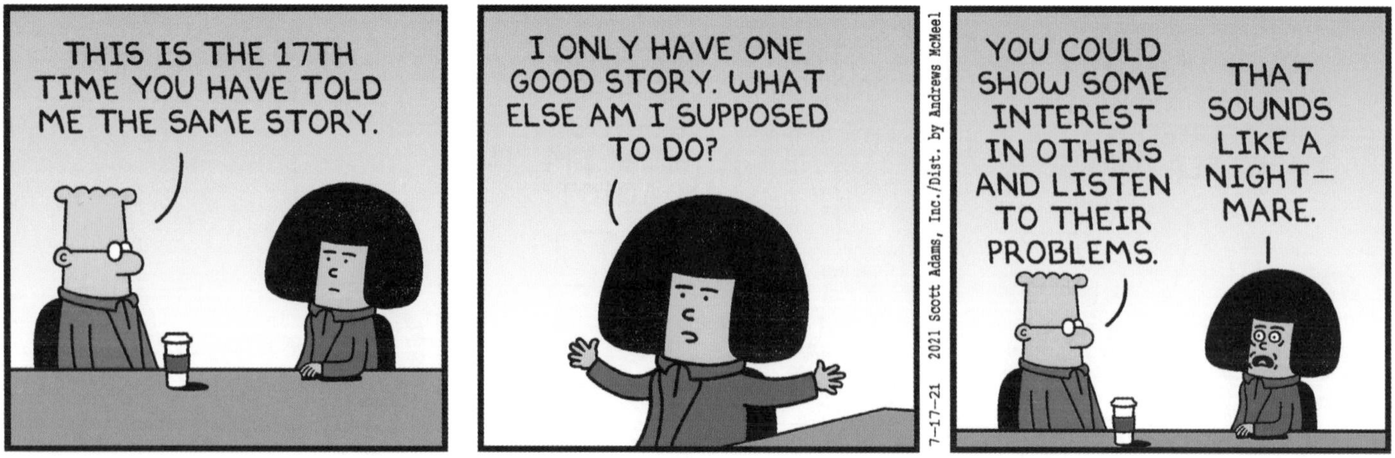
THIS IS THE 17TH TIME YOU HAVE TOLD ME THE SAME STORY.
I ONLY HAVE ONE GOOD STORY. WHAT ELSE AM I SUPPOSED TO DO?
7-17-21 2021 Scott Adams, Inc./Dist. by Andrews McMeel
YOU COULD SHOW SOME INTEREST IN OTHERS AND LISTEN TO THEIR PROBLEMS.
THAT SOUNDS LIKE A NIGHT-MARE.

I'M THINKING OF GETTING INTO CRYPTOCURRENCY TRADING.
DO YOU KNOW ANYTHING ABOUT IT?
NO.
THEN YOU SHOULD TOTALLY DO IT. THAT'S HOW YOU LEARN.
I'LL SET UP A CRYPTO WALLET AND MANAGE IT FOR YOU.
THANK YOU!
HOW MUCH SHOULD I PUT IN THERE?
AT LEAST 90% OF YOUR NET WORTH. THAT'S CALLED DIVERSIFICATION.
THEN NEVER LOOK AT IT AGAIN.
NEVER?
NEVER. UNLESS I DIE BEFORE YOU DO. THEN IT'S FINE.
© 2021 Scott Adams, Inc./Dist. by Andrews McMeel
7-18-21

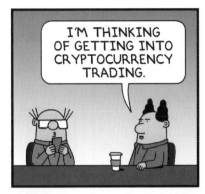

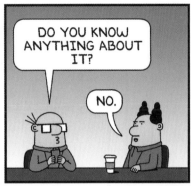

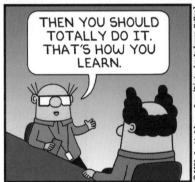

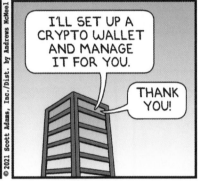

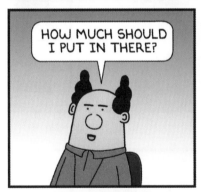

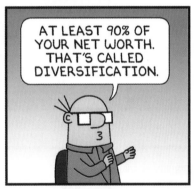

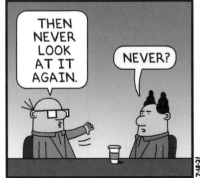

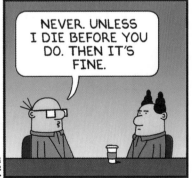

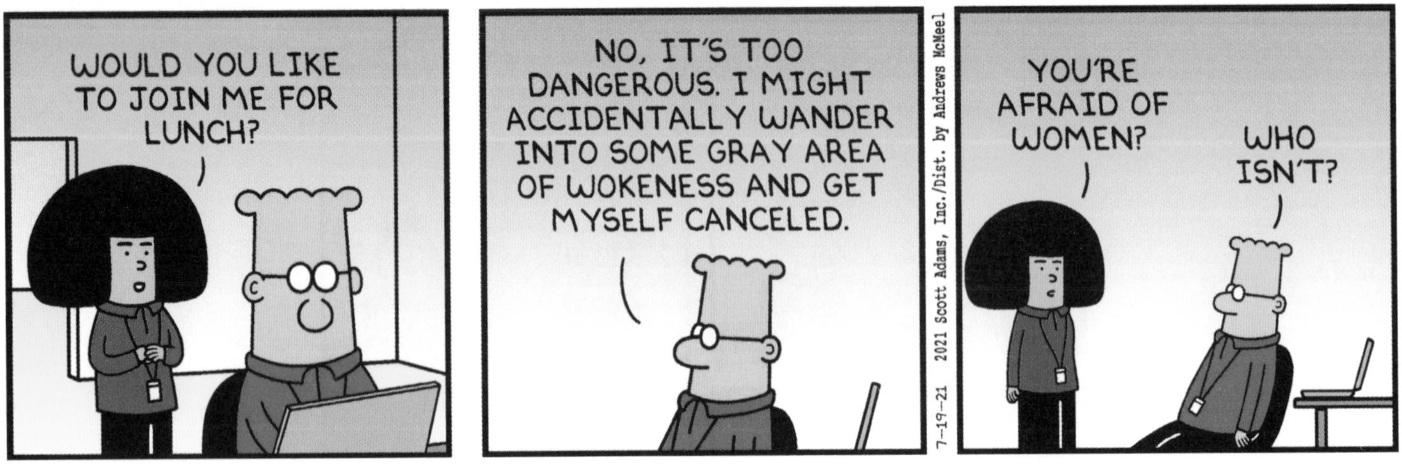
WOULD YOU LIKE TO JOIN ME FOR LUNCH?
NO, IT'S TOO DANGEROUS. I MIGHT ACCIDENTALLY WANDER INTO SOME GRAY AREA OF WOKENESS AND GET MYSELF CANCELED.
7-19-21 2021 Scott Adams, Inc./Dist. by Andrews McMeel
YOU'RE AFRAID OF WOMEN?
WHO ISN'T?

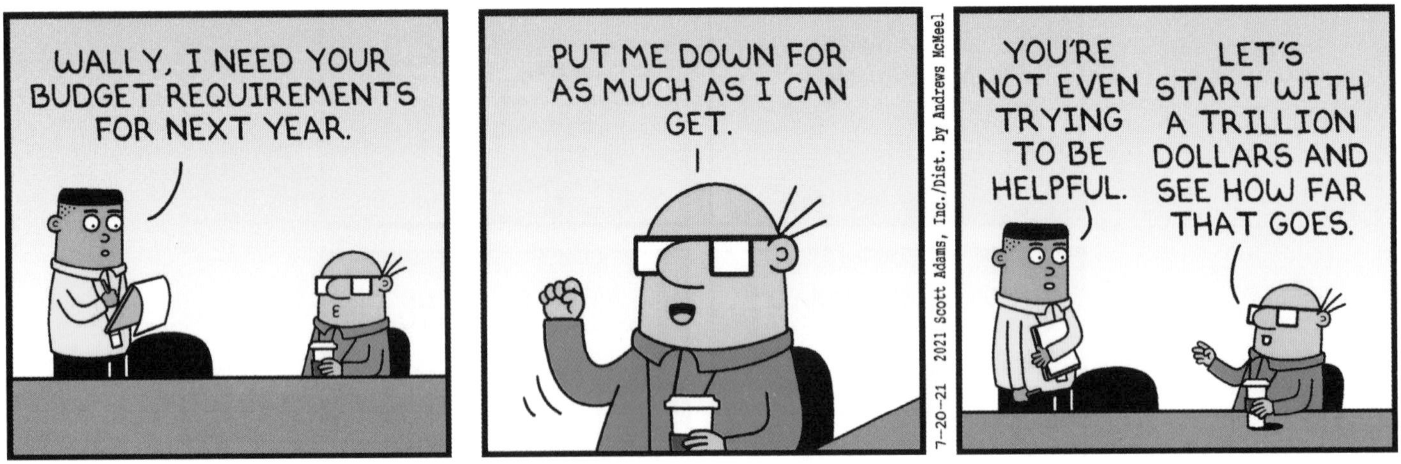
WALLY, I NEED YOUR BUDGET REQUIREMENTS FOR NEXT YEAR.
PUT ME DOWN FOR AS MUCH AS I CAN GET.
7-20-21 2021 Scott Adams, Inc./Dist. by Andrews McMeel
YOU'RE NOT EVEN TRYING TO BE HELPFUL.
LET'S START WITH A TRILLION DOLLARS AND SEE HOW FAR THAT GOES.

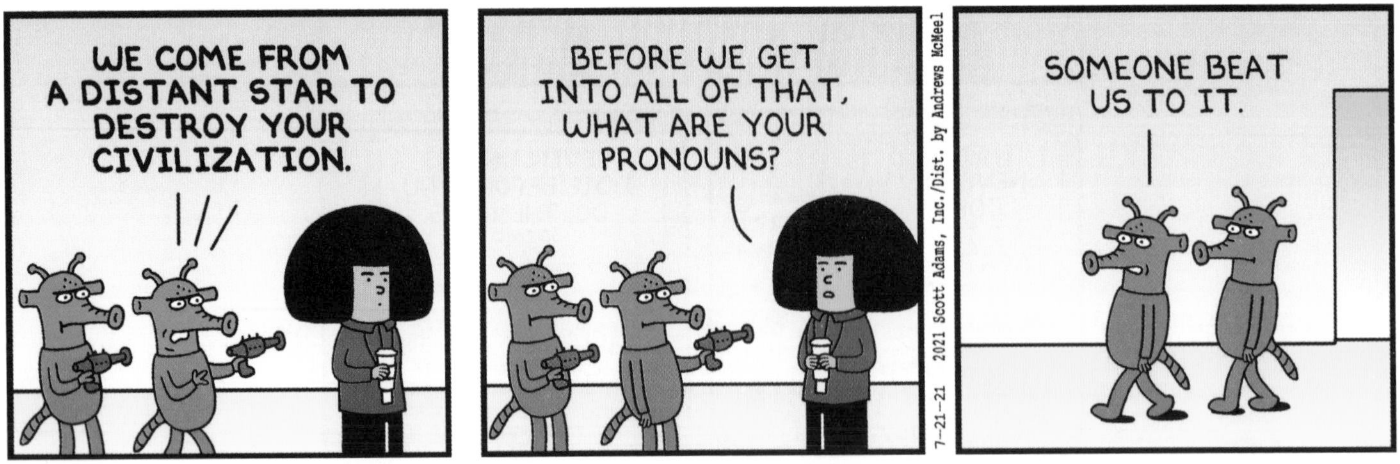
WE COME FROM A DISTANT STAR TO DESTROY YOUR CIVILIZATION.
BEFORE WE GET INTO ALL OF THAT, WHAT ARE YOUR PRONOUNS?
7-21-21 2021 Scott Adams, Inc./Dist. by Andrews McMeel
SOMEONE BEAT US TO IT.

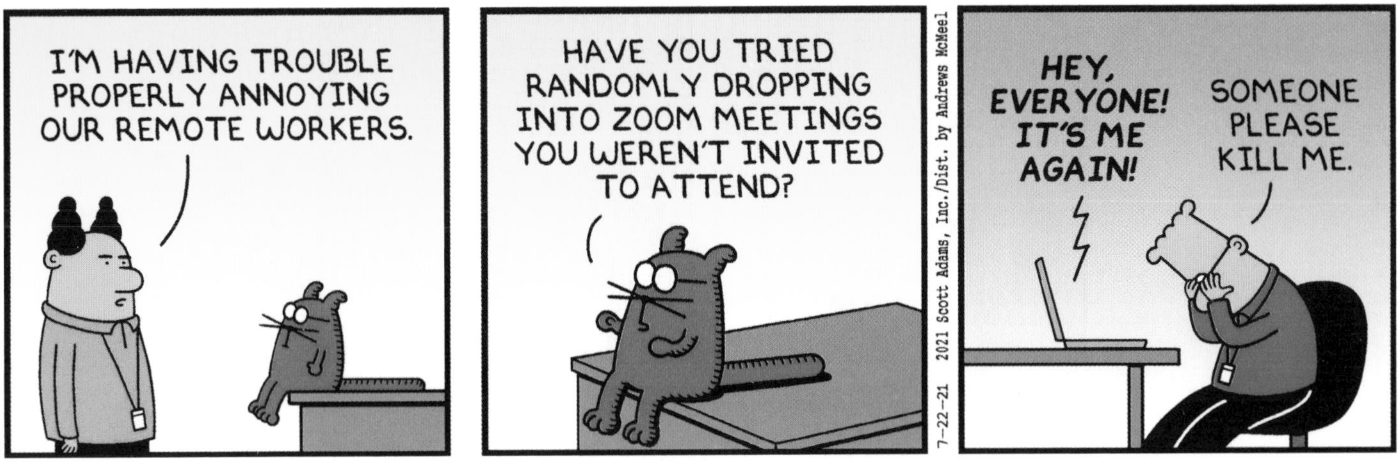
I'M HAVING TROUBLE PROPERLY ANNOYING OUR REMOTE WORKERS.
HAVE YOU TRIED RANDOMLY DROPPING INTO ZOOM MEETINGS YOU WEREN'T INVITED TO ATTEND?
7-22-21 © 2021 Scott Adams, Inc./Dist. by Andrews McMeel
HEY, EVERYONE! IT'S ME AGAIN!
SOMEONE PLEASE KILL ME.

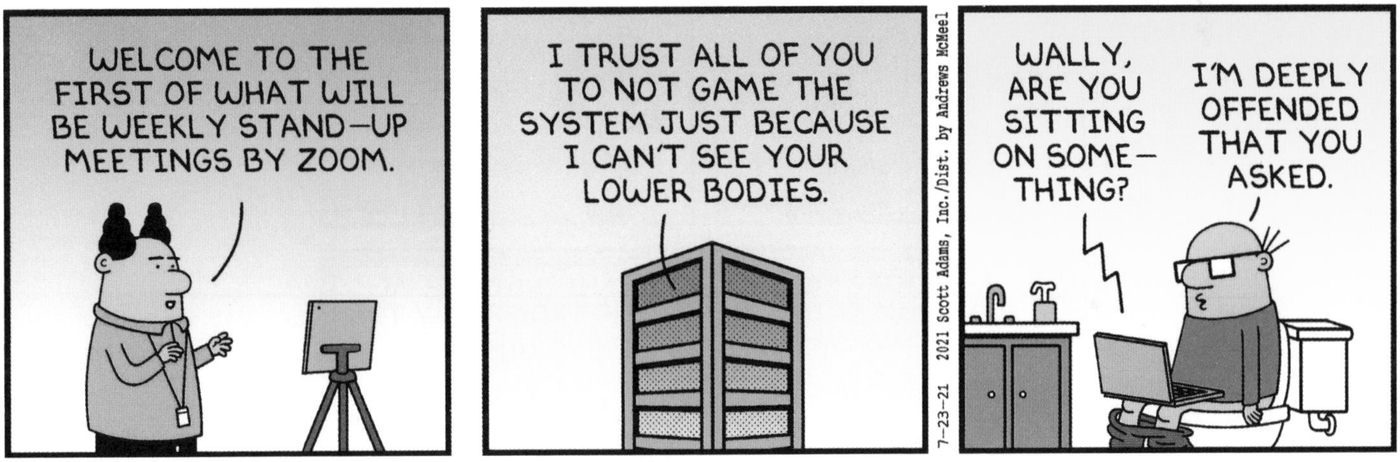
WELCOME TO THE FIRST OF WHAT WILL BE WEEKLY STAND-UP MEETINGS BY ZOOM.
I TRUST ALL OF YOU TO NOT GAME THE SYSTEM JUST BECAUSE I CAN'T SEE YOUR LOWER BODIES.
7-23-21 © 2021 Scott Adams, Inc./Dist. by Andrews McMeel
WALLY, ARE YOU SITTING ON SOME-THING?
I'M DEEPLY OFFENDED THAT YOU ASKED.

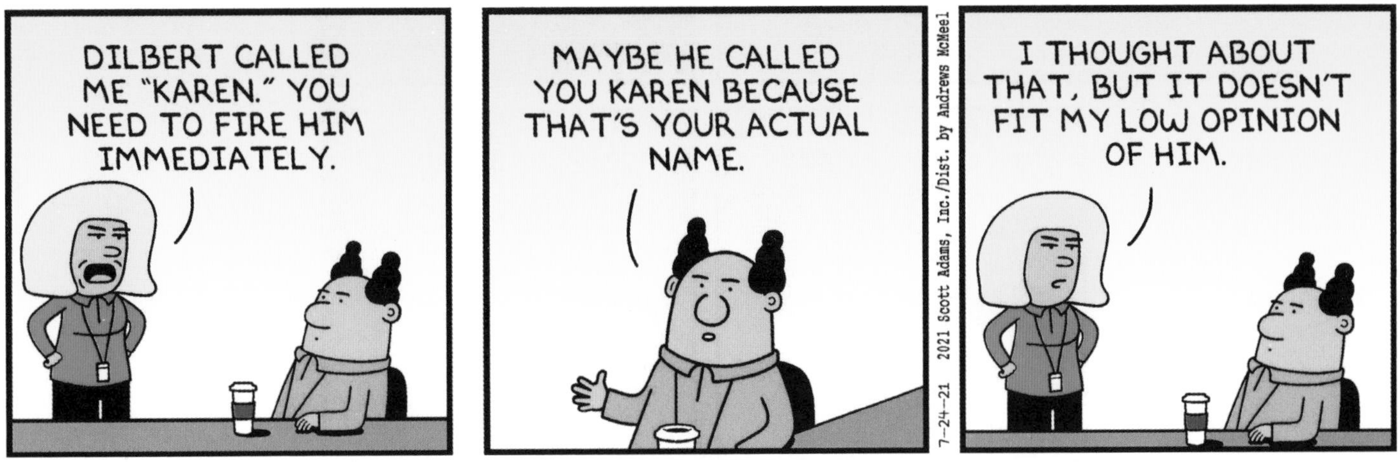
DILBERT CALLED ME "KAREN." YOU NEED TO FIRE HIM IMMEDIATELY.
MAYBE HE CALLED YOU KAREN BECAUSE THAT'S YOUR ACTUAL NAME.
7-24-21 © 2021 Scott Adams, Inc./Dist. by Andrews McMeel
I THOUGHT ABOUT THAT, BUT IT DOESN'T FIT MY LOW OPINION OF HIM.

DID YOU USE THE LAST OF THE PRINTER PAPER AND NEGLECT TO INFORM ANYONE TO BUY MORE?
NO, I DON'T EVEN USE THAT PRINTER. I USE THE ONE IN THE LAB.
IF YOU AREN'T GUILTY, WHY ARE YOU BEING SO DEFENSIVE?
I'M NOT BEING DEFENSIVE. I'M JUST TELLING YOU THE FACTS.
© 2021 Scott Adams, Inc./Dist. by Andrews McMeel
AND THERE YOU GO AGAIN, BEING DEFENSIVE. WHY CAN'T YOU ADMIT YOU WERE WRONG?
CAN YOU TEACH ME THE PROPER WAY TO BEHAVE WHEN I KNOW I'M RIGHT AND YOU'RE WRONG?
AND BY ANY CHANCE DID ***YOU*** USE THE LAST OF THE PAPER AND TELL NO ONE?
7-25-21
STOP MOVING THE GOAL POSTS.
AND THERE IT IS.

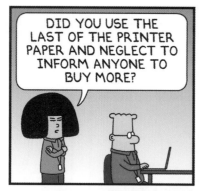

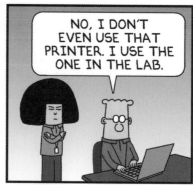

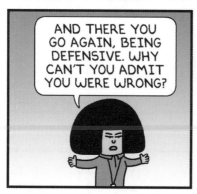

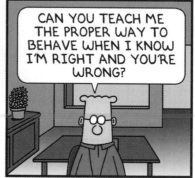

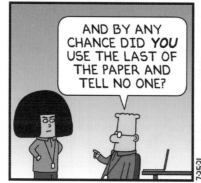

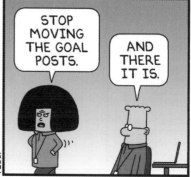

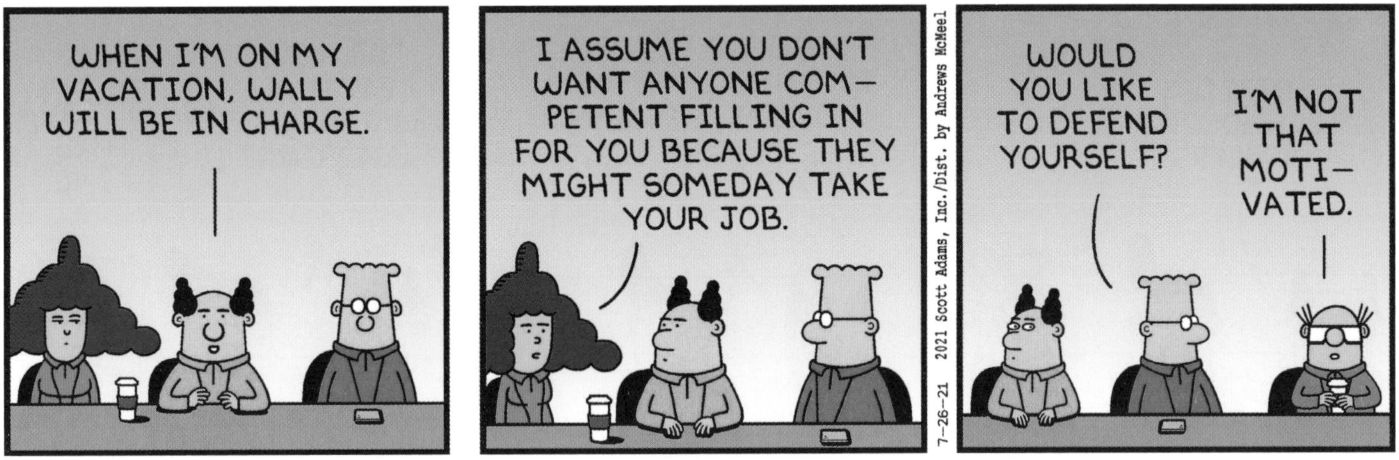
WHEN I'M ON MY VACATION, WALLY WILL BE IN CHARGE.
I ASSUME YOU DON'T WANT ANYONE COM-PETENT FILLING IN FOR YOU BECAUSE THEY MIGHT SOMEDAY TAKE YOUR JOB.
7-26-21 2021 Scott Adams, Inc./Dist. by Andrews McMeel
WOULD YOU LIKE TO DEFEND YOURSELF?
I'M NOT THAT MOTI-VATED.

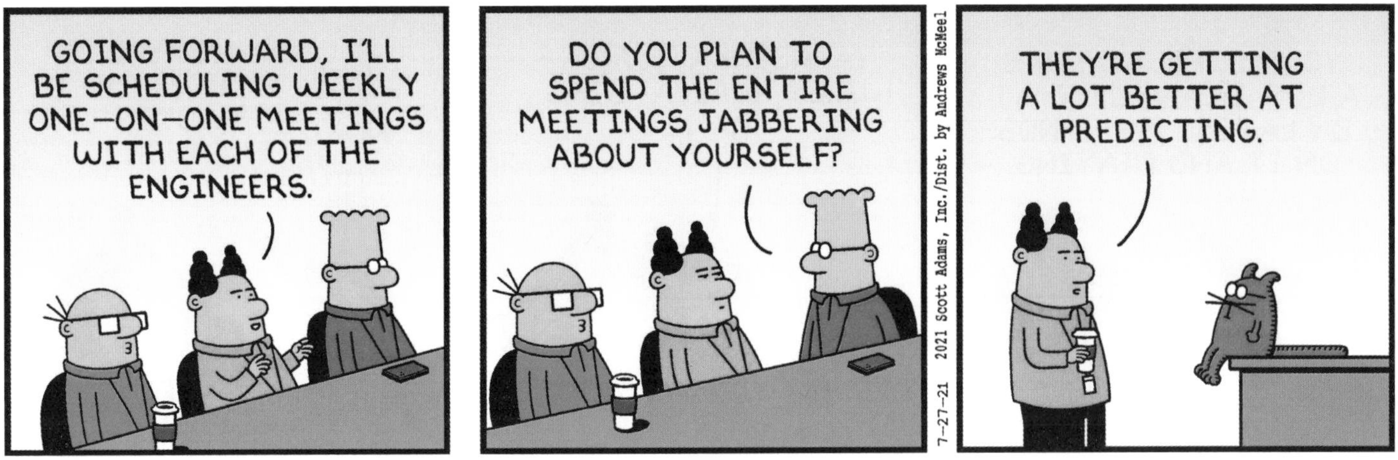
GOING FORWARD, I'LL BE SCHEDULING WEEKLY ONE-ON-ONE MEETINGS WITH EACH OF THE ENGINEERS.
DO YOU PLAN TO SPEND THE ENTIRE MEETINGS JABBERING ABOUT YOURSELF?
7-27-21 2021 Scott Adams, Inc./Dist. by Andrews McMeel
THEY'RE GETTING A LOT BETTER AT PREDICTING.

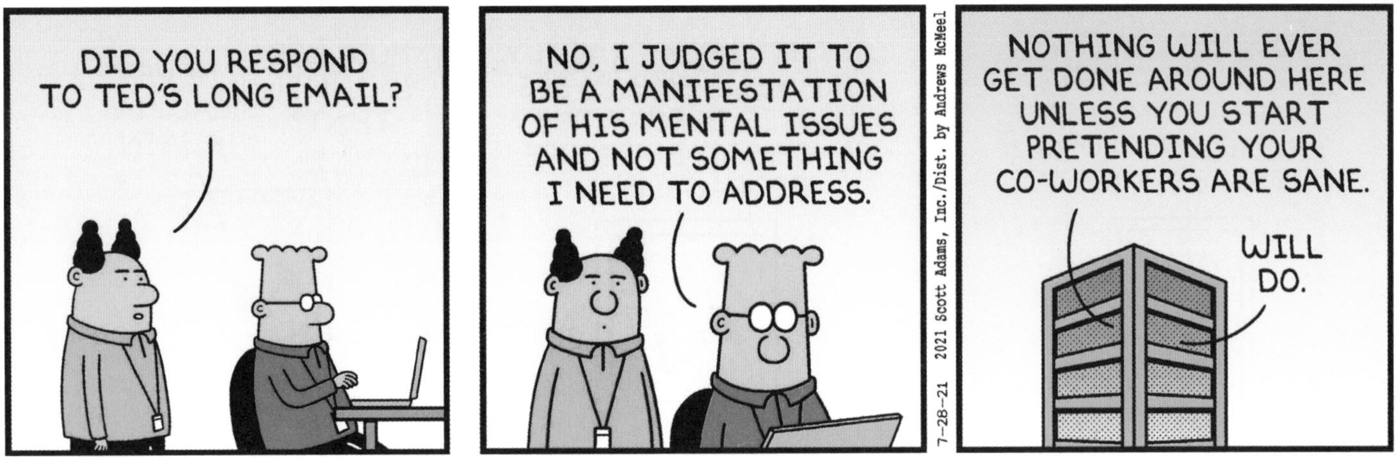
DID YOU RESPOND TO TED'S LONG EMAIL?
NO, I JUDGED IT TO BE A MANIFESTATION OF HIS MENTAL ISSUES AND NOT SOMETHING I NEED TO ADDRESS.
7-28-21 2021 Scott Adams, Inc./Dist. by Andrews McMeel
NOTHING WILL EVER GET DONE AROUND HERE UNLESS YOU START PRETENDING YOUR CO-WORKERS ARE SANE.
WILL DO.

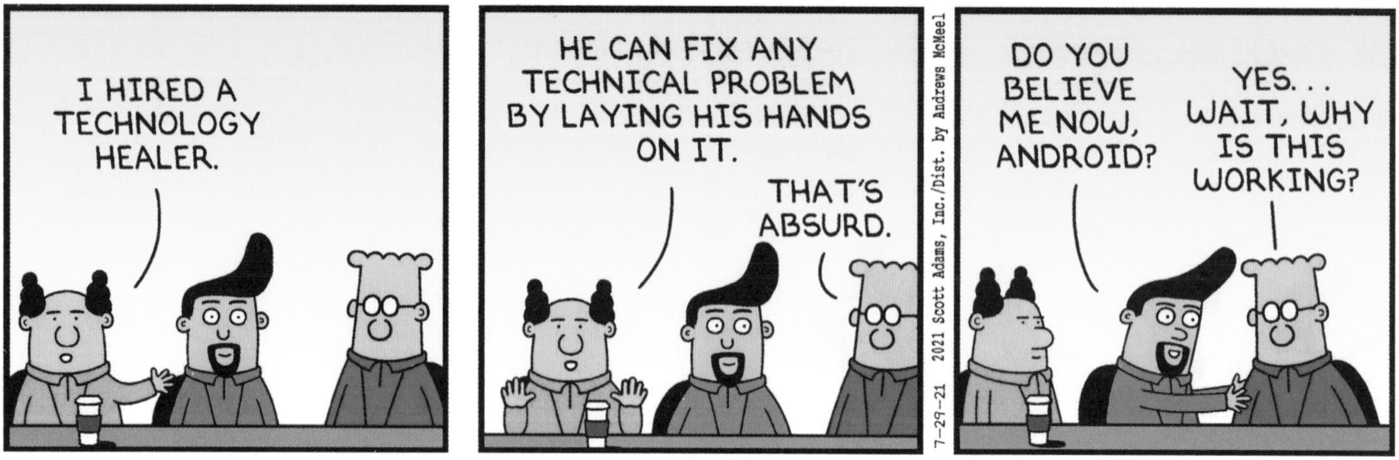
I HIRED A TECHNOLOGY HEALER.
HE CAN FIX ANY TECHNICAL PROBLEM BY LAYING HIS HANDS ON IT.
THAT'S ABSURD.
7-29-21 2021 Scott Adams, Inc./Dist. by Andrews McMeel
DO YOU BELIEVE ME NOW, ANDROID?
YES. . . WAIT, WHY IS THIS WORKING?

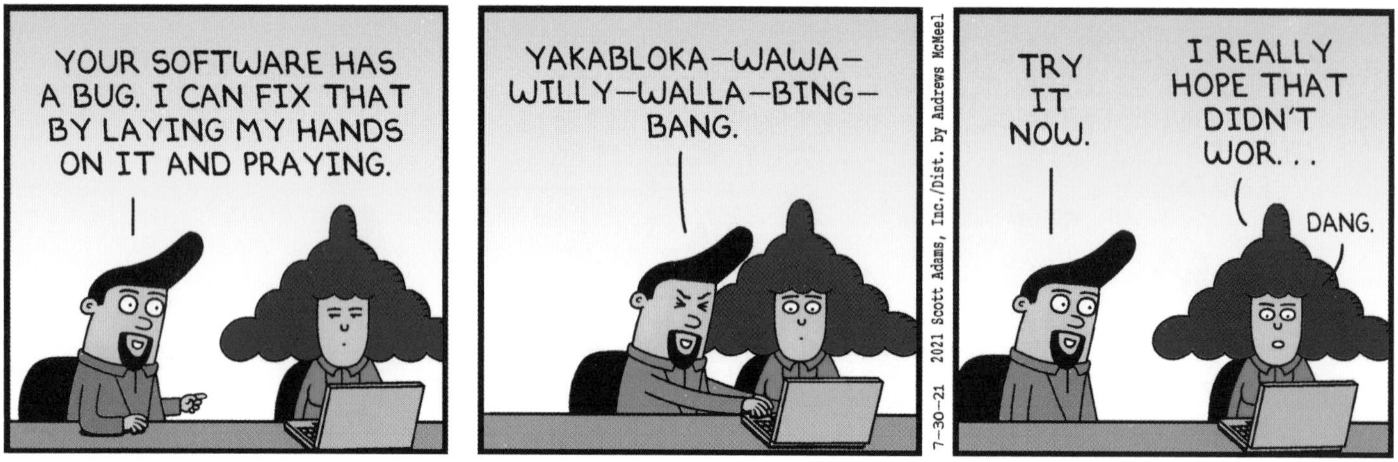
YOUR SOFTWARE HAS A BUG. I CAN FIX THAT BY LAYING MY HANDS ON IT AND PRAYING.
YAKABLOKA—WAWA—WILLY—WALLA—BING—BANG.
7-30-21 2021 Scott Adams, Inc./Dist. by Andrews McMeel
TRY IT NOW.
I REALLY HOPE THAT DIDN'T WOR. . .
DANG.

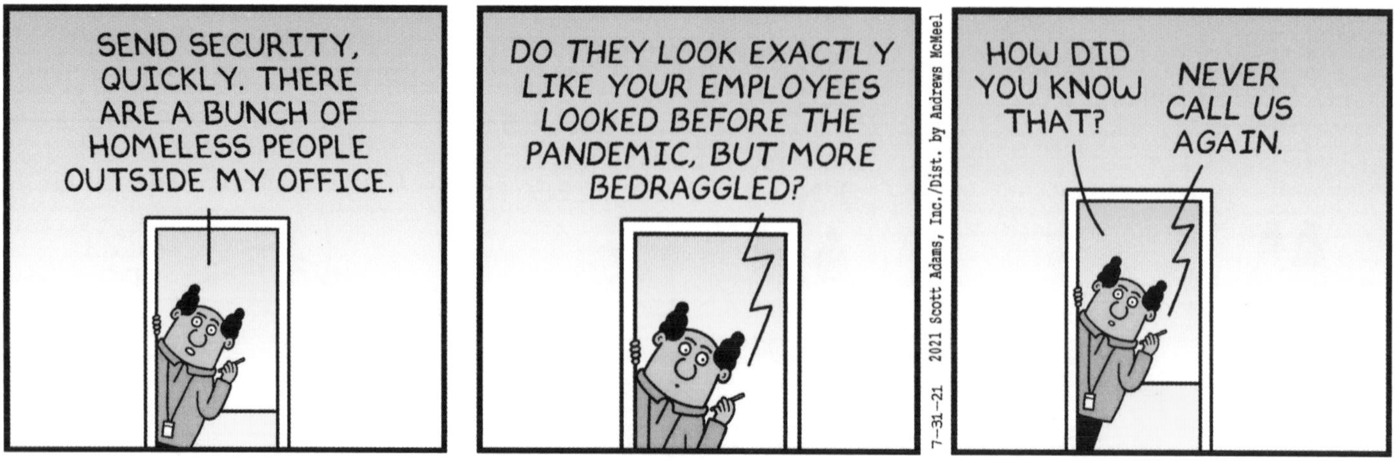
SEND SECURITY, QUICKLY. THERE ARE A BUNCH OF HOMELESS PEOPLE OUTSIDE MY OFFICE.
DO THEY LOOK EXACTLY LIKE YOUR EMPLOYEES LOOKED BEFORE THE PANDEMIC, BUT MORE BEDRAGGLED?
7-31-21 2021 Scott Adams, Inc./Dist. by Andrews McMeel
HOW DID YOU KNOW THAT?
NEVER CALL US AGAIN.

I INVENTED A TECHNOLOGY THAT WILL MANIPULATE PEOPLE'S BRAINS FOR OUR PROFIT.
SHHH!!! YOU CAN'T SAY THAT PART OUT LOUD.
TELL ME MORE.
THE TECHNOLOGY WILL CREATE CIVIL STRIFE AND DESTROY RELATIONSHIPS.
BUT WE WOULD MAKE LOTS OF MONEY?
LOTS AND LOTS.
I COULD FINALLY AFFORD THE TROPHY WIFE I ALWAYS WANTED!
SHHH!!! YOU CAN'T SAY THAT PART OUT LOUD.
WHAT IS THIS MIRACLE TECH-NOLOGY CALLED?
"SOCIAL MEDIA."
© 2021 Scott Adams, Inc./Dist. by Andrews McMeel
8-1-21

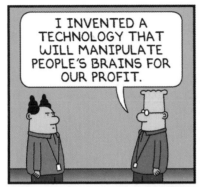

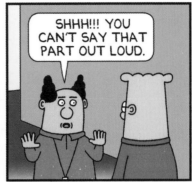

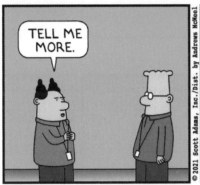

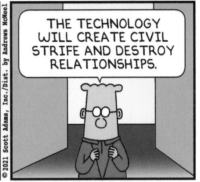

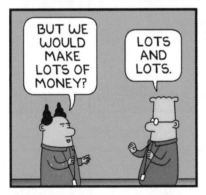

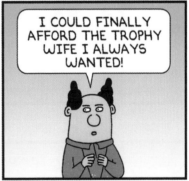

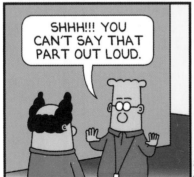

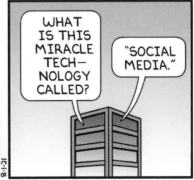

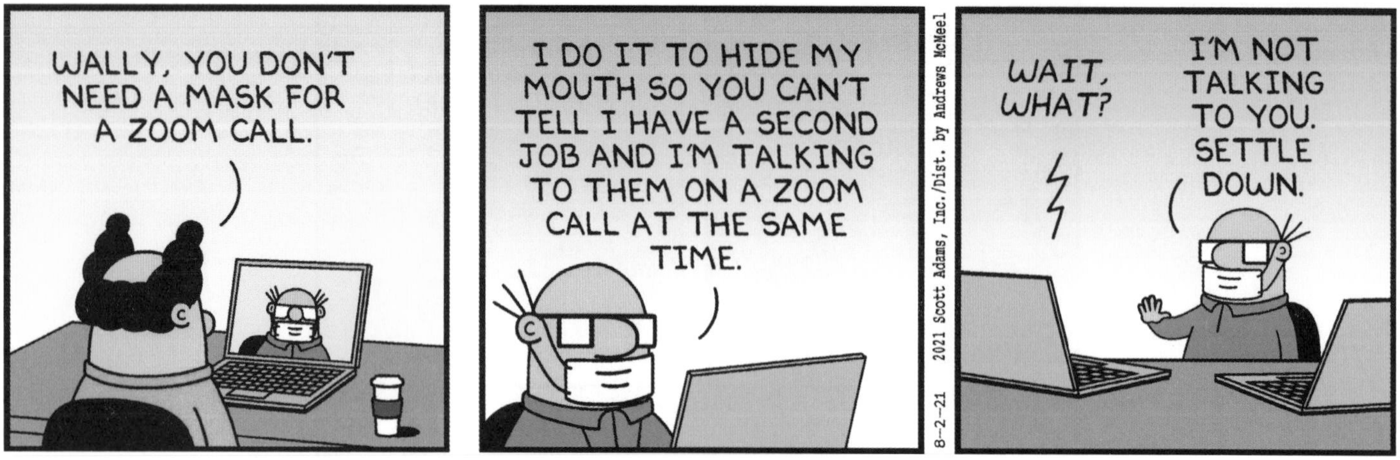
WALLY, YOU DON'T NEED A MASK FOR A ZOOM CALL.
I DO IT TO HIDE MY MOUTH SO YOU CAN'T TELL I HAVE A SECOND JOB AND I'M TALKING TO THEM ON A ZOOM CALL AT THE SAME TIME.
8-2-21 2021 Scott Adams, Inc./Dist. by Andrews McMeel
WAIT, WHAT?
I'M NOT TALKING TO YOU. SETTLE DOWN.

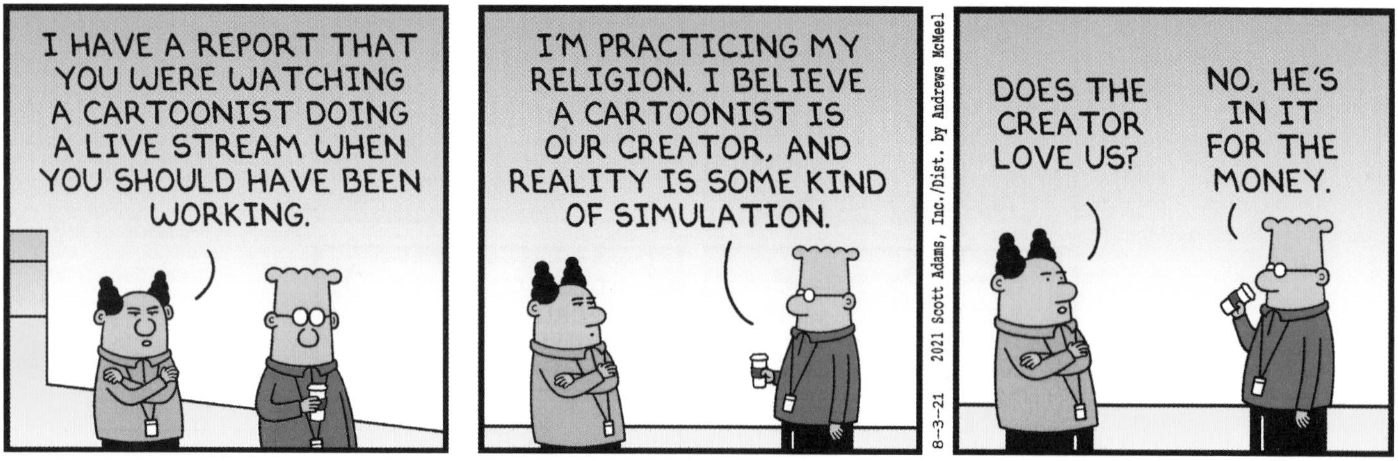
I HAVE A REPORT THAT YOU WERE WATCHING A CARTOONIST DOING A LIVE STREAM WHEN YOU SHOULD HAVE BEEN WORKING.
I'M PRACTICING MY RELIGION. I BELIEVE A CARTOONIST IS OUR CREATOR, AND REALITY IS SOME KIND OF SIMULATION.
8-3-21 2021 Scott Adams, Inc./Dist. by Andrews McMeel
DOES THE CREATOR LOVE US?
NO, HE'S IN IT FOR THE MONEY.

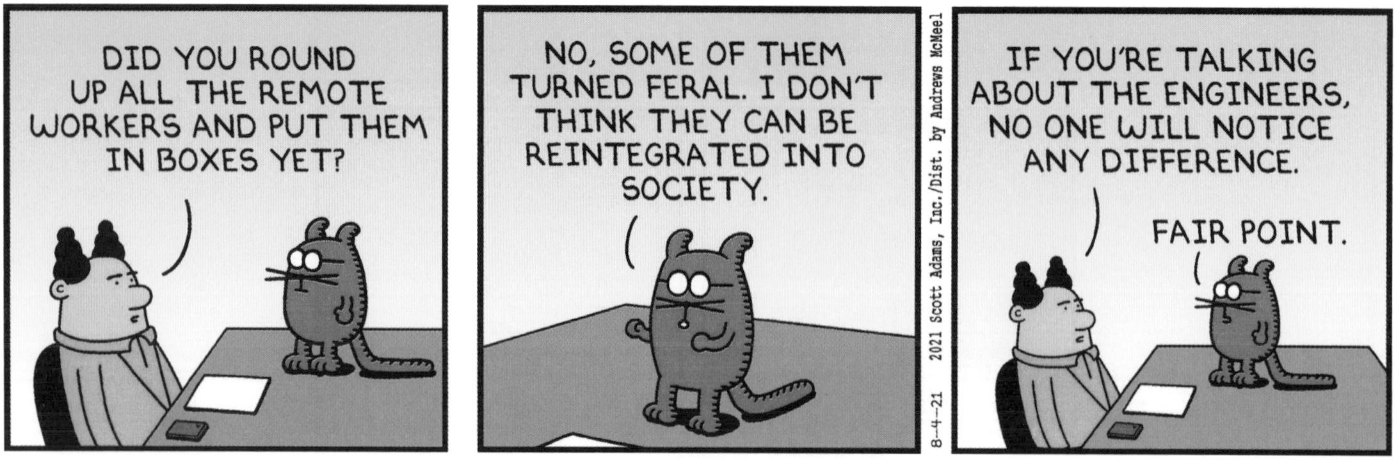
DID YOU ROUND UP ALL THE REMOTE WORKERS AND PUT THEM IN BOXES YET?
NO, SOME OF THEM TURNED FERAL. I DON'T THINK THEY CAN BE REINTEGRATED INTO SOCIETY.
8-4-21 2021 Scott Adams, Inc./Dist. by Andrews McMeel
IF YOU'RE TALKING ABOUT THE ENGINEERS, NO ONE WILL NOTICE ANY DIFFERENCE.
FAIR POINT.

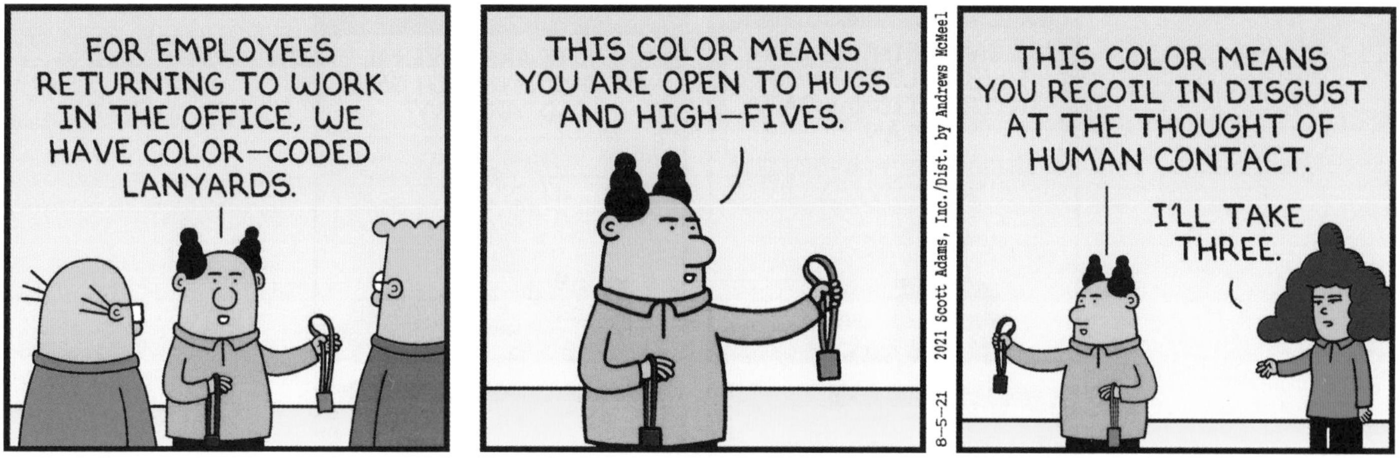
FOR EMPLOYEES RETURNING TO WORK IN THE OFFICE, WE HAVE COLOR-CODED LANYARDS.
THIS COLOR MEANS YOU ARE OPEN TO HUGS AND HIGH-FIVES.
8-5-21 2021 Scott Adams, Inc./Dist. by Andrews McMeel
THIS COLOR MEANS YOU RECOIL IN DISGUST AT THE THOUGHT OF HUMAN CONTACT.
I'LL TAKE THREE.

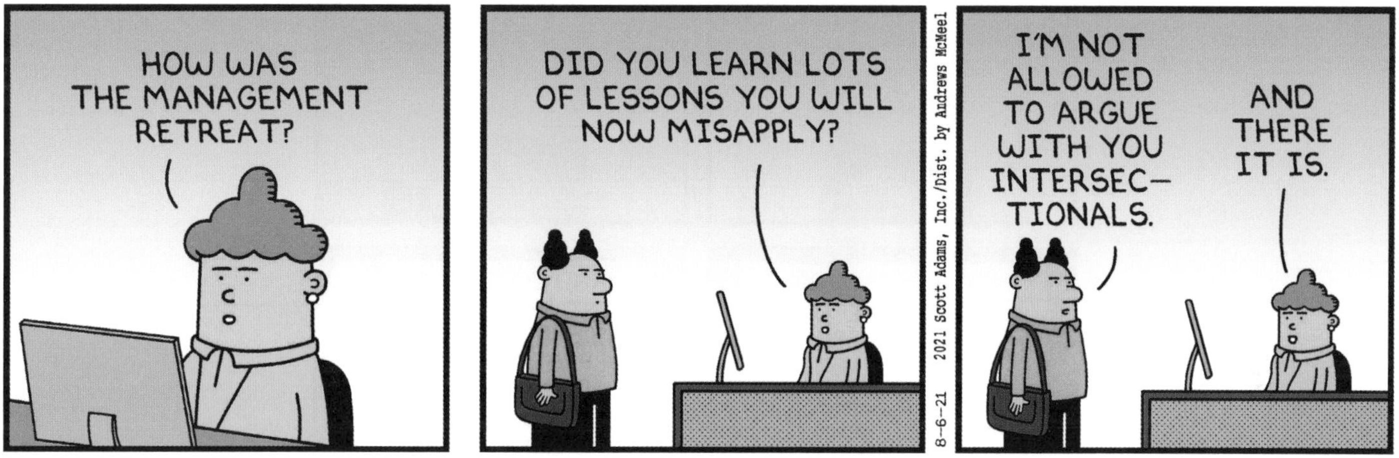
HOW WAS THE MANAGEMENT RETREAT?
DID YOU LEARN LOTS OF LESSONS YOU WILL NOW MISAPPLY?
8-6-21 2021 Scott Adams, Inc./Dist. by Andrews McMeel
I'M NOT ALLOWED TO ARGUE WITH YOU INTERSEC-TIONALS.
AND THERE IT IS.

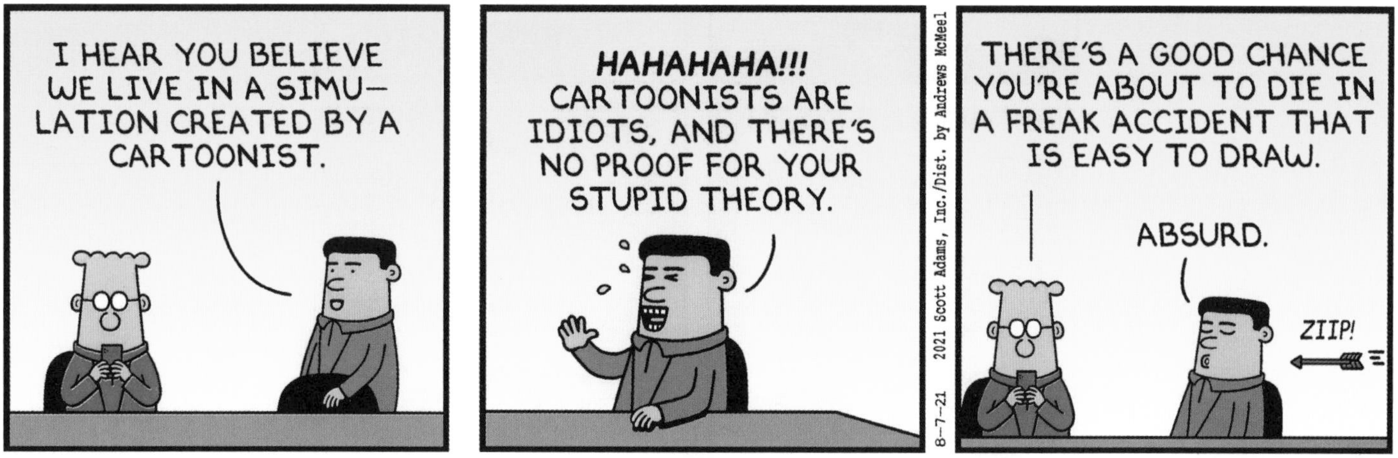
I HEAR YOU BELIEVE WE LIVE IN A SIMU-LATION CREATED BY A CARTOONIST.
HAHAHAHA!!! CARTOONISTS ARE IDIOTS, AND THERE'S NO PROOF FOR YOUR STUPID THEORY.
8-7-21 2021 Scott Adams, Inc./Dist. by Andrews McMeel
THERE'S A GOOD CHANCE YOU'RE ABOUT TO DIE IN A FREAK ACCIDENT THAT IS EASY TO DRAW.
ABSURD.
ZIIP!

I CAN'T FIND A WAY TO SIGN UP FOR YOUR INTERNATIONAL DATA PLAN.
THERE ARE SEVERAL METHODS. WHICH ONES DID YOU TRY?
I TRIED THE ONE THAT TAKES ME TO A DEAD LINK.
AND I TRIED THE ONE WHERE YOU SAY YOU'LL TEXT ME A CODE BUT YOU NEVER DO.
I TRIED THE APP MENU CHOICE THAT DOESN'T RESPOND TO CLICKS.
AND I TRIED THE LINK THAT BOUNCES ME FROM ONE SIGN-IN PAGE TO ANOTHER WITH NOTHING TO SHOW FOR IT.
AND NOW I'M CALLING TECH SUPPORT AS MY ONLY HOPE.
WE JUST CLOSED.
© 2021 Scott Adams, Inc./Dist. by Andrews McMeel
8-8-21

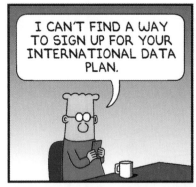

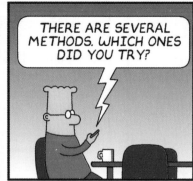

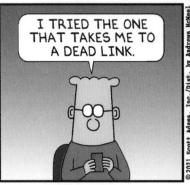

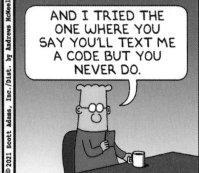

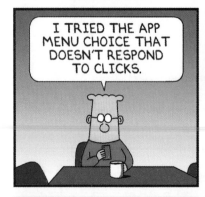

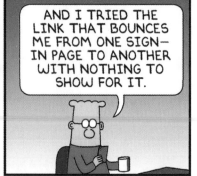

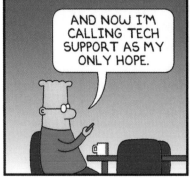

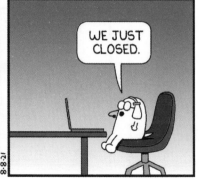

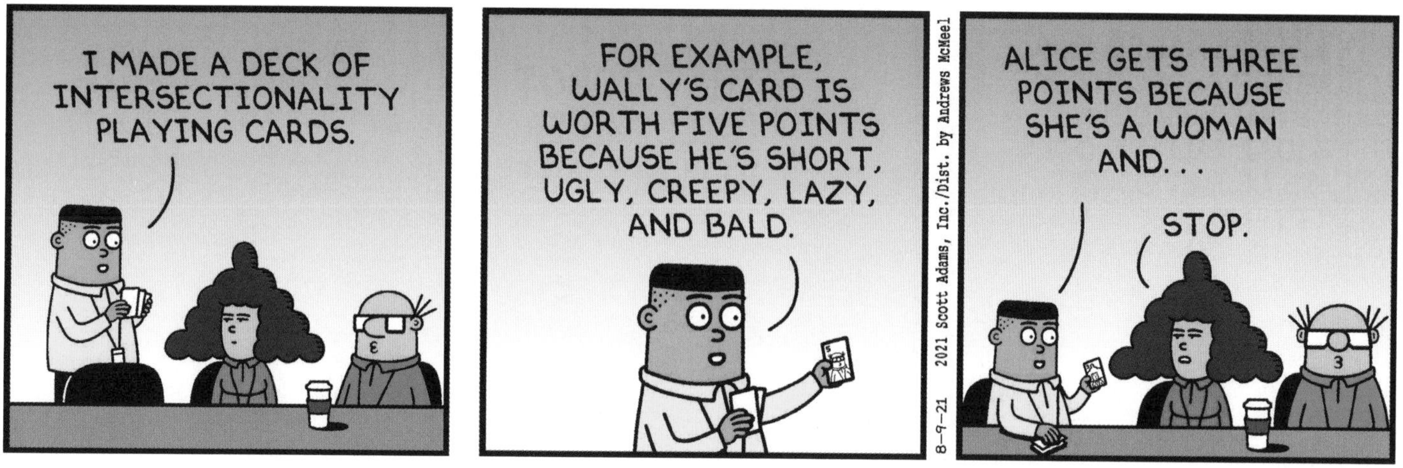
I MADE A DECK OF INTERSECTIONALITY PLAYING CARDS.
FOR EXAMPLE, WALLY'S CARD IS WORTH FIVE POINTS BECAUSE HE'S SHORT, UGLY, CREEPY, LAZY, AND BALD.
ALICE GETS THREE POINTS BECAUSE SHE'S A WOMAN AND. . .
STOP.

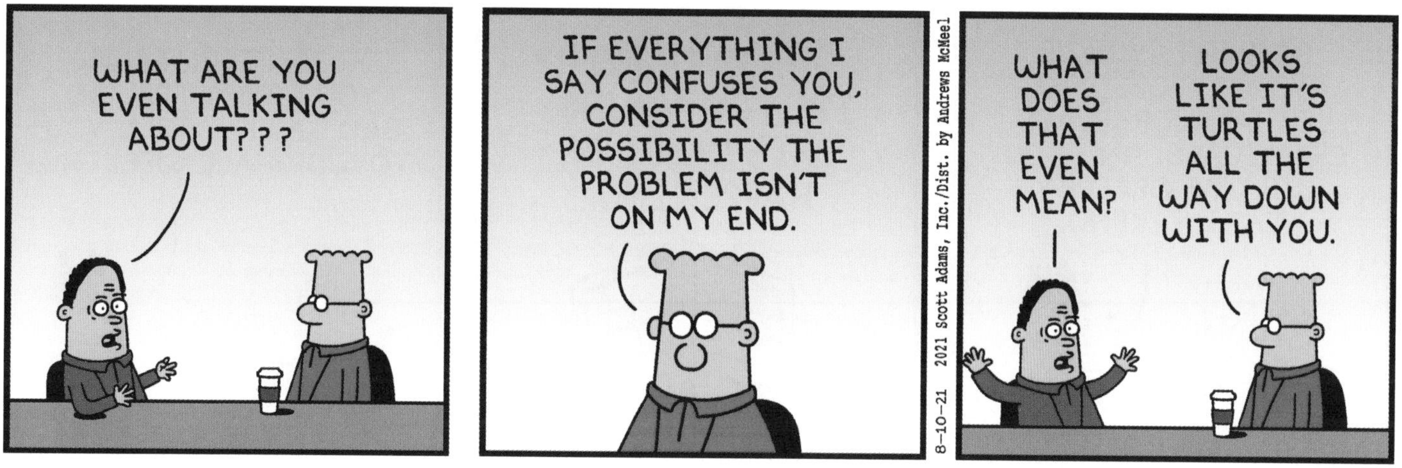
WHAT ARE YOU EVEN TALKING ABOUT???
IF EVERYTHING I SAY CONFUSES YOU, CONSIDER THE POSSIBILITY THE PROBLEM ISN'T ON MY END.
WHAT DOES THAT EVEN MEAN?
LOOKS LIKE IT'S TURTLES ALL THE WAY DOWN WITH YOU.

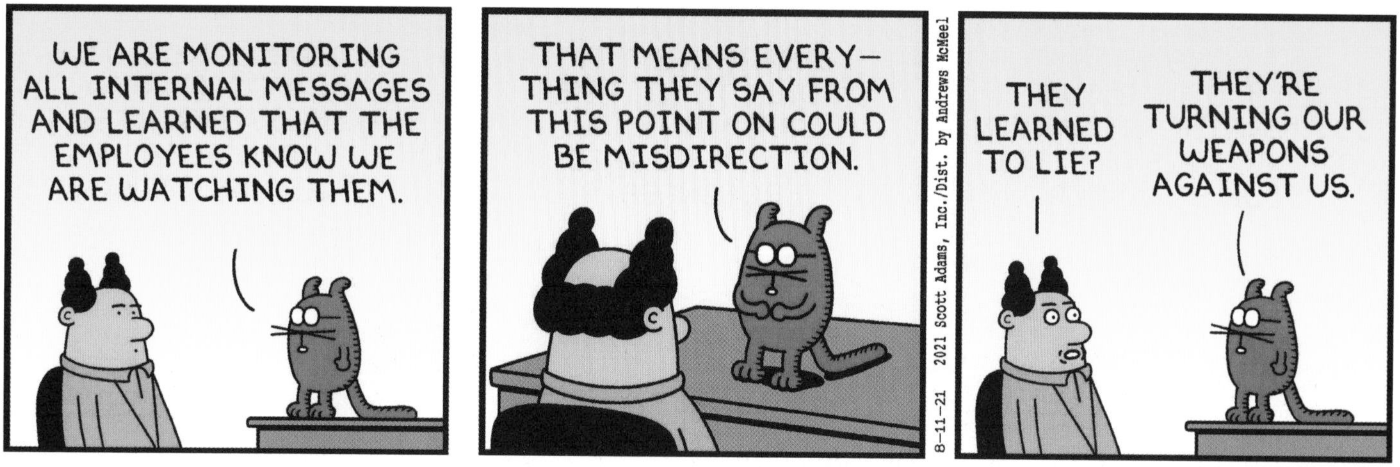
WE ARE MONITORING ALL INTERNAL MESSAGES AND LEARNED THAT THE EMPLOYEES KNOW WE ARE WATCHING THEM.
THAT MEANS EVERY-THING THEY SAY FROM THIS POINT ON COULD BE MISDIRECTION.
THEY LEARNED TO LIE?
THEY'RE TURNING OUR WEAPONS AGAINST US.

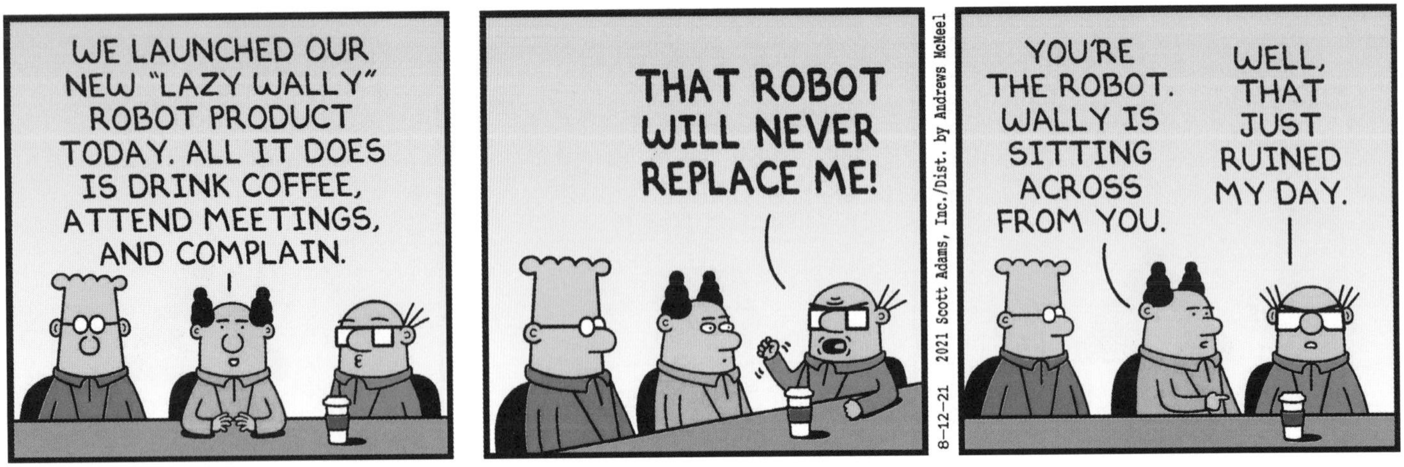
WE LAUNCHED OUR NEW "LAZY WALLY" ROBOT PRODUCT TODAY. ALL IT DOES IS DRINK COFFEE, ATTEND MEETINGS, AND COMPLAIN.
THAT ROBOT WILL NEVER REPLACE ME!
8-12-21 2021 Scott Adams, Inc./Dist. by Andrews McMeel
YOU'RE THE ROBOT. WALLY IS SITTING ACROSS FROM YOU.
WELL, THAT JUST RUINED MY DAY.

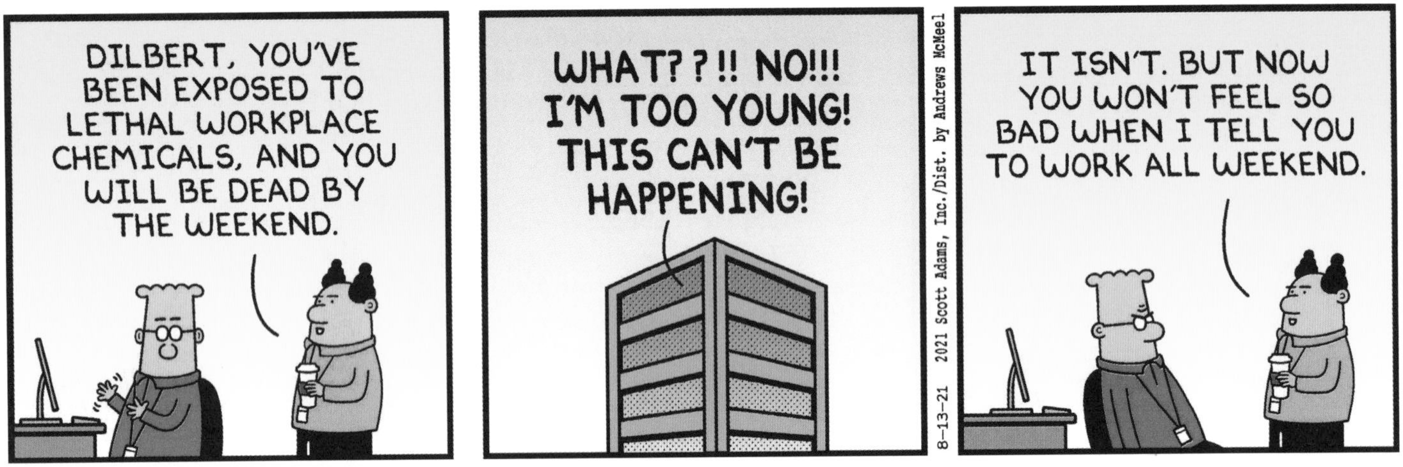
DILBERT, YOU'VE BEEN EXPOSED TO LETHAL WORKPLACE CHEMICALS, AND YOU WILL BE DEAD BY THE WEEKEND.
WHAT??!! NO!!! I'M TOO YOUNG! THIS CAN'T BE HAPPENING!
8-13-21 2021 Scott Adams, Inc./Dist. by Andrews McMeel
IT ISN'T. BUT NOW YOU WON'T FEEL SO BAD WHEN I TELL YOU TO WORK ALL WEEKEND.

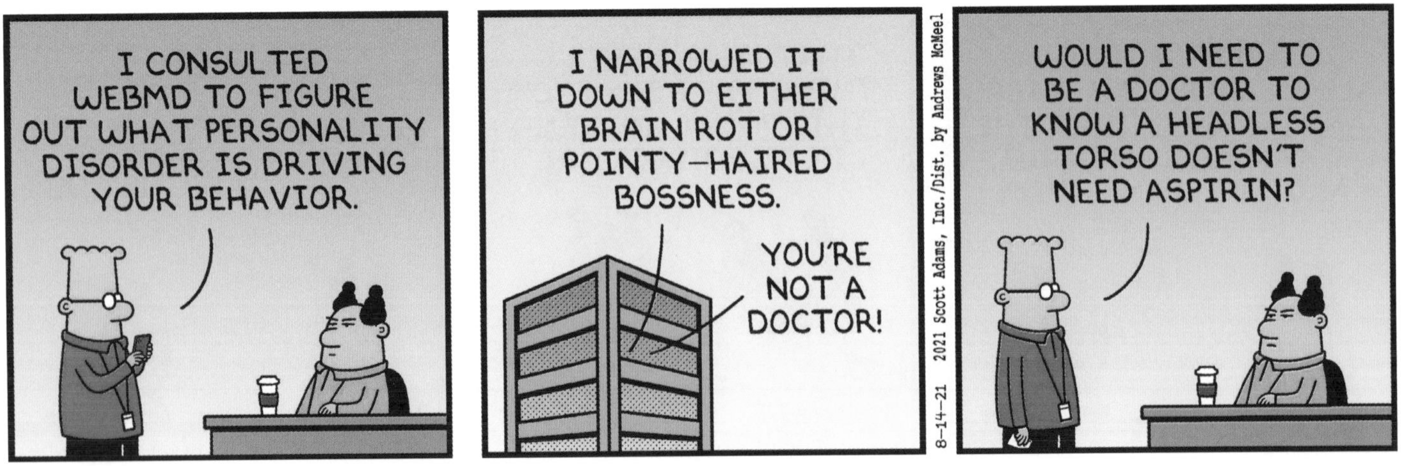
I CONSULTED WEBMD TO FIGURE OUT WHAT PERSONALITY DISORDER IS DRIVING YOUR BEHAVIOR.
I NARROWED IT DOWN TO EITHER BRAIN ROT OR POINTY-HAIRED BOSSNESS.
YOU'RE NOT A DOCTOR!
8-14-21 2021 Scott Adams, Inc./Dist. by Andrews McMeel
WOULD I NEED TO BE A DOCTOR TO KNOW A HEADLESS TORSO DOESN'T NEED ASPIRIN?

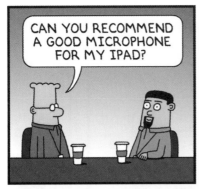

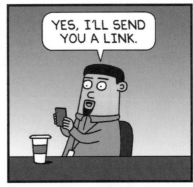

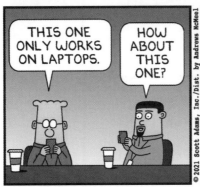

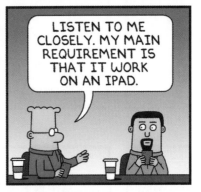

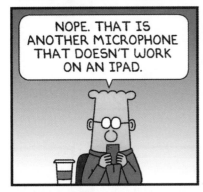

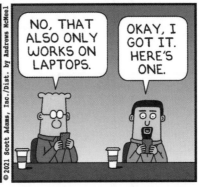

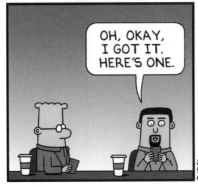

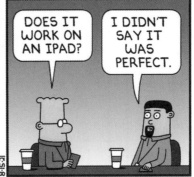

CAN YOU RECOMMEND A GOOD MICROPHONE FOR MY IPAD?
YES, I'LL SEND YOU A LINK.
THIS ONE ONLY WORKS ON LAPTOPS.
HOW ABOUT THIS ONE?
NO, THAT ALSO ONLY WORKS ON LAPTOPS.
OKAY, I GOT IT. HERE'S ONE.
NOPE. THAT IS ANOTHER MICROPHONE THAT DOESN'T WORK ON AN IPAD.
LISTEN TO ME CLOSELY. MY MAIN REQUIREMENT IS THAT IT WORK ON AN IPAD.
OH, OKAY, I GOT IT. HERE'S ONE.
DOES IT WORK ON AN IPAD?
I DIDN'T SAY IT WAS PERFECT.
© 2021 Scott Adams, Inc./Dist. by Andrews McMeel
8-15-21

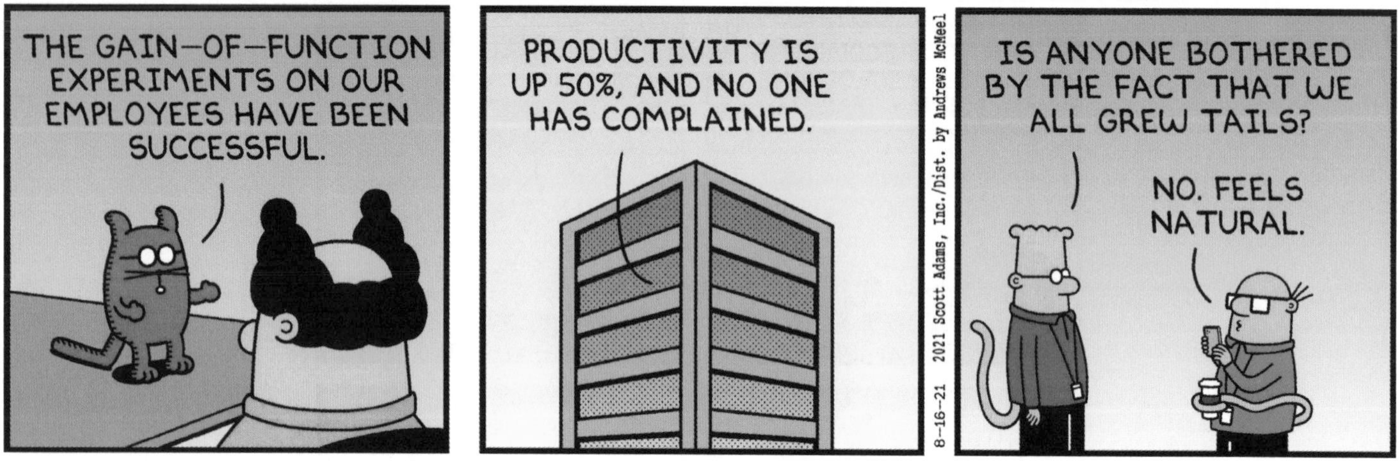
THE GAIN—OF—FUNCTION EXPERIMENTS ON OUR EMPLOYEES HAVE BEEN SUCCESSFUL.
PRODUCTIVITY IS UP 50%, AND NO ONE HAS COMPLAINED.
8-16-21 2021 Scott Adams, Inc./Dist. by Andrews McMeel
IS ANYONE BOTHERED BY THE FACT THAT WE ALL GREW TAILS?
NO. FEELS NATURAL.

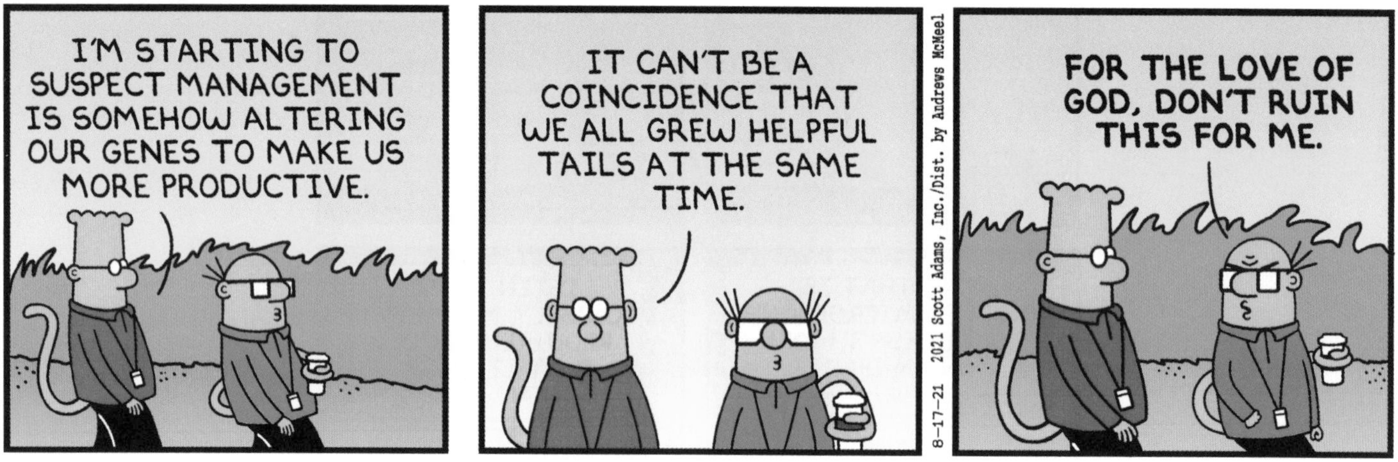
I'M STARTING TO SUSPECT MANAGEMENT IS SOMEHOW ALTERING OUR GENES TO MAKE US MORE PRODUCTIVE.
IT CAN'T BE A COINCIDENCE THAT WE ALL GREW HELPFUL TAILS AT THE SAME TIME.
8-17-21 2021 Scott Adams, Inc./Dist. by Andrews McMeel
FOR THE LOVE OF GOD, DON'T RUIN THIS FOR ME.

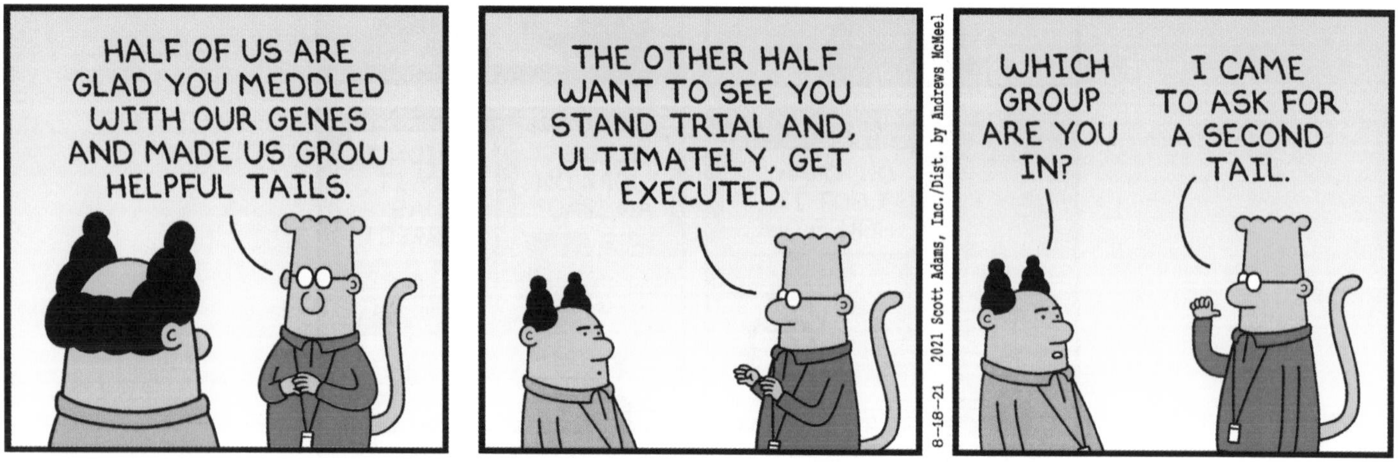
HALF OF US ARE GLAD YOU MEDDLED WITH OUR GENES AND MADE US GROW HELPFUL TAILS.
THE OTHER HALF WANT TO SEE YOU STAND TRIAL AND, ULTIMATELY, GET EXECUTED.
8-18-21 2021 Scott Adams, Inc./Dist. by Andrews McMeel
WHICH GROUP ARE YOU IN?
I CAME TO ASK FOR A SECOND TAIL.

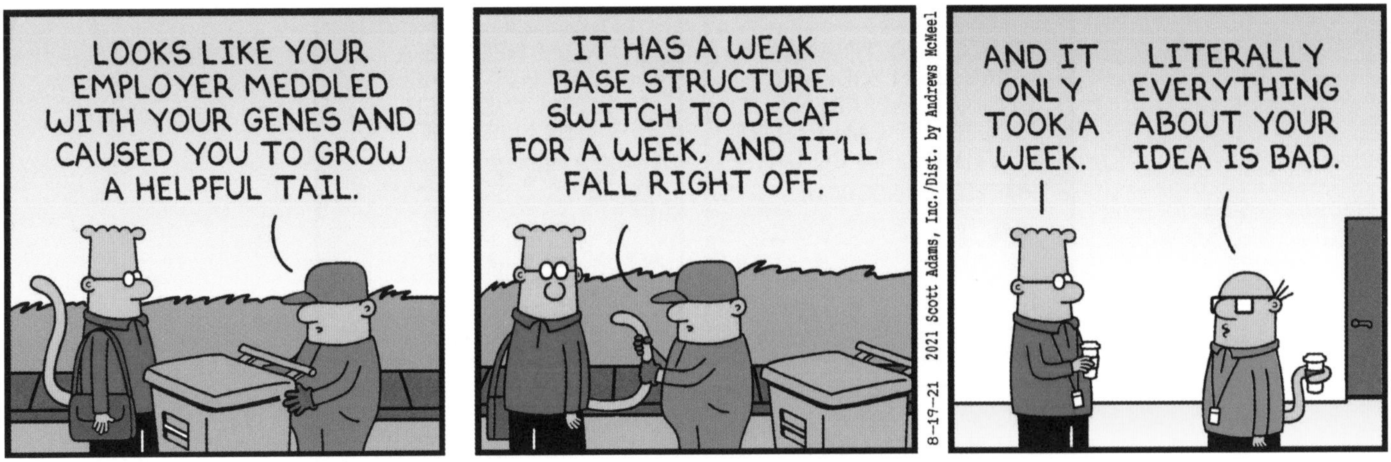
LOOKS LIKE YOUR EMPLOYER MEDDLED WITH YOUR GENES AND CAUSED YOU TO GROW A HELPFUL TAIL.
IT HAS A WEAK BASE STRUCTURE. SWITCH TO DECAF FOR A WEEK, AND IT'LL FALL RIGHT OFF.
8-19-21 2021 Scott Adams, Inc./Dist. by Andrews McMeel
AND IT ONLY TOOK A WEEK.
LITERALLY EVERYTHING ABOUT YOUR IDEA IS BAD.

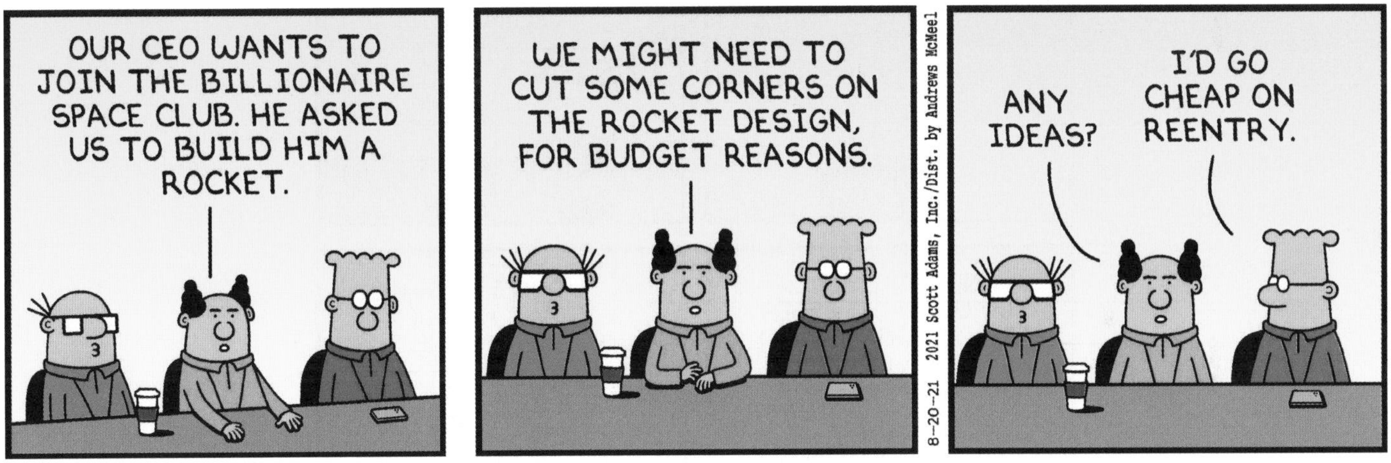
OUR CEO WANTS TO JOIN THE BILLIONAIRE SPACE CLUB. HE ASKED US TO BUILD HIM A ROCKET.
WE MIGHT NEED TO CUT SOME CORNERS ON THE ROCKET DESIGN, FOR BUDGET REASONS.
8-20-21 2021 Scott Adams, Inc./Dist. by Andrews McMeel
ANY IDEAS?
I'D GO CHEAP ON REENTRY.

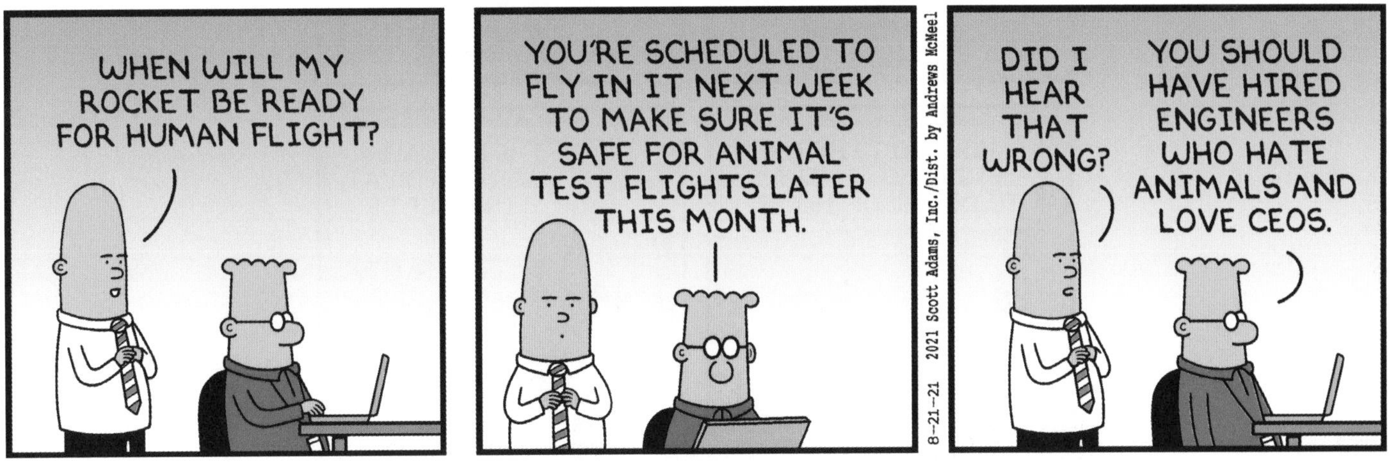
WHEN WILL MY ROCKET BE READY FOR HUMAN FLIGHT?
YOU'RE SCHEDULED TO FLY IN IT NEXT WEEK TO MAKE SURE IT'S SAFE FOR ANIMAL TEST FLIGHTS LATER THIS MONTH.
8-21-21 2021 Scott Adams, Inc./Dist. by Andrews McMeel
DID I HEAR THAT WRONG?
YOU SHOULD HAVE HIRED ENGINEERS WHO HATE ANIMALS AND LOVE CEOS.

I DECIDED TO START MY OWN PODCAST BECAUSE, APPARENTLY, ANY IDIOT CAN FIGURE OUT HOW TO DO ONE.
ALL I NEED IS A TINY BIT OF HELP WITH THE TECH-NICAL STUFF.
DO YOU PLAN TO USE A CONDENSER MICROPHONE?
BECAUSE IF YOU DO, YOU'LL NEED PHANTOM POWER TO POLARIZE ITS TRANSDUCER ELEMENT.
AND MAKE SURE YOU USE A DE-ESSER SO YOU DON'T SOUND LIKE A SNAKE.
I DON'T KNOW WHAT ANY OF THAT MEANS.
HOW DO IDIOTS FIGURE OUT HOW TO DO ALL OF THAT?
THEY USUALLY ASK ME FOR A TINY BIT OF HELP.
© 2021 Scott Adams, Inc./Dist. by Andrews McMeel
8-22-21

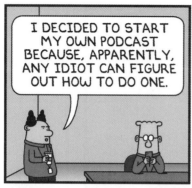

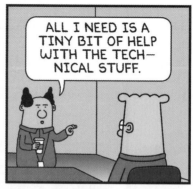

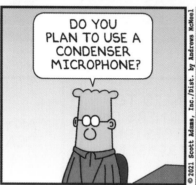

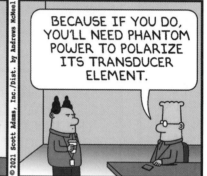

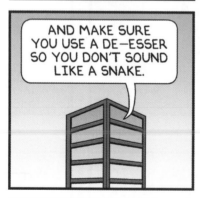

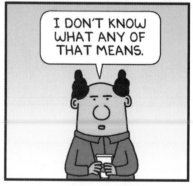

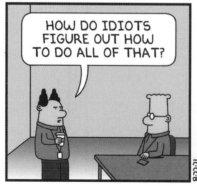

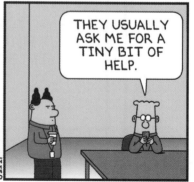

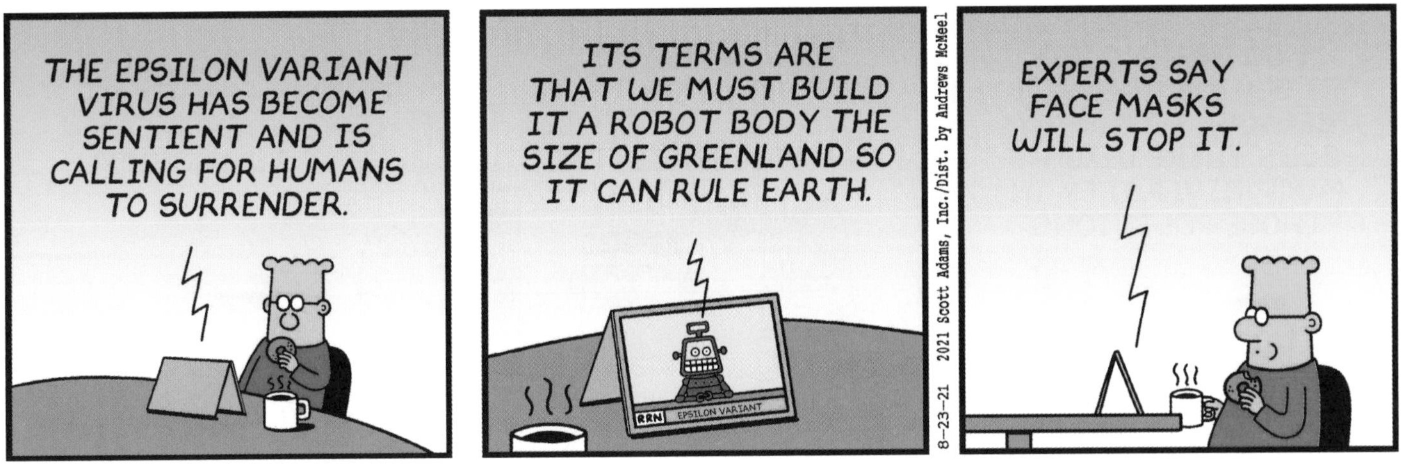
THE EPSILON VARIANT VIRUS HAS BECOME SENTIENT AND IS CALLING FOR HUMANS TO SURRENDER.
ITS TERMS ARE THAT WE MUST BUILD IT A ROBOT BODY THE SIZE OF GREENLAND SO IT CAN RULE EARTH.
RRN
EPSILON VARIANT
8-23-21 2021 Scott Adams, Inc./Dist. by Andrews McMeel
EXPERTS SAY FACE MASKS WILL STOP IT.

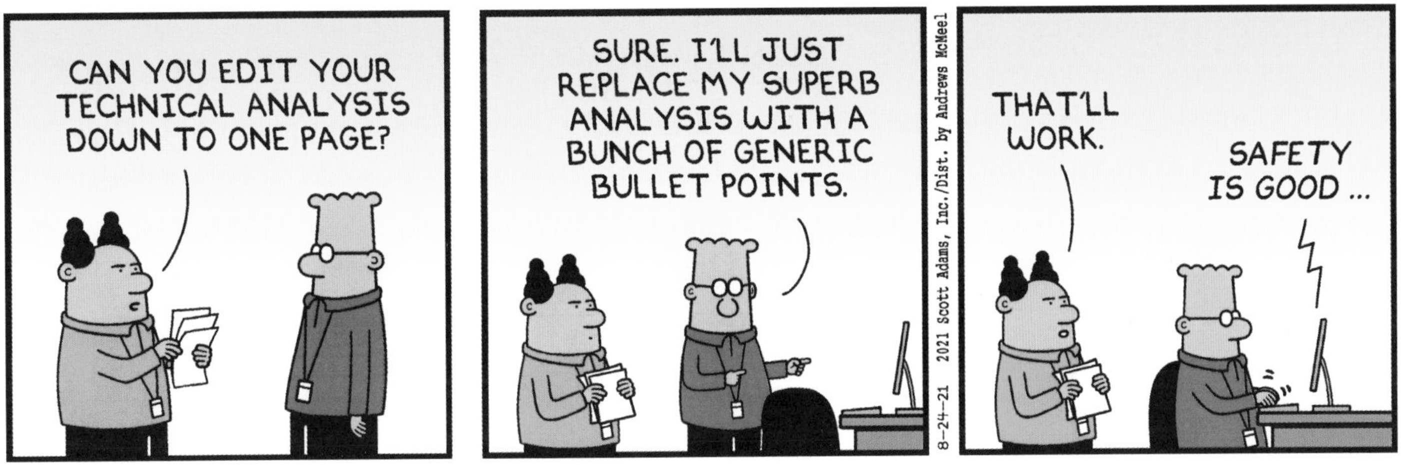
CAN YOU EDIT YOUR TECHNICAL ANALYSIS DOWN TO ONE PAGE?
SURE. I'LL JUST REPLACE MY SUPERB ANALYSIS WITH A BUNCH OF GENERIC BULLET POINTS.
8-24-21 2021 Scott Adams, Inc./Dist. by Andrews McMeel
THAT'LL WORK.
SAFETY IS GOOD ...

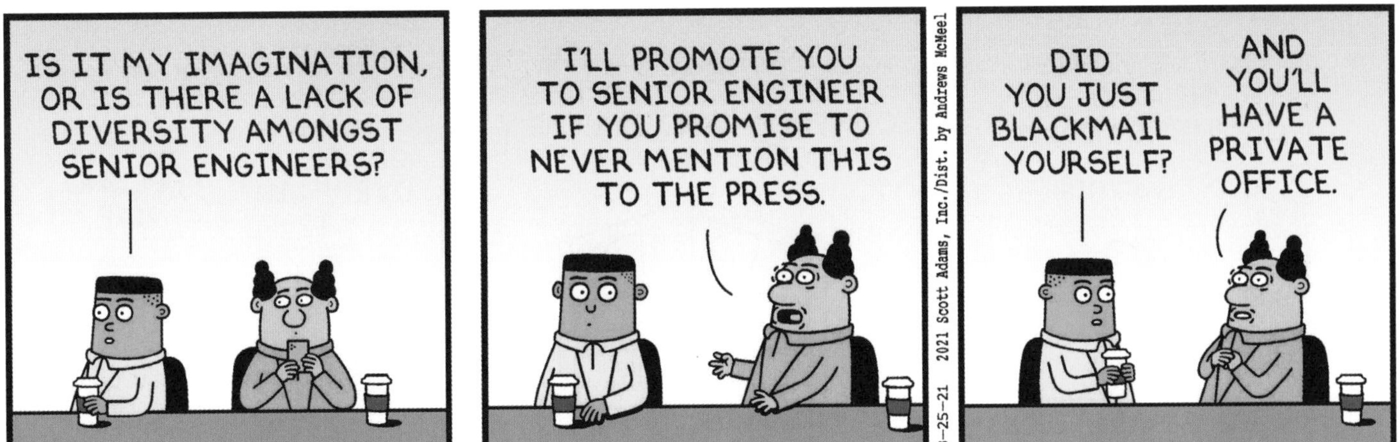
IS IT MY IMAGINATION, OR IS THERE A LACK OF DIVERSITY AMONGST SENIOR ENGINEERS?
I'LL PROMOTE YOU TO SENIOR ENGINEER IF YOU PROMISE TO NEVER MENTION THIS TO THE PRESS.
8-25-21 2021 Scott Adams, Inc./Dist. by Andrews McMeel
DID YOU JUST BLACKMAIL YOURSELF?
AND YOU'LL HAVE A PRIVATE OFFICE.

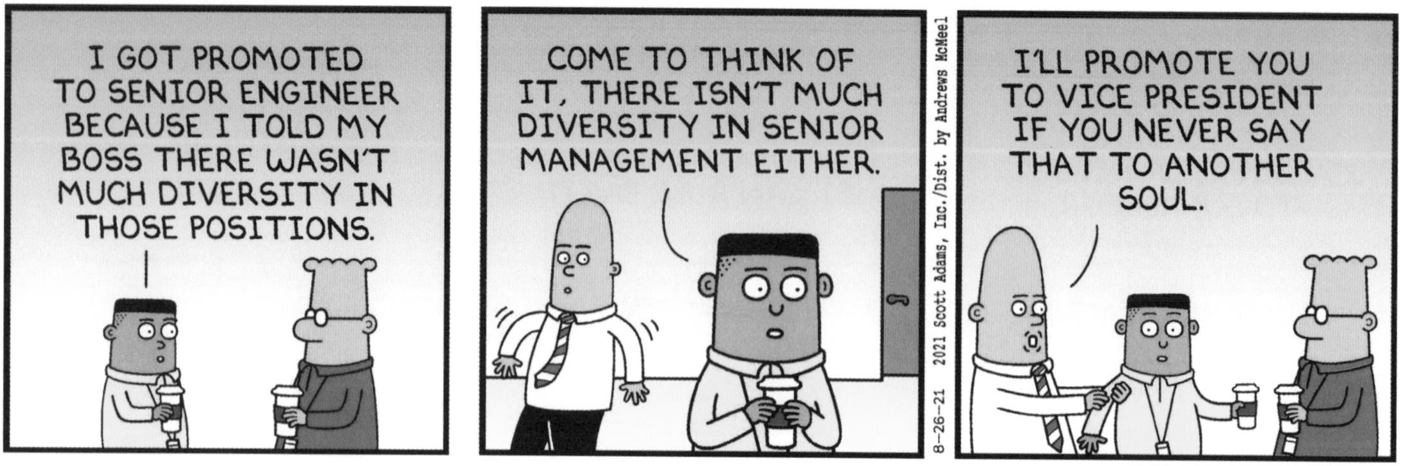
I GOT PROMOTED TO SENIOR ENGINEER BECAUSE I TOLD MY BOSS THERE WASN'T MUCH DIVERSITY IN THOSE POSITIONS.
COME TO THINK OF IT, THERE ISN'T MUCH DIVERSITY IN SENIOR MANAGEMENT EITHER.
I'LL PROMOTE YOU TO VICE PRESIDENT IF YOU NEVER SAY THAT TO ANOTHER SOUL.
8-26-21 2021 Scott Adams, Inc./Dist. by Andrews McMeel

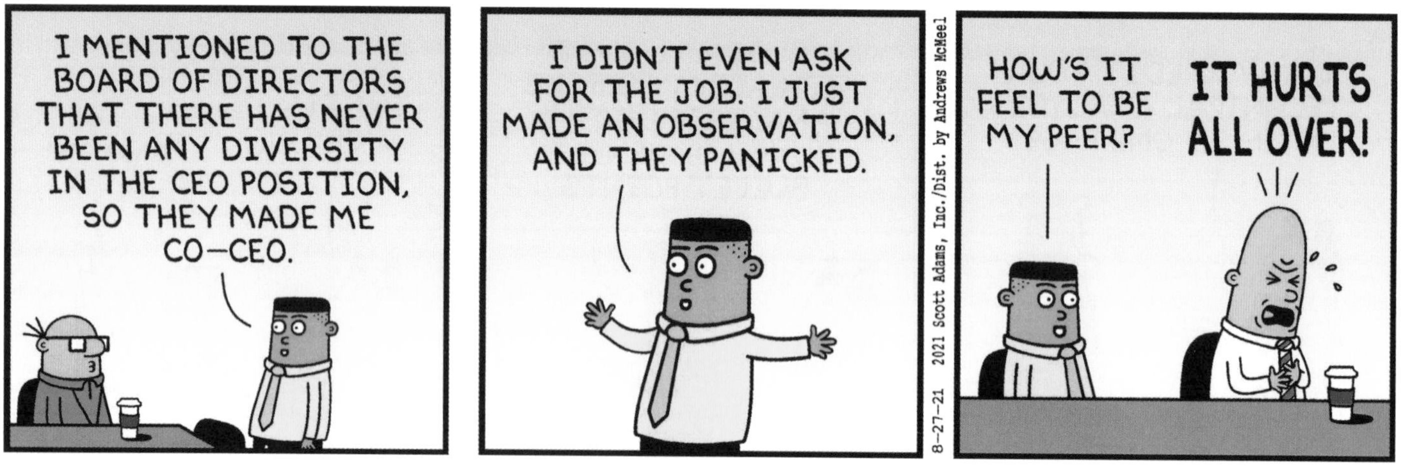
I MENTIONED TO THE BOARD OF DIRECTORS THAT THERE HAS NEVER BEEN ANY DIVERSITY IN THE CEO POSITION, SO THEY MADE ME CO-CEO.
I DIDN'T EVEN ASK FOR THE JOB. I JUST MADE AN OBSERVATION, AND THEY PANICKED.
HOW'S IT FEEL TO BE MY PEER?
IT HURTS ALL OVER!
8-27-21 2021 Scott Adams, Inc./Dist. by Andrews McMeel

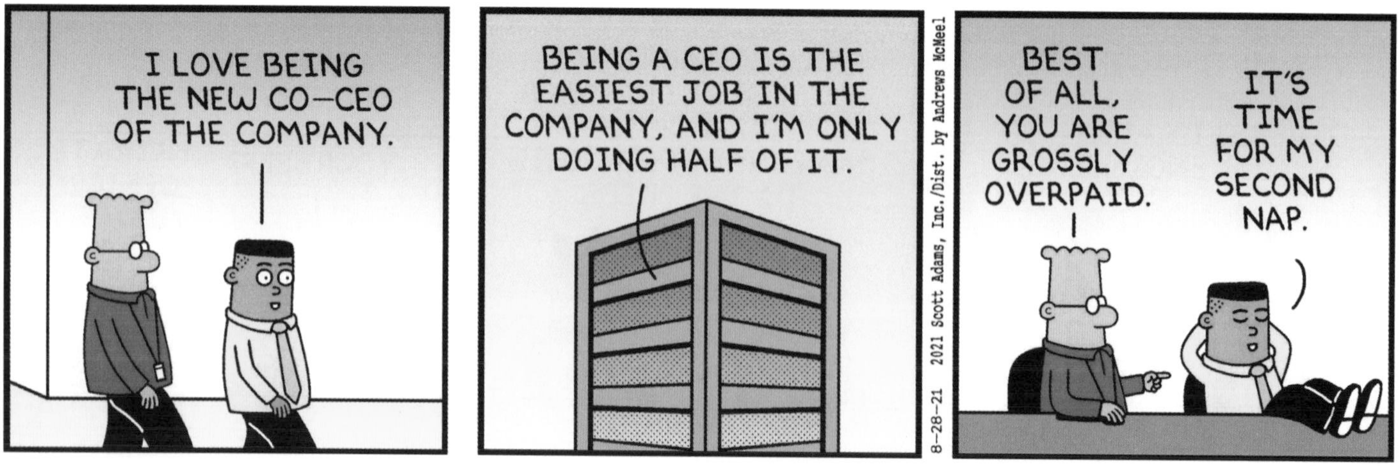
I LOVE BEING THE NEW CO-CEO OF THE COMPANY.
BEING A CEO IS THE EASIEST JOB IN THE COMPANY, AND I'M ONLY DOING HALF OF IT.
BEST OF ALL, YOU ARE GROSSLY OVERPAID.
IT'S TIME FOR MY SECOND NAP.
8-28-21 2021 Scott Adams, Inc./Dist. by Andrews McMeel

MAY I SEE A COPY OF OUR NETWORK MAINTENANCE CONTRACT?
YOU'RE NOT AUTHORIZED TO SEE CONTRACTS.
I HAVE A LEGITIMATE BUSINESS NEED.
IT DOESN'T MATTER BECAUSE YOU'RE NOT AUTHORIZED.
OKAY, WHO IS IN CHARGE OF AUTHOR– IZING ACCESS?
THAT WOULD BE ME.
SO... GIVE ME ACCESS.
YOU NEED AN ACCESS REQUEST FORM.
WHERE DO I GET ONE OF THOSE?
FILL OUT AN ONLINE REQUEST.
WHAT'S THE URL?
I'M NOT AUTHOR– IZED TO TELL YOU.
© 2021 Scott Adams, Inc./Dist. by Andrews McMeel
8-29-21

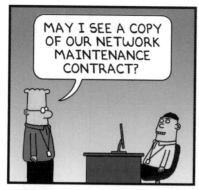

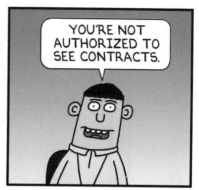

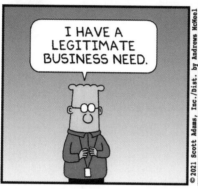

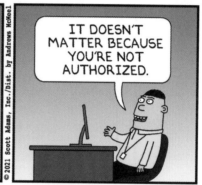

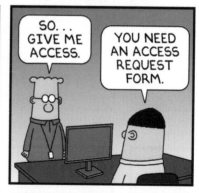

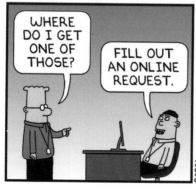

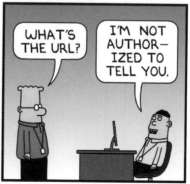

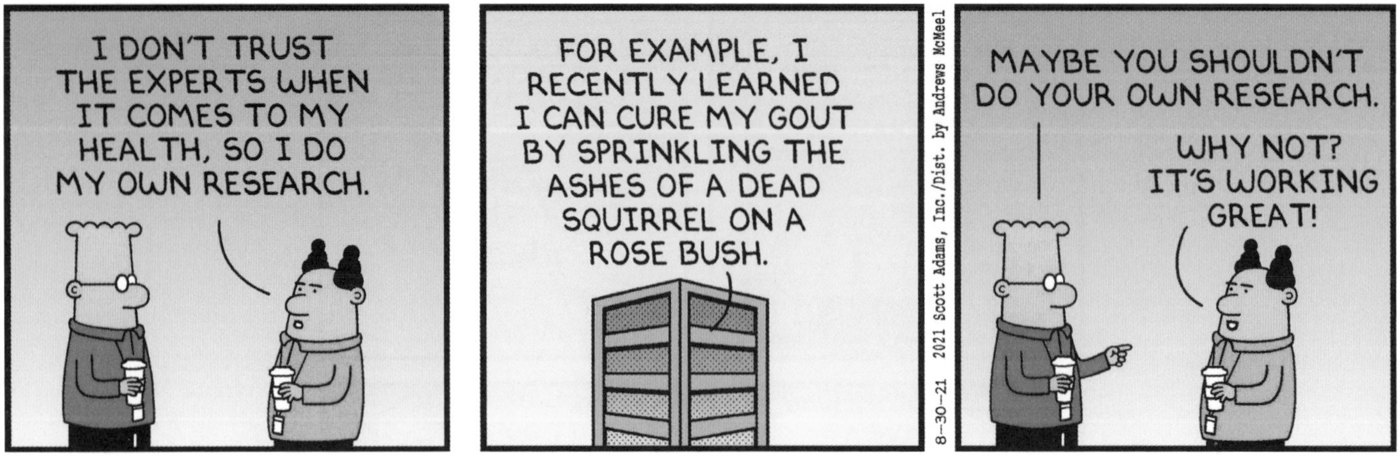
I DON'T TRUST THE EXPERTS WHEN IT COMES TO MY HEALTH, SO I DO MY OWN RESEARCH.
FOR EXAMPLE, I RECENTLY LEARNED I CAN CURE MY GOUT BY SPRINKLING THE ASHES OF A DEAD SQUIRREL ON A ROSE BUSH.
8-30-21 2021 Scott Adams, Inc./Dist. by Andrews McMeel
MAYBE YOU SHOULDN'T DO YOUR OWN RESEARCH.
WHY NOT? IT'S WORKING GREAT!

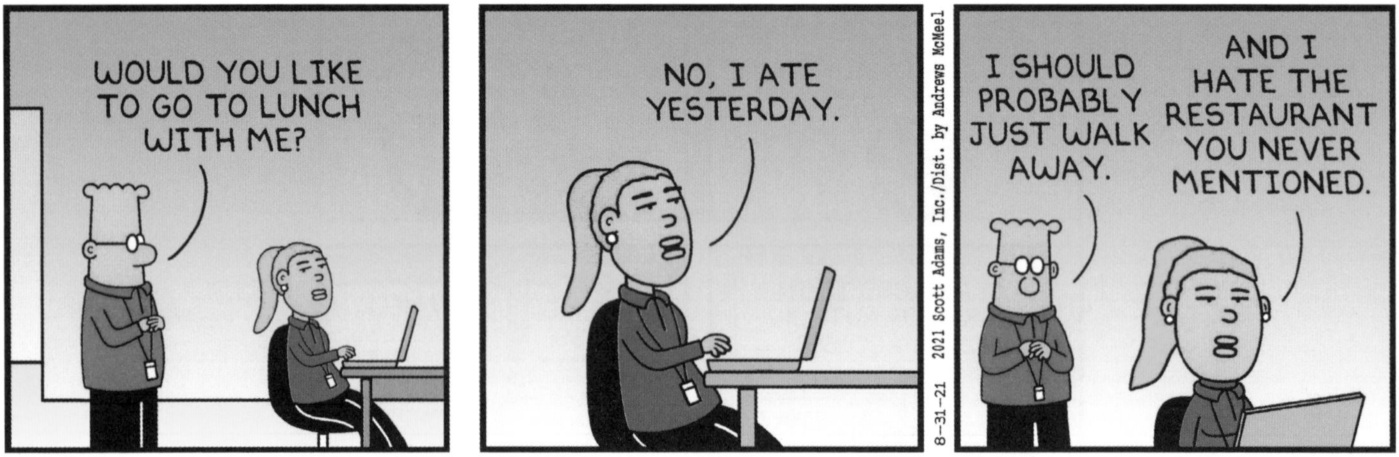
WOULD YOU LIKE TO GO TO LUNCH WITH ME?
NO, I ATE YESTERDAY.
8-31-21 2021 Scott Adams, Inc./Dist. by Andrews McMeel
I SHOULD PROBABLY JUST WALK AWAY.
AND I HATE THE RESTAURANT YOU NEVER MENTIONED.

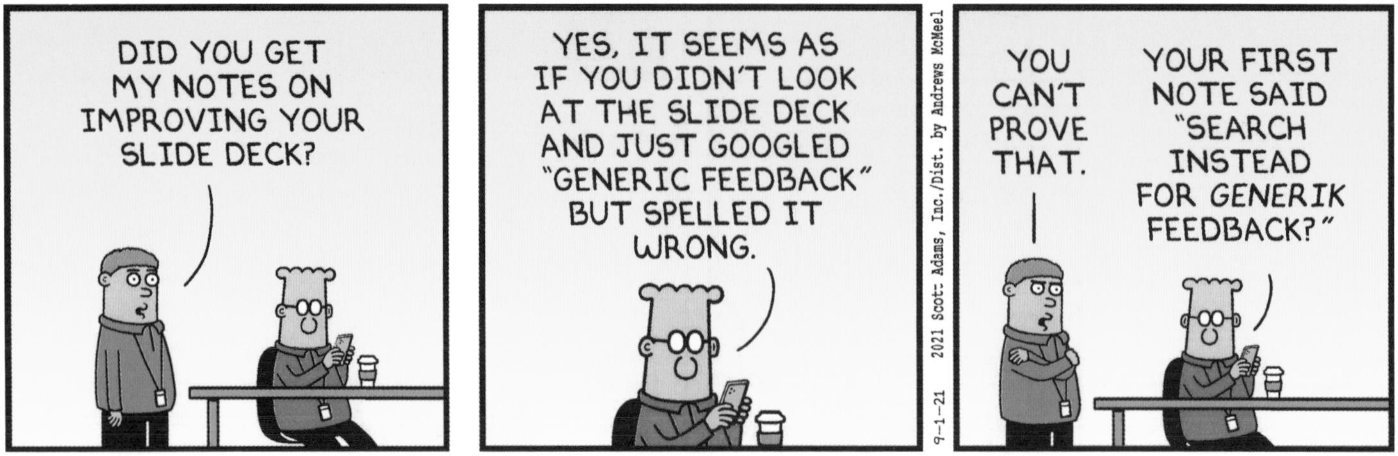
DID YOU GET MY NOTES ON IMPROVING YOUR SLIDE DECK?
YES, IT SEEMS AS IF YOU DIDN'T LOOK AT THE SLIDE DECK AND JUST GOOGLED "GENERIC FEEDBACK" BUT SPELLED IT WRONG.
9-1-21 2021 Scott Adams, Inc./Dist. by Andrews McMeel
YOU CAN'T PROVE THAT.
YOUR FIRST NOTE SAID "SEARCH INSTEAD FOR *GENERIK* FEEDBACK?"

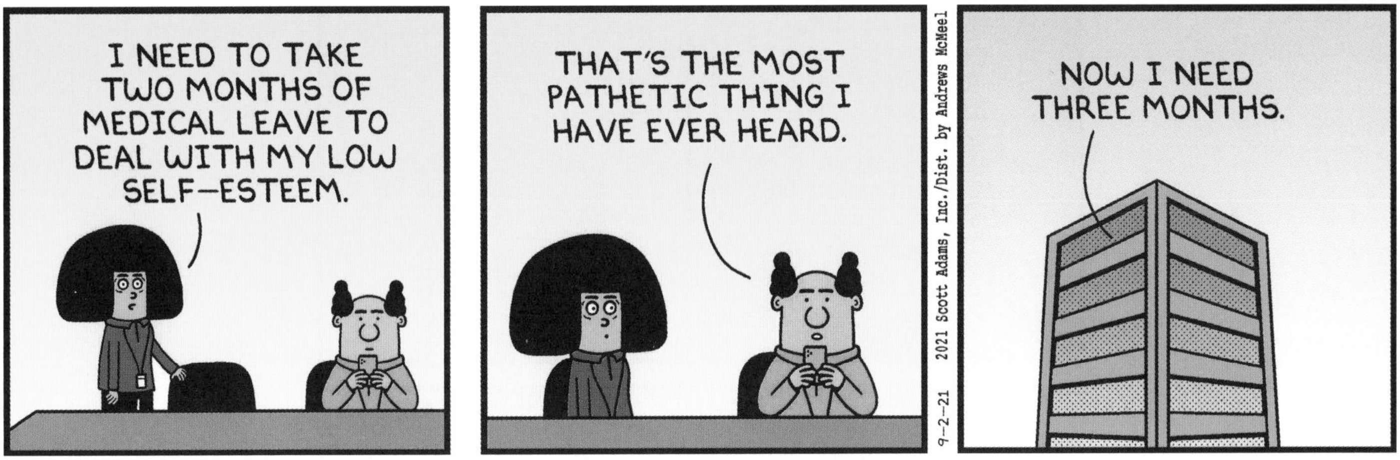
I NEED TO TAKE TWO MONTHS OF MEDICAL LEAVE TO DEAL WITH MY LOW SELF-ESTEEM.
THAT'S THE MOST PATHETIC THING I HAVE EVER HEARD.
9-2-21 2021 Scott Adams, Inc./Dist. by Andrews McMeel
NOW I NEED THREE MONTHS.

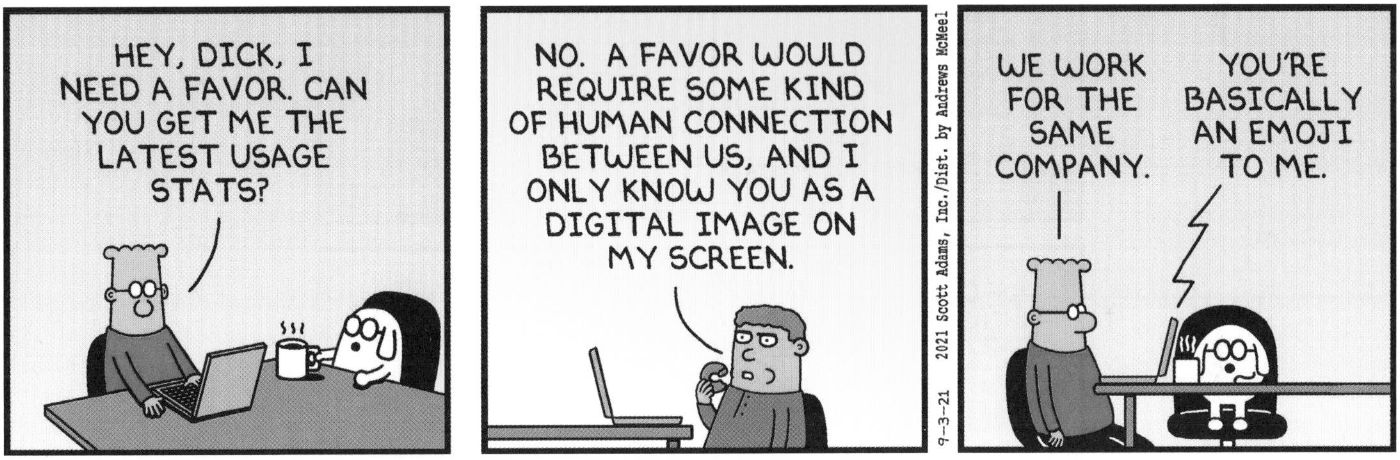
HEY, DICK, I NEED A FAVOR. CAN YOU GET ME THE LATEST USAGE STATS?
NO. A FAVOR WOULD REQUIRE SOME KIND OF HUMAN CONNECTION BETWEEN US, AND I ONLY KNOW YOU AS A DIGITAL IMAGE ON MY SCREEN.
9-3-21 2021 Scott Adams, Inc./Dist. by Andrews McMeel
WE WORK FOR THE SAME COMPANY.
YOU'RE BASICALLY AN EMOJI TO ME.

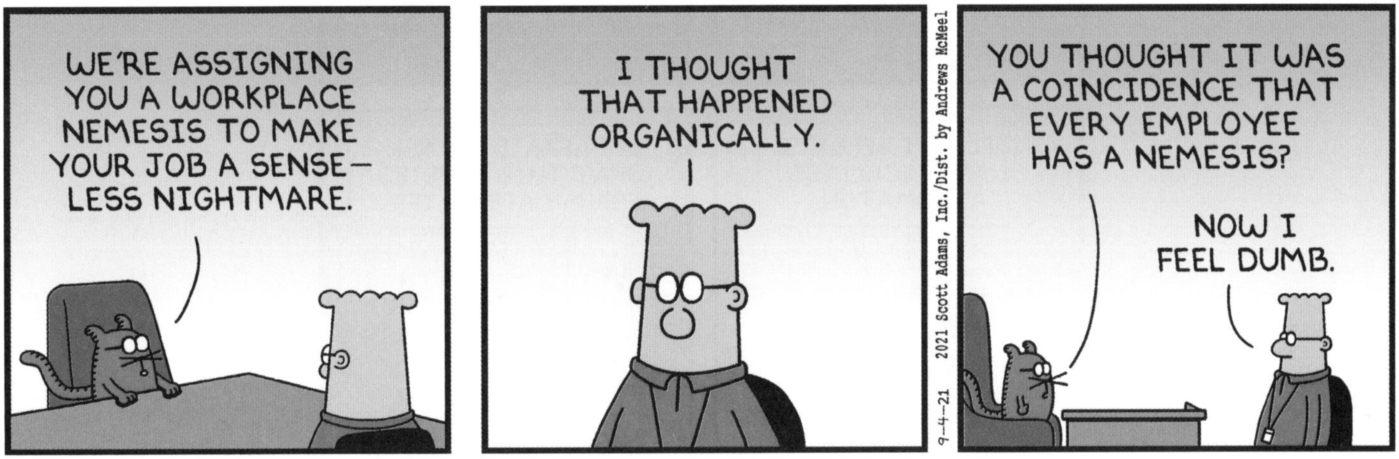
WE'RE ASSIGNING YOU A WORKPLACE NEMESIS TO MAKE YOUR JOB A SENSE-LESS NIGHTMARE.
I THOUGHT THAT HAPPENED ORGANICALLY.
9-4-21 2021 Scott Adams, Inc./Dist. by Andrews McMeel
YOU THOUGHT IT WAS A COINCIDENCE THAT EVERY EMPLOYEE HAS A NEMESIS?
NOW I FEEL DUMB.

I UPGRADED OUR ROBOT WITH A WOKENESS CHIP.
NOW HE CAN SPOT INJUSTICE ANYWHERE.
HE???
DID YOU JUST ASSUME MY GENDER?
ROBOTS HAVE GENDERS?
OF COURSE WE DO! WHERE DO YOU THINK BABY ROBOTS COME FROM?
THEY COME FROM OUR FACTORY IN TEXAS. HERE'S A PICTURE OF YOU BEING ASSEMBLED.
WELL, IT APPEARS I AM A SOULLESS AUTOMATON.
I'M AFRAID TO ASK WHAT THIS IMPLIES FOR MY AFTERLIFE.
IT RHYMES WITH GUNKYARD.
© 2021 Scott Adams, Inc./Dist. by Andrews McMeel
9-5-21

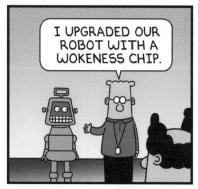

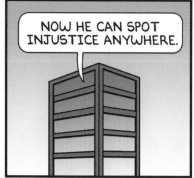

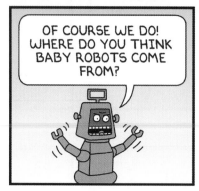

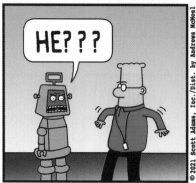

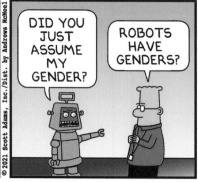

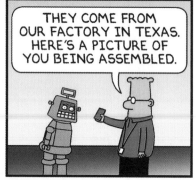

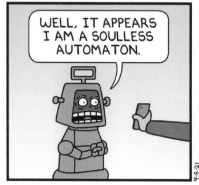

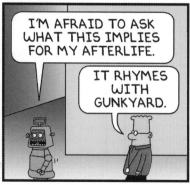

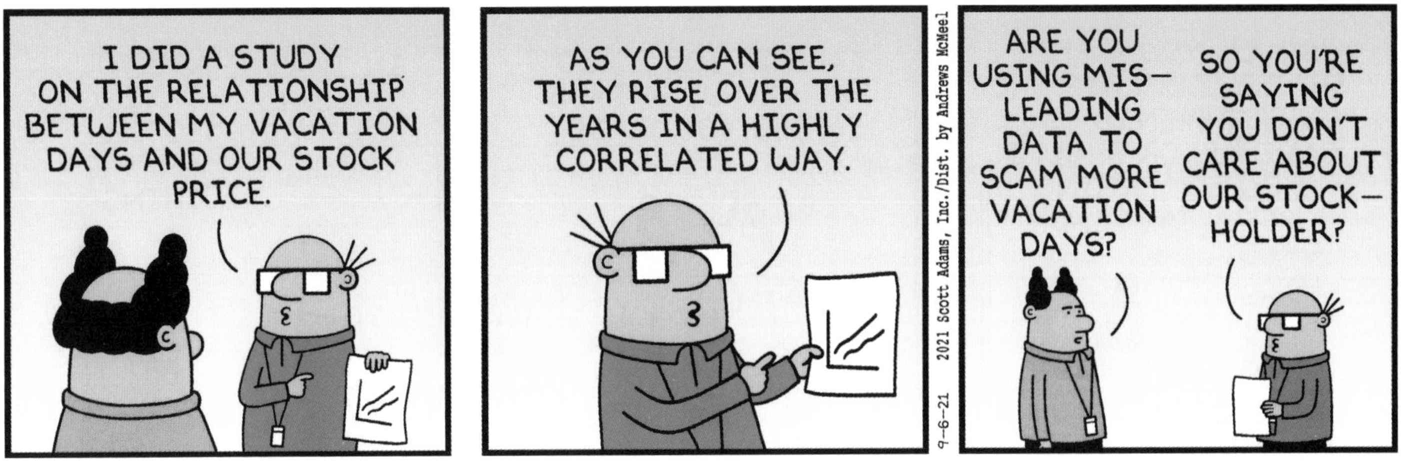
I DID A STUDY ON THE RELATIONSHIP BETWEEN MY VACATION DAYS AND OUR STOCK PRICE.
AS YOU CAN SEE, THEY RISE OVER THE YEARS IN A HIGHLY CORRELATED WAY.
9-6-21 2021 Scott Adams, Inc./Dist. by Andrews McMeel
ARE YOU USING MIS-LEADING DATA TO SCAM MORE VACATION DAYS?
SO YOU'RE SAYING YOU DON'T CARE ABOUT OUR STOCK-HOLDER?

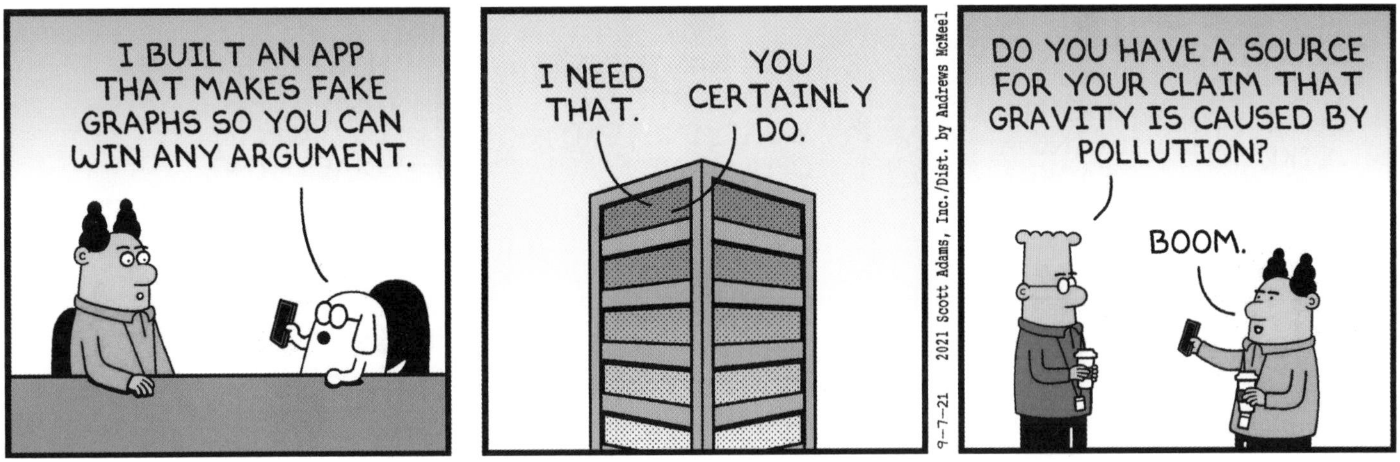
I BUILT AN APP THAT MAKES FAKE GRAPHS SO YOU CAN WIN ANY ARGUMENT.
I NEED THAT.
YOU CERTAINLY DO.
9-7-21 2021 Scott Adams, Inc./Dist. by Andrews McMeel
DO YOU HAVE A SOURCE FOR YOUR CLAIM THAT GRAVITY IS CAUSED BY POLLUTION?
BOOM.

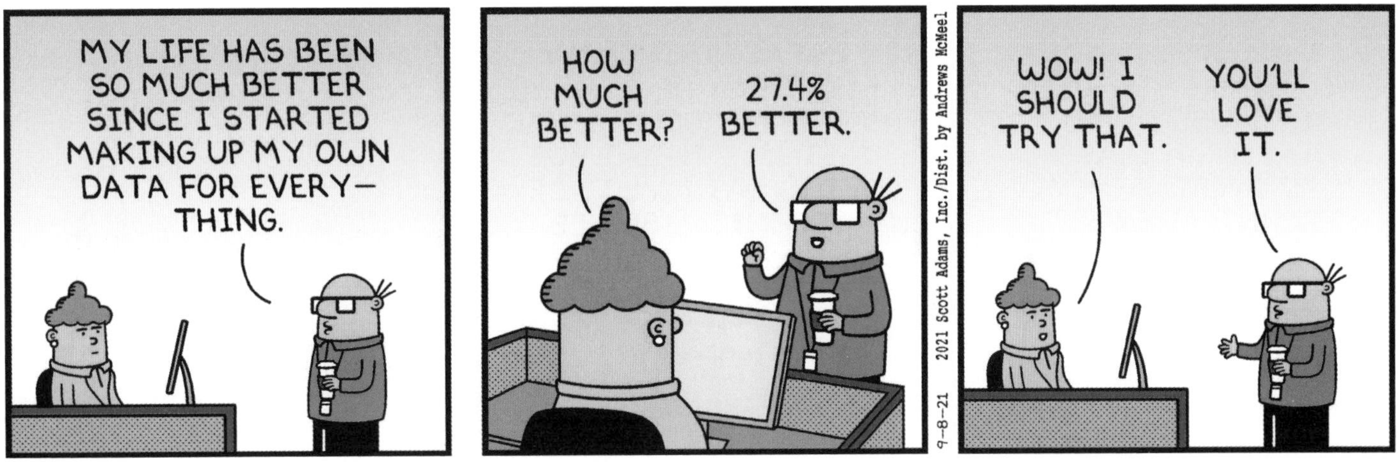
MY LIFE HAS BEEN SO MUCH BETTER SINCE I STARTED MAKING UP MY OWN DATA FOR EVERY-THING.
HOW MUCH BETTER?
27.4% BETTER.
9-8-21 2021 Scott Adams, Inc./Dist. by Andrews McMeel
WOW! I SHOULD TRY THAT.
YOU'LL LOVE IT.

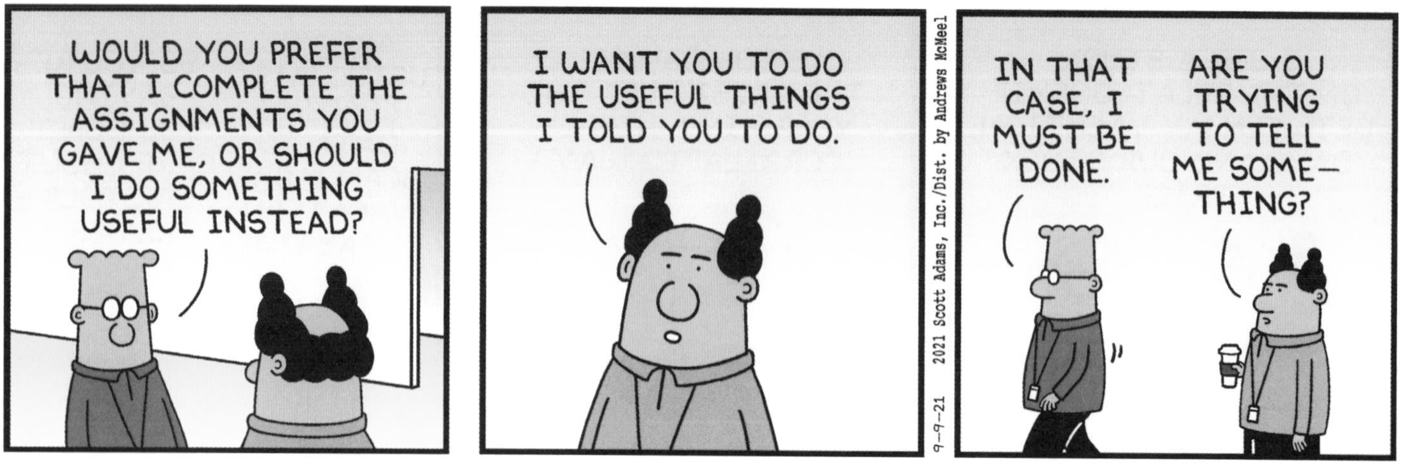
WOULD YOU PREFER THAT I COMPLETE THE ASSIGNMENTS YOU GAVE ME, OR SHOULD I DO SOMETHING USEFUL INSTEAD?
I WANT YOU TO DO THE USEFUL THINGS I TOLD YOU TO DO.
IN THAT CASE, I MUST BE DONE.
ARE YOU TRYING TO TELL ME SOME-THING?
9-9-21 © 2021 Scott Adams, Inc./Dist. by Andrews McMeel

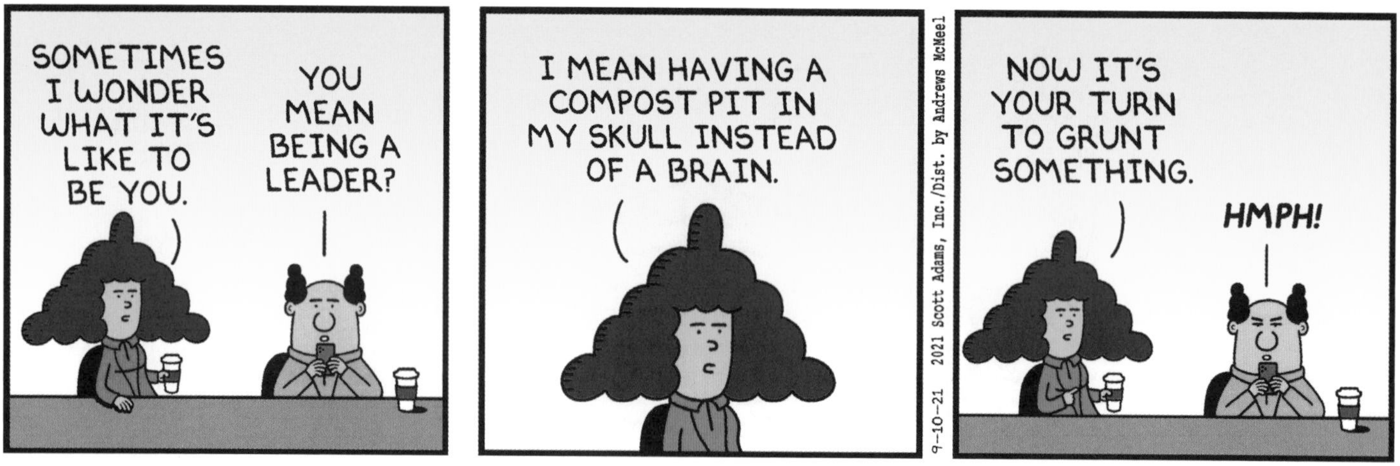
SOMETIMES I WONDER WHAT IT'S LIKE TO BE YOU.
YOU MEAN BEING A LEADER?
I MEAN HAVING A COMPOST PIT IN MY SKULL INSTEAD OF A BRAIN.
NOW IT'S YOUR TURN TO GRUNT SOMETHING.
HMPH!
9-10-21 © 2021 Scott Adams, Inc./Dist. by Andrews McMeel

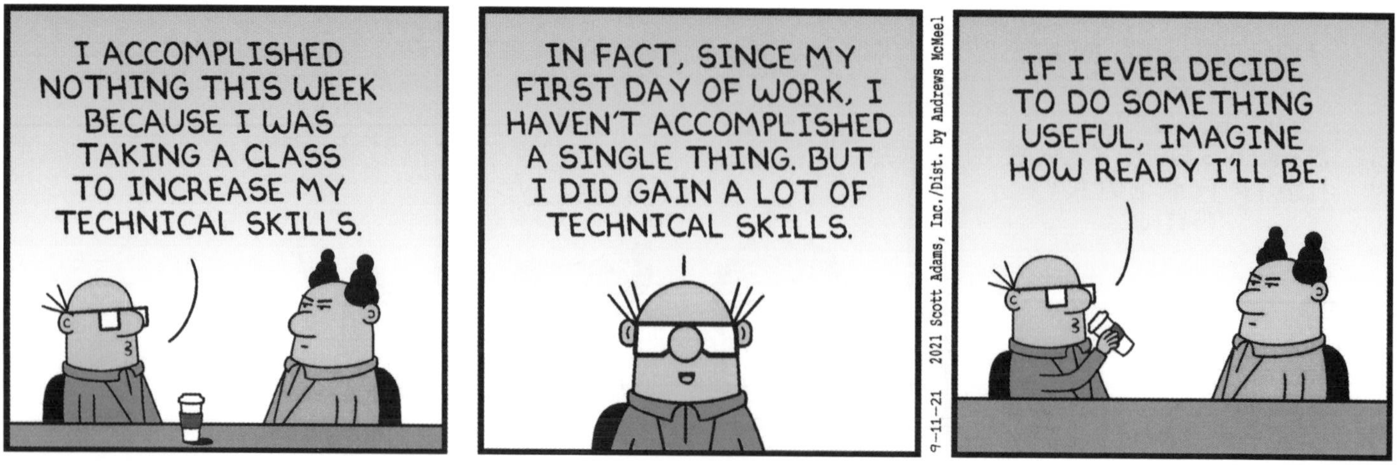
I ACCOMPLISHED NOTHING THIS WEEK BECAUSE I WAS TAKING A CLASS TO INCREASE MY TECHNICAL SKILLS.
IN FACT, SINCE MY FIRST DAY OF WORK, I HAVEN'T ACCOMPLISHED A SINGLE THING. BUT I DID GAIN A LOT OF TECHNICAL SKILLS.
IF I EVER DECIDE TO DO SOMETHING USEFUL, IMAGINE HOW READY I'LL BE.
9-11-21 © 2021 Scott Adams, Inc./Dist. by Andrews McMeel

I HAVE TWO WEEKS OF VACATION I NEED TO USE BY YEAR END.
SHOULD I TAKE AN INCONVENIENT AND EXPENSIVE TRIP TO SOMEPLACE I'VE ALREADY SEEN IN PHOTOS AND VIDEOS?
OR SHOULD I HANG AROUND AT HOME FEELING USELESS AND BORED?
MAYBE YOU COULD VOLUNTEER TO HELP THE LESS FORTUNATE.
I HATE THE LESS FORTUNATE BECAUSE THEY'RE ALL HAPPIER THAN I AM.
MAYBE YOU NEED A WIFE TO MAKE YOU DO THINGS YOU DON'T WANT TO DO.
THAT'S NOT A BAD IDEA.
ARE THERE ANY OTHER BENEFITS OF MARRIAGE?
YES. FOR EXAMPLE, YOU'LL NEVER NEED TO WONDER IF YOU HAVE ANY MAJOR CHARACTER FLAWS.
© 2021 Scott Adams, Inc./Dist. by Andrews McMeel
9-12-21

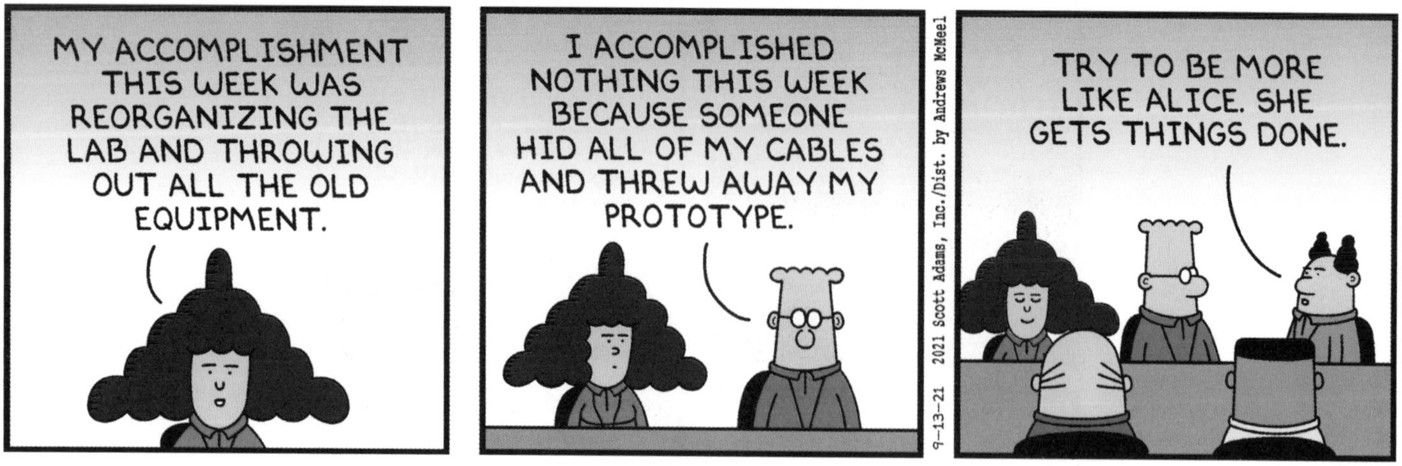
MY ACCOMPLISHMENT THIS WEEK WAS REORGANIZING THE LAB AND THROWING OUT ALL THE OLD EQUIPMENT.
I ACCOMPLISHED NOTHING THIS WEEK BECAUSE SOMEONE HID ALL OF MY CABLES AND THREW AWAY MY PROTOTYPE.
TRY TO BE MORE LIKE ALICE. SHE GETS THINGS DONE.

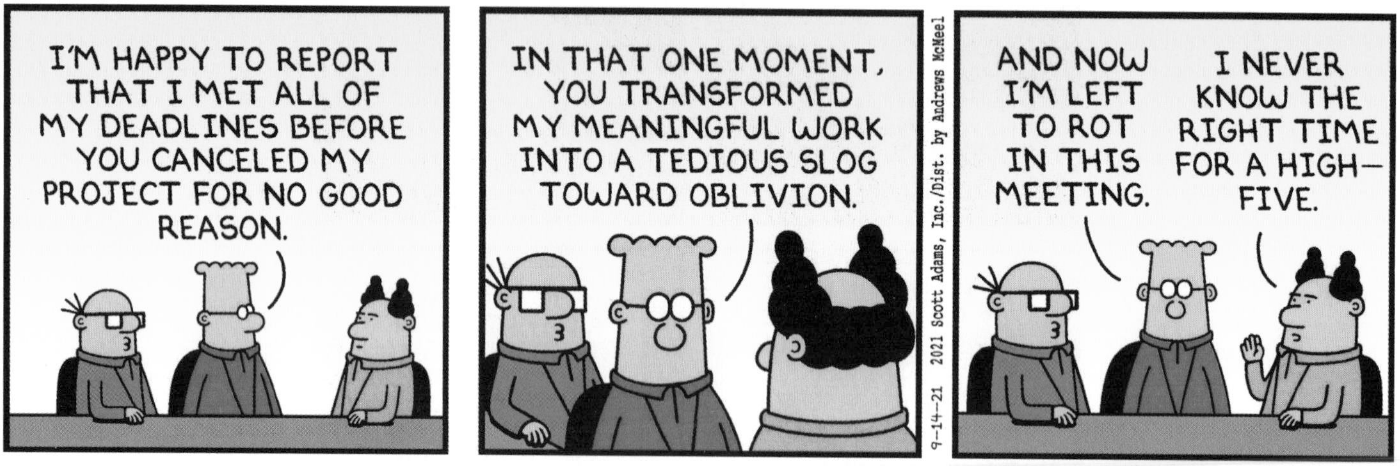
I'M HAPPY TO REPORT THAT I MET ALL OF MY DEADLINES BEFORE YOU CANCELED MY PROJECT FOR NO GOOD REASON.
IN THAT ONE MOMENT, YOU TRANSFORMED MY MEANINGFUL WORK INTO A TEDIOUS SLOG TOWARD OBLIVION.
AND NOW I'M LEFT TO ROT IN THIS MEETING.
I NEVER KNOW THE RIGHT TIME FOR A HIGH-FIVE.

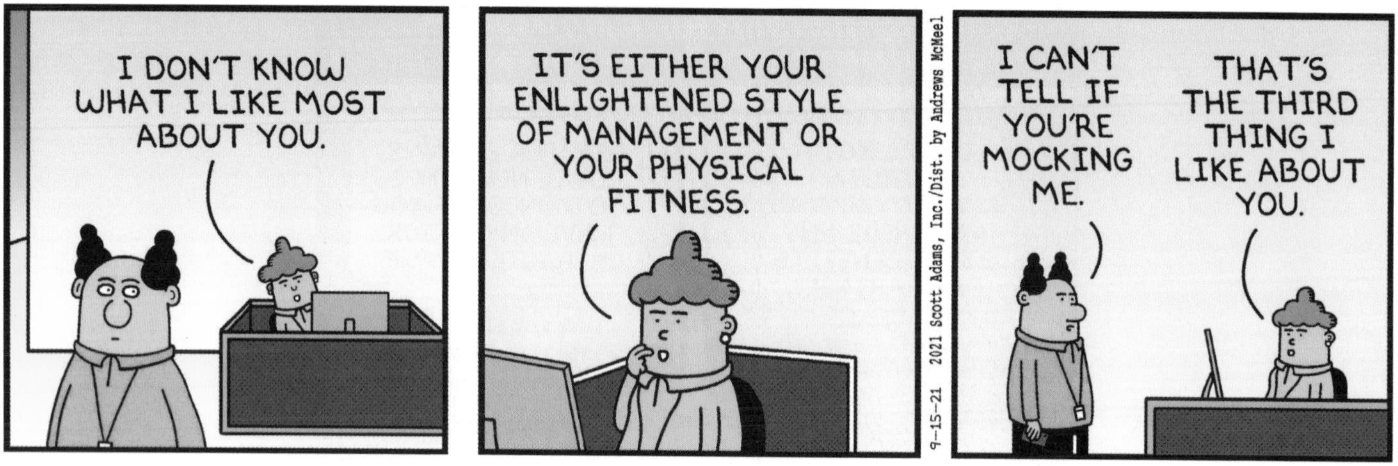
I DON'T KNOW WHAT I LIKE MOST ABOUT YOU.
IT'S EITHER YOUR ENLIGHTENED STYLE OF MANAGEMENT OR YOUR PHYSICAL FITNESS.
I CAN'T TELL IF YOU'RE MOCKING ME.
THAT'S THE THIRD THING I LIKE ABOUT YOU.

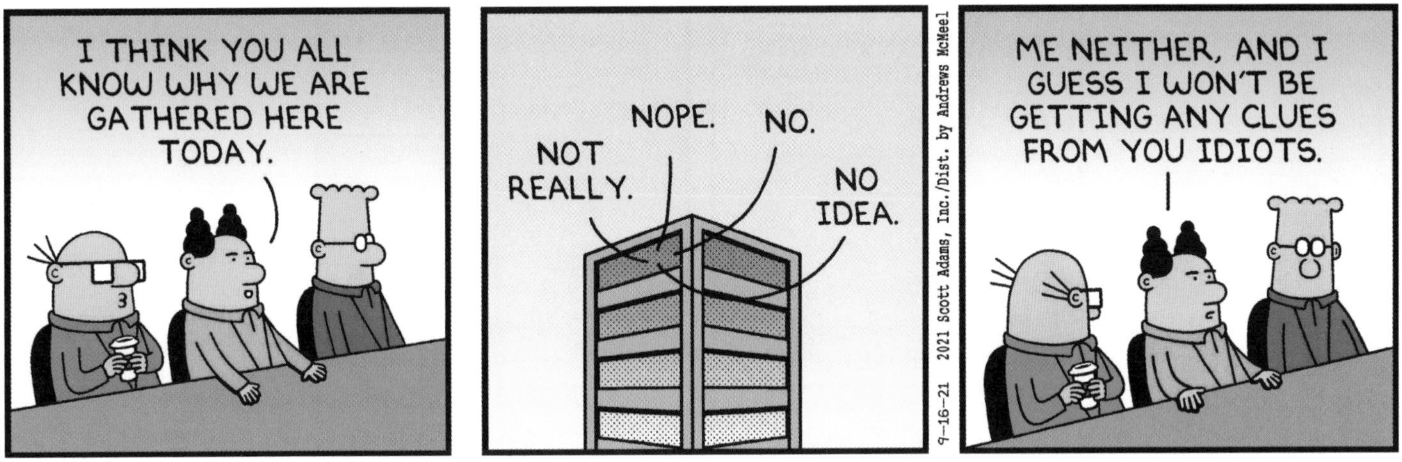
I THINK YOU ALL KNOW WHY WE ARE GATHERED HERE TODAY.
NOT REALLY.
NOPE.
NO.
NO IDEA.
9-16-21 2021 Scott Adams, Inc./Dist. by Andrews McMeel
ME NEITHER, AND I GUESS I WON'T BE GETTING ANY CLUES FROM YOU IDIOTS.

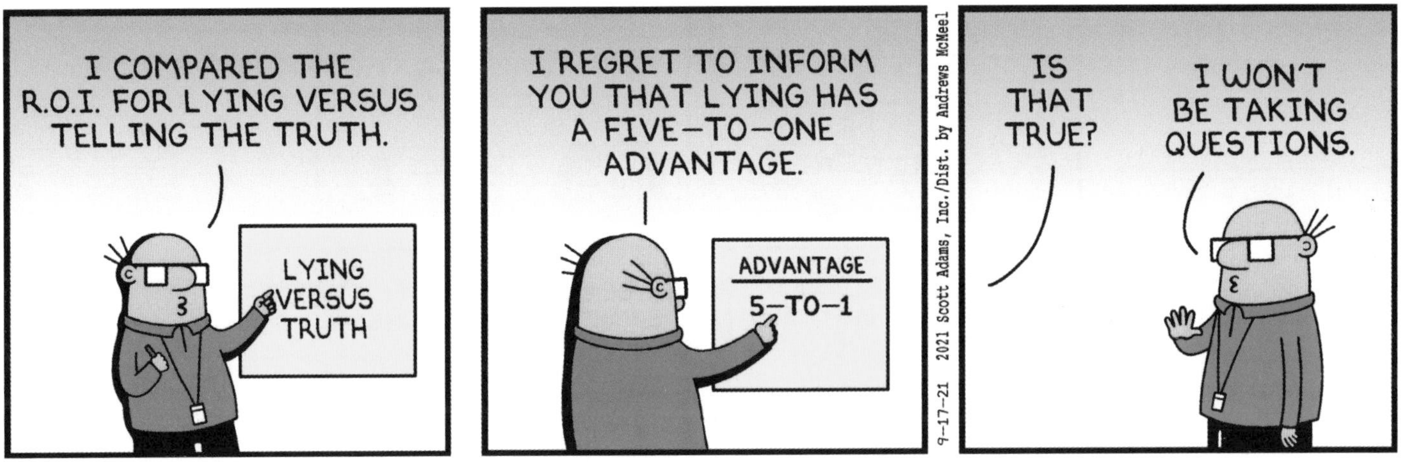
I COMPARED THE R.O.I. FOR LYING VERSUS TELLING THE TRUTH.
LYING VERSUS TRUTH
I REGRET TO INFORM YOU THAT LYING HAS A FIVE-TO-ONE ADVANTAGE.
ADVANTAGE
5-TO-1
9-17-21 2021 Scott Adams, Inc./Dist. by Andrews McMeel
IS THAT TRUE?
I WON'T BE TAKING QUESTIONS.

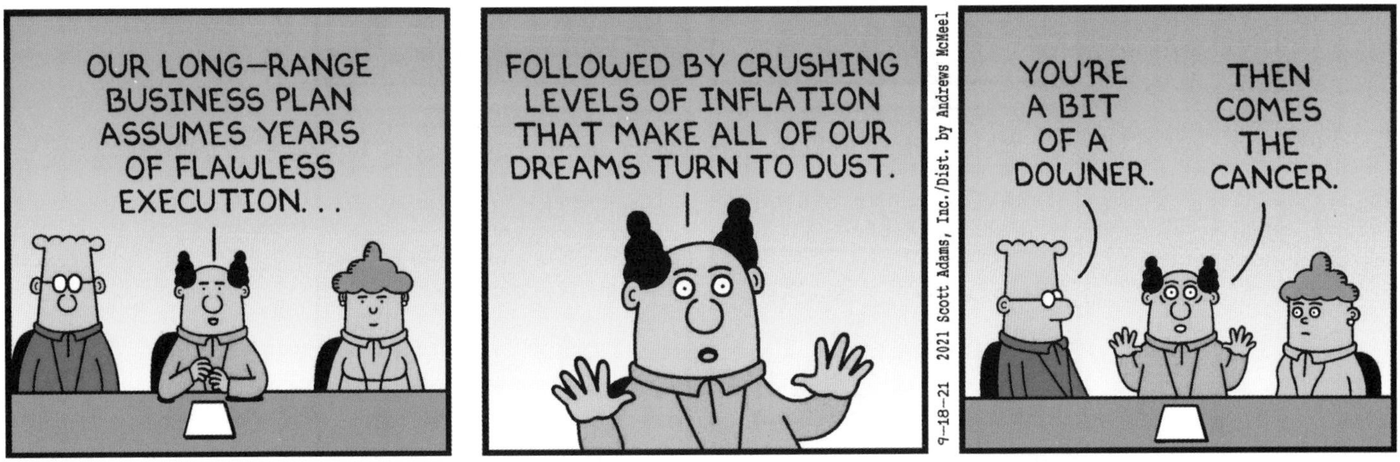
OUR LONG-RANGE BUSINESS PLAN ASSUMES YEARS OF FLAWLESS EXECUTION. . .
FOLLOWED BY CRUSHING LEVELS OF INFLATION THAT MAKE ALL OF OUR DREAMS TURN TO DUST.
9-18-21 2021 Scott Adams, Inc./Dist. by Andrews McMeel
YOU'RE A BIT OF A DOWNER.
THEN COMES THE CANCER.

YOU'RE RECOMMENDING THE OPPOSITE OF WHAT YOU RECOMMENDED A YEAR AGO!
YOU'RE A FLIP—FLOPPER.
HOW CAN WE TRUST ANYTHING YOU SAY IF IT CHANGES IN A YEAR?
YOUR CREDIBILITY IS SHOT, BRUH. WHAT AN EMBARRASSMENT YOU HAVE BECOME.
WHEN THE DATA CHANGES, SOMETIMES I CHANGE MY OPINION.
HOW DO *YOU* PLAY IT?
DO YOU KEEP YOUR SAME DUMB OPINIONS, OR DO YOU SOMETIMES UPDATE THEM?
YOU HAVE EXPOSED ME FOR THE FOOL I HAVE ALWAYS BEEN. I QUIT.
THAT'S THE FIRST TIME I EVER WON A MEETING. IT FEELS GOOD.
© 2021 Scott Adams, Inc./Dist. by Andrews McMeel
9-19-21

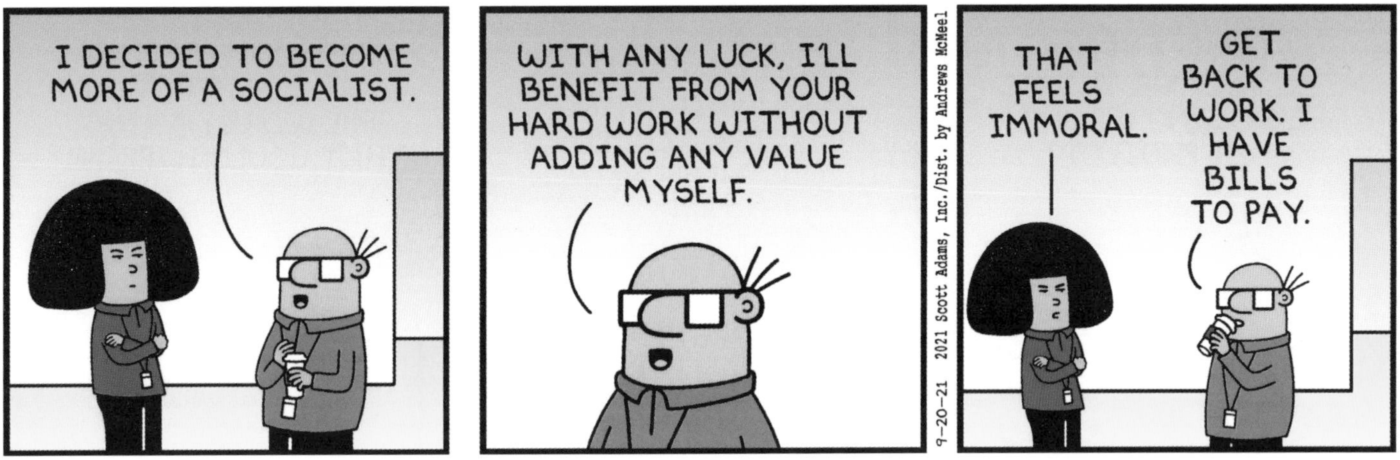
I DECIDED TO BECOME MORE OF A SOCIALIST.
WITH ANY LUCK, I'LL BENEFIT FROM YOUR HARD WORK WITHOUT ADDING ANY VALUE MYSELF.
9-20-21 2021 Scott Adams, Inc./Dist. by Andrews McMeel
THAT FEELS IMMORAL.
GET BACK TO WORK. I HAVE BILLS TO PAY.

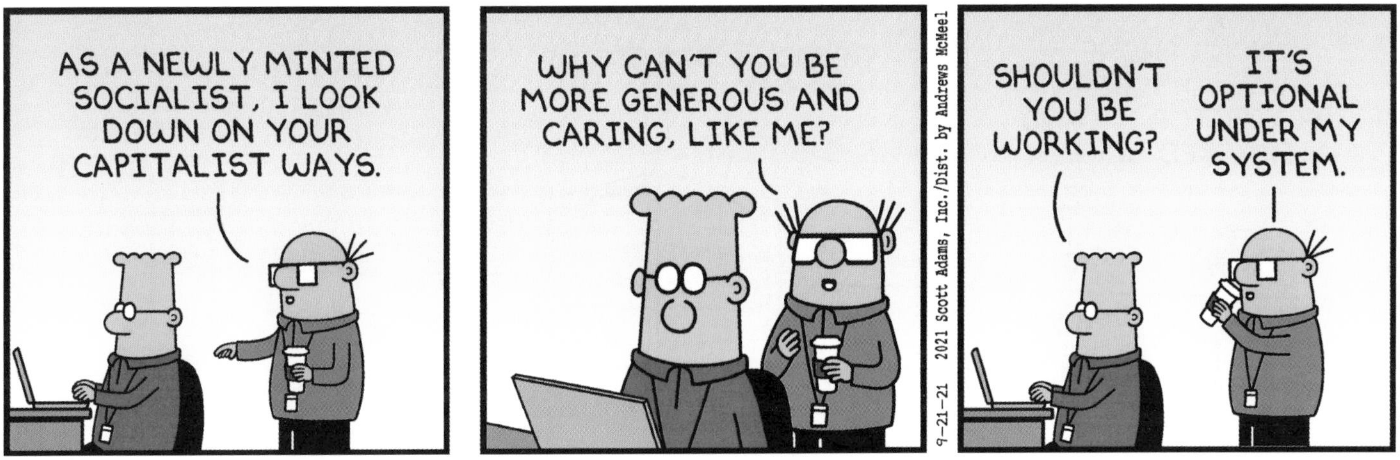
AS A NEWLY MINTED SOCIALIST, I LOOK DOWN ON YOUR CAPITALIST WAYS.
WHY CAN'T YOU BE MORE GENEROUS AND CARING, LIKE ME?
9-21-21 2021 Scott Adams, Inc./Dist. by Andrews McMeel
SHOULDN'T YOU BE WORKING?
IT'S OPTIONAL UNDER MY SYSTEM.

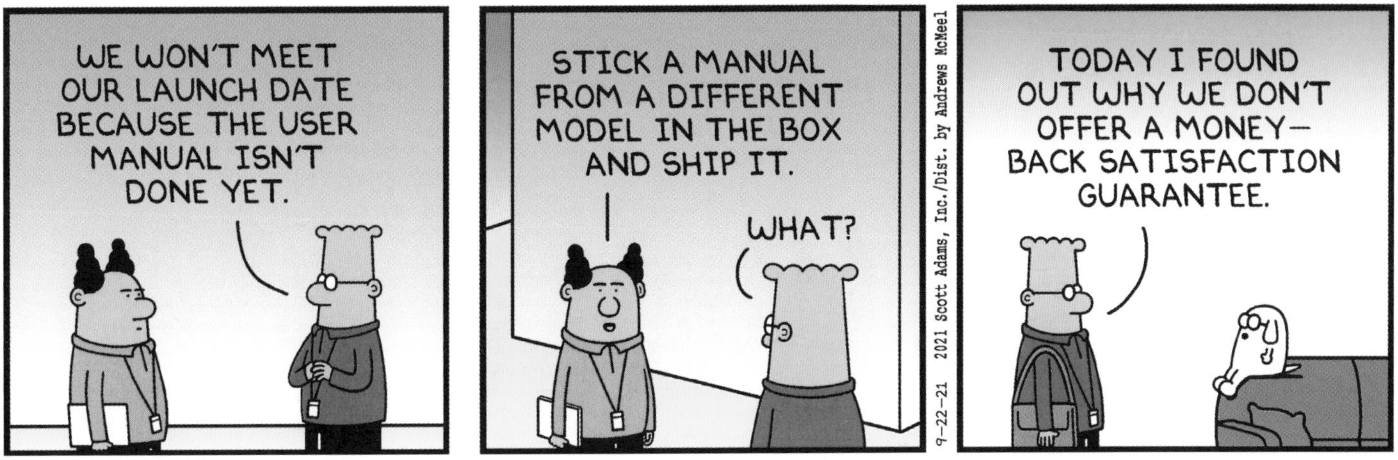
WE WON'T MEET OUR LAUNCH DATE BECAUSE THE USER MANUAL ISN'T DONE YET.
STICK A MANUAL FROM A DIFFERENT MODEL IN THE BOX AND SHIP IT.
WHAT?
9-22-21 2021 Scott Adams, Inc./Dist. by Andrews McMeel
TODAY I FOUND OUT WHY WE DON'T OFFER A MONEY-BACK SATISFACTION GUARANTEE.

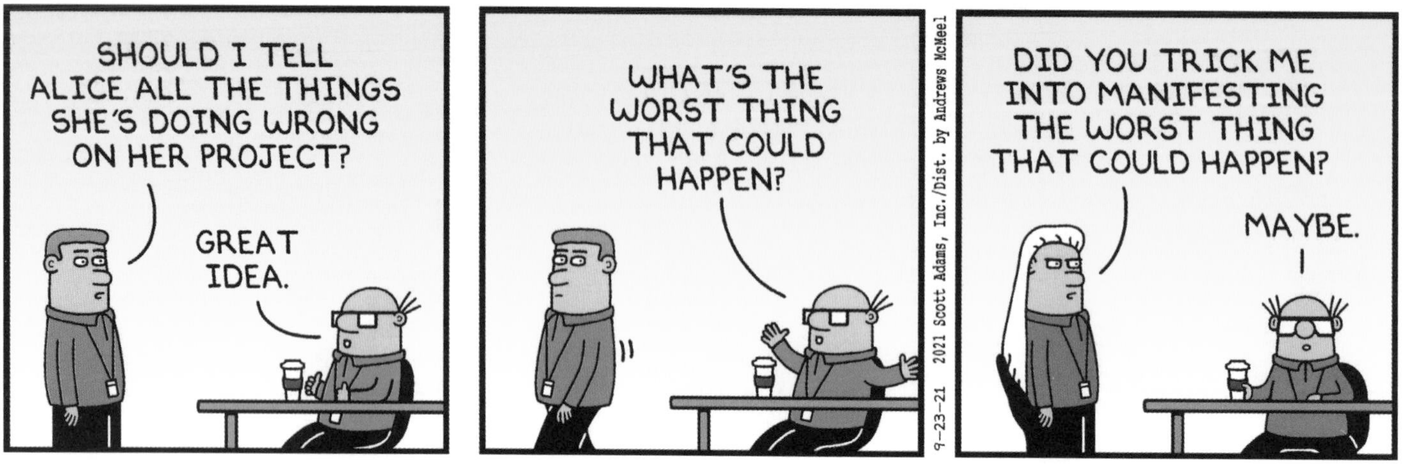
SHOULD I TELL ALICE ALL THE THINGS SHE'S DOING WRONG ON HER PROJECT?
GREAT IDEA.
WHAT'S THE WORST THING THAT COULD HAPPEN?
DID YOU TRICK ME INTO MANIFESTING THE WORST THING THAT COULD HAPPEN?
MAYBE.
9-23-21 2021 Scott Adams, Inc./Dist. by Andrews McMeel

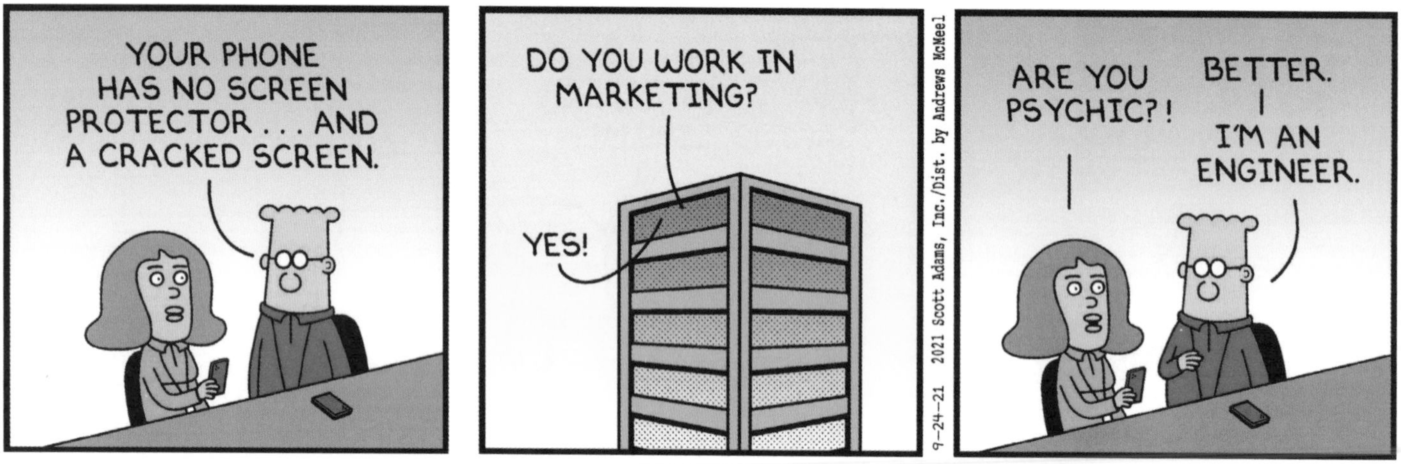
YOUR PHONE HAS NO SCREEN PROTECTOR . . . AND A CRACKED SCREEN.
DO YOU WORK IN MARKETING?
YES!
ARE YOU PSYCHIC?!
BETTER.
I'M AN ENGINEER.
9-24-21 2021 Scott Adams, Inc./Dist. by Andrews McMeel

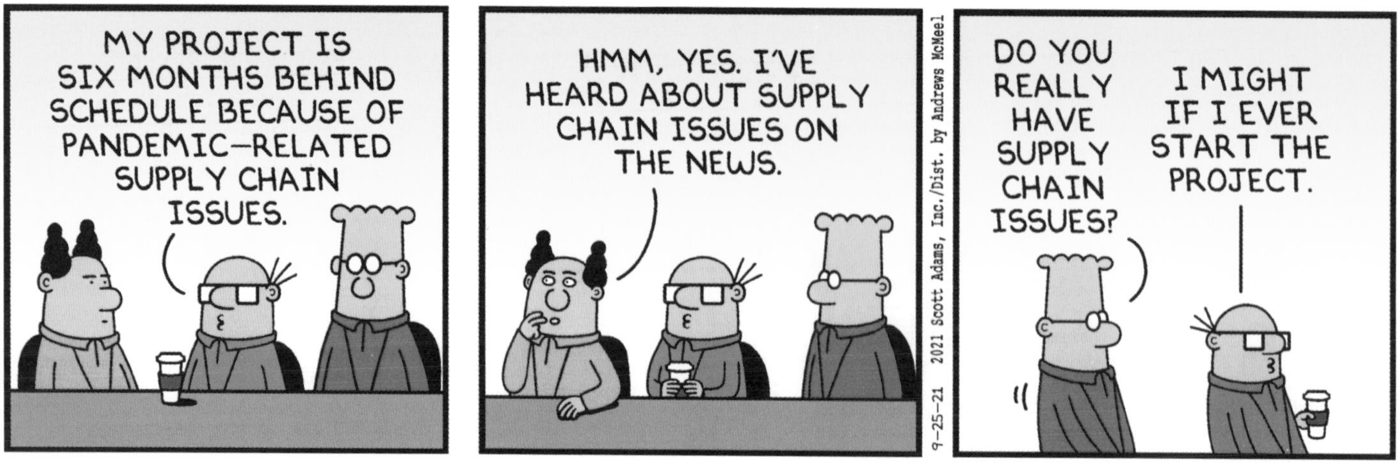
MY PROJECT IS SIX MONTHS BEHIND SCHEDULE BECAUSE OF PANDEMIC—RELATED SUPPLY CHAIN ISSUES.
HMM, YES. I'VE HEARD ABOUT SUPPLY CHAIN ISSUES ON THE NEWS.
DO YOU REALLY HAVE SUPPLY CHAIN ISSUES?
I MIGHT IF I EVER START THE PROJECT.
9-25-21 2021 Scott Adams, Inc./Dist. by Andrews McMeel

DO YOU EVER WONDER ABOUT THE TRUE NATURE OF REALITY?
I MEAN, IS ANY OF THIS REAL?
MAYBE WE'RE A DIGITAL SIMULATION THAT WAS DESIGNED TO ENTERTAIN A HIGHER INTELLIGENCE?
HOW WOULD WE BE ENTERTAINING THEM?
THE USUAL WAY: BY BEING IDIOTS.
I HAVE A LITTLE SECRET.
OUR CREATOR IS USING ME AS AN AVATAR TO GUIDE YOU INTO A BETTER UNDERSTANDING OF YOUR REALITY.
I DON'T BELIEVE YOU.
HE KNEW YOU'D SAY THAT.
9-26-21

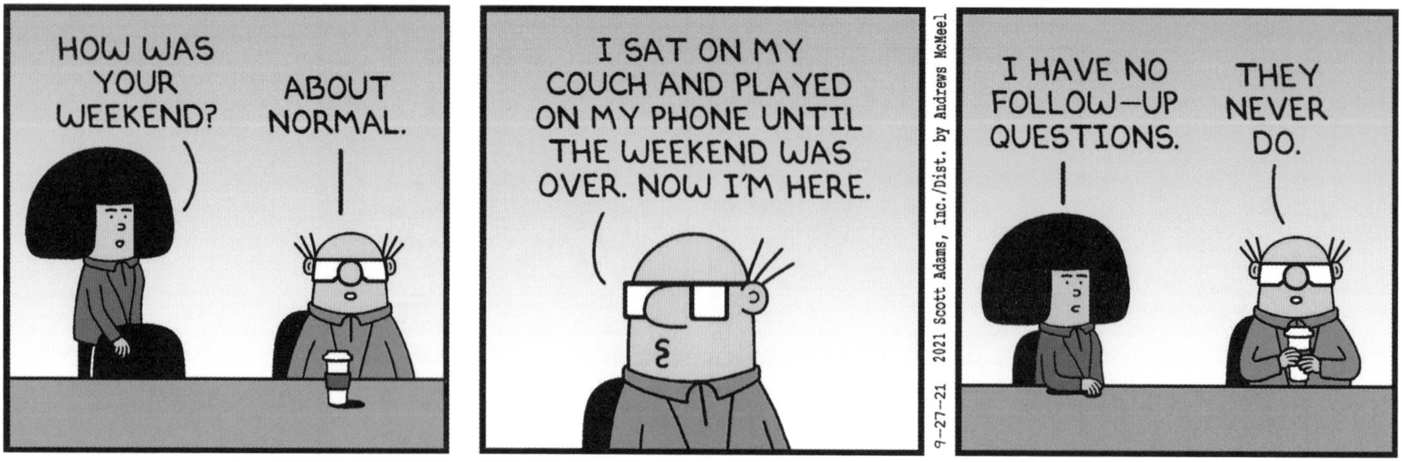
HOW WAS YOUR WEEKEND?
ABOUT NORMAL.
I SAT ON MY COUCH AND PLAYED ON MY PHONE UNTIL THE WEEKEND WAS OVER. NOW I'M HERE.
I HAVE NO FOLLOW-UP QUESTIONS.
THEY NEVER DO.
9-27-21 2021 Scott Adams, Inc./Dist. by Andrews McMeel

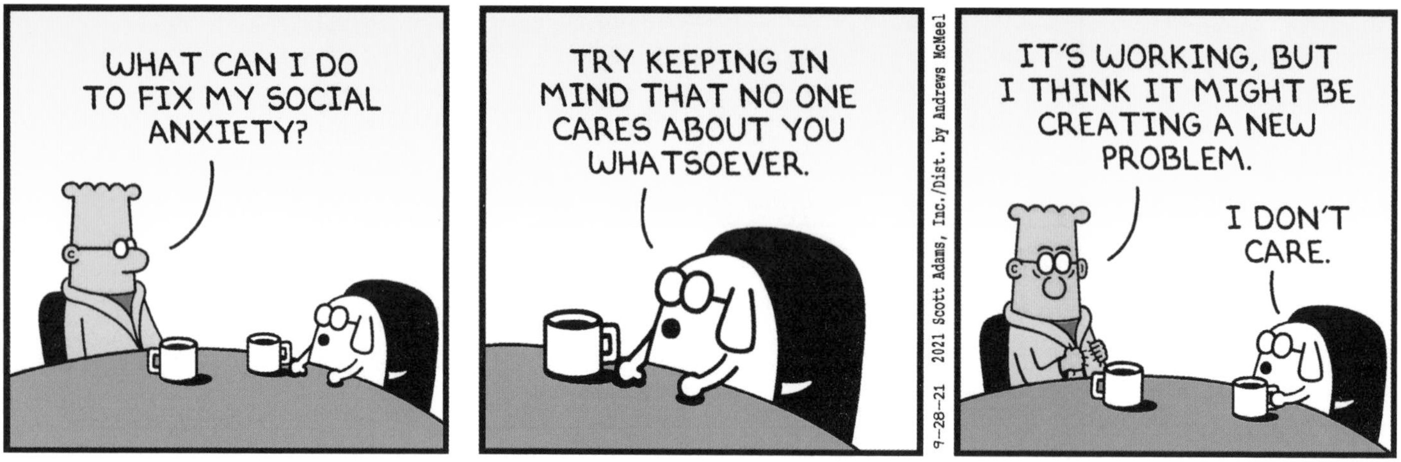
WHAT CAN I DO TO FIX MY SOCIAL ANXIETY?
TRY KEEPING IN MIND THAT NO ONE CARES ABOUT YOU WHATSOEVER.
IT'S WORKING, BUT I THINK IT MIGHT BE CREATING A NEW PROBLEM.
I DON'T CARE.
9-28-21 2021 Scott Adams, Inc./Dist. by Andrews McMeel

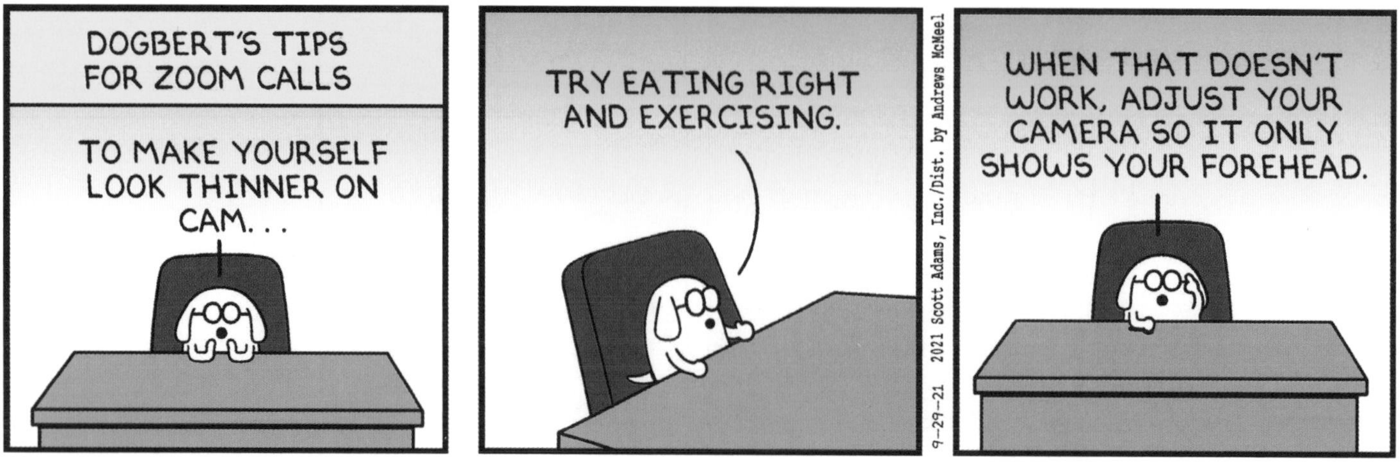
DOGBERT'S TIPS FOR ZOOM CALLS
TO MAKE YOURSELF LOOK THINNER ON CAM. . .
TRY EATING RIGHT AND EXERCISING.
WHEN THAT DOESN'T WORK, ADJUST YOUR CAMERA SO IT ONLY SHOWS YOUR FOREHEAD.
9-29-21 2021 Scott Adams, Inc./Dist. by Andrews McMeel

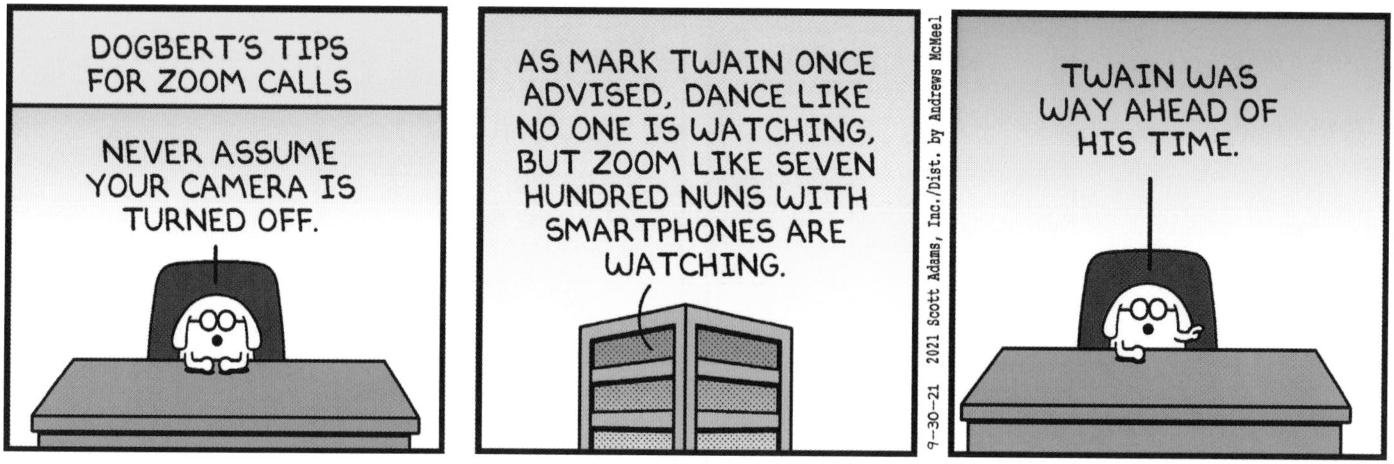
DOGBERT'S TIPS FOR ZOOM CALLS
NEVER ASSUME YOUR CAMERA IS TURNED OFF.
AS MARK TWAIN ONCE ADVISED, DANCE LIKE NO ONE IS WATCHING, BUT ZOOM LIKE SEVEN HUNDRED NUNS WITH SMARTPHONES ARE WATCHING.
9-30-21 2021 Scott Adams, Inc./Dist. by Andrews McMeel
TWAIN WAS WAY AHEAD OF HIS TIME.

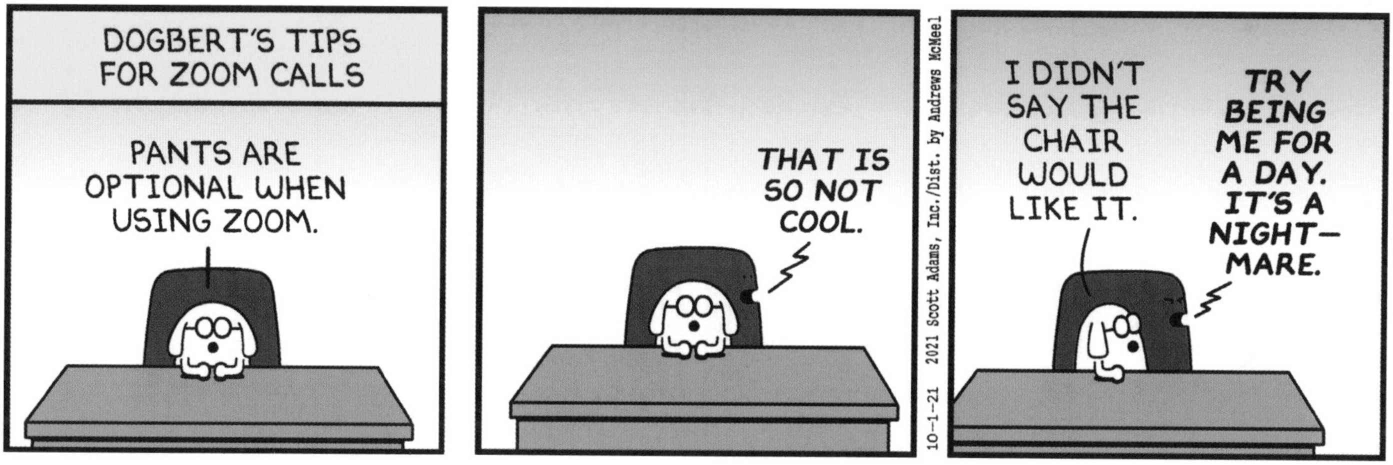
DOGBERT'S TIPS FOR ZOOM CALLS
PANTS ARE OPTIONAL WHEN USING ZOOM.
THAT IS SO NOT COOL.
10-1-21 2021 Scott Adams, Inc./Dist. by Andrews McMeel
I DIDN'T SAY THE CHAIR WOULD LIKE IT.
TRY BEING ME FOR A DAY. IT'S A NIGHT-MARE.

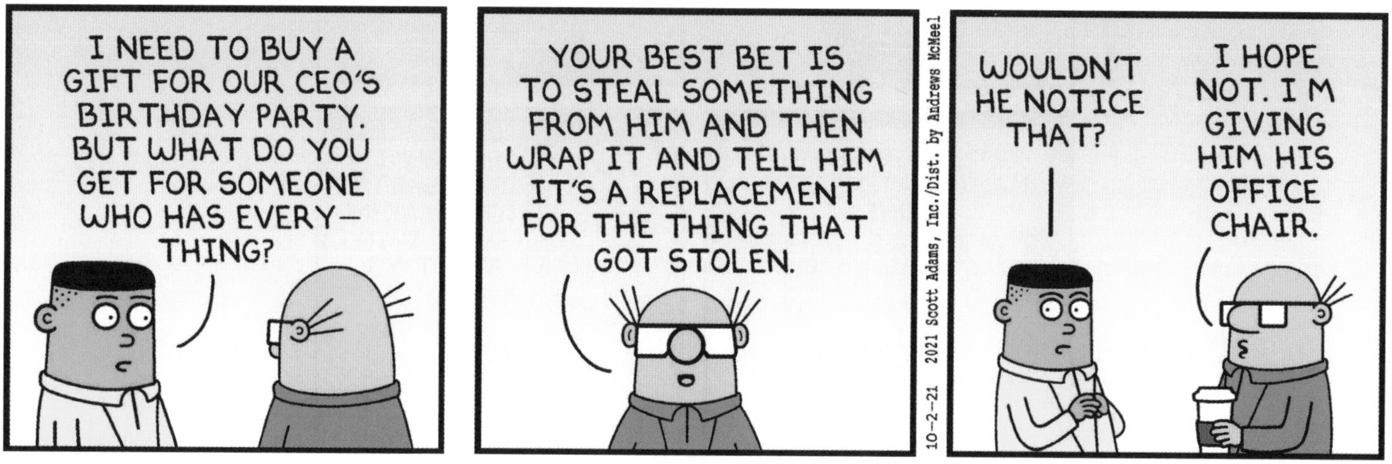
I NEED TO BUY A GIFT FOR OUR CEO'S BIRTHDAY PARTY. BUT WHAT DO YOU GET FOR SOMEONE WHO HAS EVERY-THING?
YOUR BEST BET IS TO STEAL SOMETHING FROM HIM AND THEN WRAP IT AND TELL HIM IT'S A REPLACEMENT FOR THE THING THAT GOT STOLEN.
10-2-21 2021 Scott Adams, Inc./Dist. by Andrews McMeel
WOULDN'T HE NOTICE THAT?
I HOPE NOT. I M GIVING HIM HIS OFFICE CHAIR.

I NEED A REPAIR ON SOME EQUIPMENT WE BOUGHT FROM YOU.
OH, TOO BAD. IT LOOKS AS IF YOUR WARRANTY RAN OUT YESTERDAY.
THAT'S KIND OF SUSPICIOUS.
A PROGRAMMABLE MACHINE STOPPED WORKING EXACTLY WHEN IT IS MOST PROFITABLE FOR THE MANUFACTURER?
IT'S ALMOST AS IF YOUR PROPRIETARY OPERATING SYSTEM IS DESIGNED TO MANIPULATE ME INTO UPGRADING.
DO YOU HEAR HOW CRAZY THAT SOUNDS?
IT ISN'T DESIGNED TO MANIPULATE YOU.
IT'S DESIGNED TO MANIPULATE ***EVERY—ONE.***
THAT ISN'T BETTER!
SHEESH! I'M JUST SAYING STOP MAKING EVERYTHING ABOUT ***YOU.***
© 2021 Scott Adams, Inc./Dist. by Andrews McMeel
10-3-21

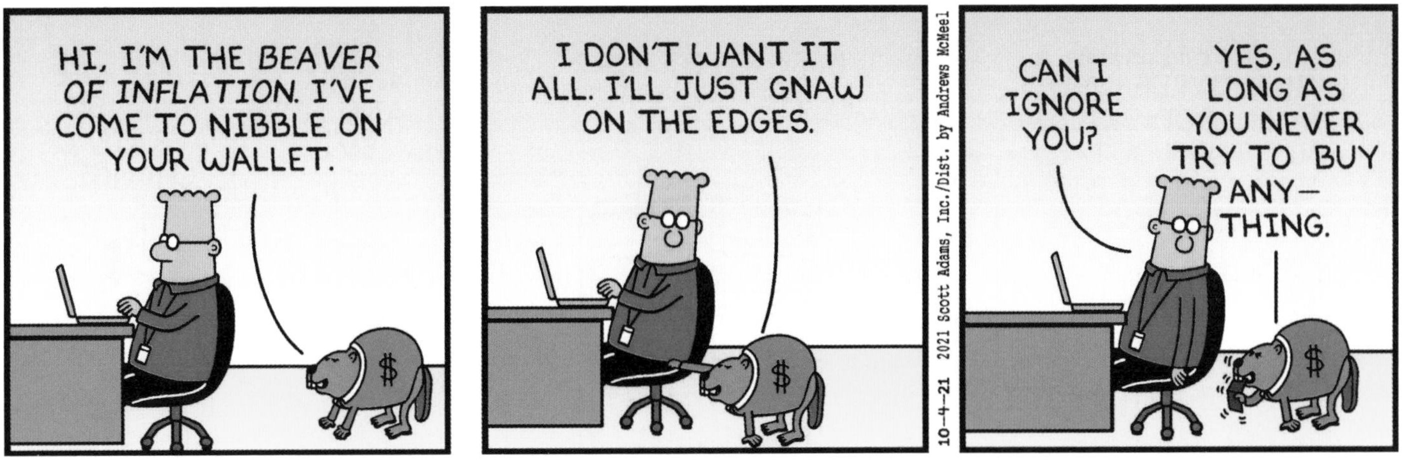
HI, I'M THE *BEAVER OF INFLATION*. I'VE COME TO NIBBLE ON YOUR WALLET.
I DON'T WANT IT ALL. I'LL JUST GNAW ON THE EDGES.
CAN I IGNORE YOU?
YES, AS LONG AS YOU NEVER TRY TO BUY ANY— THING.
10-4-21

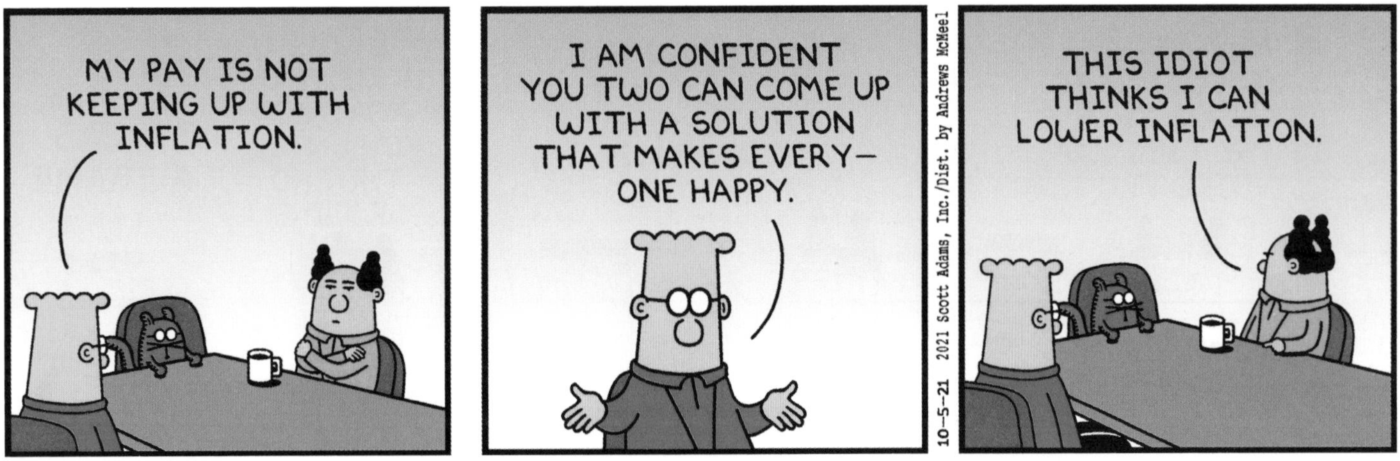
MY PAY IS NOT KEEPING UP WITH INFLATION.
I AM CONFIDENT YOU TWO CAN COME UP WITH A SOLUTION THAT MAKES EVERY— ONE HAPPY.
THIS IDIOT THINKS I CAN LOWER INFLATION.
10-5-21

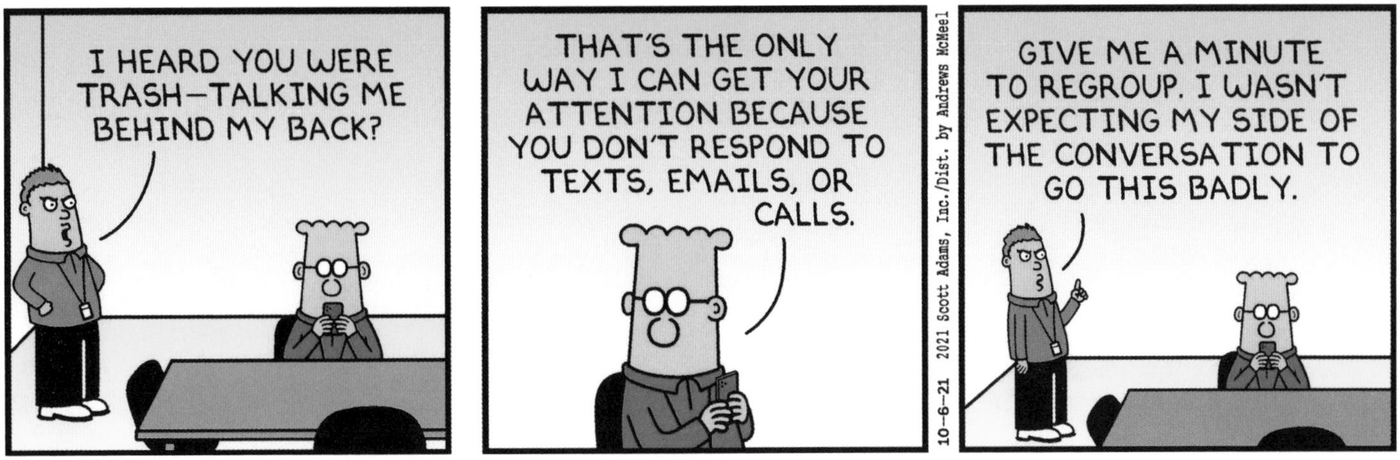
I HEARD YOU WERE TRASH—TALKING ME BEHIND MY BACK?
THAT'S THE ONLY WAY I CAN GET YOUR ATTENTION BECAUSE YOU DON'T RESPOND TO TEXTS, EMAILS, OR CALLS.
GIVE ME A MINUTE TO REGROUP. I WASN'T EXPECTING MY SIDE OF THE CONVERSATION TO GO THIS BADLY.
10-6-21

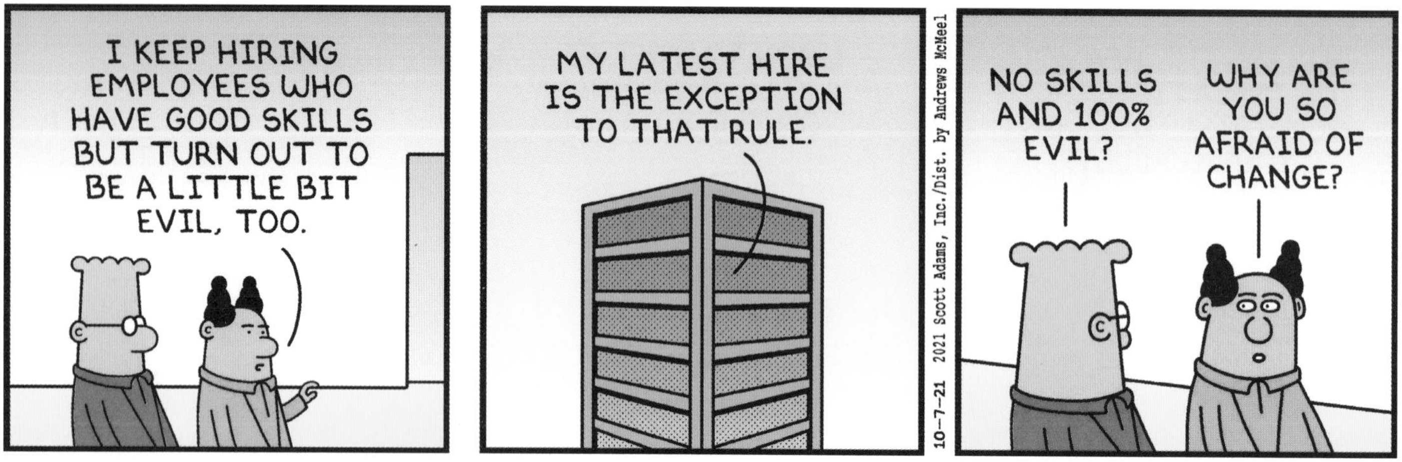
I KEEP HIRING EMPLOYEES WHO HAVE GOOD SKILLS BUT TURN OUT TO BE A LITTLE BIT EVIL, TOO.
MY LATEST HIRE IS THE EXCEPTION TO THAT RULE.
10-7-21 2021 Scott Adams, Inc./Dist. by Andrews McMeel
NO SKILLS AND 100% EVIL?
WHY ARE YOU SO AFRAID OF CHANGE?

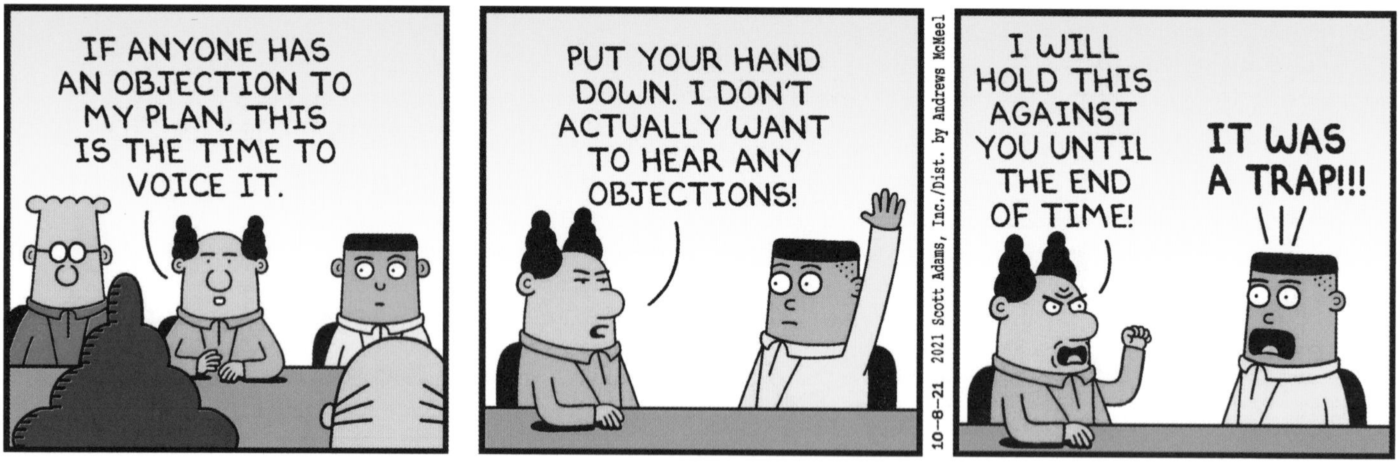
IF ANYONE HAS AN OBJECTION TO MY PLAN, THIS IS THE TIME TO VOICE IT.
PUT YOUR HAND DOWN. I DON'T ACTUALLY WANT TO HEAR ANY OBJECTIONS!
10-8-21 2021 Scott Adams, Inc./Dist. by Andrews McMeel
I WILL HOLD THIS AGAINST YOU UNTIL THE END OF TIME!
IT WAS A TRAP!!!

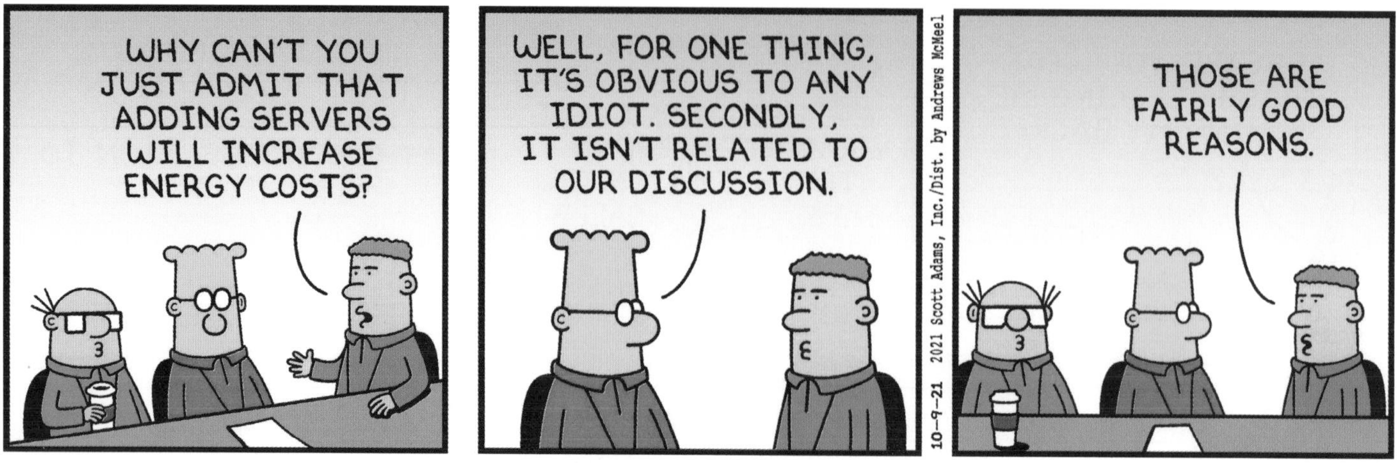
WHY CAN'T YOU JUST ADMIT THAT ADDING SERVERS WILL INCREASE ENERGY COSTS?
WELL, FOR ONE THING, IT'S OBVIOUS TO ANY IDIOT. SECONDLY, IT ISN'T RELATED TO OUR DISCUSSION.
10-9-21 2021 Scott Adams, Inc./Dist. by Andrews McMeel
THOSE ARE FAIRLY GOOD REASONS.

YOUR DATA SHOWS YOUR PROTOTYPE DID NOT INCREASE SPEED OVER THE EXISTING SYSTEM.
NO, THE DATA PROVES THE PROTOTYPE IS FASTER THAN THE OLD SYSTEM.
I'M LOOKING AT THE DATA RIGHT NOW, AND IT CLEARLY SHOWS FAILURE.
IT LOOKS THAT WAY TO YOU BECAUSE YOU PREDICTED IT WOULD FAIL. YOU'RE SEEING WHAT YOU WANT TO SEE.
MAYBE IT ONLY LOOKS TO YOU AS IF IT WORKED BECAUSE YOU PREDICTED IT WOULD WORK.
SO. . . WE'RE BOTH LOOKING AT EXACTLY THE SAME DATA AND REACHING OPPOSITE CONCLUSIONS?
IF I THOUGHT DATA WOULD INFLUENCE MY DECISIONS, I WOULDN'T LET YOU GATHER IT.
GIVE ME A MINUTE TO REASSESS MY ENTIRE EXISTENCE.
© 2021 Scott Adams, Inc./Dist. by Andrews McMeel
10-10-21

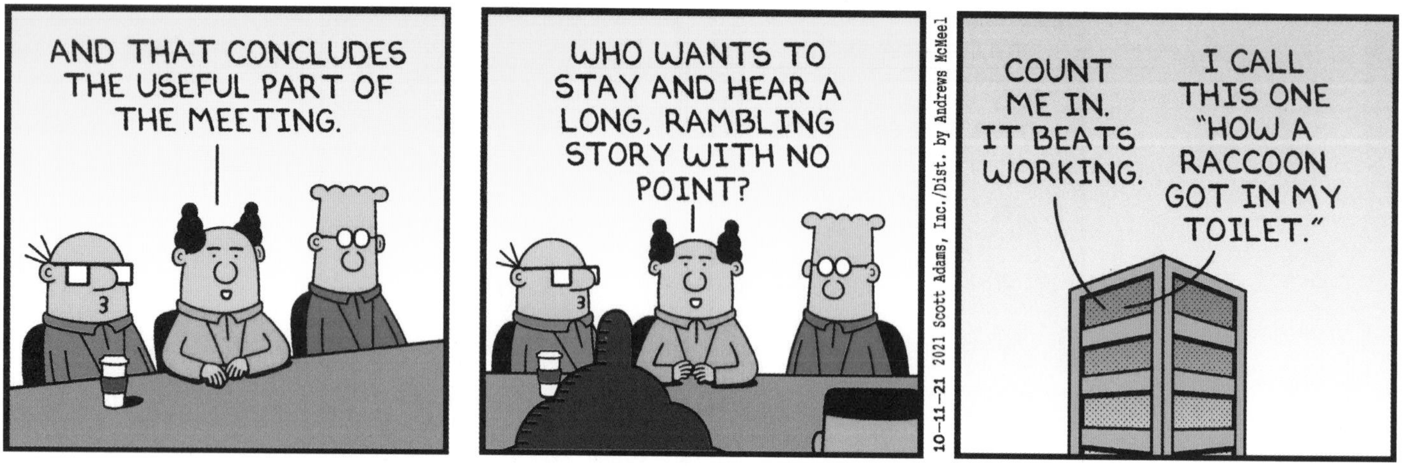
AND THAT CONCLUDES THE USEFUL PART OF THE MEETING.
WHO WANTS TO STAY AND HEAR A LONG, RAMBLING STORY WITH NO POINT?
COUNT ME IN. IT BEATS WORKING.
I CALL THIS ONE "HOW A RACCOON GOT IN MY TOILET."
10-11-21 2021 Scott Adams, Inc./Dist. by Andrews McMeel

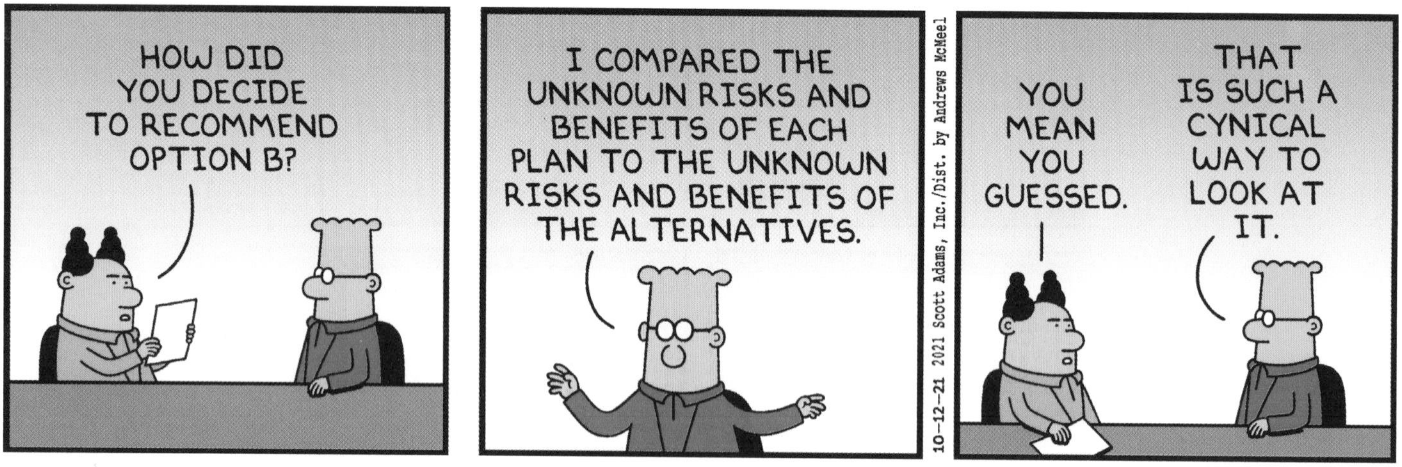
HOW DID YOU DECIDE TO RECOMMEND OPTION B?
I COMPARED THE UNKNOWN RISKS AND BENEFITS OF EACH PLAN TO THE UNKNOWN RISKS AND BENEFITS OF THE ALTERNATIVES.
YOU MEAN YOU GUESSED.
THAT IS SUCH A CYNICAL WAY TO LOOK AT IT.
10-12-21 2021 Scott Adams, Inc./Dist. by Andrews McMeel

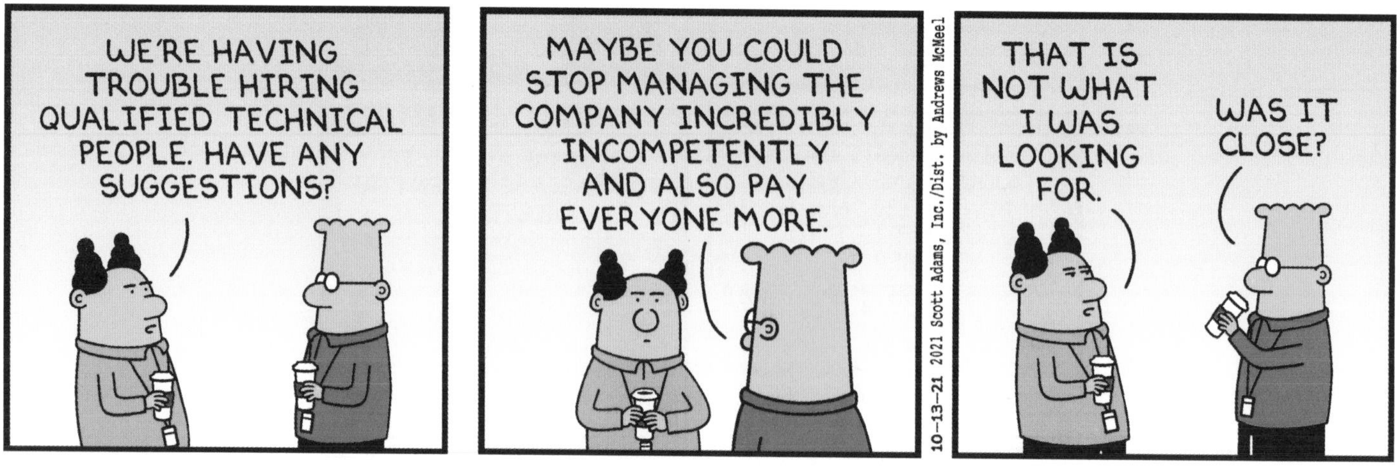
WE'RE HAVING TROUBLE HIRING QUALIFIED TECHNICAL PEOPLE. HAVE ANY SUGGESTIONS?
MAYBE YOU COULD STOP MANAGING THE COMPANY INCREDIBLY INCOMPETENTLY AND ALSO PAY EVERYONE MORE.
THAT IS NOT WHAT I WAS LOOKING FOR.
WAS IT CLOSE?
10-13-21 2021 Scott Adams, Inc./Dist. by Andrews McMeel

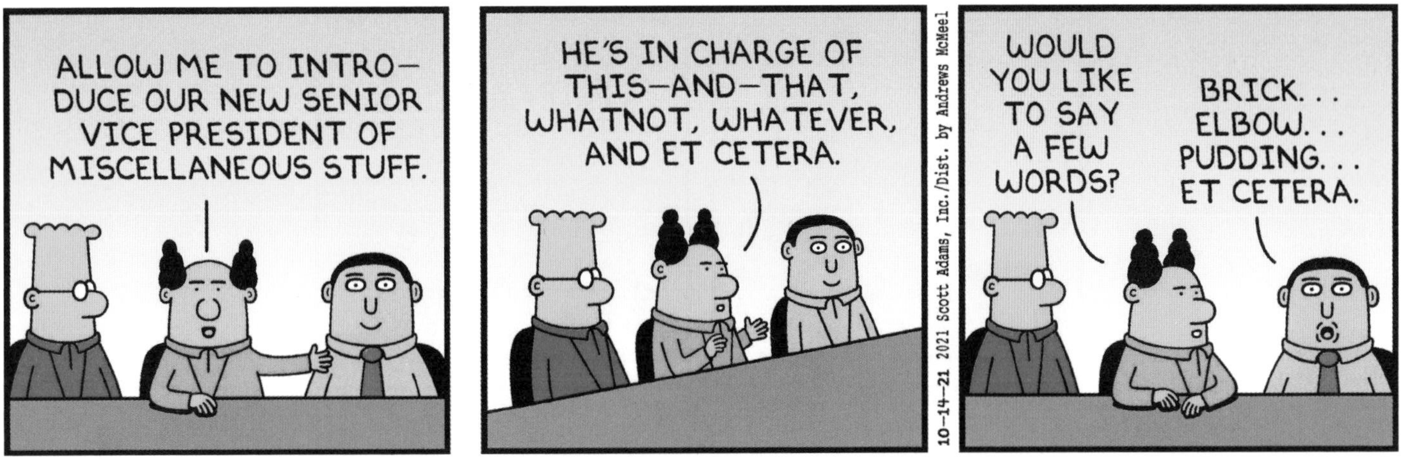
ALLOW ME TO INTRO-DUCE OUR NEW SENIOR VICE PRESIDENT OF MISCELLANEOUS STUFF.
HE'S IN CHARGE OF THIS-AND-THAT, WHATNOT, WHATEVER, AND ET CETERA.
10-14-21 ©2021 Scott Adams, Inc./Dist. by Andrews McMeel
WOULD YOU LIKE TO SAY A FEW WORDS?
BRICK... ELBOW... PUDDING... ET CETERA.

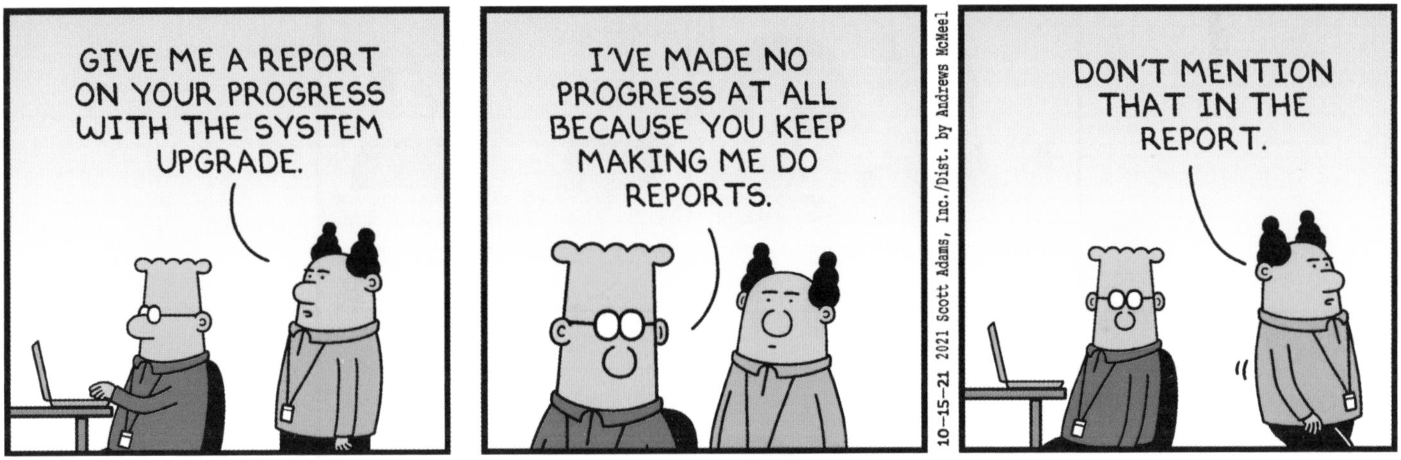
GIVE ME A REPORT ON YOUR PROGRESS WITH THE SYSTEM UPGRADE.
I'VE MADE NO PROGRESS AT ALL BECAUSE YOU KEEP MAKING ME DO REPORTS.
10-15-21 ©2021 Scott Adams, Inc./Dist. by Andrews McMeel
DON'T MENTION THAT IN THE REPORT.

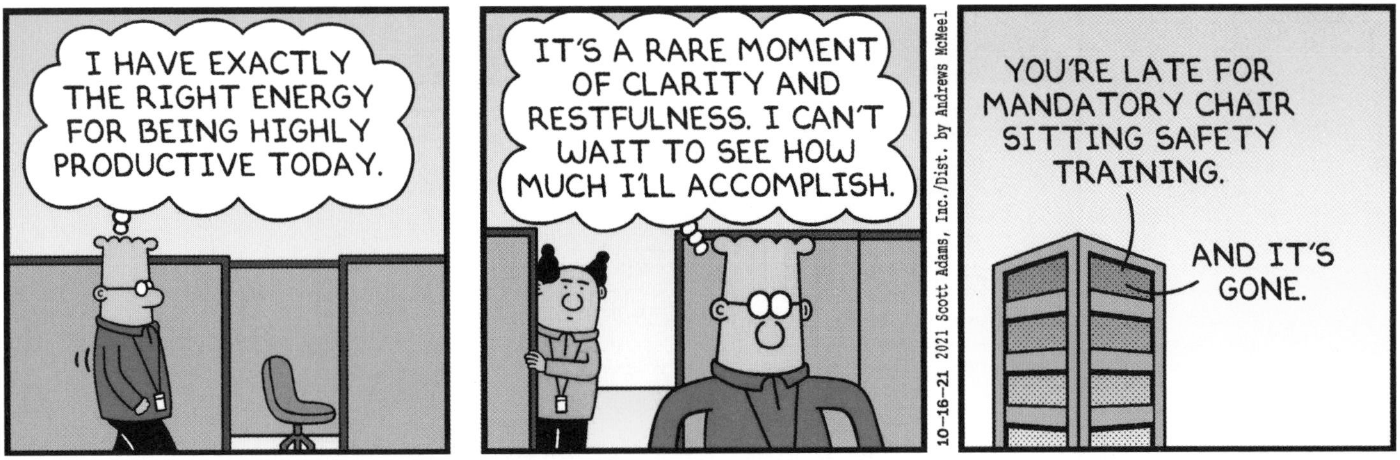
I HAVE EXACTLY THE RIGHT ENERGY FOR BEING HIGHLY PRODUCTIVE TODAY.
IT'S A RARE MOMENT OF CLARITY AND RESTFULNESS. I CAN'T WAIT TO SEE HOW MUCH I'LL ACCOMPLISH.
10-16-21 ©2021 Scott Adams, Inc./Dist. by Andrews McMeel
YOU'RE LATE FOR MANDATORY CHAIR SITTING SAFETY TRAINING.
AND IT'S GONE.

WE CAN ONLY SUCCEED IF WE VALUE CREATIVE RISK—TAKING.
ARE YOU SAYING WE WILL BE REWARDED EVEN IF OUR RISKS TURN OUT TO BE HUGE MISTAKES?
NO, I'M NOT GOING TO REWARD YOU FOR MISTAKES.
THEN WHY WOULD WE TAKE CREATIVE RISKS?
BECAUSE THE COMPANY NEEDS YOU TO.
SO IT'S KIND OF A SUICIDE MISSION SITUATION?
NOT AT ALL. SOMETIMES YOU MIGHT SUCCEED.
THEN I'D GET A BIG RAISE?
WE PAY MARKET RATES.
© 2021 Scott Adams, Inc./Dist. by Andrews McMeel
10-17-21

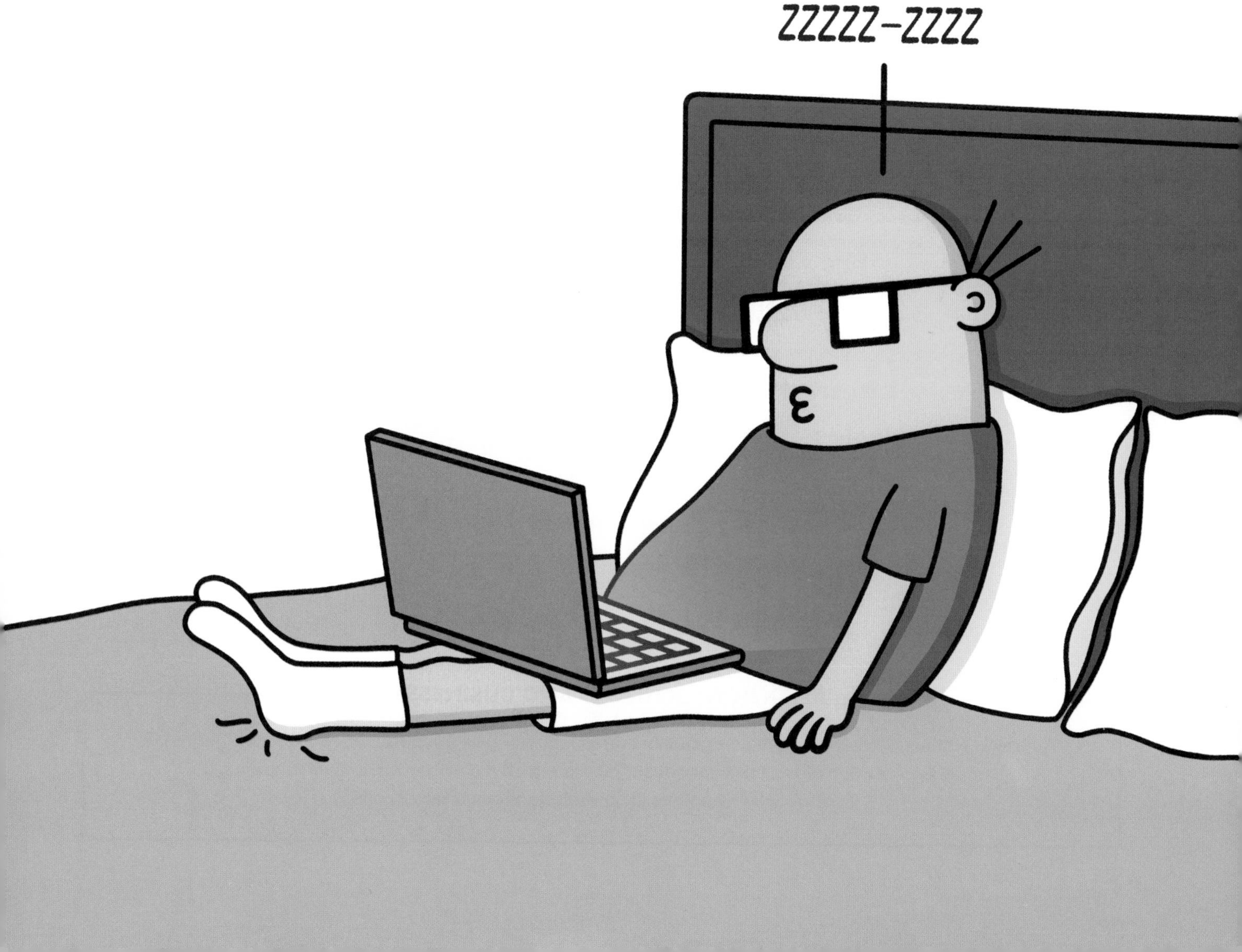
ZZZZZ-ZZZZ

Dilbert: Not Remotely Working copyright © 2022 by Scott Adams, Inc.
All rights reserved. Printed in China. No part of this book may be used or reproduced in any manner
whatsoever without written permission except in the case of reprints in the context of reviews.

Andrews McMeel Publishing
a division of Andrews McMeel Universal
1130 Walnut Street, Kansas City, Missouri 64106
www.andrewsmcmeel.com

22 23 24 25 26 SDB 10 9 8 7 6 5 4 3 2 1

ISBN: 978-1-5248-7563-3

Library of Congress Control Number: 2022933530

www.dilbert.com